D1433672

Exclusion Clauses and Unfair Contract Terms

Eleventh Edition

Exclusion Clauses and Unfair Contract Terms

Eleventh Edition

Richard Lawson LLM PhD

SWEET & MAXWELL

THOMSON REUTERS

Published in 2014 by Sweet & Maxwell, Friars House, 160 Blackfriars Road, London, SE1 8EZ
part of Thomson Reuters (Professional) UK Limited (Registered in England & Wales,
Company No 1679046.
Registered Office and address for service: Aldgate House, 33 Aldgate High Street, London
EC3N 1DL)

For further information on our products and services, visit *www.sweetandmaxwell.co.uk*

Typeset by LetterPart Typesetting Ltd, Reigate, Surrey.

Printed and bound in Great Britain by CPI Group (UK) Ltd, Croyden, CR0 4YY.

No natural forests were destroyed to make this product; only farmed timber was used and
re-planted.

A CIP catalogue record of this book is available for the British Library.

ISBN: 978-0-41403-101-2

Thomson Reuters and the Thomson Reuters logo are trademarks of Thomson Reuters.

Sweet & Maxwell ® is a registered trademark of Thomson Reuters (Professional) UK
Limited.

Crown copyright material is reproduced with the permission of the Controller of HMSO and
the Queen's Printer for Scotland.

Dedication

In loving memory of my wonderful sister Valerie: October 22, 1935–December 22, 2012.

However much I valued her, I wish I had valued her more.

Foreword

There were two main reasons for producing this new edition. The first was the steady flow of case law on such central issues as the application of the reasonableness test; what terms in consumer contracts were fair; the meaning of what counts as a "core provision"; and, as always, just how were exclusion and limitation clauses to be interpreted.

The other, more compelling, reason was the implementation of the EU Consumer Rights Directive 2011/83/EU. Though this did not in itself greatly affect the areas covered by this book, Parliament decided to introduce a Consumer Rights Bill which has the effect of repealing and re-enacting the Unfair Terms in Consumer Contracts Regulations 1999 and limiting the Unfair Contract Terms Act 1977 just to business-to-business dealings.

The Directive was meant to be implemented by June 13, 2014 but as this edition went to press, it still had not been enacted. Even so, the decision was taken to proceed with this edition. Throughout, reference is made to the Consumer Rights Act 2014, and the section numbers quoted are those of today's date. Readers can be confident that what is stated as the law will be the law, since no real changes of substance are planned by the Consumer Rights Act in the field of exclusion clauses and unfair terms. The main thrust of the Act is to enhance consumer rights in the area of the sale and supply of goods and services, not in the area of unfair terms. Because the section numbers might change in the final version of the Act, readers should check the Act for any changes in the section numbers we cite.

We noted above that the Consumer Rights Directive should have been enacted by June 13, 2014. We would just note here that, following the ruling in the *Becker* case (Case 8/61, January 19, 1992), the Directive entered automatically into force in the United Kingdom on the prescribed date. The effect of this, we feel, is best left for others to ponder.

The law as stated as at August 11, 2014.

TABLE OF CONTENTS

2. INTERPRETATION OF EXCLUSION CLAUSES

3. AVOIDANCE AND QUALIFICATION OF EXCLUSION CLAUSES

4. HARSH AND UNCONSCIONABLE BARGAINS

PART 2
Legislative Control

5. UNLAWFUL EXCLUSION CLAUSES

6. VOID AND INEFFECTIVE EXCLUSION CLAUSES

7. THE UNFAIR CONTRACT TERMS ACT 1977: SOME PRELIMINARY POINTS

8. THE UNFAIR CONTRACT TERMS ACT: AREAS OF APPLICATION

9. THE REASONABLENESS TEST

10. UNFAIR TERMS IN CONSUMER CONTRACTS

TABLE OF CASES

TABLE OF STATUTES

TABLE OF STATUTORY INSTRUMENTS

PART 1

JUDICIAL CONTROL

CHAPTER 1

INCORPORATION OF EXCLUSION CLAUSES

INTRODUCTION

It is the first essence of an exclusion clause that it be effectively incorporated into the contract. If this basic step has not been achieved, the clause will be of no effect, however suitable its drafting to exclude or limit liability for the relevant breach. The ways in which a clause can become a contractual term are discussed below.

1–001

CONTRACTUAL DOCUMENTS

Frequently, the putative terms of a contract, including exclusion clauses, are displayed about the premises where the contract is to be made. They may also be printed in a document tendered or delivered by one party to another, or referred to in such a document.

1–002

As has been said, in words endorsed by Lord Denning M.R. in *White v Blackmore*,[1] "… the court must be satisfied that the particular document relied on as containing notice of the excluding or limiting term is in truth an integral part of the contract".[2] This has meant that documents or any writing must have been intended to be contractual and not, for example, in the nature of mere receipts. The latter really represent an acknowledgment of a contract, rather than operate as a part of one.

This was explained by Mellish L.J. in the course of his judgment in *Parker v South Eastern Railway Co.*[3] He thought that:

> "there may be cases in which a paper containing writing is delivered by one party to another in the course of a business transaction, where it would be quite reasonable that the party receiving it should assume that the writing contained in it no condition, and should put it in his pocket unread. For instance, if a person driving through a turnpike gate received a ticket upon paying the toll, he might reasonably assume that the object of the ticket was that by producing it he might be free from paying toll at some other turnpike gate, and might put it in his pocket unread."[4]

The Court of Appeal relied on this statement in *Chapelton v Barry Urban DC.*[5] Deck-chairs were stacked near a notice requesting members of the public to

---

[1] [1972] 3 All E.R. 158 at 167.
[2] Cheshire, Fifoot and Furmston, Law of Contract, 14th edn (London: Butterworths, 2001), p.173.
[3] (1877) L.R. 2 C.P.D. 416.
[4] (1877) 2 C.P.D. 416 at 422.
[5] [1940] 1 K.B. 532.

obtain tickets from an attendant and retain them for inspection. The claimant took the chairs and obtained two tickets which he did not read. One of the chairs collapsed and he was injured. The Court of Appeal held that no reliance could be placed on the exclusion clauses on the tickets. No one would assume that the ticket was anything but a receipt.

This approach was accepted as correct by the House of Lords in *McCutcheon v MacBrayne*.[6] The defendants owned steamers operating between the Scottish mainland and the islands. An oral contract was made with the claimant for the shipment of a car. On the voyage, and because of the defendants' negligence, both ship and car were lost. The exclusion clauses put up by the defendants on their behalf were contained in 27 paragraphs of small print displayed both inside and outside their office. The terms were also printed on a "risk-note" which customers were usually, though not on this occasion, asked to sign. In this case, the only document to have been tendered was a receipt stating that "all goods were carried subject to the conditions set out in the notices". Neither the claimant, nor his agent through whom the contract was made, had read the words of the notices or the receipt. There was, in any case, no contractual document, and judgment was given for the claimant.

1–003   In *Burnett v Westminster Bank*,[7] the claimant had accounts at branch A and branch B of the defendant bank. The new cheque book for branch A contained a notice that "the cheques in this book will be applied to the account for which they have been prepared". No notice of contractual terms had been contained in previous cheque books. The claimant attempted to direct a cheque from the new book to branch B, but the computer could not read his instructions on the cheque. Branch A duly debited his account, even though the claimant had placed a stop notice with branch B, whither he assumed the cheque was headed. Mocatta J. found that the words in the cheque book were not contained in a contractual document and were, therefore, ineffective.

In *Grogan v Robin Meredith Plant Hire and Triact Civil Engineering Ltd*,[8] a telephone agreement had been made between Triact and Meredith Plant Hire for the supply to the former of a driver and machine. Neither of the parties referred to any particular terms as governing the contract: in particular, no reference was made to the standard terms of the Contractors' Plant Association commonly used in contracts of this particular category. At the end of the first and second weeks, time sheets were presented to Triact's site working agent, a person having authority to hire machinery on behalf of his employers. At the bottom of the sheet, above the place for signature, were the words: "All hire undertaken under CPA conditions. Copies available on request".

The Court of Appeal said that the central question was whether the time sheet fell within the class of document which the recipient knew, or would reasonably expect, to contain relevant contractual provisions. The test was stated to be whether a particular document purported to be a contract or to have contractual effect. The evidence showed that Meredith regarded the time sheet as essentially an administrative document which was designed to indicate the hours worked on

---

[6] [1964] 1 All E.R. 430.
[7] [1965] 3 All E.R. 81.
[8] [1996] C.L.C. 1127.

a particular contract. The High Court had stated that the document had been signed for a "contractual purpose" and had ruled that the particular terms had thus been incorporated into the contract. The Court of Appeal, however, rejected the argument that a document did not have to be a contractual document if it were signed, and that it was necessary to look at a signed document only to see what it said. That argument was dismissed as "too mechanistic" and "contrary to a long line of authority". It ruled that the terms had not been incorporated into the contract.

These cases should be contrasted with the decision of the Court of Appeal in *Rhone Poulenc Rorer Ltd v TGG Ltd.*[9] An agreement provided for invoices to be issued subject to TGG's standard terms and conditions, a copy of which was appended to the agreement. Invoices for air shipments were issued by TGG to Rhone stating that they were subject to certain trading conditions as they had been in the past. The Court of Appeal held that it was the invoices which were subject to the standard terms because it was always thought as between the parties as commercial entities that the invoices were the contractual documents.

INCORPORATION—ESTABLISHING THE INTENTION OF THE PARTIES

Whether or not a term is incorporated in the contract will depend on the intention of the parties, and the principles to be deployed in establishing such intention were detailed by Rix J. in *Ceval Alimentos SA v Agrimpex Trading Co Ltd.*[10] A sale contract sought to include the terms of a charterparty by use of the clause: "All other terms, conditions and exceptions as per charterparty". One such term was a diversion clause. Rix J. said that it was a "fundamental rule of construction" that one had to seek, by objective means, the true intention of the parties. To do so required the court to note a number of factors:

1–004

(1)   The incorporation clause was not especially "emphatic". "All" was immediately qualified by "other" in circumstances where the sale contract had already immediately before provided for the deemed incorporation in the charterparty of specific clauses designed to deal with the problem of war.

(2)   It was also "common ground" that "all" does not mean what it appears to mean. For instance, charterparty terms not dealing with shipment, carriage or delivery would not be incorporated; nor would terms which could not be "manipulated" to make sense in the context of a contract of sale. Ancillary terms were likewise not incorporated.

(3)   There were also factors which led to the conclusion that the diversion clause must be regarded as inconsistent with the sale contract. That contract contained various provisions dealing with the effect of war and in particular the place of delivery. There was, the judge concluded, no room for any further, fundamentally different provision relating to the same specific matter but which was "left for the sellers to deal with behind ... the curtain of incorporation". On top of this, the parties had in any event agreed an

---

[9] Unreported February 18, 1998.
[10] [1996] 2 Lloyd's Rep. 319.

amendment to the sale contract which was to operate only if the vessel could not reach the specified ports in Yugoslavia. The diversion clause, however, provided that a different port could be selected if an additional war risk premium were imposed. In agreeing to this amendment, the judge concluded, the sellers must have realised that they were agreeing on something at odds with the diversion clause, as the buyers would have realised for themselves if told of that clause.

(4) It was possible that the unusual nature of that clause of itself sufficed to exclude its incorporation. It was scarcely the case that the parties would have contemplated that the sellers would procure a contract which rendered them in breach of their obligation to secure only such contract as was reasonable. Such consideration, however, might well not by itself override a prima facie incorporation, but it was even so "highly relevant" in the consideration of what the parties must be held to have meant by the incorporation clause.

(5) Rationality and commercial common sense also had their part to play in arriving at the true intention of the parties. It was always open to the parties to agree to the inclusion of unreasonable terms of contract: where, however, this was to be done by an incorporation clause, the parties must make their position clear. The judge concluded that the incorporation of the diversion clause, in the absence of specific negotiation between the parties, lacked rationality and flew in the face of commercial common sense.

(6) There was, the judge said, no reason why that clause should be "manipulated", so as to make it effective within the sale contract. The parties had negotiated their own terms to deal with diversion in the case of war and it was not for the court to save a clause for incorporation which the sellers could have sought to negotiate expressly with the buyers.

His final conclusion that the diversion clause had not been incorporated was supported in particular, he said, by the unusual nature of the diversion clause and the fact that it conflicted with specific terms in the contract dealing with the renomination of the discharge port.[11]

A different decision on the effect of general words of incorporation was reached in *Habas Sinai Ve Tibbi Gazlar Isthisal Endustri AS v Sometal SAL*.[12] The applicant Turkish company applied to set aside an arbitration award on jurisdiction by which the tribunal decided that it had jurisdiction to entertain the claim made by the respondent Lebanese company alleging breach of a contract for sale. There had been 14 previous contracts between the same parties. The first three contracts were prepared by the applicant. The next contract was prepared by Habas Sinai and contained a London arbitration clause. The following contracts were prepared by the Lebanese party or its agent. The contracts prepared by the Lebanese contained the arbitration clause. The contracts prepared by the agent and those prepared by the Lebanese set out the terms relating to material, quantity, price and shipment but those prepared by the agent, unlike those prepared by the Lebanese, did not set out terms relating to quality, demurrage,

---

[11] See para.1–018 and following for the discussion of unusual clauses.
[12] [2010] EWHC 29 (Comm). Reference should be made also to the cases cited in this judgment.

force majeure or law and arbitration. Instead the contracts prepared by the agent provided that: "The rest will be agreed mutually"; "The rest will be as per previous contracts"; or "All the rest will be same as our previous contracts".

The final contract, on which the Lebanese relied, was prepared by their agent. Accordingly, it did not contain the arbitration clause but provided that: "All the rest will be same as our previous contracts". The Lebanese alleged that the applicant had repudiated the contract by failing to take delivery. The arbitral tribunal held that the reference to the terms of "our previous contracts" could not have referred to the contracts prepared by the applicant or to those prepared by the agent which did not contain any relevant additional terms or themselves referred to previous contracts. Therefore the reference was to the terms of the contracts prepared by the Lebanese containing the arbitration clause. The applicant argued that:

(1)   for a clause such as the arbitration clause to be incorporated into a contract there had to be an express reference to the clause or wording that showed a clear intention to incorporate it and that that requirement was not satisfied; and

(2)   even if general words were capable of incorporating such a clause, the words used here were not apt for the purpose.

It was held that, in principle, English law accepted incorporation of standard **1–005** terms by the use of general words. The principle did not distinguish between a term which was an arbitration clause and one which addressed other issues. A stricter rule was applied in charterparty/bills of lading cases. There was a material distinction between incorporation of the terms of a contract made between the same parties, a "single contract" case, and incorporation of the terms of a contract made between different parties, even if one of them was a party to the contract in suit, a "two contract" case. In relation to the latter a more restrictive approach to incorporation was required. In such a case it might not be evident that the parties intended not only to incorporate the substantive provisions of the other contract but also provisions such as an arbitration clause, particularly if a degree of verbal manipulation was needed for the incorporated arbitration clause to work. Those considerations did not, however, apply to a single contract case, and the stricter rule was not to be extended to single contract cases since that would involve the exception swallowing up the rule, The instant case was not to be regarded as a two contract case. In a single contract case, the independent nature of the arbitration clause should not determine whether it was to be incorporated, general words of incorporation were capable of incorporating terms which included an arbitration clause without specifically referring to it and the question was whether in the instant case they did so. It was further said that the court should not be astute to find that the words used had no effect at all. It was not to be assumed that the words of incorporation were intended to refer to all the previous contracts, and it was clear that they did not refer to the first three contracts drafted by the applicant. Nor could they refer to the contracts in which it was agreed that the rest of the terms would be agreed. The remaining contracts either contained the London arbitration clause or incorporated it by reference. It was therefore clear that the words of incorporation in the last contract were apt to incorporate the London arbitration clause. Application of the arbitration clause did not require any linguistic manipulation. When the parties referred to "all the rest" being the same there was no good reason to treat them as meaning all of the rest except the arbitration clause.

The same broad approach can be seen in *Rooney v CSE Bournemouth Ltd.*[13] The first respondent was the owner of the second respondent company that was the registered owner of an aircraft that had been leased to a third party company (E). The aircraft was maintained by C, an aircraft maintenance company, under a maintenance support contract and a continuing airworthiness management support contract with E. Under the contractual arrangements the maintenance company's practice was for the scope of maintenance works to be carried out on the aircraft to be defined on a work order form. Its work order forms contained the statement "terms and conditions available on request". On a particular occasion, the maintenance company negligently carried out works, pursuant to a work order form, on the aircraft with the result that it sustained damage on a subsequent flight. E assigned its right of claim against the company to the first respondent. The respondents subsequently brought a claim for losses incurred by them and E as result of the damage suffered by the aircraft. The respondents applied for summary judgment in their claim on the basis that, inter alia, the maintenance company had no real prospect of showing that the work order form was a contractual document or that it incorporated the maintenance company's terms and conditions. The High Court held that it was reasonably arguable that the work order was a document intended to have contractual effect. The judge held, however, that the statement "terms and conditions available on request" did not incorporate the maintenance company's standard conditions of trading because they conveyed no more than that there were terms and conditions available, and they did not purport to incorporate any particular terms and conditions into a contract. The company contended that the High Court erred by adopting too linguistic an approach and failed to look at the commercial context in which the work order form and the statement on it was made, and that, if it had, it ought to have found that it was at least arguable that it was intended that work carried out by the maintenance company pursuant to a work order form was subject to its conditions of trading.

The Court of Appeal held that the High Court had erred in finding that the words used could not be said to have incorporated the maintenance company's standard conditions of trading. The work order form was a contractual document that took its place in a contractual maintenance scheme whereby the work order form activated the work, and nature of work, to be done on the aircraft. Whilst the High Court's interpretation of the words used might have been correct grammatically, in a business context, the Court of Appeal felt that it would be "odd" if a contractual binding order such as the work order form contained no commercial terms but left them only for inclusion at a customer's request. It was

---

[13] [2010] EWCA Civ 1364, considered in *Salkeld Investments Ltd v West One Loans Ltd* [2012] EWHC 2701. An email footer stated that contracts would be documented by means other than email. The court said that, despite this, the contract was plainly constituted by email and that a client agreement, containing an exclusion clause, had only been incorporated, if at all, if it had been discussed prior to the formation of the contract.

at least arguable that a reasonable person would have understood the words used as referring to contractual terms upon which the maintenance company had agreed to work on the aircraft.

The general rules of construction also fell to be applied in *OK Petroleum v Vitol Energy*.[14] By two contracts of sale, OK Petroleum sold quantities of gasoline to Vitol. Both contracts expressly provided that demurrage was to be "as per charterparty" and also contained specific terms as to laytime. OK then proceeded to charter two vessels, one for each contract, on standard form terms. Both charterparties specifically incorporated OK's standard charterparty terms and conditions. Included in those terms and conditions was a provision that the charterers were not to be held liable for demurrage or costs incurred under the charterparty unless notification of any claim was received within a specific 90-day period.

1–006

Under both contracts, the buyers took longer than the laytime to discharge the cargo. The sellers claimed demurrage under both contracts, but Vitol reckoned that the sellers' claim was time-barred under the 90-day provision in the charterparty. This left for resolution by the High Court the question whether the time bar in the charterparty was incorporated into the contracts of sale.

The court ruled against incorporation. As there was no clear trade usage in this regard, it was necessary to apply the general rules of construction. Although there were differences in contractual structure and context between a sale contract and a bill of lading contract, principles of construction relating to the latter were of assistance. In this particular context, it had been held that only such provisions will be incorporated as are, in substance, relevant or germane to, and, if incorporated, capable of being operated in conjunction with, the subject-matter of a bill of lading. There was, the court said, no logical basis for confining such an approach to bills of lading. The time-bar provision, although exclusively applicable to claims for demurrage under the charterparty, was in essence ancillary to the substantive or subject-matter provisions of that contract relating to demurrage. The words of incorporation in the sale contracts, being in general terms, did not "clearly express" a mutual intention to incorporate into those contracts any provision of the charterparty not part of the demurrage subject-matter of the contract, but which was clearly ancillary to it. The court therefore held that the sellers' claim was not time-barred.[15]

REASONABLE SUFFICIENCY OF NOTICE

It was established in *Parker v South Eastern Railway Co*[16] that a term will only become incorporated in the contract if notice of the term has been given and that notice is reasonably sufficient in all the circumstances of the case. This is a

1–007

---

[14] [1995] 2 Lloyd's Rep. 160.
[15] See also *Extrudakerb v Whitemountain Quarries Ltd* [1996] C.L.C 1747; *BCT Software Solutions Ltd v Arnold Laver & Co Ltd* [2002] 2 All E.R. (Comm) 85; *Hackwood Ltd v Areen Design Services Ltd* [2005] EWHC 2322 (TCC); *Dalkia Energy and Technical Services Ltd v Bell Group* [2009] EWHC 73 (TCC); *Midgulf International Ltd v Groupe Chimiche Tunisien* [2009] EWHC 1684 (Comm).
[16] (1877) L.R. 2 C.P.D. 416.

question of fact, "in answering which the tribunal must look at all the circumstances and the situation of the parties".[17]

In the *Parker* case itself, the claimant had deposited a bag in the cloakroom of a railway station belonging to the defendants. He was given a ticket declaring "See back"; and on the back were conditions including a clause limiting liability to £10. The claimant had not read the clause, but was held bound by it. The defendants had done enough to notify the claimant of the clause. The ticket, it may be supposed, was a contractual document.

A clear statement of the applicable principles was made by Judge Waksman in *Allen Fabrications Ltd v ASD Metal Services Ltd.*[18] He said that a party's standard terms could be incorporated into a contract in two principal ways other than where they are expressly agreed to for example by being signed:

> "(1) They may be on or referred to in a document which is "contractual" that is to say provided to the other party prior to or at the time when the contract is made (leaving aside "battle of the forms" cases); or
>
> (2) They may be on or referred to in a document not itself contractual but post-contractual, like the advice notes and invoices here, but which are nonetheless held to have been incorporated because of a prior course of dealing between the parties using those documents from which it can be inferred, objectively, that the parties must have intended to contract on those terms."

He went on to consider the case where such terms have not actually been read by the other party or where that party was not aware of their import or effect. In such a case, the basic principles governing their incorporation are:

(1) if the person receiving the document did not know there was writing or printing on it, he is not bound;

(2) if he knew that the writing or printing on it contained or referred to conditions, he is bound;

(3) (if the answer to question 1 is "yes" but the answer to question 2 is "no") that party will be bound by the conditions if the tendering party did what was reasonably sufficient to give the other party notice of the conditions. He went on to say that, if this requirement is satisfied, it matters not that the party in question was (still) not subjectively aware of them. In the normal course, the judge said, the fact that the document contains the terms on its face or clearly refers to them as being on the reverse or being available elsewhere, is likely to be sufficient.

In *F.G. Wilson Engineering Ltd v John Holt Ltd*,[19] the statement of principle was expressed thus by Popplewell J.: "Where a party seeks to incorporate standard terms and conditions into a contract by reference, they will be incorporated if that party has taken such steps as are sufficient to give reasonable notice of the terms. ... What is reasonable depends upon the circumstances of

---

[17] *Hood v Anchor Line* [1918] A.C. 837 at 844, per Lord Haldane. See also *John Snow and Co Ltd v DBG Woodcroft and Co Ltd* [1985] B.C.L.C. 54.
[18] [2012] EWHC 2213.
[19] [2012] EWHC 2477.

each case and the term or condition which is relied upon. Generally the more unusual or onerous the term, the greater the notice that must be given of it".

The need to bring the terms and conditions to the attention of the other contracting party was well illustrated in *SSL International Plc v LRC Products*.[20]

In that case, S, an English company, manufactured and marketed condoms. T, an Indian company, formed a joint venture with S under which T was obliged to supply condoms to S. S generated a purchase order that referenced S's standard terms and conditions which included an exclusive jurisdiction clause. However, the purchase order was never seen by T. T ceased supplying the condoms to S. S served a claim form in respect of alleged breaches of contract on one of the directors that it had nominated to T's board who was within the jurisdiction. S submitted that its standard terms and conditions had been incorporated in the contract.

The way the parties operated meant that, a contract, or contracts, arose every month for the supply of condoms for delivery, by and large, in the following month, sometimes in the month after that. The final step in the formation of the contract was the purchase order, or the communication of purchase order number.   **1–008**

It was the court's opinion that this was "an odd procedure". The purchase order, on the evidence it had seen, was not actually sent to India. The Indian company, therefore, never saw the purchase order and, on all the evidence, had never seen a purchase order in all the years for which this procedure had been operating, but it knew that it was to supply because it had got the purchase order number and was told to which goods it related. The purchase order itself, which was a one or two sheet document, stayed in England and was not communicated, despite the fact it seemed to be addressed to the Indian company.

The court noted that the purchase order had a reference to the claimant's standard terms of supply on the bottom of it. However, not being a document which was ever communicated to the other side, it was not presented in a way in which the defendant could ever have been alerted to the existence of the terms or invited to subscribe to them.

The reference on the bottom of these untransmitted purchase orders was the only relevant reference to the supply conditions. There was a reference to them on the website but the court did not see how that could be the basis of an acceptance of their incorporation by the Indian company.

The result was that the contract was governed by Indian law since the clause as to English jurisdiction had not been incorporated into the contract.

In *Frank Maas (UK) Ltd v Samsung Electronics (UK) Ltd*,[21] the relevant clause   **1–009**
was a term of the standard contract drawn up by the British International Freight Association. In the course of negotiations between the parties, Maas had stated that the contract was to be subject to BIFA terms. A good number of invoices were also sent to Maas that contained the same statement as to the BIFA terms. While there was no document in which Samsung formally accepted these terms as applicable, there was equally none which denied their applicability. There had,

---

[20] [2011] EWHC 1695. An appeal was allowed but not on matters relevant here: [2013] EWCA Civ 1232.
[21] [2004] EWHC 1502.

though, been a meeting between the parties where reference had been made to the BIFA terms and also to those of the United Kingdom Warehousing Association "as appropriate". It was explained in evidence that BIFA terms were used for "transit movements" and the UKWA terms for "storage accounts". There was also a letter from Maas to Samsung where Maas stated that deliveries of mobile phones and computers would be subject to UKWA terms, and that road haulage would be subject to BIFA terms. Samsung replied that they accepted these terms. There was, though, a later email from Maas which sought to confirm that trading between the parties would be on BIFA terms.

In resolving this issue, the court returned to the distinction made in evidence between transit movements (BIFA terms) and storage accounts (UKWA terms). The warehouse where the phones had been lodged was what was known as an Enhanced Remote Transit Shed, approved by Customs & Excise. Goods can be transferred directly to such a shed, and customs formalities dealt with there. This meant that the goods did not have to be left in the storage facilities of the air carrier. It was also the case that the goods could be re-packaged in the shed so that they could be despatched immediately after C&E clearance had been obtained. Such goods would usually be transferred from the shed in a matter of days. Samsung accepted in evidence that the shed was not a true storage warehouse, but was more a short-transit lounge. Maas made no charge for storage since, as far as it was concerned, this was not a storage account.

The court found that Maas had done what was necessary to give reasonable notice of the BIFA terms. Had the UKWA terms never been referred to, the court said that it would have had no difficulty in ruling that the BIFA terms had been incorporated by conduct or by way of business dealing. Despite such reference, however, the court still found that the contract was governed by the BIFA terms. Even if the UKWA terms had supplanted BIFA, the latter had been reasserted when Maas had emailed Samsung with a statement that they traded under BIFA terms. Samsung had replied that they had mislaid their copy of the terms and requested a replacement. The court also pointed to the use of the shed and concluded that the BIFA terms were applicable because the deposit of the phones was more in the nature of a transit movement than of a true storage.

The court also pointed to the inherent improbability, in a commercial context, of the contract being subject to no standard terms at all. At best, it could only be said that Maas did not emphasise the BIFA terms since they did not wish to jeopardise an important business client. For their part, Samsung were reluctant to acknowledge such terms, which they knew were intended to apply so as to preserve some plausible room to manoeuvre in the event of a claim.

Location of notification

1–010   Although each case depends upon its facts, it has almost become a rule of law that failure to state on the front of the ticket "for conditions see over" (or an equivalent phrase) will render the exclusion clauses ineffective.[22]

---

[22] See *Henderson v Stevenson* (1875) L.R. 2 H.L (sc) 1470.

In *Sugar v London, Midland & Scottish Railway Co*,[23] the words "For conditions see back" were obliterated when the tickets were stamped with the date. The right conclusion in such cases:

> "is that the railway company did not take reasonable steps to bring the conditions to the notice of the passenger, for the obvious reason that it is no use printing words in much clearer type than anything else printed on the ticket if the next thing they do is to blot the words out."[24]

A not dissimilar case is *Richardson Spence & Co v Rowntree*.[25] The claimant contracted with the defendants to be taken as a passenger on a steamer from Philadelphia to Liverpool. She paid her fare and received a ticket containing a number of terms, one of which limited the liability of the defendants to £100. The ticket was presented to her folded up, the conditions also being obliterated in part by a stamp in red ink. A jury found that the claimant knew there to be writing on the ticket although she did not know that the writing contained terms of the contract. The question posed was whether reasonably sufficient notice had been given and the decision of the jury was that it had not. The House of Lords declined to interfere with this finding.

In *Lacey's Footwear Ltd v Bowler International*,[26] the defendant carriers had been soliciting business from the claimants, sending them mailshots and visiting them at their place of work. The first approach had been by telephone in May 1986 and this had been followed by a letter, the bottom of which bore a reference to the defendants' terms and conditions. These were on the reverse of the letter and "in print so small and so faint as to be legible only to one of such tender years that he or she would be far too young to comprehend the meaning of them". The reverse of the letter did, however, add that a larger print version was available, and this statement was itself in larger print. No contract was made at that stage.

A fresh approach was made two years later, a letter being tendered to the claimants which contained terms and conditions on the reverse. Still no contract materialised, nor did an approach in 1991 come to anything. In October 1992, however, the claimants sought quotations from a number of carriers, including the defendants. They prepared a document which referred to terms of trading and then phoned the claimants. In the proceedings which followed, the claimants did not dispute that the letters emanating from the defendants had those tiny terms and conditions on the back, but the claimants' managing director, with whom the negotiations had been conducted, said that he never read them and that "he never read trading terms as their function usually was to limit or exclude liability", an attitude described by the judge as showing an "ostrich-like approach". The judge did, though, acknowledge that:

> "Every time I receive an unsolicited communication from a double glazing company, a life insurance company or a credit card company anxious to sell me its wares, I cannot be expected to read the terms and conditions set out in the small print in the advertisement."

---

[23] [1941] 1 All E.R. 172.
[24] [1941] 1 All E.R. 172 at 174, per Lord Caldecote C.J. See also *Nunan v Southern Railway Co* [1924] 1 K.B. 223; and *Penton v Southern Railway Co* [1931] 2 K.B. 103.
[25] [1894] A.C. 217.
[26] [1997] 2 Lloyd's Rep. 369.

1–011   The key question, he said, was whether there had been reasonable notice of the terms and conditions. The opening move had been made by a call from the claimants followed by the defendants' brief covering letter. This had small print at the foot of the page: "Trading Conditions—See reverse". There was no other effort made to bring the defendants' conditions to the claimants' notice. The defendants' rate proposal specifically referred to the terms of trading in block capitals, but that reference specifically detailed "from FOB Alicante to delivered London E2. Excluding customs clearance". There was nothing in the proposal to refer back to the small print on the reverse side of the covering letter. The court ruled that, on these facts, reasonable notice of the terms and conditions had not been given. The court said that, in reaching such conclusion, it had borne in mind that this was an oral contract negotiated over the telephone and made in a hurry. The rate proposals, which formed the basis of the contract, did not refer to the conditions of contract: they made no reference to the conditions set out on the reverse side of the accompanying letter.[27]

The position taken in *Parker v South Eastern Railway Co* was endorsed in *Shepherd Homes Ltd v Encia Remediation Ltd*.[28] The court was required to determine a preliminary issue as to whether a liability limitation clause in the standard terms and conditions of the third party sub-contractor had been incorporated into its contract with the defendant civil engineering contractor. The latter had employed the former to carry out piling work on a housing development. Following a meeting in which the parties had made an agreement in principle, the sub-contractor had sent a letter to the other party setting out its offer "as detailed in the attached documents". It enclosed its standard terms and conditions of contract which included a clause limiting its liability to the contract price. The engineering contractor's reply instructed the sub-contractor to commence work the following week. It also changed the allocation of risk in relation to ground conditions and thus amounted to a counter-offer. Shortly afterwards, the parties attended a meeting with an engineering firm instructed by the contractors, in which changes to the design of piles were discussed. The sub-contractor proposed its own design for the pile heads and backed its offer by stating that it had professional indemnity cover in the sum of £1 million. In the event, the claimant developer brought proceedings against the contractor for damages after properties constructed on the site began to show signs of cracking. The claim included an allegation that the piling design was defective. The contractor argued that the sub-contractor had failed to give adequate notice of the liability limitation clause; and that the discussion relating to insurance amounted to a revision of the terms offered so as to exclude the liability limitation clause.

1–012   It was held, applying *Parker v South Eastern Railway Co*, that there was no doubt that the sub-contractor's standard conditions formed part of its offer. The contractor's representative had read and considered the terms and conditions and it had been reasonable for the sub-contractor to infer that he had done so. In any event, the latter's offer was sufficient to incorporate the limitation clause when considered in the light of the authorities on the rules of notice. The court endorsed the following statement of principle:

---

[27] See also *Gregg & Co (Knottingley) Ltd v Emhart Glass Ltd* [2005] EWHC 804.
[28] [2007] EWHC 70.

"The rules which have been laid down by the courts regarding notice in such circumstances are three in number:
(1)   If the person receiving the document did not know that there was writing or printing on it, he is not bound.
(2)   If he knew that the writing or printing contained or referred to conditions, he is bound.
(3)   If the party tendering the document did what was reasonably sufficient to give the other party notice of the conditions, and if the other party knew that there was writing or printing on the document, but did not know it contained conditions, then the conditions will become the terms of the contract between them."

This was broadly the line adopted in *Kingspan Environmental v Borealis AS.*[29] The crucial facts as found by the High Court were that company officials within Kingspan were well aware, as indeed they accepted, that polymer suppliers contracted on standard terms and that Borealis was supplying Borecene on its conditions. The relevant Kingspan officer received and signed hundreds of invoices and knew that they had terms and conditions. He was also broadly aware that Borealis gave no warranty "when we turned it into green tanks". Kingspan did not have terms on its purchase orders. Borealis' invoices made plain on their face that all sales were exclusively governed by Borealis General Terms and Conditions as printed on the last page. Those terms were printed on a single page in clear and legible typescript. They were never objected to. Borealis Denmark, the court adjudged, "was reasonably entitled to believe that they were accepted".
Christopher Clarke J. went on to say:

"In those circumstances I am quite satisfied that, as a matter of English law, those terms were incorporated into the contracts of sale which are the subject of these proceedings ... It does not appear from the evidence that anyone at Kingspan ever read or addressed their minds to the content of the invoices other than the amounts. But that does not alter the position. The test for incorporation is an objective one."

It should be noted that the Consumer Rights Act 2014[30] provides for the potential **1–013** unfairness, and hence invalidity, of irrevocably binding terms with which the consumer had no real opportunity of becoming acquainted with before the conclusion of the contract.[31] On a number of occasions, the Office of Fair Trading (now the Competition and Markets Authority) had sought amendment of a contract which contains such clauses. For instance, at the instigation of the OFT, a clause in a home furnishing contract was deleted when it referred to a separate guarantee that the consumer was required to comply with, a copy being made available only on request; in another, a term in a contract for a domestic cleaning services agency contained a term irrevocably binding a consumer to an insurance policy, the terms of which the consumer did not have a reasonable opportunity to examine. The contract was revised by the addition of the main terms of the insurance policy.[32]

---

[29] [2012] EWHC 1147.
[30] The Act in so providing repeats the provisions of the Unfair Terms in Consumer Contracts Regulations 1999/2083, which it repealed.
[31] See generally Ch.10.
[32] See Unfair Contract Terms Bulletin 19.

POSSIBLE ILLEGALITY

1–014   There is an arguable case for saying that exclusion or limitation clauses which are not presented properly to a consumer have been rendered illegal by the Consumer Protection from Unfair Trading Regulations 2008.[33] The Regulations make illegal any misleading omission committed in the course of a commercial practice. A misleading omission embraces a commercial practice which "hides material information [or which] provides material information in a manner which is unclear, unintelligible, ambiguous or untimely". "Material information" means— (a) the information which the average consumer needs, according to the context, to take an informed transactional decision; and (b) any information requirement which applies in relation to a commercial communication as a result of a Community obligation. "The matters which have to be taken into account when deciding if there has been a material omission are:" (a) all the features and circumstances of the commercial practice; (b) the limitations of the medium used to communicate the commercial practice (including limitations of space or time); and (c) where the medium used to communicate the commercial practice imposes limitations of space or time, any measures taken by the trader to make the information available to consumers by other means". It can be said that obliterating or rendering unreadable a statement such as "for terms and conditions see reverse",[34] or where terms are not drawn to a party's attention prior to the contract being made, are each illegal under the Regulations. So would be any form of presentation of a document (perhaps by the way it is folded) which actually hid the relevant provision.[35]

DISABLED PARTIES

1–015   Rather special factors come into play where the claimant, even if he were inclined to do so, could not read the appropriate conditions, because he was illiterate, blind, or unable to comprehend English. In *Thompson v London, Midland & Scottish Railway Co*[36] the claimant was unable to read. Her niece bought for her a railway ticket which on its face contained the familiar words: "For conditions see back". The back of the ticket made reference to timetables and excursion bills. The bills themselves referred to the timetables, which contained a clause exempting the company from liability in respect of any injury, however caused. The Court of Appeal held that the illiteracy had no effect since enough had been done to bring the terms to the attention of those members of the public to which the claimant belonged.

It appears, however, that where the special disability is known to the other party, that will suffice to disapply the particular clauses. The relevant case is

---

[33] SI 2008/1277 as amended by the Consumer Protection (Amendment) Regulations 2014 (SI 2014/870).
[34] See *Sugar v London, Midland & Scottish Railway Co* [1941] 1 All E.R. 172.
[35] There are no equivalent provisions in the Business Protection from Misleading Marketing Regulations 2008 (SI 2008/1276).
[36] [1930] 1 K.B. 41.

Geier v Kujawa.[37] A notice in English was displayed in a car, stating that passengers rode at their own risk. This was held not to bind one particular passenger who, to the driver's own knowledge, spoke German but little English. If the railway company in the previous case had known of the passenger's illiteracy, and had she on that occasion been unaccompanied, presumably she would not have been bound by the clauses unless told of their existence in general or specific terms.

It should also be noted that under the Equality Act 2010 there is a duty to make reasonable adjustments to ensure that a disabled person is not at a disadvantage. In appropriate circumstances this could, for example, require Braille copies of contracts to be provided.

PROVIDING COPIES

An interesting variation on the usual problems of incorporation arose in *Smith v South Wales Switchgear Co Ltd*.[38] A contractual document provided that the general conditions were available on request. There were three editions, the last being March 1970. No copy was requested, but the 1969 version was sent. This was done because of a misunderstanding over another contract between the same parties. The House of Lords held that the 1970 version had been incorporated into the contract. The meaning reasonably attributed to the reference was that the conditions referred to were the current ones. It was common experience that general conditions of contract were periodically revised. Had a copy been requested, the recipients would reasonably have expected to receive the 1970 edition.

    1–016

In contrast, where an out-of-date set of conditions was handed to the other party in error, but with the intention that they should form the basis of the contract, these were the terms which were incorporated into the contract.[39]

UNAVAILABILITY OF COPIES

A particular problem which has not yet been litigated arises where a party asks for copies of conditions, where his attention is drawn to them before the contract is made, only to be told that they are unavailable, for whatever reason. If the party making the request proceeds nonetheless to make the contract, it is not clear whether he is bound by those contract terms. On the assumption that he was free to turn around and decline the contract, there is reason for saying that he must therefore be bound by those terms. Equally, though, the party who invites reference to those terms, but then fails to proffer them when a reasonable request is made, may be said to have lost the chance to incorporate those terms. As a practical matter, it is likely that in the instant case the attitude and reaction of the party seeking a copy of those terms will do much to clarify the position. If the

    1–017

---

[37] [1970] 1 Lloyd's Rep. 364.
[38] [1978] 1 All E.R. 18. See too *UCB Ltd v Spooner Industries Ltd and Forbo Siegling (UK) Ltd* [2013] CSOH 150.
[39] *St Albans City and District Council v International Computers Ltd* [1995] F.S.R. 686.

attitude of the party making the request is that "it does not really matter", the terms will probably be implied against him. If, in contrast, his attitude is that he is proceeding with the contract on the basis of the inapplicability of those terms, then indeed they will surely be inapplicable.

WHERE THE CLAUSE IS UNUSUAL

1–018   If the particular condition relied upon by the party seeking exemption is one that is unusual in that class of contract, that party, it now seems clear, will have to show that he took special measures fairly to bring the condition to the attention of the other party. In *Spurling Ltd v Bradshaw*,[40] Denning L.J. gave it as his view, *obiter dicta*, that:

> "the more unreasonable a clause is, the greater the notice which must be given of it. Some clauses which I have seen would need to be printed in red ink on the face of the document with a red hand pointing to it before the notice could be held to be sufficient."[41]

In *Thornton v Shoe Lane Parking Ltd*,[42] a notice outside a car park bore the legend "All cars parked at owners' [sic] risk". When a driver approached the entrance, a ticket emerged from an automatic machine and he would then proceed into the car park. The ticket contained printed wording to the effect that it was issued subject to the conditions displayed on the premises. These conditions were lengthy and included words exempting the defendants not only from liability for damage to cars, but also from liability for any injury to the customer howsoever caused, while his car was in the car park.
Lord Denning regarded the clause as:

> "so wide and so destructive of rights that the court should not hold any man bound by it unless it is drawn to his attention in the most explicit way . . . In order to give sufficient notice, it would need to be printed in red ink with a red hand pointing to it, or something equally startling."[43]

Megaw L.J. continued with this basic theme. Where the condition relied on involves a restriction not usual in a particular class of contract, a defendant "must show that his intention to attach an unusual condition of that particular nature was fairly brought to the attention of the other party".[44] That had not been done here, since there had been no clear indication which would lead an ordinary sensible person to suppose that a term relating to personal injury had been included in the contract. He did not think that the stage had yet been reached wherein such terms were an accepted aspect of such contracts as featured in this particular case.[45]

---

[40] [1956] 2 All E.R. 121.
[41] [1956] 2 All E.R. 121 at 125.
[42] [1971] 1 All E.R. 686.
[43] [1971] 1 All E.R. 686 at 690.
[44] [1971] 1 All E.R. 686 at 692.
[45] [1971] 1 All E.R. 686 at 692.

It is always arguable that such a practice as is described above constitutes a misleading and hence criminal omission, since presentation of the ticket is untimely, given that there is nothing the driver can do in relation to the terms and conditions.[46]

The line of argument in these two cases was firmly endorsed by the Court of Appeal in the major case of *Interfoto Picture Library Ltd v Stiletto Visual Programmes Ltd*.[47] The defendant advertising agency required photographs of the 1950s for a presentation for a client. It telephoned the claimants on March 5, 1984, asking if they had any photographs which might be suitable for the presentation. The defendants had not dealt with the claimants, who ran a library of photographic transparencies, on any previous occasion. On the same day, the claimants dispatched to the defendants transparencies packed in a bag with a delivery note which clearly specified that the transparencies were to be returned by March 19 and which, under the heading "Conditions", prominently stated nine printed conditions in four columns. The heading "Conditions" was printed prominently in capitals. Condition 2 stated that all transparencies were to be returned within 14 days from the date of delivery and that a "holding fee of £5 plus VAT per day will be charged for each transparency which is retained by you longer than the said period of 14 days". The defendants did not use the transparencies for their presentation and put them on one side and forgot about them. The transparencies were not returned until April 2. The claimants sent the defendants an invoice for £3,783.50 being the holding charge calculated at £5 per transparency per day from March 19 to April 2. The defendants refused to pay and the claimants brought an action against them for the amount of the invoice. The Court of Appeal ruled that where a condition in a contract was particularly onerous or unusual and would not be generally known to the other party, the party seeking to enforce the condition had to show that it had been fairly and reasonably brought to the other party's attention. Condition 2 was an unreasonable and extortionate clause which the claimants had not brought to the attention of the defendants and therefore it did not become part of the contract and the defendants were not bound by it.

1–019

According to Dillon L.J.:

"At the time of the ticket cases in the last century it was notorious that people hardly ever troubled to read printed conditions on a ticket or delivery note or similar document. That remains the case now. In the intervening years the printed conditions have tended to become more and more complicated and more one-sided in favour of the party who is imposing them, but the other parties, if they notice that there are printed conditions at all, generally still tend to assume that such conditions are only concerned with ancillary matters of form and are not of importance. In the ticket cases the courts held that the common law required that reasonable steps be taken to draw the other parties' attention to the printed conditions or they would not be part of the contract. It is in my judgment a logical development of the common law into modern conditions that it should be held as it was in *Thornton v Shoe Lane Parking Ltd*[48] that, if one condition in a set of printed conditions is particularly onerous or unusual, the party seeking to enforce it must show that the particular condition was fairly brought to the attention

---

[46] See the consideration of the Consumer Protecting from Unfair Trading Regulations at para.1–014.
[47] [1988] 1 All E.R. 348.
[48] [1971] 1 All E.R. 686. See para.1–018.

of the other party. In the present case, nothing whatever was done to draw the defendants' attention to Condition 2, in particular; it was merely one of four columns' width of conditions printed across the delivery note."[49]

It was, however, held that these other conditions, which were in common form and were usual terms regularly encountered in this business, were incorporated into the contract.

The *Interfoto* case was followed in *AEG (UK) Ltd v Logic Resource Ltd.*[50] In response to an order from buyers, sellers despatched a confirmation note which set out details of the equipment ordered and which added at the bottom, in small capital letters, the words: "ORDERS ARE SUBJECT TO OUR CONDITIONS OF SALE—FOR EXTRACT SEE REVERSE". The reverse set out five conditions, headed: "Extracts from our Conditions of Sale". These conditions were followed by: "A copy of the full Conditions of Sale is available on request". The buyers made no such request. One of the clauses provided that: "The purchaser shall return the defective parts at his own expense to the supplier immediately on request of the latter". This clause was, however, a subclause in what was called a "warranty". The other subclauses in this warranty contained a guarantee that the goods were free from defects caused by faulty materials and bad workmanship, adding that, if the goods were not in fact manufactured by the sellers, then the latter would warrant them only to the extent of any warranty provided by the manufacturers. A further subclause required buyers to notify the suppliers of any defect within seven days of its discovery and also to tender proof of purchase and guarantee. Once the goods were with the suppliers, buyers were to allow them "the time and opportunity requested as estimated" by the suppliers. Buyers were also required to pay the costs of any tests run on the goods if the suppliers denied liability. This warranty also provided that: "All other warranties or conditions are hereby expressly excluded" adding that the suppliers were not to be "liable in any event for any consequential loss". The District Judge ruled that the phrase: "Subject to our conditions of sale—for extract see reverse" sufficed to incorporate the full terms and conditions: "I am satisfied that these words give the purchaser sufficient notice that terms and conditions exist and are an adequate tender of those conditions". The Court of Appeal referred to the *Thornton* and *Interfoto* cases and, by a majority, reversed the lower court. It was held that the disputed clause had to be read in context and, so judged, it could only be judged "extremely onerous". Since nothing had been done to bring it specifically to the attention of the buyer, it was not binding.

1–020   Hobhouse L.J. dissented, though only on the question of whether the clause was unusual, and not from the *Interfoto* case. He said that the whole of the warranty clause dealt with a topic:

---

[49] See [1988] 1 All E.R. 348 at 352. It has been pointed out that Dillon L.J. would not have accepted the onerous term being part of the contract, "whereas Bingham L.J. held that the relevant condition was to be relieved against, a rather different approach". See *Debenhams Retail Plc v Customs & Excise Commissioners* [2004] EWHC 1540. The judge in this case preferred the approach of Bingham L.J.

[50] [1996] C.L.C. 265. See also *Cubitt Building & Interiors Ltd v Richardson Roofing (Industrial) Ltd* [2008] EWHC 1020 (TCC).

> "normally dealt with. It is in no way unusual for standard conditions to qualify obligations for sellers under a contract of sale. The clauses deal with a topic one would expect to be dealt with in the Conditions of Sale and they cover the type of points which would be commonly dealt with."

He added that, if every clause were to be given close scrutiny, to determine if it is "entirely reasonable, then one is distorting the ordinary mechanisms of making contracts and an element of uncertainty will be introduced".[51]

In *Picardi Architects v Cuniberti*,[52] a contract by which architects were engaged sought to incorporate the standard terms of the Royal Institute of British Architects. One of these terms related to adjudication on disputes arising between the parties. It was the case that the adjudication clause was incorporated by virtue of s.108 of the Housing Grants, Construction and Regeneration Act 1996, but that s.106 of that Act provided that such provision was not to apply to private residents, such as the defendant in this case. The court concluded that the adjudication clause in this case was so unusual that it should have been brought to the attention of the defendant and individually negotiated. It was felt to be significant that RIBA's own guidance notes indicated that the adjudication clause should be brought specifically to the attention of the other contracting party.

Using the *Interfoto* case as providing inferential support, it has also been said that, where a contract contains "stringent" terms, a party will not secure the incorporation of those terms, where he does not comply with his own stipulations as to how the contract is to be made.[53]

A clause found not to fall foul of the *Interfoto* ruling was the following, in a contract for the lease of a photocopier to a business:

> "Our Exclusion and Limitation. The equipment and the supplier have been selected by you relying entirely on your own judgment. If you require any warranties or guarantees in respect of the equipment, its maintenance or suitability for any purpose, you must obtain them from the supplier. We exclude all express or implied warranties, conditions or guarantees from this agreement, and in no event will our liability under this agreement exceed the aggregate of the rentals paid by you at the time the liability arises. In no event will we be liable to you in contract, tort or otherwise including any liability for negligence:
> (a)   for any loss of revenue, business, anticipated savings or profits, or any loss of use or value; or
> (b)   for any indirect or consequential loss howsoever arising. 'Anticipated savings' means any expense which you expect to avoid incurring or to incur in a lesser amount than would otherwise have been the case."

The court held that, while this clause was widely drawn, "it is plainly to be expected that clauses of that nature would be found in equipment leasing contracts with finance companies". Furthermore, the facts disclosed that the

---

[51] In *HIH Casualty & General Insurance Ltd v New Hampshire Insurance Co* [2001] EWCA Civ 735, Rix L.J. doubted if the Interfoto principle extended to clauses which were merely unusual.
[52] [2002] EWHC 2923 (TCC).
[53] *Jonathan Wren & Co Ltd v Microdec Plc* (1999) 65 Con. L.R. 157. See also *Munkenbeck & Marshall v Harold* [2005] EWHC 356 (TCC). As to whether Interfoto could be used to imply a term as to good faith, see *Berkeley Community Villages Ltd v Fred Daniel Pullen* [2007] EWHC 1330.

lessee had looked at the terms and conditions and "therefore, probably, understood the nature of what he was signing". The *Interfoto* case was therefore distinguished.[54]

1–021   The *Interfoto* case was also distinguished in *O'Brien v MGN Ltd*.[55] Rule 5 of a scratchcard game stated that if more prizes were claimed than were available in any prize category a draw would take place for the prize. The Court of Appeal ruled that, although this rule 5 did turn an apparent winner into a loser, it could not by any normal use of language be called "onerous" or "outlandish": it did not impose any extra burden on the claimant, nor did it seek to absolve the defendant from liability for personal injuries negligently caused (reference being made here to *Thornton v Shoe Lane Parking*). It merely deprived the claimant of a windfall for which he had done very little in return. He had bought two newspapers, although in fact he could have acquired a card and discovered the hotline number without doing either. He had made a call to a premium rate number, which would have cost him some money and gained the newspaper some, but only a matter of pennies not pounds. The court did observe, however, that the defendants had only done "just about enough" to draw the rules to the claimant's attention.[56]

Interfoto was further distinguished in *Carlsberg-Tetley Brewing Ltd v Gilbarco Ltd*.[57] The relevant contract document bore at the bottom the abbreviation "CONT", and the following sheet was headed "CONTINUATION SHEET". The judge, who was also impressed by the fact that the claimants in this case had more relevant expertise than the defendants, dismissed the contention that more could have been done to bring the terms to the claimant's notice. He said it was "difficult to imagine what else the defendants could have done apart from typing 'Continued' in red on the first page and typing the second page also in red ... [Interfoto] is a thousand miles away from the facts of this case".

Although each case must be judged on its individual facts, the trend has been to find that a disputed clause is not unusual or onerous, as the following instances show:

(1)   In *Ocean Chemical Transport Inc v Exnor Craggs Ltd*,[58] a clause provided that all liability whatsoever would cease unless a suit was brought within six months after delivery of the goods. This clause was neither extreme nor unexpected and it had, furthermore, been drawn to the attention of the other party.

(2)   In *Debenhams Retail Plc v Customs & Excise Commissioners*,[59] Debenhams introduced a new scheme in relation to credit and debit card payment for the purpose of reducing its liability to VAT. Certain "notification

---

[54] *Danka Rentals Ltd v Xi Software Ltd* (1998) 17 Tr. L.R. 74. In *Bankway Properties Ltd v Dunsford* [2001] EWCA Civ 528, Arden L.J. indicated that, while a particular rent review clause was onerous, clear attention had been drawn to it by the landlord in a pre-contract letter, thus incorporating it into the agreement.

[55] [2001] EWCA Civ 1279.

[56] [2001] EWCA Civ 1279, *per* Butler-Sloss L.J.

[57] Unreported March 31, 1999 TCC. See also *Photolibrary Group Ltd v Burda Senator Verlag GmbH* [2008] EWHC 1343 (QB).

[58] [2001] 1 All E.R. (Comm) 519.

[59] [2004] EWHC 1540 (Ch).

words", alerting the customer to the new scheme were posted at the store doors and tills. It was held that, while the notification words did not operate as terms of the necessary contracts, they were sufficient indications both of the terms on which the business would be willing to enter into contracts for the supply of goods in return for card payment and, of the broad nature of the service provided and any detriment to the customer was minor and there were countervailing benefits to be derived from the use of the cards.

(3)   In *Shepherd Homes Ltd (claimant) v Encia Remediation Ltd*,[60] it was held that limitation of a contractor's liability to the contract price could not be said to be particularly unusual or onerous. In any case, sufficient notice of such clause had been given.

(4)   In *Sumukan Ltd v Commonwealth Secretariat*,[61] the contract between the parties provided for disputes to be referred to the Commonwealth Secretariat Arbitral Tribunal for settlement by arbitration in accordance with its statute which formed part of the contract and was available on request. The statute provided that the judgment of the tribunal was to be final and binding on the parties and not subject to appeal. The court held that the exclusion agreement was not some form of unusual or onerous clause to which attention had to be drawn specifically before it could be relied on. It pointed out that the policy of the Arbitration Act 1996 was to encourage the notion that persons should arbitrate and keep the resolution of their disputes out of the courts.

(5)   In *Otto Chan v Barts and the London NHS Trust*,[62] the claimant employee sought various declarations against the defendant following his summary dismissal for gross misconduct. Paragraph 190 of the Terms and Conditions for Hospital and Medical and Dental Staff, which had been incorporated into his contract of employment when he joined the trust, provided for an appeal to the Secretary of State for Health against an unfair termination of employment by sending a notice of appeal during the period of notice of termination of the appointment. He was informed by the trust in 2003 that it would be adopting a new standard consultant contract which was to be adopted nationally. The new contract removed the para.190 procedures. It was held that the loss of the right of appeal was not such a fundamental change and was not so onerous or unusual as to require explicit and clear notification to the claimant.

(6)   In *Do-Buy 925 Ltd v National Westminster Bank Plc*,[63] a contract between a jeweller, in relation to his acceptance of credit card payments, and a bank as merchant acquirer, contained this clause: "You agree that as between You and Us it is Your responsibility to prove to Our Satisfaction that the debit of a cardholder's account was authorised by the genuine cardholder". The court ruled that *Interfoto* did not apply. This was said not to be an extreme case nor one in which there was any cause to depart from the rule that a party was bound by its signature to a document. The court pointed out that

---

[60] [2007] EWHC 70 (TCC).
[61] [2007] EWCA Civ 243.
[62] [2007] EWHC 2914 (QB).
[63] [2010] EWHC 2862 (QB).

the signature was immediately below a statement that the signatory had read the terms and conditions, and this came at the end of a section marked: "Important—you should read this carefully". The court also said that the clause was neither a particularly unusual or onerous term in allocating the risk of identity fraud to the merchant:

> "In any event the Bank did more than was sufficient fairly to draw the attention of Do-Buy to this allocation of risk. It is expressly identified in the Merchant Operating Instructions. It is part and parcel of the system of chargebacks, which are also clearly identified in the contractual literature".

(7) In *Allen Fabrications Ltd v ASD Metal Services*,[64] the disputed clauses were these:

> "We are not liable for any other loss or damage (including indirect or consequential loss, financial loss, loss of profits or loss of use) arising from the contract or the supply of goods or their use, even if we are negligent.
> For all other liabilities not referred to elsewhere in these conditions our liability is limited in damages to the price of the goods".

1–022 The court noted that, in *Interfoto*, the relevant clause in a one-off contract for the hire of transparencies imposed a penal rate when they were not returned on time. It said that the Court of Appeal in that case, having reviewed the authorities, had said that if one condition was particularly onerous or unusual the party seeking to enforce it must show that it (and not merely the standard terms generally) was fairly brought to the attention of the other party:

> "The tendency of the English authorities has…been to look at the nature of the transaction in question and the character of the parties to it; to consider what notice the party alleged to be bound was given of the particular condition said to bind him; and to resolve whether in all the circumstances it is fair to hold him bound by the condition in question.[65]"

The court in the present case, though, said it would make a couple of observations on this. First, it was not always clear what amounted to an "onerous" clause. In *Interfoto*, the court had said that the clause in question was "unreasonable and extortionate" and referred to "particularly" onerous clauses. The court also pointed to *Circle Freight v Mideast Gulf Exports*,[66] where there were international freight forwarding standard terms which limited the carrier's liability to cases of wilful neglect and which provided a ceiling on the amount paid by reference to the lowest of three different formulae. In the case itself this meant that only £192 would be payable against a claim for £6,371. These clauses were not unusual because they were in common use. But they were not held to be onerous either. The court had said that they were not "draconian". The court in

---

[64] [2012] EWHC 2213. For another example of a clause being regarded as neither unfair nor onerous, see *Mortgage Express v Sawali* [2010] EWHC 3054.
[65] *Interfoto Picture Library Ltd v Stiletto Visual Programmes Ltd* [1988] 1 All E.R. 348 per Bingham L.J. at p.357.
[66] [1988] 2 Lloyd's Rep 427.

the *Allen* case thus concluded that the mere fact that the clause was a limitation or exclusion clause did not seem to render it onerous without more. It said that much would depend on the context.

The court thought that if a clause was in very common use, then it was less likely properly to be regarded as onerous "especially between two commercial parties since that is the business in which they knowingly operate". The court also made the point that if the dispute term was subject to the provisions of the Unfair Contract Terms Act, it was arguable that a more flexible approach to what is truly "onerous" could be taken.

It was also noted that it had been suggested that the "onerous" class of terms extended to ones which, whether onerous or unusual, abrogated statutory rights. The court, though, felt that this view should be approached with caution. The point had, however, not been taken in the present case and was not considered further.

The court concluded that the assessment of fairness and reasonableness in the present case was "clearly fact-sensitive and regard must be had in particular to (a) the nature of the clause, (b) what actual steps were taken to draw it to the other party's attention, (c) the character of the parties, and (d) their particular dealings".   **1–023**

The court made the interesting observation that "some adjustment of the principle must be called for" where the other party already knows not merely that the document contains terms but also that it contains, or is likely to contain terms, of the type complained of even though they have not read this actual clause. As the court explained, the "whole concept of reasonably bringing it to the attention of the other party" is to avoid the mischief of their ignorance of it. In many of the reported cases, the court said, it was common ground that not only had the terms not been read, the other party did not know the onerous term was there. If, though, the other party is in general terms aware that it was, "then notice is not necessary. Put another way, the requirement that a contracting party knew that the writing or printing on it contained or referred to conditions can be rephrased for onerous terms: 'If he knew that the writing or printing on it contained or referred to the onerous condition relied upon or conditions of the same type, he is bound.'" The court said that the alternative way to put it was to say that in such a case, what will constitute bringing the clause fairly and reasonably to the attention of the other party is likely to be little more than what is necessary in respect of the conditions as a whole.

The court concluded that any argument based on the alleged onerous nature of the disputed clauses in this case failed. The relevant terms here were not unusual in this industry. The buyers knew that suppliers like ASD would (like it did itself) have exclusion clauses in respect of which buyers like Allen would have to protect themselves by insurance and using such terms themselves. On that footing, the court judged, it was impossible to see what further steps were required of ASD other than to satisfy the normal "notice" test for incorporation and course of dealing which, it had been conceded, they did.

The court made the further point that, unlike other cases, this was not a single dealing between the parties, nor was the party affected an individual consumer:

"This was a commercial customer who had already dealt with ASD on over 250 occasions usually 3–4 times a month. It had had the actual terms on numerous occasions albeit on advice notes normally only seen by those working in the yard. It had a clear reference to the terms on invoices which would be seen by the buyers' relevant officers".

ONEROUS CLAUSES IN CONSUMER CONTRACTS

1–024 When the Consumer Rights Bill was first presented to Parliament, the position with regard to unusual or onerous contracts would have been given statutory force. Such measure was, however, dropped from the 2014 Act. No doubt this was because an unusual or onerous term would in any event have been subject to the test of fairness.

THE EFFECT OF SIGNATURE

1–025 Although it has never been formally decided, it seems that the principles of the *Interfoto* case will not apply where the relevant document has been signed. This must, though, now be limited to contracts with a business since the provisions of s.71 just discussed would appear to rule out giving any effect to a consumer's signature.

In *Jonathan Wren & Co Ltd v Microdec Plc*,[67] it was said that "it is unlikely that the approach adopted in the *Interfoto* case would be applied to a written contract actually signed by the parties". Again, in *Bankway Properties v Dunsford*,[68] Arden L.J. thought it not clear that the *Interfoto* doctrine applies to a contract which a party signs. In *Ata v American Express Ltd*,[69] Rix J. was quite specific that the *Interfoto* principle did not apply to documents which had been signed. Although the point has not been authoritatively decided, it appears to be the case that the *Interfoto* principle will apply to signed contracts only in extreme cases.[70]

INTERFOTO ANALYSED

1–026 In the *Interfoto* case, Bingham L.J. had said that the cases on sufficiency of notice were to be judged on two levels.[71] At one level, they involved issues of "pure contractual analysis", dealing with the question whether one party had done enough to give the other notice of incorporation of a contract term. At the other level, such terms were concerned with the different question as to whether it would be fair or reasonable in all the circumstances to hold that a party was

---

[67] (1999) 65 Con. L.R. 157.
[68] [2001] EWCA Civ 528.
[69] Unreported October 7, 1996. The matter was not considered in the appeal: The Times, June 26, 1998, CA (Civ Div).
[70] See *JP Morgan Chase Bank v Springwell Navigation Corp* [2008] EWHC 1186 (Comm) and the cases there cited. See also *J Sweeney v Peninsula Business Services Ltd* [2003] UKEAT 1096_02_0104; *Do-Buy 925 Ltd v National Westminster Bank Plc* [2010] EWHC 2862 (QB) and *Allen Fabrications Ltd v ASD Metal Services* [2012] EWHC 2213.
[71] See [1988] All E.R. 348 at 353.

bound by unusual or stringent terms. This analysis found favour in *Lacey's Footwear Ltd v Bowler*.[72] Brooke L.J. stated that:

> "In my judgment it is infinitely better for the common law to be able to fashion a fair result in a case like this by adopting the approach which was identified by Bingham L.J. in *Interfoto* and which is well founded on authority than to have to resort to interpretative devices of almost Byzantine sophistication to arrive at a result that the words of a contract do not mean what, on the face of it, they clearly do mean. It would, in my judgment, be a reproach to the common law if a court had to resort to such devices in order to do justice in a case like this."

The disputed clause was as follows:

> "(3)   In no case whatsoever shall any liability of the Company, howsoever arising, and notwithstanding that the cause or loss or damage be unexplained exceed:
> (a)   The value of the relevant goods or
> (b)   A sum at the rate of £800 per metric tonne on the gross weight of the goods or
> (c)   £15,000 in respect of any one claim whichever shall be the least."

Brooke L.J. said that the court should not be:

> "willing to apply [the disputed clause]... Standing back from the detail of the case and looking at the overall justice of the situation, I consider that this would be a just result. It neither compels the court to make a finding of wilful misconduct when it would be unfair to do so because of the inherent weaknesses in the available evidence, nor does it force the court to give effect to a standard small-print trading condition when it would be manifestly unjust to do so."[73]

In *Amiri Flight Authority v BAE Systems Plc*,[74] Tomlinson J. expressed reservations about the approach adopted by Bingham L.J. when the contract was of some magnitude and sophistication, concluded between "large and powerful commercial interests who have available to them skilled legal advice". He said that the Lord Justice's test involves consideration as to whether a clause could be said to have been fairly and reasonably brought to the other party's notice, and that it "must be obvious that fairness and reasonableness will take their colour from the nature of the transaction and the nature of the parties thereto". He added that the structure of a "complex contract" was part of the context in the light of which the contract, or any part of it, was to be construed. Tomlinson J. also found that the particular clause had been fairly brought to the notice of the other side, pointing to the fact that it was in capital letters; its meaning was clear and obvious and it was properly positioned within the contract itself.

INTERFOTO AND ARBITRATION CLAUSES

It has been said that the *Interfoto* principles: **1–027**

> "are applicable to contracts containing arbitration clauses but, plainly, all the relevant circumstances must be taken into account in deciding whether or not the particular arbitration

---

[72] See [1997] 2 Lloyd's Rep. 369.
[73] In fact, this finding was *obiter dicta* since the Court of Appeal agreed that the pleadings had disclosed no reliance on the provisions of the Unfair Contract Terms Act 1977.
[74] [2002] EWHC 2481 (Comm).

agreement in issue is unusual or onerous and, if it is, whether it has been brought fairly and reasonably to the attention of the other party."[75]

When the Terms to be Incorporated do not yet Exist

1–028   In *Ceval Alimentos SA v Agrimpex Trading Co Ltd,*[76] a clause sought to incorporate: "All other terms, conditions and exceptions as per charterparty". The court had to decide if this sufficed to introduce into a sale contract a diversion clause which was to be found in the charterparty, this latter not then being in existence. The court observed that it was typical of c.i.f. contracts for the seller to be obliged to enter into carriage contracts by the terms of an earlier sale contract. The sale contract would frequently refer to the terms then unknown, such as the demurrage provisions. It was also the case that, through the bill of lading, the buyer was in turn to become party to all the terms of the contract of carriage arranged between seller and shipowner. There was always the danger that allowing incorporation of a future contract would expose a party to the danger of contracting on terms over which he had no control, but this was limited by "well-known" doctrines, such as the requirement that any term to be incorporated must be such that it could be read consistently and sensibly in the context of the parent contract.

When Acceptance Cannot be Avoided

1–029   In the *Thornton* case, it was thought by Megaw L.J. to be a "highly relevant factor", in considering whether the matter was fairly brought to the attention of the claimant, that the first attempt to bring the conditions to his attention was when it was "practically impossible" for him to withdraw from the premises. One can well imagine, the Lord Justice continued, the chaos which would ensue should customers, after seeing the reference on the tickets, leave their cars blocking the entrance to the garage "in order to search for, find and peruse the notices"![77]

This was the effective introduction of a novel concept. The fact that a party has virtually no option but to proceed with his acceptance of the offer is not to deny of itself that he was even so fully informed of the terms of agreement, or the fact that there were such terms. Impractical though it may have been, the option still lay with the individual not to proceed with the agreement. Indeed, Megaw L.J. viewed such matters only as supporting his view that reasonable notice had not been supplied.

Sir Gordon Willmer, however, took a more robust line. In the case of a ticket proffered by an automatic machine, he said, there is something quite irrevocable: "it seems to me that any attempt to introduce conditions after the irrevocable step

---

[75] *Kaye v Nu Skin UK Ltd* [2009] EWHC 3509 (Ch), per Kitchin J. citing *Stretford v Football Association Ltd* [2007] EWCA Civ 238; [2007] 2 All E.R. (Comm) 1 and *Sumukan v Commonwealth Secretariat* [2007] EWCA Civ 243; [2007] 2 All E.R. (Comm) 23.
[76] [1996] 2 Lloyd's Rep. 319.
[77] [1971] 1 All E.R. 686 at 693.

has been taken of causing the machine to operate must be doomed to failure".[78] In the case of tickets proffered by human hand, in contrast, there remains the opportunity to say: "I do not like your conditions. I will not have this ticket".[79]

The same basic point has been made by the Court of Appeal in *Burnett v British Waterways Board*.[80] The claimant in that case was a lighterman in a barge which was part of a convoy being moved forward into a lock. The rope pulling his barge forward snapped, because of the negligence of the defendants, and the claimant was injured, for which injury he later brought an action. The defendants maintained that their liability had been excluded by a notice at the entrance to the lock which was held, by the High Court and the Court of Appeal, to contain wording which was apt to cover the damage which had occurred. In the Court of Appeal, agreeing with the court below that the exclusion clause was of no avail, Lord Denning quoted with approval the words of Waller J.:

1–030

> "The claimant was not somebody arriving on his own at the entrance to the lock and saying: 'Well, I will not go in because of this notice.' He was an employee on a barge, part of a train of barges, and by the time he had got to the lock it was certainly beyond his ability to make a choice and not go in... The plain fact, as I see it, is that the claimant was not really in a position to exercise a free choice."[81]

The full implications of this approach have yet to be worked out. Although couched in terms of automatic machines, there is no reason why tickets offered by human hand cannot also come within the above principles. Where tickets are proffered at the head of a lengthy queue, as at a football match or railway booking office, it is essentially impossible not to accept the offered terms. The same might be said of the passenger who has boarded a bus which then moves off.[82]

AT OR BEFORE THE TIME OF CONTRACTING

It is settled law that no clause is effective unless adequately brought to the other party's attention before the time the contract is made. A well-known example is *Olley v Marlborough Court Ltd*.[83] A husband and wife arrived at a hotel and paid for board and residence in advance. They went to the room allotted to them, and on one of the walls was this notice: "The proprietors will not hold themselves responsible for articles lost or stolen unless handed to the manageress for safe custody". In their absence, clothing was stolen from the room. The Court of Appeal held that the contract was completed before the guests went up to their room and that no subsequent notice could affect their rights.

1–031

---

[78] [1971] 1 All E.R. 686 at 693.
[79] [1971] 1 All E.R. 686 at 693.
[80] [1972] 2 All E.R. 1353; [1973] 2 All E.R. 631 CA.
[81] [1972] 2 All E.R. 1353 at 1358.
[82] See also the discussion of the effect of the Consumer Rights Act 2014 at para.10–025 and the reference to the indicative list.
[83] [1949] 1 All E.R. 127.

The same point was made by Mocatta J. in *Burnett v Westminster Bank Ltd*.[84] The defendants in that case were in effect seeking to alter the terms of a contract already made, quite apart from any question whether the cheque book was or was not a contractual document. It may also be pointed out that had the ticket in *Chapelton v Barry Urban DC*[85] constituted a contractual document, it would have been ineffective in that it had been given to the claimant after he had accepted the offer to hire a chair, and hence after the contract was made.

Another useful example is *Hollingworth v Southern Ferries*.[86] B booked a passage for P and himself on D's vessel, and was later given tickets containing an exclusion clause. It was held that the contract was concluded before the ticket was delivered and, accordingly, D could not rely on the exclusion clause.

The problem of when a contract is made if done through the agency of a machine was considered by Lord Denning in *Thornton v Shoe Lane Parking*.[87] It was his view that the contract was concluded when the money was put into the machine. The whole business could be translated into the dogma of offer and acceptance in this way. The offer:

> "is made when the proprietor of the machine holds it out as being ready to receive the money. The acceptance takes place when the customer puts his money into the slot. The terms of the offer are contained in the notice placed in or near the machine stating what is offered for the money. The customer is bound by those terms as long as they are sufficiently brought to his notice beforehand, but not otherwise. He is not bound by the terms printed on the ticket if they differ from the notice, because the ticket comes too late. The contract has already been made."[88]

1–032   This approach, while attractive, must be treated with considerable caution, not least because the proprietor holding out the machine as ready to receive money is surely more akin to an invitation to treat. Lord Denning himself also found more traditional grounds for avoiding the exclusion clause (that not enough notice had been given) while both Megaw L.J. and Sir Gordon Willmer expressly reserved judgment on this issue.[89]

What this case does highlight, of course, is the clear need to bear in mind the distinction between an offer and an invitation to treat. This also arose (albeit it did not create much difficulty) in *Levison v Patent Steam Carpet Cleaning Co*.[90] Over the telephone, the owner of a carpet had requested that it be picked up and taken away for cleaning. When the cleaning company called for it, the owner was presented with a form, containing exclusion clauses, which he duly signed. The Court of Appeal was unanimous in its decision that the document had been incorporated into the contract, albeit no firm reason was given why. Lord Denning M.R. felt that the document had become incorporated through the course of dealing between the parties.[91] Orr L.J. felt that the document would have been

---

[84] [1966] 1 Q.B. 742.
[85] [1940] K.B. 532.
[86] [1977] 2 Lloyd's Rep. 70. See also *Dillon v Baltic Shipping Co* [1990] 1 Lloyd's Rep. 579.
[87] [1971] 1 All E.R. 686.
[88] [1971] 1 All E.R 686 at 689.
[89] [1971] 1 All E.R 686 at 692 and 693, respectively.
[90] [1977] 3 All E.R. 498.
[91] [1977] 3 All E.R. 498 at 502. See further the discussion at para.1–034.

part of the contract even "in the absence of any previous dealing between the parties",[92] a view with which Sir David Cairns agreed.[93]

In this latter case, one must view the telephone conversation as merely inviting the defendants to come to the claimant's house and offer to take away the carpet for cleaning. It may be asked if this is entirely acceptable: the telephone conversation was more specific than that ("Can you come and collect and when?—Yes, July 17")[94] and it may be wondered if the two judges would have held to their view had the defendants arrived in their van only to be turned away because the claimant had changed his mind. It is thought that Lord Denning's clear assumption that a contract had been concluded over the telephone is the correct one.

Yet if this had been a binding contract, and one not concluded on the basis of a usual course of dealing, Sir David Cairns still saw a way to incorporate the exclusion clauses. When the telephone conversation had taken place, reference had been made only to the carpet. Yet when the van arrived, a carpet and a rug were tendered and taken away. This allowed Sir David to suggest a novation: "A fresh contract was made on July 17 when an additional item, a white rug, was offered for cleaning and accepted".[95] Manifestly, such acceptance was on the basis of the written terms contained in the document.

While this is acceptable on the special facts of the case, there are inherent dangers. If a contract is agreed upon, and subsequently a document containing exclusion clauses is tendered and accepted, this arguably constitutes a novation. The original contract has been replaced by another incorporating the terms of the document. There is more force in this argument, perhaps, when the document is signed. Yet this is probably to take the argument further than its merits. There was no difficulty in this particular case since new goods were added to the contract: where this is not so, very clear evidence indeed will be needed to show that both parties intended to replace one agreement with another.

It is also the case that, provided terms have been brought to the other side's notice before the contract is made, any such terms, including exclusion or limitation clauses, can be incorporated into the contract even if acceptance of the contract is not in the form specified. In *Edmund Murray Ltd v BSP International Foundations Ltd*,[96] the writing paper used by the suppliers, BSP, contained a printed notice at the foot of the first page which stated that: "all goods and services are supplied subject to the company's conditions of sale … ". In addition, when BSP sent their quotation to these buyers, it was accompanied by three sheets which set out these terms of sale. The buyers argued that these terms had not been incorporated since the contract terms also stated:

1–033

> "When the sellers confirm their acceptance of the buyer's order, any quotation sent out, the buyer's order and the seller's confirmation of acceptance form shall alone constitute the contract between the sellers and the buyers and no other terms, conditions, warranties or exceptions shall form part of this contract."

---

[92] [1977] 3 All E.R. 498 at 506.
[93] [1977] 3 All E.R. 498.
[94] See the judgment of Lord Denning, [1977] 3 All E.R. 498 at 501.
[95] [1977] 3 All E.R. 498 at 506.
[96] (1992) 33 Con. L.R. 1.

In fact, BSP had no confirmation of acceptance form, but the Court of Appeal still held that the various terms had been incorporated into the contract. It reasoned that the condition was inserted to minimise the risk of the suppliers being liable on the basis of terms contained in documents other than those mentioned; and that the particular provision itself made it clear that the quotation was to be dealt with as an invitation to treat and that the order was an offer, not an acceptance. This meant, the Court of Appeal said, that BSP were not precluded by this term from giving an unequivocal acceptance by some means other than a confirmation of acceptance form.

THE COURSE OF DEALING

1–034   It is possible that, far from being an isolated transaction, the particular agreement between the parties was one of a regular series of such agreements. If, over that period, the parties have regularly and specifically incorporated certain exclusion clauses, it needs to be asked what the effect will be when, perhaps by an oversight, there has been no such specific incorporation.

One point can easily be dealt with. In an *obiter dictum* expressed in *McCutcheon v MacBrayne*,[97] Lord Devlin had urged that a term could be introduced by a course of dealing only where there was actual knowledge of the content of that term as opposed to knowledge of its existence.[98] This view was rejected by the House of Lords in *Henry Kendall & Sons v William Lillico & Sons*.[99]

The latter case is also instructive as to when a course of dealing operates to incorporate particular clauses. There had been a verbal contract followed the next day by a "sold note" which contained an exclusion clause. There had been more than 100 similar contract notes in a course of dealing stretching back three years. The recipients knew of the existence of the written conditions but had never raised any query or objection, although they had never read them. As Lord Pearce summarised:

> "The only reasonable inference from the regular course of dealing over so long a period is that SAPPA were evincing an acceptance of, and a readiness to be bound by, the printed conditions of whose existence they were aware although they had not troubled to read them. Thus, the general conditions became part of the oral contract."[100]

Similarly, in *Allen Fabrication Ltd v ASD Metal Services*,[101] a course of dealing was held to be established when the parties had dealt with each other on over 250 occasions and the buyers had received the actual terms on advice notes and there had been a clear reference to the terms on invoices which would have been seen by them.

---

[97] [1964] 1 All E.R. 430.
[98] [1964] 1 All E.R. 430 at 437.
[99] [1968] 2 All E.R. 444 at 474 and 481, per Lords Guest and Pearce respectively.
[100] [1968] 2 All E.R. 444 at 481.
[101] [2012] EWHC 2213 (TCC).

These authorities can be usefully contrasted with the findings in *McCutcheon v MacBrayne*.[102] Here, the claimants' agent had dealt with the defendants on a number of occasions: sometimes he had signed a risk note containing the relevant exclusion clauses and sometimes he had not. He had not so signed on the relevant occasion. Holding that the clauses were not part of the contract, Lord Pearce maintained that the defendants were:

> "seeking to establish an oral contract by a course of dealing which always insisted on a written contract. It is the consistency of a course of conduct which gives rise to the implication that in similar circumstances a similar contractual result will follow. When the conduct is not consistent, there is no reason why it should still produce an invariable contractual result."

As Lord Pearce later added: "The ordinary course of business was therefore no help to the carrier, since the transaction did not follow the ordinary course".[103]

The same finding was made in *Hollier v Rambler Motors Ltd*.[104] The claimant telephoned the defendants asking for some repair work to be done. The defendants agreed to attend to the defects in due course. These were the only terms of that agreement. It was established that during the previous five years the claimant, on three or four occasions, had had repairs done by the defendants. On the last two of these occasions, the claimant signed a note containing exclusion clauses. This had not happened on this latest occasion. Salmon L.J., with whom Stamp L.J. and Latey J. concurred, found it impossible to hold that the exclusion clauses had been incorporated into the latest contract. If it were not possible to rely on a course of dealing in *McCutcheon v MacBrayne*, "still less would it be possible to do so in this case, when the so-called course of dealing consisted only of three or four transactions in the course of five years".[105] In contrast, though noting that every case must depend on its facts, it was held in *Knight Machinery (Holdings) Ltd v Rennie*[106] that a particular clause had been incorporated into a contract when the parties had contracted on five previous occasions and the particular condition had been used.

Further guidance as to just when it can be shown that there has been a previous course of dealing, such as would act to incorporate terms on the latest occasion, came in *Petrotrade Inc v Texaco Ltd*.[107] In the words of Langley J.:

> "There is now evidence of numerous contracts for the sale of fuel products over some four and a half years preceding the disputed contract made between Petrotrade and Texaco and between Petrotrade and other companies in the Texaco group. Petrotrade (rightly in my judgment) does not seek to rely upon the latter. All these contracts, where Petrotrade was the seller, and the transactions were of the same nature as the present, were without exception 'confirmed' on Petrotrade's terms and conditions including the two clauses Petrotrade rely upon. Texaco submits that the evidence does not show that Petrotrade has any standard terms and conditions or if it did how they were incorporated into the contracts. Although it is true that no standard printed form has been produced or relied upon I cannot accept that submission. The whole thrust and detail of the evidence shows a method and course of trading including the use of the clauses in question. Moreover, Texaco has not even suggested (let alone produced any

1–035

1–036

---

102 [1964] 1 All E.R. 430.
103 [1964] 1 All E.R. 430 at 439–440.
104 [1972] 1 All E.R. 399.
105 [1972] 1 All E.R. 399 at 404.
106 [1995] S.L.T. 166.
107 [1999] EWHC 291 (Comm).

evidence) that any other or different terms were ever used or that there ever was a relevant contract where they were not used. The point is taken that many of the previous transactions relied upon were with other divisions of Texaco or for other specific fuel products, but even excluding these (albeit I do not think it is right to do so) there is no dispute that over the 13 or so months prior to the contract there were 5 other contracts for the sale of similar if not the same product between Petrotrade as seller and Texaco as buyer on the same terms and effected in the same manner. In my judgment that is sufficient of itself to establish a course of trading. It is the more so in the context of the total number of contracts between the same parties of which there were 22 in the previous 12 months."

In *Motours Ltd v Euroball (West Kent) Ltd*,[108] the parties had entered into around 14 contracts during a period of some 18 months. Many were in writing with the defendants' terms and conditions on the reverse. The claimant did not read the terms and conditions and they were not explained to him. He had in the past signed the forms immediately after a statement which provided that the contract was subject to the terms and conditions overleaf. The court concluded that:

"the claimant, by continuing business with the defendants after having had notice many times of the terms and conditions, and indeed copies of them, did lead the defendants reasonably to believe that he had accepted their terms."

1–037   An unusual example of how terms can be incorporated through the course of dealing came about in *Lamport & Holt Lines Ltd v Coubro & Scrutton (M&I Ltd) and Coubro & Scrutton (Riggers & Shipwrights) Ltd*.[109] The second defendants were a subsidiary of the first, the two companies having been separated in 1975 when nationalisation was threatened. The terms and conditions of contract used by the second defendants were exactly the same as those used by the first defendants, with whom the claimants had contracted for many years. The matter was slightly complicated by the fact that, when the stationery for the second defendants was printed, and because of a printer's error, the terms and conditions of contract were not printed on the reverse of the invoices. The evidence showed that, when work was to be done for the claimants, a form of acknowledgment was sent out on the reverse of which were the standard conditions. It was immaterial to the claimants which of the two defendants did the particular work on any occasion, the decision being left to the defendants. If the work was allotted to the second defendants, the acknowledgment was sent out on their form, on the back of which were printed their terms and conditions, these being, as stated above, identical to those of the parent company. The evidence also showed that the claimants had been well aware that the second defendants were being incorporated to do the riggers' and shipwrights' work originally done by the first defendants. By September 1975, when the contract in question was made, there had been numerous transactions between the claimants and the second defendants when acknowledgments of order were dispatched with the latter's terms and conditions printed on the back. Only one of these acknowledgments could now be found, but Goff J. concluded that "on the evidence before the court, I have no doubt that on each occasion they were sent", and that there cannot be the

---

[108]   [2003] EWHC 614 (QB).
[109]   [1981] 2 Lloyd's Rep. 659; [1982] 2 Lloyd's Rep. 42.

"slightest hesitation" in holding that the terms and conditions of the second defendants were incorporated into the contract in question.[110] This was not contested in the Court of Appeal.

In *Rinaldi & Patroni v Precision Mouldings*,[111] the defendants were cartage contractors, and the claimants were builders of large fishing boats. An oral agreement was made for the transport of a particular boat. En route, while following the pilot vehicle, the cargo was taken under a low bridge. The boat struck the underside of the bridge and was extensively damaged. It was conceded by Rinaldi that they had been negligent, but they pleaded in their defence that a clause had been incorporated into the contract which gave them a defence in such circumstances. The evidence showed that, over six months, Rinaldi had carried goods for Precision Mouldings on some nine or ten occasions. Rinaldi's drivers had in their possession a book of cart notes. The top was white, and was prepared so that it would be signed by the consignee. A blue form and a yellow form were located under the white form. They were all in identical terms, except that the white note was headed "Customer's Copy". Once the goods were delivered, the costing was done on the blue note, and these details would also appear on the yellow note. This latter would then be stapled to an invoice and would then be sent to the consignor for payment. On the face of each cart note, there appeared the words: "All goods accepted subject to conditions on reverse". It appeared that, when the parties had contracted with each other, on three occasions the white note had not been signed. On the seven occasions when it had been signed, three times the signature was that of Precision Mouldings' production manager. Once it had been signed by the company's foreman. The other signatures could not be identified. It was also the practice, once a job had been done, for the invoice and yellow note to go to Precision Mouldings' purchasing officer. Once he had satisfied himself that the work had been authorised, had been done and correctly charged for, he would then pass the invoice for payment. He knew that there were words printed on the back of the yellow note but he never read them. The court found that, on the evidence of the dealings between the parties, the contract terms in general, and the exclusion clause in particular, had not been incorporated into the contract.

Ultimately, everything depends on the facts, and a decision as to whether there has been a sufficient course of dealing can be difficult to make. This was acknowledged by Judge Havelock Allan in *Capes (Hatherden) Ltd v Western Arable Services Ltd*[112]:

> "In the present case, the course of dealing between the parties consists of four contracts in the same year, with an interval of 5 months between the last of them and the two contracts in question. Although a different crop was involved, the procedure by which the previous contracts were concluded was substantially the same. On each occasion the claimant received a contract note referring to Contract 1/04: but he was not required to respond positively to it (e.g. by signing and returning a copy). He did not in fact notice the reference to Contract 1/04 and it was never expressly discussed or drawn to his attention. In my judgment these facts fall right on the borderline. If there had been any persuasive evidence, either that the terms of

---

[110] [1981] 2 Lloyd's Rep. 659 at 661.
[111] [1986] W.A.R. 131.
[112] [2009] EWHC 3065 (QB). See also *SIAT v Tradax* [1978] 2 Lloyd's Rep. 470 and *Circle Freight International Ltd v Medeast Gulf Exports Ltd* [1988] 2 Lloyd's Rep. 427.

Contract 1/04 were the usual terms on which grain merchants purchase grain from U.K. producers, or that Mr Capes knew that grain merchants commonly employed standard terms which provided for disputes to be settled by arbitration, I would have been likely to hold that Contract 1/04 was incorporated. In the absence of such evidence, I do not think that the previous contracts justify the conclusion that the AIC terms were incorporated. To put it another way, the limited course of dealing between the parties is not in my view such that an impartial observer would conclude that the parties had reached a common understanding that Contract 1/04 applied."

THE COMMON UNDERSTANDING OF THE PARTIES

1–038 The "course of dealing" as an argument for the incorporation of exemption clauses may be supplemented, indeed superseded, by the "understanding of the parties". This is well illustrated by *British Crane Hire Corp v Ipswich Plant Hire*.[113] Both parties were companies engaged in the hiring out of earth-moving equipment. The defendants needed a dragline crane urgently and contacted the claimants by telephone who agreed to supply one on hire. Nothing was said as to the conditions of hire. Subsequently, a printed form containing the appropriate conditions was sent for signature, but it was never signed. From the evidence, it appeared that there had been two previous agreements within the preceding year which had been effected on the basis of the written terms. These transactions were not known to the defendants' manager when he ordered the crane. In the circumstances, Lord Denning doubted "whether those two would be sufficient to show a course of dealing".[114]

The evidence further showed, however, that the defendants knew that firms in the trade imposed conditions as to the hire of plant. Indeed, the defendants did so themselves. In such circumstances, Lord Denning did not doubt but that the written conditions had been incorporated into the contract. He:

> "would not put it so much on the course of dealing, but rather on the common understanding which is to be derived from the conduct of the parties, namely, that the hiring was to be on the terms of the claimants' usual conditions ... it is just as if the claimants had said, 'we will supply it on our usual conditions', and the defendants said, 'of course, that is quite understood'."[115]

Sir Eric Sachs was of like mind. The machine had been damaged, and under the printed conditions the defendants were to indemnify the claimants. The "business realities of the situation", Sir Eric declared, were "plain". If the defendants had declared to the claimants when the contract was made that risk of damage lay with the latter, the reply would have been "That is nonsense, and you don't get the machine".[116] Moreover, he said, "to hold that the claimants did take the risk impliedly would be unrealistic and obviously contrary to the mythical

---

[113] [1974] 1 All E.R. 1059.
[114] [1974] 1 All E.R. 1059 at 1061.
[115] [1974] 1 All E.R. 1059 at 1062–1063.
[116] [1974] 1 All E.R. 1059 at 1064.

officious bystander's view".[117] In any case, Sir Eric concluded, the matter goes further: both sides knew "that contracts of this type are normally subject to printed conditions".[118]

Support for the above line of argument is to be found in *Keeton Sons & Co Ltd v Carl Prior Ltd*.[119] The defendants, as official shipping and handling agents to a trade association, advised the claimants, machine tool manufacturers, of their appointment by a letter which stated "All business transacted in accordance with Standard Conditions of the Company—copies on application". One of those conditions was that the defendants would not be responsible for any damage to goods unless it was proved that the damage occurred while the goods were in their custody and under their actual control and that such damage was due to the wilful neglect or default of the defendants or their servants. A circular some six weeks later detailed the defendants' services in relation to a forthcoming exhibition in the US and contained the same reference to their trading conditions. The claimants duly engaged the defendants for the shipment of the machine tools. Subsequently, the defendants sent them a telex reminding the claimants of the last date for dispatch of the machines. This telex referred to the earlier circular. In due course, the machines were delivered to the US. It was later agreed that the defendants would arrange for the return to the UK of one of the machines. On its return, that machine was found to be seriously damaged because of the way in which the defendants had packed it. In an action for damages for breach of contract, the judge found that the defendants' terms and conditions had not been incorporated into the contract.

An appeal was allowed. The Court of Appeal stated that it was always a question of fact whether reasonable notice had been given of the incorporation of standard trading terms into a contract between parties. Since the claimants had conceded that they expected to be contracting on the defendants' conditions, and since it was normal that such items would include a clause seeking to exclude liability, it was clear that the claimants had expected and accepted that they would be trading with the defendants on terms which would include limiting and excluding terms. The letter and circular did no more than confirm the obvious, namely that the defendants traded subject to standard conditions and that they could be inspected on request.

The approach taken in the *Keeton* case was adopted in *Lacey's Footwear Ltd v Bowler*.[120] The question had been put as to whether certain terms had been incorporated into the contract, the judge below finding that they had not. There had been nothing in the rate proposal sent under cover of a letter which drew attention to the terms on the reverse side of the covering letter. Although, from 1986 onwards, on at least half a dozen occasions, Bowler had written to Lacey's attempting to secure their business on notepaper which similarly carried the terms and conditions, the recipient could not reasonably be expected to read every unsolicited communication to see what terms and conditions were likely to apply. Accordingly, the judge had held that reasonable notice had not been given and

1–039

---

[117] [1974] 1 All E.R. 1059 at 1064.
[118] [1974] 1 All E.R. 1059 at 1064.
[119] [1986] B.T.L.C. 30.
[120] [1997] 2 Lloyd's Rep. 369.

that consequently the terms were not incorporated in the contract. The Court of Appeal thought that, in coming to this conclusion, the judge had overlooked evidence which had been given under cross-examination by the recipient of that correspondence. His attention had been drawn to the trading conditions of the Institute of Freight Forwarders of 1984 which were referred to in earlier correspondence and counsel had asked:

> "Q: So you accept that you would both have known about the fact that the company was trading on standard terms and that you probably would have noticed them even if you did not read them. Is that right?
>
> A: I suppose I would have noticed them, yes."

He accepted that he was an experienced businessman importing shoes since 1983 and he was then asked:

> "Q: You have some nine years' experience in the international sale and carriage of goods by 1992 and in that time there is no reason in my suggestion why you should not have familiarised yourself with the important and special conditions that were described to you in the quotations that you had received over those years?
>
> A: As I say, those conditions in my mind did not apply to me for the simple reason that I always insisted on my goods being insured.
>
> Q: So the conditions did not apply?
>
> A: In my mind they did not because the conditions normally on the back are a way of allowing the transport people to get out of something and as long as I am fully insured they cannot hurt me and that was all I was interested in.
>
> Q: How did you know they were always intending to get the carriers out of something?
>
> A: Why have conditions?
>
> Q: Sometimes they might describe the nature of the business that is being carried on, the nature of the contract, the nature of their obligations. Was that not important?
>
> A: The nature of their obligations or whatever as long as they delivered the shoes to me on time and they were covered for risk that is all I was interested in. I am not a lawyer. I do not read these things. I just cover myself properly with insurance, pensions, everything. I am meticulous in that way. As long as I am covered I am happy. I do not have time. I do not understand them to start reading them."

1–040 From this series of questions and answers, the Court of Appeal said that it appeared that the only reasonable inference was that Lacey's knew that carriers and forwarding agents such as Bowler did contract on terms and conditions which limited or were likely to limit their liability as carriers though they did not bother to read them because, as was said, they were meticulous about insuring the goods. Whether the steps taken by Bowler to draw the conditions to their attention were adequate was beside the point. Lacey's were judged to be well aware that there most probably were terms and conditions and, had they chosen to do so, they could have read them (with some difficulty) and informed themselves of them. Beldam L.J. summed up the position thus:

> "I would hold that [Lacey's] frame of mind was that [they were] prepared to enter into the contract of carriage on the basis of the terms and conditions whatever they were because [they were] going to take steps to see [that they were] properly insured. Thus I would hold that the terms and conditions did apply to this contract of carriage."

It is also the case that the common understanding of the parties might be that there would be no exclusion clauses, or at least that liability would not be excluded. In *Mostcash Plc v Fluor Ltd*,[121] the claimant argued that it had been the parties' joint intention that the contract would not exclude the defendant's liability for design defects and that provisions were to be included in the contract to make it clear that the defendant warranted that its work would be carried out with reasonable skill and care, so that the end product would be of merchantable quality, and that the defendant would be liable in damages if any of those warranties were breached. Much detailed negotiation took place on the inclusion of such provisions, but they did not actually appear in the contract. Referring to this evidence, the judge held that the parties had proceeded on the basis of a common mistake, where both believed that such liability would not be excluded by the contract, when in fact it did contain an exclusion clause. It would therefore be inequitable for the defendant to rely on the exclusion clause and the contract would be rectified to follow the intention of the parties that the contract would not exclude liability for design defects.

The *British Crane* case and the *Lacey's Footwear* case were also distinguished in **1–041** *Scheps v Fine Art Logistic Ltd*.[122] The claimant sought damages from the defendant in respect of the loss of a sculpture which the claimant had purchased while it was being stored by an auction house. He had engaged the defendant to collect the sculpture and store it before it was taken to the artist's studio for some restoration work. When required the sculpture could not be found in any of the defendant's storage units. The latter's view was that it had by accident been destroyed. The defendant maintained that the agreement between the parties incorporated its standard terms and conditions which limited liability for the loss of the sculpture to £350 per cubic metre of its volume. The defendant submitted that it was usual in the transport and storage trade for services to be provided on standard terms and conditions that limited liability and that the claimant must have been aware of that as a result of his considerable experience of arranging for the transport of works of art.

After considering these two cases, the court ruled against the defendant. It pointed out that the defendant at no stage provided the claimant with a copy of its terms and conditions or with a document which referred to them. The claimant was a private customer, and there was nothing about the status in which the claimant dealt with the defendant which might have led the defendant to believe that the claimant was dealing with the defendant on the basis of the defendant's terms and conditions. Nor was there anything done or said by the claimant which might have led the defendant to believe that the claimant was contracting with the defendant upon the basis of the defendant's terms and conditions. Although it is more likely than not that the claimant understood that the defendant would probably supply its services pursuant to certain terms and conditions which might well include limits on the defendant's liability, that did not, the court said:

> "entitle the defendant to rely upon its terms and conditions against the claimant because the defendant at no stage mentioned its terms and conditions and, objectively, there was no reason why the defendant might reasonably conclude that the claimant intended to contract with the defendant on the basis of the defendant's terms and conditions."

---

[121] Unreported April 11, 2002 (TCC).
[122] [2007] EWHC 541 (QB). See also *Balmoral Group Ltd v Borealis (UK) Ltd* [2006] EWHC 1900 (Comm).

1–042 It must be appreciated that this line of argument, based on the common understanding of the parties, is a potentially dangerous one. Most consumers, without being unduly cynical, now expect to have whatever rights they have negated by the small print of the agreement and no doubt contract on that assumption, whether or not presented with the appropriate document. The Court of Appeal in the *British Crane* case was certainly alive to this possibility. Lord Denning pointed to *Hollier v Rambler Motors Ltd*, observing that in contrast to the instant case, the claimant "was not of equal bargaining power with the garage company".[123] Sir Eric Sachs was also at pains to stress that nothing in his judgment was relevant to the "position where the owner and user are in wholly different walks of life, as in *Hollier's* case" (the point of course being taken in the *Scheps* case)—"where one, for instance, is an expert in a line of business and the other is not".[124]

No authority was cited for these propositions, and it is indeed difficult to accept them at face value. If there is such a thing as a common understanding, it must apply without discrimination. The fact that one party is of inferior bargaining power can scarcely affect his understanding of the contract. Indeed, the weaker a party, the more he may suppose that certain terms, especially exclusion clauses, will be inserted into the contract. The plain truth is, of course, that simple morality ordains a more solicitous view when unequal parties make an agreement.

INCORPORATION BY CONDUCT

1–043 It is also possible that, on the right occasion, terms can be incorporated by the conduct of the parties. In the *Cuniberti* case,[125] the argument had been put that, since the customer had made stage payments to the architect, that had sufficed to incorporate the RIBA terms and conditions into the contract. The court rejected this because the payments made by the customer, properly construed, were referable to certain agreed percentage fees. The payments made referred to a subsequent agreement that, pending conclusion of a more detailed agreement, if such could be agreed, the architect could charge in accordance with the agreed percentages and in accordance with the stages in the RIBA contract. The terms set out in the contract were never agreed to by the customer and were not incorporated into the contract.

SIGNATURE

1–044 The effect of signing a written document was first indicated by Mellish L.J. in *Parker v South Eastern Railway Co.*[126] In the ordinary case, he said:

---

[123] [1974] 1 All E.R. 1059 at 1062.
[124] [1974] 1 All E.R. 1062 at 1064.
[125] [2002] EWHC 2923 (TCC).
[126] (1877) L.R. 2 C.P.D. 416.

> "where an action is brought on a written agreement which is signed by the defendant, the agreement is proved by proving his signature, and, in the absence of fraud, it is wholly immaterial that he has not read the agreement and does not know its contents."[127]

This was accepted as correct by the Court of Appeal in *L'Estrange v F Graucob Ltd*.[128] The claimant, the owner of a café, agreed to buy from the defendants an automatic slot-machine for cigarettes. The agreement was to pay by instalments, and it contained an exemption clause excluding liability for breaches of warranty or condition. The claimant signed the agreement without reading its terms. The machine proved faulty, and the claimant purported to terminate the contract for breach of condition.

It was held that she could not do so since she was bound by the terms of the exclusion clause. The words of Scrutton L.J. were unambiguous:

> "In cases in which the contract is contained in a railway ticket or other unsigned document, it is necessary to prove that an alleged party was aware, or ought to have been aware, of its terms and conditions. These cases have no application when the document has been signed. When a document containing contractual terms is signed, then, in the absence of fraud, or, I will add, misrepresentation, the party signing it is bound, and it is wholly immaterial whether he has read the document or not."[129]

Despite signature, however, and even in the absence of fraud or misrepresentation, there is still scope for enquiring whether the particular party was misled in some way, which would go towards negating his consent to one or more terms of the document. In *Harvey v Ventilatoren-Fabrik*,[130] negotiations between an English buyer and a German seller were conducted in English, and the oral agreement confirmed in writing. The buyer was sent two sets of acknowledgment of order, signing one and returning the other. This latter contained terms in German printed on the back, while the former contained no such terms. There had been no references on the face of either set to printed conditions on the back and no relevant discussions during the negotiations. The Court of Appeal said that, viewed objectively, a reasonable person in the position of the English buyer could naturally conclude that the printed material on the back, which he did not understand, could be regarded as irrelevant. The court could therefore draw the inference that the buyer was misled by the difference between the two sets of documents and did not in reality assent to the incorporation of those terms.

FRAUD AND MISREPRESENTATION

As both Mellish and Scrutton L.JJ. observed, a party can escape the full consequences of his signature if he can show that the contract was tainted with fraud or misrepresentation. In such cases, the innocent party is entitled to rescind the contract and claim damages. Where the misrepresentation is otherwise than fraudulent, the court, acting under s.2(2) of the Misrepresentation Act 1967, may   **1–045**

---

[127] (1877) L.R. 2 C.P.D. 416.

[128] [1934] 2 K.B. 394.

[129] [1934] 2 K.B. 394 at 403. For the effect of a signature on the application of the *Interfoto* principle, see para.1–025.

[130] (1989) 8 Tr. L.R. 138.

declare the contract subsisting and award damages in lieu of rescission. Where the misrepresentation is entirely innocent (i.e. made free of fraud or negligence) it is only under s.2(2) that damages may be awarded.[131] It is now well established that where the misrepresentation constitutes a negligent breach of the duty of care, there is a common law right to rescind the contract and claim damages.[132] Section 2(1) of the 1967 Act also provides such a remedy. The statutory remedy is more amenable to the claim of one who asserts a misrepresentation, since the onus is placed on the defendant to show that he was not negligent, this being the reverse of the common law position.[133]

NON EST FACTUM

1–046   A final word can be said on the plea of *non est factum*. This arises where a person claims that he so misunderstood a document to which he put his signature, that he has not therefore assented to its terms, and that the agreement is thus void. It appears from the decision of the House of Lords in *Gallie v Lee*[134] that the plea will avail a mistaken party if he satisfies the court that the document is radically different from that which he intended to sign and that his mistake is not due to his carelessness. As Lord Wilberforce said, however:

> "there still remains a residue of difficult cases. There are still illiterate or senile persons who cannot read, or apprehend, a legal document; there are still persons who may be tricked into putting their signature on a piece of paper which has legal consequences different from anything they intended... to eliminate it [the plea of *non est factum*] would, in my opinion, deprive the courts of what may be, doubtless, on sufficiently rare occasions, an instrument of justice."[135]

Where an illiterate person signs a bank guarantee without reading it or telling the bank that he cannot read, but in reliance on the bank's misrepresentations as to its nature, he can rely on *non est factum*, as well as on the bank's negligent misrepresentation.[136]

Where a person signs a document in blank, the plea of *non est factum* is not strictly applicable. If, however, a document is so signed, leaving another to fill in the terms in accordance with an oral agreement, no agreement exists if the completed agreement does not accord with that oral agreement.[137]

---

[131] See *Whittington v Seale-Hayne* (1900) 82 L.T. 49. See the discussion in Cheshire, Fifoot and Furmston, *Law of Contract*, pp.314, 325. Damages cannot, however, be awarded where it is no longer possible to rescind the contract: *Government of Zanzibar v British Aerospace (Lancaster House) Ltd* [2000] C.L.C. 735. Nor can damages be awarded when a consumer has a right to redress under the Consumer Protection from Unfair Trading Regulations 2008/1277. See Consumer Protection (Amendment) Regulations 2014/870; reg.5.

[132] *Esso Petroleum Co Ltd v Mardon* [1976] 2 All E.R. 5.

[133] See *Howard Marine & Dredging Co Ltd v Ogden* [1978] 2 All E.R. 1134.

[134] [1970] 3 All E.R. 961. See also *Chiswick Investments v Pevats* [1990] 1 N.Z.L.R. 169.

[135] [1970] 3 All E.R. 961 at 971.

[136] *Lloyds Bank Plc v Waterhouse* [1993] 2 F.L.R. 97.

[137] See *Anson's Law of Contract*, 26th edn (Oxford: OUP, 1984) p.281.

CHAPTER 2

INTERPRETATION OF EXCLUSION CLAUSES

Once an exclusion clause has, by whatever means, been incorporated into a particular contract, the next question is whether it has been drafted so as to cover the particular loss or damage which has arisen. **2–001**

THE GENERAL APPROACH TO INTERPRETATION

The modern approach to the interpretation of contract terms has been stated as follows[1]: **2–002**

(1) Interpretation is the ascertainment of the meaning which the document would convey to a reasonable person having all the background knowledge which would reasonably have been available to the parties in the situation in which they were at the time of the contract.

(2) The background was referred to by Lord Wilberforce as the "matrix of fact", but this phrase is, if anything, an understated description of what the background may include. Subject to the requirement that it should have been reasonably available to the parties and to the exception to be mentioned next, it includes absolutely anything which would have affected the way in which the language of the document would have been understood by a reasonable man.

(3) The law excludes from the admissible background the previous negotiations of the parties and their declarations of subjective intent. They are admissible only in an action for rectification. The law makes this distinction for reasons of practical policy and, in this respect only, legal interpretation differs from the way we would interpret utterances in ordinary life. The boundaries of this exception are in some respects unclear.

(4) The meaning which a document (or any other utterance) would convey to a reasonable man is not the same thing as the meaning of its words. The meaning of words is a matter for dictionaries and grammars; the meaning of the document is what the parties using those words against the relevant background would reasonably have been understood to mean. The background may not merely enable the reasonable man to choose between the possible meanings of words which are ambiguous but even (as occasionally happens in ordinary life) to conclude that the parties must, for

---

[1] *Investors Compensation Scheme Ltd v West Bromwich Building Society; Alford v West Bromwich Building Society* [1998] 1 All E.R. 98 at 114–115, per Lord Hoffmann.

whatever reason, have used the wrong words or syntax. See *Mannai Investments Co Ltd v Eagle Star Life Assurance Co Ltd*.[2]

(5) The "rule" that words should be given their "natural and ordinary meaning" reflects the common sense proposition that we do not easily accept that people have made linguistic mistakes, particularly in formal documents. On the other hand, if one would nevertheless conclude from the background that something must have gone wrong with the language, the law does not require judges to attribute to the parties an intention which they plainly could not have had. Lord Diplock made this point when he said in *The Antaios Compania Neviera SA v Salen Rederierna AB*[3]:

> "... if detailed semantic and syntactical analysis of words in a commercial contract is going to lead to a conclusion that flouts business commonsense, it must be made to yield to business commonsense."[4]

If, though, the words have only one possible meaning, then that is how the words must be interpreted.

Contractual intent

2–003   In interpreting an exclusion clause, the courts will not so interpret it so as to rid the contract of any contractual intent. In *Kudos Catering Ltd v Manchester Central Convention*,[5] by a written agreement, M appointed K the exclusive supplier of catering services at its venues for a five-year period. After three years, M purported to terminate the agreement. K responded by purporting to treat M's actions as a repudiatory breach of the agreement and to accept that as terminating the agreement. K claimed loss of profits that would have been earned during the remaining term of the agreement. M denied repudiation and argued that K's claim for loss of profits was precluded by cl.18.6 of the agreement which provided that M should "have no liability whatsoever in contract, tort (including negligence) or

---

[2] [1997] 2 W.L.R. 945.
[3] [1985] A.C. 191 at 201.
[4] This statement was adopted by Morritt L.J. in *WRM Group Ltd v Wood* [1998] C.L.C. 189 and approved by Thomas J. in *Kumar v AGF Insurance Ltd* [1998] 4 All E.R. 788. The same principles have been expressed in many other cases too. See, for example, *Cambridge Antibody Technology Ltd v Abbott Biotechnology Ltd* [2004] EWHC 2974 (Pat); *Sirius International Insurance Co (Publ) v FAI General Insurance Ltd* [2004] UKHL 54; *Wiltshire CC v Crest Estates Ltd* [2005] EWCA Civ 1087; *Grosvenor v High-Point Rendell Plc* [2004] EWHC 2407 (TCC); *Artpower Ltd v Bespoke Couture Ltd* [2005] EWCA Civ 981; *Fairbriar Plc v Van Rey* [2007] EWHC 2510 (Ch); *Prudential Assurance Co Ltd v David Monroe Ayres* [2008] EWCA Civ 52; *Chartbrook Ltd v Persimmon Homes Ltd* [2008] EWCA Civ 183; *Fenice Investments Inc v Jerram Falkus Construction Ltd* [2009] EWHC 3272 (TCC); *William Hare Ltd v Shepherd Construction Ltd, CT Reynolds (Construction) Ltd v Shepherd Construction Ltd* [2010] EWCA Civ 283; *Global Coal Ltd v London Commodity Brokers* [2010] EWHC 1347; *Wincanton Group Ltd v Garbe Logistics UK 1 SNARL* [2011] EWHC 905; *Rainy Sky SA v Bookman Bank* [2011] UKSC 50; *Coulson v Newsgroup Newspapers Ltd* [2011] EWHC 3482; [2012] EWCA Civ 1547; *Earl of Cardigan v John Moore* [2012] EWHC 1024; *Orion Publishing Group Ltd v Novel Entertainment Ltd* [2012] EWHC 1951; *Abbas v Rotary International Ltd* [2012] NIB 41; *Belfair's Management Ltd v (1) Matthew Sutherland (2) Christine Jane Sutherland* [2013] EWCA Civ 185; *Anderson v London Fire & Emergency Planning Authority* [2013] EWCA Civ 321; *Fujitsu Services Ltd v IBM United Kingdom Ltd* [2014] EWHC 752.

otherwise for any loss of goodwill, business, revenue or profits . . . suffered by the Contractor or any third party in relation to this Agreement". The judge determined as a preliminary issue that clause 18.6 excluded M's liability for K's loss of profits.

The Court of Appeal reversed this decision, saying that if the judge's construction of cl.18.6 was adopted, the agreement would be effectively devoid of contractual content since there was no sanction for non-performance by M. It was inherently unlikely that the parties intended the clause to have that effect.

Although less obviously so, this also appeared to be the approach taken in *Proton Energy Group SA v Orlen Leituva*[6]: a clause provided that "in no event shall the seller have any liability for any . . . loss of profit . . . or any type of special indirect or consequential loss". The court said that if the words relied on by Proton were taken literally there would be no right to damages at all for breach of the warranty of quality or in respect of short delivery because the loss will always be almost entirely that of profit. It declined to accept any such interpretation.

The *contra proferentem* rule

The so-called *contra proferentem* rule amounts to this: that a person who, by reference to an exclusion clause, seeks to avoid a liability which otherwise would fall upon him must do so by reference to words which clearly and unequivocally apply to the case in hand. The words of Scrutton L.J. in *Szymonowski & Co v Beck & Co*[5] are to the point:

2–004

> "Now I approach the consideration of that clause applying the principle repeatedly acted upon by the House of Lords and by this court that if a party wishes to exclude the ordinary consequences that would flow in law from the contract that he is making he must do so in clear terms."

He quoted Lord McNaughton as saying, "an ambiguous clause is no protection".[6]

In *Thomas Witter Ltd v TBP Industries Ltd*,[7] the judge stressed that, if an exclusion clause is to have effect, then the party seeking that protection cannot be "mealy-mouthed in his clause. He must bring it home that he is limiting his

---

[5] [2013] EWCA Civ 38.

[6] [1923] 1 K.B. 457 at 466. The reference is to *Elderslie Steamship Co Ltd v Northwick* [1905] A.C. 93 at 96. "In the event of any ambiguity, the clause must be construed against the drafter of the clause"; *Kingsway Hall Hotel Ltd v Red Sky IT (Hounslow) Ltd* [2010] EWHC 965 (TCC), per Toulmin J.; "It is of course axiomatic that exclusion clauses of this type have to be construed strictly. They also have to be construed *contra proferentem*. On either approach, it seems to me that I have to give the claimant the benefit of any doubt arising from the words used by the defendant in their standard terms and conditions"; *Elvanite Full Circle Ltd v AMEC Earth & Environmental (UK) Ltd* [2013] EWHC 1191, per Coulson J. See too *Fujitsu Services Ltd v IBM United Kingdom Ltd* [2014] EWHC 752 (TCC) per Carr J.: where a clause permits of two possible constructions, the court is entitled to prefer the construction that is consistent with business common sense and to reject the other... however, "where the parties have used unambiguous language the court must apply it"

[7] [1996] 2 All E.R. 573.

liability".[8] He later stated that an artificial approach to exclusion clauses was unnecessary "now that the Unfair Contract Terms Act 1977 exists to destroy unreasonable exclusion clauses . . . If a party wants to exclude liability for certain sorts of misrepresentation, it must spell those sorts out clearly".[9]

An excellent example of how this rule is applied exists in *Lee & Son Ltd v Railway Executive*.[10] The claimants leased a warehouse from the defendants. In the lease was a clause purporting to provide an exemption from liability "for loss or damage (whether by act or neglect of the company or their servants or agents or not) which but for the tenancy hereby created . . . would not have arisen". Goods in the warehouse were damaged by fire owing to the alleged negligence of the defendants in allowing a spark or some such combustible matter to escape from their railway engines. Applying the *contra proferentem* rule, the Court of Appeal held that the exclusion clause applied to liabilities which arose only by reason of the relationship of landlord and tenant created by the lease; this being the impact of the words in the lease "but for the tenancy hereby created". Certainly, this clause was capable of bearing a wider interpretation, but it had to be construed against the defendants who were, therefore, not protected.

2–005 It is clear from this that the courts will interpret exemption clauses strictly and will, in particular, attribute precise legal meanings to technical expressions. In *Wallis, Son & Wells v Pratt & Haynes*,[11] the claimant purchased from the defendant certain seed described as "common English sainfoin". The seed was in fact a different, lower quality, seed known as "giant sainfoin". The contract contained a clause excluding liability for breach of all warranties, whether express or implied. The defendant, of course, was in breach of the condition, implied by s.13 of the Sale of Goods Act 1893 (now repealed and re-enacted by s.13 of the Sale of Goods Act 1979), requiring the goods to correspond with their description.

If this had been all, the court could easily have avoided the exclusion clause, since it referred only to warranties, and not to conditions. The problem which arose was that the claimant had accepted the goods within s.11(1)(c)[12] and so was compelled to treat the breach of condition as a breach of warranty. Even so, the House of Lords held the sellers unable to rely on the clause. The term in question, although it fell to be treated as a warranty, did not for that reason ever cease from being a condition.

The reasoning of this case was later relied on by the Court of Appeal in *Baldry v Marshall*.[13] The signed contract for the sale and purchase of a motor car contained a term excluding "any other guarantee or warranty express or otherwise". The purchaser complained that it was not reasonably fit for its purpose, the condition implied by s.14(1) of the Sale of Goods Act 1893 (now s.14(3) of the Sale of Goods Act 1979). According to Bankes L.J., if "there is one thing more clearly established than another it is the distinction between a

---

[8] [1996] 2 All E.R. 573 at 596.
[9] [1996] 2 All E.R. 573 at 598.
[10] [1949] 2 All E.R. 581.
[11] [1911] A.C. 394.
[12] Since property had passed. This provision was amended by the Misrepresentation Act 1967 s.4(1).
[13] [1924] All E.R. 155.

warranty and a condition".[14] This particular clause, he affirmed, whether speaking of "a guarantee" or "a warranty" speaks of "nothing but what the law would recognise as a warranty ... there [is] here no exclusion of any implied condition".[15] Atkin L.J. agreed that it was proper to distinguish a guarantee, or warranty, "as being different from, certainly as not including, a condition".[16]

Both these cases were given a thorough examination in *KG Bominflot Bunkergesellschaft fr Mineraloele mbH & Co v Petroplus Marketing AG*[17] where, in relation to a breach of an implied condition, the following clause was relied on:

> "There are no guarantees, warranties or representations, express or implied, of merchantability, fitness or suitability of the oil for any particular purpose or otherwise which extend beyond the description of the oil set forth in this agreement ... It is a condition of this agreement that buyer complies with its obligations under this clause. In the event that buyer is in breach of any of the provisions of this clause in whole or part, seller shall be entitled to terminate this agreement immediately."

With what can be fairly called a certain amount of reluctance, the Court of Appeal followed the precedent of the previous cases despite showing sympathy for the argument that a less rigorous approach would be justified given the principles now espoused in cases such as *Investors Compensation Scheme Ltd v West Bromwich Building Society*.[18]   **2–006**

There is, though, more than a hint of a move away from the strict interpretation of conditions and warranties in *Air Transworld Ltd v Bombardier Inc.*[19]

A sale agreement provided that the:

> "warranty, obligations and liabilities of the seller and the rights and remedies of the buyer in the agreement were exclusive and were in lieu of, and the buyer waived and released, all other warranties, obligations, representations or liabilities, express or implied, arising by law, in contract, civil liability or in tort, or otherwise including but not limited to any implied warranty of merchantability or of fitness for a particular purpose."

It was argued that this did not extend to the conditions implied by the Sale of Goods Act. The court did not agree and said that the "language must necessarily be taken to refer to the implied conditions of the Sale of Goods Act, because they are obligations and liabilities implied, arising by law". Since the same could be said of the contract terms referred to in the cases from the *Wallis* case onwards, it may be that any future case will be treated more in the line of this particular case and thus more closely adhere to the principles set out in the *West Bromwich* case.[20]

Yet further examples of the strict interpretation of exclusion clauses can be found. In *Webster v Higgin*,[21] a term in a hire purchase contract provided that "no

---

[14] [1924] All E.R. 155 at 158.
[15] [1924] All E.R. 155 at 158.
[16] [1924] All E.R. 155 at 160. See too *The Marconi Lady* [2009] EWHC 1088.
[17] [2010] EWCA Civ 1145.
[18] [1998] 1 All E.R. 98.
[19] [2012] EWHC 243.
[20] The approach adopted in this case was approved by Flaux J. in *Dalmare SpA v (1) Union Maritime Ltd (2) Valor Shipping Ltd* [2012] EWHC 3537. See further at para.10–039.
[21] [1948] 2 All E.R. 127.

warranty, condition or description is given", it being held that this failed to exclude liability for an undertaking which had previously been given. In *Houghton v Trafalgar Insurance Co Ltd*,[22] a motor insurance policy provided that the insurer was not to be liable "while the car is carrying any load in excess of that for which it was constructed". Here, it was held that the provision did not serve to exclude liability where the car carried an excess of passengers. Passengers were not embraced by the term "load".[23]

Consumer contracts

2–007   Since enactment of the Consumer Rights Act 2014, there are only implied terms in consumer contracts. References to conditions and warranties have disappeared. They do of course remain in the case of businesses contracts.

Statutory intervention

2–008   The *contra proferentem* principle was taken a stage further in the Unfair Terms in Consumer Contracts Regulations 1999 and the Consumer Protection from Unfair Trading Regulations 2008.[24]

The first-mentioned Regulations have now been repealed and replaced by s.69 of the Consumer Rights Act which provides that if a term in a consumer contract, or a consumer notice, could have different meanings, the meaning that is most favourable to the consumer is to prevail. The repealed Regulations had also stated that the language used had to be plain and intelligible. This requirement has been dropped from the Act with little impact on the position. The Regulations did, however, refer only to written terms which the Act does not. As a result, oral terms are now within the *contra proferentem* rule, but this is probably no real change in practice.

The *contra proferentem* provisions of the Act do not apply, however, in any application for an injunction against the use of clauses rendered automatically void by the Act when seeking to exclude a particular obligation.[25] Thus, an ambiguous clause will allow an injunction to be obtained without the need to show that, once construed, it did not actually have the effect of excluding that liability.

As for the 2008 Regulations, there is a serious risk that unintelligible terms could actually be illegal in the case of a consumer contract. Under the Regulations, a commercial practice is misleading, and hence illegal, if it contains "material information" which is ambiguous or unintelligible. "Material information" is defined to include "the information which the average consumer needs, according to the context, to take an informed transactional decision". There

---

[22] [1953] 2 All E.R. 1409.
[23] See too *Dixons Group Plc v Murray-Obodynski* [1999] EWCA 1775.
[24] SI 2008/1277, as amended by the Consumer Protection (Amendment) Regulations 2014 (SI 2014/870).
[25] Consumer Rights Act 2014 Sch.3 para.3 as applied by s.69(2). For the void exclusion clauses, see Chapter 8.

cannot be much doubt that this would include an exclusion or limitation clause. An action for damages lies in respect of a breach of the Regulations.

Negating the statutory implied terms

Section 55(2) of the Sale of Goods Act 1979, and s.16(2) of the Supply of Goods and Services Act 1982, each provide that an express condition or warranty will only negative a condition or warranty implied by the respective enactments if "inconsistent with it". In *Salvage Association v CAP Financial Services Ltd,*[26] a term in a contract governed by the 1982 Act provided that "liability ... shall be in lieu of any warranty or condition of any kind, express or implied, statutory or otherwise as to the merchantability or fitness for a particular purpose of the Service or any part thereof". It was held that this clause purported only to exclude any warranty or condition as to merchantability and fitness for purpose; it did not purport to exclude liability for breach of any term that the particular party carry out the service with reasonable care and skill implied by s.13 of the 1982 Act.

2–009

Consumer contracts

The foregoing provisions are disapplied in the case of consumer contracts by virtue of the Consumer Rights Act 2014.[27]

2–010

Strict interpretation of exclusion clauses

It was said by Scrutton L.J. in *Gordon Alison & Co Ltd v Wallsend Slipway & Engineering*[28] that if "a person is under a legal liability and wishes to get rid of it, he can only do so by using clear words".[29] The words of the exclusion clause must be apt precisely to cover the liability which is sought to be excluded.

2–011

This is well illustrated by the decision in *Internet Broadcasting Corp Ltd and (t/a NETTV) v MAR/LLC*.[30] In ruling that an exclusion clause did not apply to acts of deliberate repudiation, the court laid down the principles to be deduced from the decided cases:

(1)   There is no rule of law applicable and the question is one of construction.

---

[26] [1995] F.S.R. 654.

[27] Consumer Rights Act 2014 Sch.1.

[28] (1927) 43 T.L.R. 323.

[29] (1927) 43 T.L.R. 323 at 324. See also *Photo Production Ltd v Securicor Transport Ltd* [1980] A.C. 827 at 850, per Lord Diplock. Lord Diplock's approach was accepted as correct by Coulson J. in *Decoma UK Ltd v Haden Drysys International Ltd* [2005] EWHC B12 (TCC). In *Stocznia Gdynia SA v Gearbulk Holdings Ltd* [2008] EWHC 944 (Comm), it was argued that the enactment of the Unfair Contract Terms Act 1977 and the Unfair Terms in Consumer Contracts Regulations 1999 (SI 1999/2083) have rendered the "clear words" principle inapplicable to exclusion clauses since it is less necessary for the courts to find a strained interpretation in order to seek to do justice between the parties. The court did not rule specifically on the issue which is in any case rejected by the *Internet Broadcasting* case.

[30] [2009] EWHC 844 (Ch). See also *Red River UK Ltd v Sheikh* [2010] EWHC 961 (Ch).

(2)   There is a presumption, which appears to be a strong presumption, against the exemption clause being construed so as to cover deliberate, repudiatory breach.

(3)   The words needed to cover a deliberate, repudiatory breach need to be very "clear" in the sense of using "strong" language such as "under no circumstances. . .".

(4)   There is a particular need to use "clear", in the sense of "strong", language where the exemption clause is intended to cover deliberate wrongdoing by a party in respect of a breach which cannot, or is unlikely to be, covered by insurance. Language such as "including deliberate repudiatory acts by [the parties to the contract] themselves . . ." would need to be used in such a case.

(5)   Words which, in a literal sense, cover a deliberate repudiatory breach will not be construed so as to do so if that would defeat the "main object" of the contract.

(6)   The proper function between commercial parties at arm's length and with equal bargaining power of an exemption clause is to allocate insurable risk, so that an exemption clause should not normally be construed in such cases so as to cover an uninsurable risk or one very unlikely to be capable of being insured, in particular deliberate wrongdoing by a party to the contract itself (as opposed to vicarious liability for others).

(7)   Words which in a literal sense cover a deliberate repudiatory breach cannot be relied upon if they are "repugnant".

An excellent example is also afforded in *Henry Kendall & Sons v Williams Lillico & Sons*.[31] The question arose whether a term excluding liability for latent "defects" sufficed to exclude liability for failure to comply with the term implied by s.14(1) of the Sale of Goods Act 1893 (now s.14(3) of the Sale of Goods Act 1979) that goods be reasonably fit for their purpose. Finding that it did not, Lord Morris argued that the word "defects" related:

> "Prima facie to the quality of goods. Goods might be fit for a known particular purpose and yet have certain defects. Any latent defects covered by the clause are such as do not prevent the goods being reasonably fit for their purpose. As the clause does not refer to the conditions which, being implied, are part of the contract between the parties and as, in my view, the clause does not either expressly or by necessary inference negative or cancel any of the conditions, it must be construed as referring to such latent defects as do not prevent compliance with the conditions."[32]

This was also the view (as it was of the entire House of Lords) accepted by Lord Pearce. The clause, he said, does not necessarily exclude the implied term. The goods:

> "might have had defects of quality which did not make them unfit for their purpose. It is to these defects that the clause should be read as applicable. If it was intended to cut down the

---

[31] [1968] 2 All E.R. 444.
[32] [1968] 2 All E.R. 444 at 462–463.

condition as to fitness in respect of all latent defects, the clause should have said so in clear and unambiguous terms, referring expressly to the condition which it was limiting."[33]

Further illustrations

There are a number of other cases which may serve to illustrate the point. In *Beck & Co v Szymonowski & Co*,[34] the purchasers had bought 2,000 gross six-cord sewing cotton thread reels, each reel stated to be 200 yards in length. It was said in the contract that:

2–012

> "The goods delivered shall be deemed to be in all respects in accordance with the contract, and the buyers shall be bound to accept and pay for the same accordingly, unless the sellers shall within 14 days after the arrival of the goods at their destination receive from the buyers notice of any matter or thing by reason whereof they may allege that the goods are not in accordance with the contract."

The reels had only 188 yards of cotton, not 200 yards, a fact discovered long after 14 days had expired. The House of Lords held that, comprehensive though it appeared, the clause was ineffective. The damages are claimed not in respect of the goods delivered but in respect of goods which were not delivered.[35]

The same approach can be seen in *Pegler Ltd v Wang (UK) Ltd.*[36] The relevant clause provided that "no action . . . arising out of the transaction in relation to this contract may be brought by either party more than 2 years after the cause of action has accrued". The court held that, on its true construction, this clause applied only to events arising once the products had been supplied: it did not apply in the case of late or non-delivery.

In *Minister of Materials v Steel Bros & Co*[37] a contract for the sale of goods limited the right to complain as to matters of quality to a period of 60 days. The goods were damaged as a result of defective packing. The Court of Appeal ruled that the clause was ineffective since the ground of complaint was not the quality of the goods. This is a particularly good illustration of judicial hostility to exclusion clauses since in *Niblett Ltd v Confectioners' Materials Co Ltd*,[38] it was held that the quality of goods includes the state of the packing, and that if this is unsatisfactory the goods are not of merchantable quality.

Similarly, in *Edmund Murray Ltd v BSP International Foundations Ltd*,[39] the supplier gave itself the right to repair or replace goods which were defective "by reason solely of faulty materials or workmanship supplied or performed". The purpose for which the goods were wanted had been made known, and the supplier was relied on to supply a rig fit for that purpose. The buyers said that the failure of the goods did not come about because of faulty materials or workmanship, but because of a design fault or exaggeration in the relevant specifications, the result being that the above clause had no effect. The Court of Appeal, reversing the

2–013

---

[33] [1968] 2 All E.R. 444 at 482.
[34] [1924] A.C. 43.
[35] [1924] A.C. 43 at 50.
[36] [2000] EWHC 137 (TCC).
[37] [1952] 1 T.L.R. 499.
[38] [1921] 3 K.B. 387.
[39] [1992] 33 Con. L.R. 1.

High Court, agreed. In the circumstances, the supplier had undertaken an obligation to supply goods designed and suitable for the buyer's purpose. If "and insofar as any failure of performance was due to the underlying design of the rig or to its incapacity to match up to what was known to be required as detailed in the specification, the ruling of the High Court was wrong".

In *Merlin Distribution Ltd v Somerfield Stores Ltd*,[40] a clause read:

> "If this agreement terminates for any reason [Somerfield are to pay] liquidated damages equal to the aggregate of such amount as may then be due and payable by [Merlin] in financing arrangements which [Merlin] may have entered from time to time in respect of the vehicles."

In response to the argument that this clause was an exclusion clause which had the effect of restricting any liability on the part of the supermarket to the relevant sum, Evans L.J. said that, as a matter of principle, the exclusion or limitation "must be express or at least unambiguously clear". It was held that the words of the clause were "not words of exclusion" and could be sufficiently explained by giving them a much more limited effect.

In *Econoler v GEC Alsthom*,[41] the relevant clause ran as follows:

> "After the risk in the Goods shall have passed to the Buyer, the Seller's liability to the Buyer for any damages whatsoever shall be limited as follows:
> 'Subject to Clause 18 above all representations, warranties, conditions, guarantees and liabilities express or implied statutory or otherwise (whether as to fitness for purpose, quality, description, standard of workmanship or otherwise) in respect of all or any of the Goods are hereby expressly excluded to the maximum extent permitted by law and the provisions hereof shall override any alleged representation or collateral agreement to the contrary. The Seller shall in no event be liable to any person, firm, or company (including but not limited to the Buyer) at any time whether in contract or tort or otherwise for any direct or indirect costs, damages or expenses relating to damage occasioned by any defect in or failure of the Goods or any part thereof or replacement therefor howsoever any such defect or failure may be caused and for the avoidance of doubt, the Seller shall not be liable in any event at any time for any consequential loss or damage (including but not limited to any loss of production or of profits) howsoever caused suffered by the Buyer or any other person, firm or company. The Buyer shall keep the Seller fully and effectively indemnified against all and any liability mentioned in the last preceding sentence. In particular and without prejudice to the foregoing provisions of this Clause the Buyer shall keep the Seller indemnified against any liability the Seller may incur at any time whether in tort or otherwise to any servant or agent of the Buyer in respect of any defect or failure of the Goods or any part thereof or replacement therefor howsoever caused.'"

2–014 The judge felt it "far from clear" just what was the precise ambit of this clause, saying that the first two exclusions might well cover liability in respect of goods, but did not appear apt to cover liability in respect of the supply of services, such as installation, commissioning or maintenance. He also expressed the "tentative" view that the clause was not drafted so as to exclude the effect of express words of description, quality or fitness for purpose. He felt that the same was true insofar as any lack of merchantable quality or lack of conformity with description arose from any failure by the defendants in relation to the supply of such services.

In *Brewer v Mann*,[42] a clause read:

---

[40] Unreported *The Buyer*, May 1996.
[41] Unreported April 16, 1999.
[42] [2010] EWHC 2444 (QB).

"the Customer agrees:—

1. That (apart from any of the following which have been expressly given to [sic] the Owner itself to the customer in writing) no condition, warranty, stipulation or representation whatsoever of any kind has been given by the Owner, its servants or agents in relation to the goods (other than a warranty that the Owner will pass to the customer upon exercise by the customer of the rights conferred on it by Clauses 4.1, 4.3 or 8.1 such title to the goods as the manufacturer or supplier pass to it);"

The defendant argued that this provision had the effect that the contractual description of the car as a "1930 Bentley Speed Six Car" was a "condition, warranty, stipulation or representation whatsoever of any kind" that had been given by the owner, its servants or agents in relation to the goods. Thus, the defendant had not given that condition, warranty, stipulation or representation and could not be liable for the misdescription it contained. The judge rejected this submission, saying that the disputed clause did not exclude the hire being by description:

"This is because the description in this case is not provided by [the defendant] as a contractual condition, warranty, stipulation or representation. The description is provided as an express term of the contract which [the defendant] approved. Thus, clause 5.1 does not extend to this provision and is not applicable to this term."

In the *Econoler* case, a further clause stated: **2–015**

"The Contract contains the entire agreement between the parties relating to the sale of the Goods and supersedes all prior written or oral communication between the Seller and the Buyer. The Buyer acknowledges that it does not place and has not placed any reliance on any representations, agreements, statements or undertakings (oral or written) made prior to the Acknowledgement of Order other than those expressly incorporated in any manner except by an instrument in writing signed by duly authorised representatives of both parties."

The judge said he found it difficult to regard such a clause as "effective to exclude liability under the express terms in the written 'bespoke' contract".[43] The action had been to strike out a statement of claim as being unarguable, but the court felt that certain terms were arguable, but made no final decision, which would have to await a full trial.

In *ED&F Man Sugar Ltd v Transportgesellschaft MBH*,[44] fire broke out at a terminal thus causing delay. The charterers relied on this clause to avoid having to make the appropriate payment:

"In the event that whilst at or off the loading place ... the loading ... of the vessel is prevented or delayed by any of the following occurrences: strikes, riots, civil commotions, lock outs of men, accidents and/or breakdowns on railways, stoppages on railway and/or river and/or canal by ice or frost mechanical breakdowns at mechanical loading plants, government interferences, vessel being inoperative or rendered inoperative due to the terms and conditions of appointment of the Officers and crew time so lost shall not count as laytime."

The High Court rejected reliance on this clause, saying that, as a matter of "ordinary language and common sense", the destruction of an item (or even its

---

[43] For the effectiveness generally of non-reliance clauses, see para.2–050.
[44] [2012] EWHC 2879.

partial destruction) could not be said to be within the scope of the term "breakdown", still less within the term "mechanical breakdown".

The same approach of requiring a strict interpretation is applied to clauses by which a measure of liability is imposed on the other contracting party. In *Dorset CC v Southern Felt Roofing Co*,[45]a party was engaged to carry out works of repair and renewal to a flat roof at a primary school. During the course of the works, the school caught fire because of the defendant's negligence, and the building's contents were severely damaged. A term in the contract provided that the defendant would indemnify the claimant against "any liability, loss, claim or proceedings in respect of injury or death to persons or damage to property". It was held that this clause was directed exclusively to claims by third parties and that, in consequence, the claim by the claimants based on this clause must fail.

2–016 In *Bovis Construction (Scotland) Ltd v Whatlings Construction Ltd*,[46] a clause limited damages in respect of "time-related costs". Head contractors sought to end the employment of sub-contractors on the ground that they were not proceeding diligently and claimed damages in excess of the amount provided for in the clause. The House of Lords ruled that a clause which limited liability should state "clearly and unambiguously the scope of the limitation and would be construed 'with a degree of strictness', albeit not to the same extent as an exclusion or indemnity clause".

Much the same point was made in *Bikam Ood v Adria*[47] where a limitation clause was under consideration. It recognised that, traditionally, the courts had taken a very severe view of exclusion clauses. They had to be drafted very carefully indeed. In this case, though, the court was prepared was prepared to step back from such a rigorous approach. For one thing, a more modern view was to look at the contract and to recognise that parties to commercial contracts are entitled to apportion the risk of loss as they saw fit and that provisions which limit or exclude liability must be construed in the same way as other terms. The other point was to recognise that the courts were far less inclined to attack limitation clauses (such as the one in the present case) which accepted a degree of liability, than they were in the case of clauses which excluded liability altogether. The court concluded that the contract in dispute before the court involved a calculated allocation of risk and remuneration. The limitation clause accordingly applied.

In *Meditek Laboratory Services Ltd v Purolator Courier Ltd*,[48] a clause in a carrier's contract provided that there could be no liability in excess of a given sum and that this maximum applied regardless of "negligence or gross negligence". A particular parcel was misdelivered because of negligence, but a further breach took place when the delivery sheets were deliberately completed incorrectly. The carrier's inability to trace the missing goods and complete delivery in time "was a result of the false completion of its own documents. That misconduct did not come within the scope of the limitation of liability". The clause was therefore held not to apply to the particular breach.

---

[45] (1990) 6 Const. L.J. 37.
[46] [1995] N.P.C. 153.
[47] [2012] EWHC 621.
[48] Unreported *The Buyer*, March 1996.

A clause will also be cut back in effect if its literal reading would be inimical to **2–017** the sense of the contract. In *Mitsubishi Corp v Eastwind Transport Ltd*,[49] the relevant terms of the contract were as follows:

> "4. Carrier's exemption clause. Subject to clause 1 hereof the Carrier shall not be responsible for loss or damage to or in connection with the Goods of any kind whatsoever (including deterioration, delay or loss of market) however caused (whether by unseaworthiness or unfitness of the vessel or any other vessel, tender, lighter or craft or any other mode of conveyance whatsoever or by faults, errors or negligence, or otherwise howsoever).
> In particular and without prejudice to the generality of the foregoing
>
> A.   The Carrier shall be under no such responsibility:
>   (i)   at any time prior to the loading of the Goods on to and subsequent to the discharge of the Goods or part thereof from the vessel when but for the provisions of this clause such goods would be the responsibility of the Carrier and
>   (ii) in the case of live animals or of cargo which in this Bill of Lading is stated as being carried on deck and is so carried none of which is subject to the Convention or legislation referred to in Clause 1 hereof at any time when, but for the provisions of this clause such goods would be the responsibility of the carrier.
>
> B.   Unless this Bill of Lading is subject to the Hague-Visby Rules in accordance with paragraphs (A) and/or (E) of Clause 1 or to the Hague Rules in accordance with paragraphs (B) and/or (D) of Clause 1, the carrier shall not be liable for loss of or damage to or in connection with the Goods or part thereof of any kind whatsoever (including deterioration, delay or loss of market) arising or resulting from: unseaworthiness (whether or not due diligence shall have been exercised by the Carrier, his servants or agents or others to make the vessel seaworthy); Act, neglect of default of the Master, mariner, pilot or the servants or agents of the Carrier in the navigation or in the management of the vessel or in the care of the cargo; fire, perils, dangers and accidents of the sea or other navigable waters; act of God; act of War; act of public enemies; arrest or restraint of princes, rulers or people, or seizure under legal process; quarantine restrictions; act or omission of the Shipper, Consignee, Owner of the Goods, or Holder of this Bill of Lading, his agents or representatives, strikes or lock-outs or stoppage or restraint of labour from whatever cause, whether partial or general; riots and civil commotions; saving or attempting to save life or property at sea; wastage in bulk or weight or any other loss or damage arising from inherent defect, quality or vice of the Goods; insufficiency of packing; insufficiency or inadequacy of marks; latent defects; any other cause whatsoever, whether or not of a like kind to those above mentioned, and including negligence on the part of the Carrier, his servants, agents or others."

In its ruling, the court pointed out that the disputed clause was plainly intended to relieve the carrier of liability for loss of or damage to the goods shipped caused by, amongst other things, the unseaworthiness or uncargoworthiness of the vessel, or the negligence of the carrier, its servants or agents. This meant that, if effective, the clause would clearly protect the defendants against the claims made in the present action, which blamed the alleged damage to the goods shipped on their negligence and the unseaworthiness, or uncargoworthiness, of their ship.

The court accepted that, read literally the words, "however caused", "or otherwise howsoever", and "arising or resulting from ... any other cause whatsoever ..." could comprehend any cause of loss of, or damage to, the goods shipped, including a deliberate refusal on the part of the carrier to perform its contract at all, or even theft by the carrier of the goods entrusted to it. On this construction the clause would operate to exclude liability for every potential

---

[49] [2004] EWHC 2924 (Comm).

cause of loss or damage and the holder of the bills of lading would have no remedy for any breach of contract by the carrier at all. As the court noted, the claimants were indeed arguing that the clause should be read in this way and that, with this meaning, it was therefore repugnant to the main object of the contracts, and should be rejected altogether.

2–018   The court countered this argument by saying that the common law's approach to the construction of contracts was, however, not a literalist one. It had been established in the previous cases that, if giving words in a contract, "their full and complete meaning", would produce a result at odds with the main object of the contract, then the court would put upon those words a restricted meaning. Indeed, this would lead the court to reject words, or even whole provisions, if they were inconsistent with the main purpose of the contract. It was, however, more common, the court said, that the court would attribute, wherever possible, to the words used a meaning consistent with the underlying purpose of the contract.

In the present case, the court felt it plain that the words, "however caused", "or otherwise howsoever" and "arising or resulting from ... any other cause whatsoever", when considered in their context as parts of contracts for the carriage of goods from one port to another, did not operate to relieve the carrier of liability for any and every breach of contract. Those words bore a restricted meaning. They did not cover, for example, loss or damage caused by dishonesty on the part of the carrier. Whether that was because of a rule of law, or a principle of construction did not matter: "the result is that the carrier would be liable for a breach of contract caused by its dishonesty. Moreover the words would not be strong enough to relieve the carrier from liability for loss of or damage to the goods caused by it arbitrarily refusing to ship them to the port of discharge at all".

The court accepted that the clause operated to shift most risks which might result in loss of or damage to the goods shipped from the carrier to the holder of the bill of lading. That, though, was not inconsistent with the purpose of a commercial contract of carriage where the bearer of a risk can insure against it. The court thus concluded that it was unnecessary, and indeed impossible, to imagine all circumstances in which it might be said by the carrier that the disputed clause applied, and where a court might have to decide whether it does or not. The fact that the application of the clause might have to be determined case by case does not, it said, make its meaning uncertain. It was certainly a principle of construction that, in cases of doubt a contractual provision would be construed against the person who produced it, and for whose benefit it operated, but that did not extend to construing a contractual provision as widely as possible so as to render it repugnant to the main object of the contract read as a whole when it could be given a meaning consistent with that object. In the present case, this meant that the clause could not be given the wide meaning sought by the claimants, and that it was therefore not repugnant to the aim of the contract.

2–019   The claimants' case was that some of the goods shipped were damaged as a result of the negligence of the defendants, or the unseaworthiness or uncargoworthiness of their vessel. In the court's judgment, properly construed, there was no reason to reject the clause which protected the carrier where damage to the goods shipped resulted from such causes. It was therefore effective to exempt the defendants from any potential liability for those claims.

These cases can be contrasted with *China Shipbuilding Corp v Nippon Yusen Kabukishi Kaisha.*[50] China Shipbuilding agreed to build three vessels for Nippon under shipbuilding agreements on the Shipbuilding Association of Japan form with variations. Article IX.1 provided for a one-year guarantee by China Shipbuilding of materials and workmanship. Article IX.3(a) further provided that defects were excluded when discovered after the end of the guarantee period as were defects other than those specified in art.IX.1. The obligation under the guarantee was limited to the repair and replacement of defects. After the guarantee period had expired, defects were discovered. China Shipbuilding relied on art.IX.3(a), arbitrators holding that the terms of the contract did not in the circumstances exempt the builder from liability. The Commercial Court remitted the matter to arbitration, ruling that art.IX.3 was a complete code for dealing with defects discovered after delivery. Article IX.3(a) was intended to, and did, exclude liability arising from breach of an express term of the contract unless there was liability under the terms of art.IX.1.

Negligence liability

Nowhere has the animosity of the judges toward exclusion clauses been better displayed than in their attitude to the exclusion of liability for negligence. The position has, of course, been drastically affected by the Unfair Contract Terms Act 1977 and the Consumer Rights Act 2014 which have reduced the need to give a strained construction to exclusion and limitation clauses.[51] Yet wide though the impact of these enactments is, there will nevertheless remain an area where common law precedent remains paramount. This is because a substantial number of types of contract are excluded from the purview of these enactments: and because, even within them, certain types of exclusion clause relating to negligence liability remain valid if reasonable. But even if reasonable and hence valid, they will remain to be interpreted, and this explains the continued relevance of much of what was decided before the two Acts.

2–020

The special problems relating to negligence liability have been put thus:

> "it may happen that, apart from the contract, [the person inserting the clause] may find himself in a situation where the law casts upon him not only a duty of care but also some form of strict liability. In such a case, unless the language of the contract manifestly covers both types of obligation he will be taken to have excluded only the latter."[52]

This is neatly illustrated by *White v Warwick.*[53] The claimant hired a bicycle from the defendants. It was a term of the agreement that "nothing in this agreement shall render the owners liable for any personal injuries to the riders of the machine hired". The saddle tipped over and the claimant was hurt. He brought

---

[50] *China Shipbuilding Corp v Nippon Yusen Kabukishi Kaisha (The Seta Maru, The Saikyo and The Suma)* [2000] 1 Lloyd's Rep. 367; [2000] C.L.C. 566 QBD (Comm).
[51] The provisions of the 1977 Act in relation to negligence liability have been disapplied in the case of consumer contracts or notices by the 2014 Act Sch.4.
[52] See Cheshire, Fifoot and Furmston, *Law of Contract* (London: Butterworths, 1986), p.157. Although not repeated verbatim in later editions, the extract is still an accurate statement of the law.
[53] [1953] 2 All E.R. 1021.

an action, suing alternatively for breach of contract and in tort for negligence. Since liability could be grounded in either negligence or strict liability for breach of contract, the Court of Appeal felt able to hold that the exclusion clause extended only to a claim concerning the latter. Accordingly, the defendants remained liable in negligence.

It must be appreciated that there are limits in the application of this particular case. In *Lamport & Holt Lines Ltd v Coubro & Scrutton (M&I Ltd) and Coubro & Scrutton (Riggers and Shipwrights) Ltd*,[54] where reliance was placed by the defendants on the *White* case, Goff J. stressed that the earlier case "was concerned with a clause which exempted the defendant from liability both in contract and in tort, the liability in contract being wider than the liability in tort".[55] In the *White* case itself, Denning L.J. had himself observed that:

> "The liability for breach of contract is more strict than the liability for negligence. The owners may be liable in contract for supplying a defective machine, even though they were not negligent... In these circumstances, the exemption clause must, I think, be construed as exempting the owners only from their liability in contract, and not from their liability in negligence."[56]

2–021   When the *Lamport & Holt* case reached the Court of Appeal, Donaldson L.J. made the trenchant observation that:

> "The basis of the decision was that the contract, on its true construction, would, in the absence of this clause, have imposed a warranty of fitness for the purpose. The clause was therefore held to negative this warranty, while leaving liability in tort unaffected. But I know of no case in which words of exclusion have been held to operate in relation to a liability for breach of an obligation in contract, but not to affect liability for breach of the self-same obligation in tort. Indeed, the whole concept of a hypothetical discussion between two parties, other than law students, which led to such an agreement is patently absurd."[57]

The general point is also well illustrated by the opinion of the Privy Council in *Canada Steamship Lines Ltd v The King*.[58] The terms of the lease of a shed provided that the lessee "shall not have any claim" for damage to goods. An indemnity clause required the lessee to indemnify the lessor against all claims in any manner based upon "any action taken or thing done". Owing to the negligence of the lessor's servants, a fire broke out, destroying the shed and all its contents. The lessees, and others whose property was destroyed, sought damages from the lessors. Lord Morton considered that in approaching such clauses as were contained in this particular contract, three principles fell for consideration[59]:

(i)   If the clause contains language expressly exempting a party from the consequences of his negligence, effect must be given to that provision.

(ii)   If there is no such express reference, the court must consider whether, given their natural meaning, the words extend to cover negligence.

---

[54] [1982] 2 Lloyd's Rep. 42; [1981] 2 Lloyd's Rep. 659.
[55] [1981] 2 Lloyd's Rep. 659 at 665.
[56] [1953] 2 All E.R. 1021 at 1025.
[57] [1982] 2 Lloyd's Rep. 42 at 46.
[58] [1952] 1 All E.R. 305.
[59] [1952] 1 All E.R. 305 at 310. See also *Rutter v Palmer* [1922] 2 K.B. 87 at 92, per Scrutton L.J.

(iii)   If the words are sufficiently wide, then the court must consider whether the head of damage may be based on some ground other than that of negligence. Such other ground must not be so fanciful or remote that the party seeking to rely on it cannot be supposed to have sought protection from it. Subject to such a qualification, the existence of a possible head of damage other than that of negligence is fatal even if the words used are *prima facie* wide enough to cover negligence.

Applying these rules, the following findings were made. The lessors had failed to limit liability in respect of negligence in clear terms and hence the clause was to be construed as relating to a liability not based on negligence. Turning to the indemnity clause, the Privy Council was of the opinion that it also failed to cover negligent acts. It was at least doubtful that the words "any action taken or things done . . . by virtue hereof" could be applied to a negligent act done in the course of carrying out an obligation. But even if they were wide enough, the principle remained that the head of damage might be based on some ground other than that of negligence. Finally, the meaning and effect of the indemnity clause were far from clear, and liability on an indemnity clause must be imposed by clear words. Lord Morton summarised the lessor's position when he said that there "would have been no difficulty in inserting an express reference to negligence" if these clauses had been intended to protect the lessors against the consequences of negligence.[60]

Lord Morton's approach was given close scrutiny in *Monarch Airlines Ltd v London Luton Airport Ltd*.[61] Damage had been done to an aircraft, the cause of such damage being negligence and breach of duty on the part of the defendants. The relationship between the parties was governed by a contract, one of the terms of which was:

2–022

> "Neither the airport company nor its respective servants or agents shall be liable for loss or damage to the aircraft, its parts or accessories or any property contained in the aircraft, occurring while the aircraft is in the airport, or being removed or dealt with elsewhere . . . arising directly or indirectly from any act, omission, neglect or default on the part of the airport company or its servants or agents unless done with intent to cause damage or recklessly and with knowledge that damage would probably result."

The airline submitted that Lord Morton's criteria were not satisfied by this clause. There was no specific reference to negligence; it was not wide enough in its ordinary meaning to cover negligence; or, if it did cover negligence, there were possible bases of liability other than negligence which were excluded by the clause. For its part, the airport submitted that this was not the kind of clause which Lord Morton had in mind, but was rather one which could be described as a "not liable unless" or "only liable if" clause.

The court first noted that:

---

[60] [1952] 1 All E.R. 305 at 313.
[61] [1997] C.L.C. 698.

"Like all rules of construction, Lord Morton's test is a guide designed to ascertain the true intention of the parties. It should not be applied rigidly or mechanically so as to defeat their intentions."[62]

Referring to the clause in dispute, the court said that, under it, there was to be no liability arising from any act, omission, neglect or default unless done with intent, recklessly, and with knowledge that damage would probably result. This meant that there would only be liability in any of these cases if there were an intention to cause damage or if there were relevant recklessness. The court accepted that the clause did not refer specifically to recklessness, but "it would make a nonsense of the clause if the airport was to be liable for what might be called ordinary negligence, but only liable for other neglect or default if the test of intention or recklessness was satisfied". The court was prepared to accept the argument that the words "neglect or default", as used in the present clause, were "clearly intended" to exclude liability for negligent acts, so that: "It follows that the clause passes Lord Morton's first test". This finding rendered it strictly unnecessary to consider whether the clause was wide enough in any event to cover negligence, but the court did say that it was.

Lord Morton's third test had asked if there were another head of liability, one not relating to negligence, which the clause could be read as covering. In the present case, it had been argued that there were two possible such heads of liability, relating to private nuisance and breach of statutory duty. The court, however, said of private nuisance that "the chances that either the draftsman or the parties had any such liability in mind are very remote indeed". It did accept, though, that the clause had been drafted with breach of statutory duty in mind. This finding did not, however, ultimately help the airline, since the court, as it pointed out, had already held that the clause was clearly intended to protect the airport from acts of negligence except where there was any intent, recklessness and knowledge that damage would probably result.

2–023   The same warning against a mechanistic approach to the *Canada Steamship* principles was voiced in *Mir Steel UK Ltd v Morris*.[63] The fourth respondent R4 was a company which manufactured steel. It had entered into a contract for C to provide a hot strip mill at its premises. The mill remained C's property. R4 went into administration. The first, second and third respondents (X) were its administrators. They offered R4's assets for sale, including the mill. C sent them formal notification of its claim to ownership of the mill, but they hived down all of the assets into M, a wholly-owned subsidiary company. In cl.9.5 of the hive down agreement M agreed to be responsible for settling "any claim" made against it by C concerning the mill. M was then purchased by another company

---

[62] "These guidelines are only guidelines and all the more plainly so in the case of limitation clauses": *Cert Plc v George Hammond Plc* [1999] 2 All E.R. (Comm) 976. See also the statement that: "Lord Morton was giving helpful guidance on the proper approach to interpretation and not laying down a code. The passage does not provide a litmus test which applied to the terms of the contract, yields a certain and predictable result. The courts' task of ascertaining what the particular parties intended, in their particular commercial context, remains": *HIH Casualty & General Insurance Ltd v Chase Manhattan Bank*[2003] 2 Lloyd's Rep. 61, per Lord Bingham. Lord Bingham's words were endorsed by Hamblen J. in *Onego Shipping & Chartering BV v JSC Arcadia Shipping* [2010] EWHC 777 (Comm).
[63] [2012] EWCA Civ 1397.

(L). C brought proceedings against M and L for conversion, inducing a breach of contract and unlawful means conspiracy. M accepted that cl.9.5 covered the conversion claim. It sought permission to join X and R4 as defendants, on the basis that it had prospective claims against them for a contribution in relation to C's inducement and conspiracy claims.

Counsel acknowledged, that, taken at face value, the words 'any claim' did cover all claims against Mir Steel. He submitted, however, in reliance on *Canada Steamship* that that was not enough. Whilst he accepted that the words undoubtedly extended to the claim in conversion, and so imposed any liability for that exclusively upon Mir Steel, he did dispute that they ought to be read as also imposing upon it the exclusive burden of bearing the consequences of torts said to have been committed being torts which had at their heart intentional wrongdoing: namely, inducing a breach of the 3 April 2000 contract and conspiracy. Counsel added that it was only if cl.9.5 had expressly spelt out that it was intended to have that latter, and wider, effect that it could properly be construed as covering even such claims.

In response, Rimer L.J. cautioned that that case "should not be applied mechanistically and ought to be regarded as no more than guidelines. They do not provide an automatic solution to any particular case. The court's function is always to interpret the particular contract in the context in which it was made. It would be surprising if it were otherwise". After noting the principles set out in the *West Bromwich*[64] case, the Court of Appeal said that the court's task was to approach the interpretation of cl.9.5 in light of the overall commercial purpose of the hive down agreement, and to determine whether it was "inherently improbable" that it was directed at releasing the respondents not just from liability to contribute to a claim in conversion, but also from liability to contribute to any other claim that C might bring against M in respect of the mill. It found that the commercial purpose of the hive down agreement was obvious to all the parties. R4 had entered into administration and X was under a statutory duty to achieve the purpose of administration as quickly and efficiently as reasonably practicable. They resolved to perform that duty by selling R4's business and assets to M, their objective being to achieve a prompt realisation and distribution of proceeds to creditors. M's objective, as purchaser, was to acquire the business and assets with a view to exploiting them for its own commercial advantage. However, unlike most such cases, when X, R4 and M entered into the hive down agreement they all knew that C had asserted a claim to the ownership of the mill, and they were aware of the factual basis upon which C might assert its title. X was admittedly selling M an asset to which the title was possibly flawed, but M was nevertheless prepared to buy it, and, by cl.9.5 to assume responsibility for "settling any claim made against it" by C in respect of the mill. Therefore, if C made claims against M in respect of the mill, it could not realistically have been the parties' intention that M would then be entitled to claw back from X and R4 part of the price that it had agreed to pay for the mill, being a price it had agreed in full knowledge of the possible flaw in the mill's title, and of the risk of claims by C. Further, if the sale to M involved any wrongdoing, whether by conversion, inducing a breach of contract or conspiracy, the parties to the hive down

---

[64] See para.2–002.

agreement were all engaged in it together, and M should have realised that. The whole point of cl.9.5 was therefore to shift to M the entire risk and burden of any claim that C might make in respect of the mill. Its words extended to all the claims that C had in fact brought and the lower court had been correct to refuse to join X and R4 as parties to the claims.

2–024   With these observations in mind, we can consider the following cases in which the principles of *Canada Steamship* were considered. BHP ordered a pipeline from British Steel subject to a contract containing a clause excluding "all liability" for defects in the pipeline save and except for those defects becoming apparent within two years of the date of the purchase order. BS maintained that this clause was sufficiently clear and comprehensive enough to cover all latent defects which were not apparent within two years of the date of delivery, and had the effect of excluding all liability of any nature, including liability in negligence. BHP argued that the wording "all liability" should be construed *contra proferentem* and that the clause operated only to confer additional mutual rights for a limited period. Specifically, BHP maintained that there was an obligation on BS to repair within the specified period and for BHP to permit them to do so rather than seeking recompense in damages. BHP contended that it was only liability arising from this additional right which was subject to the time limitation imposed.

It was held, applying the principles laid down in the *Canada Steamship* case, that the clause was effective to exclude all liability for the specified period, including any liability in negligence which had not become apparent within two years from the date of delivery. This was held to be so for the following reasons:

(a)   the phrase "all liability of the supplier relating to the work" contained within the clause was wider than the rectification obligation;

(b)   taken at face value, the wording used was clearly sufficient to exclude far more than liability to rectify within a specified period;

(c)   the wider construction was supported by a consideration of the contract conditions as a whole; and

(d)   there was no reason why the principles applicable to monetary limitation were not equally applicable to time limitation.

In *Macquarie Internationale Investments Ltd v Glencore (UK) Ltd*,[65] under a sale and purchase agreement M had agreed to buy, and G agreed to sell to M, the shares in a company (C) which headed an energy group. Under the agreement M had the benefit of various warranties given by G which, by arrangement with the other sellers, was the sole warrantor. M had issued proceedings against G alleging breaches of warranty in that the accounts and books of C and its subsidiaries did not fairly reflect their financial position. G brought claims against R and S, who were respectively the finance director and managing director of C at the time of the sale, alleging breaches of common law duties of care and fiduciary duties. The applicants relied on cl.6.8 which ran as follows:

---

[65]   [2008] EWHC 1716 (Comm).

"The Sellers shall not (if a claim is made against any of them in connection with the sale of the Shares to the Purchaser) make any claim against the Company or any of the Subsidiaries or against any director, employee, agent or officer of the Company or any of the Subsidiaries on whom any of the Sellers may have relied before agreeing to any term of this Agreement or the Deed of Tax Covenant or authorising any statement in the Disclosure Letter. The Sellers acknowledge that they have no rights to make any such claim. This shall not prevent any Seller from claiming against any other Seller under any right of contribution or indemnity to which he may be entitled. The rights of the Company or any of the Subsidiaries and any director, employee, agent or officer of the Company or any of the Subsidiaries under this clause are subject to the provisions of Clause 17.4 (No Rights of Third Parties)."

The suggested proviso to cl.6.8 that claims against directors were barred only if **2–025** the relevant acts or omissions were within the scope of their employment did not feature in the wording of cl.6.8 and was never satisfactorily explained by G. Such a proviso was inconsistent with the commercial purpose of cl.6.8, which was to bar claims against C lest the value of the warranties be undermined and in the same way to make sure that the sellers could not circumvent the prohibition on suing C by suing natural persons. Collateral claims by G against directors or employees of C would also be damaging in terms of the impact of such claims upon staff morale and management time. There were thus good commercial reasons for barring such claims irrespective of whether relevant actions or omissions were alleged to have been within the scope of employment. Moreover, R and S had received a reduced bonus because they were unwilling to give personal warranties in any sale and purchase agreement for C. That gave a further reason why they had a legitimate interest in being reassured that under cl.6.8 they could prevent claims being made against them. There was no principled or practical basis for distinguishing between assuming tortious responsibility in the course of acting as a director and doing so when not in the course of so acting. The court said that the "the obvious claim" against R and S, which everyone must have had in mind when cl.6.8 was drafted, was a claim in negligence.

It is useful, at this point, to refer to the decision in the *Lamport & Holt* case. What had actually happened there was that a derrick on which certain work was being done was being restowed on the claimants' vessel when the tumbler of the mast topping block carried away or fractured with the result that the derrick damaged a closed hatch cover. At first instance, Goff J. turned to consider the principles discussed above as set out by Lord Morton. The clause in dispute had excluded liability "for any damage ... suffered by you ... and which may arise from or be in any way connected with any act ... of any person or corporation employed by us or by any subcontractors or engaged in any capacity herewith ...". It was contended by the claimants that those words were wide enough to cover heads of liability other than negligence and which were not, as Lord Morton had insisted, too "fanciful or remote". The other possible heads were said to be:

(a)   late delivery of the derrick;
(b)   restowing it in the wrong position; and
(c)   in reliance on *White v Warwick*, the fact that there could also be liability in contract.

The last possibility was rejected on the grounds referred to above. The first alleged alternative head was rejected for being too "fanciful", the point being that other clauses in the contract would have applied in the event of breach by late delivery. The remaining contention, that of excluding liability for restowing the derrick in the wrong position, was likewise outside the clause since, on its true construction, "the condition cannot... exempt R&S from a simple failure to carry out the works which they had contracted to do. So to apply the condition would be to defeat the very purpose of the contract itself".[66]

When the *Lamport & Holt* case reached the Court of Appeal, Donaldson L.J. was keen to stress that Lord Morton's opinion is likely to mislead "unless full force is given to his caveat that the 'other ground' must not be so fanciful or remote that the *proferens* cannot be supposed to have desired protection against it".[67] Before the Court of Appeal, the claimants had recast the other possible grounds:

> "the very doing of which suggests that it is by no means clear that there was an alternative substantial, *i.e.* not fanciful, ground of liability. Late delivery has become the delayed provision of services. Misperformance remains, as does a contractual liability parallel with a tortious liability, but [counsel] now adds nuisance, conversion and detinue."[68]

2–026 The idea of delay being covered by this condition was rejected because other contract terms were more appropriate. Parallel liability in contract and tort was likewise rejected for reasons earlier noted.[69] Misperformance was likewise discounted since there was no obvious reason why, when the clause in dispute was being framed, "the parties should have been, or be deemed to have been, addressing their minds to contractual neglect rather than tortious neglect or vice versa".[70] As for the newcomers, nuisance, conversion and detinue:

> "Suffice it to say that I am not surprised that [counsel] has only now thought of this. If the officious bystander had raised the point with the parties when they were negotiating the contract, I think that he would be trying to explain to them what he had in mind."[71]

There was concern also on the part of May and Stephenson L.JJ. that a correct understanding be had of the possible other heads of liability argument. According to the former, the court is to discard, when turning its attention to alternative heads of liability outside negligence, any ground to which, on a reasonable assessment:

> "of all the circumstances at the time the underlying contract was made, it is unlikely that the parties would have addressed their mind ... the exercise upon which the court is engaged in these cases is one of construction, that is one of deciding what the parties meant or must be deemed to have meant by the words they used."[72]

---

[66] See para.2–020.
[67] [1981] 2 Lloyd's Rep. 659 at 665.
[68] [1982] 2 Lloyd's Rep. 42 at 45.
[69] See para.2–021.
[70] [1982] 2 Lloyd's Rep. 42 at 46.
[71] [1981] 2 Lloyd's Rep. 659 at 665.
[72] [1981] 2 Lloyd's Rep. 659 at 665.

Stephenson L.J. agreed that, if there is another head of damage, then the clause will cover that damage, and will not extend to damage resulting from negligence:

"If there is no such head of damage, the court is under no duty to seek out, or think up, remote and far-fetched possibilities in order to defeat the intention, which would otherwise be derived from the plain meaning of the clause, to protect the party relying on it from liability."[73]

The Privy Council opinion was followed in *Dorset CC v Southern Felt Roofing Co.*[74] Applying the *Canada Steamship* case, the court held that the clause was capable of exempting the defendant from tortious liability under common law but since there were risks not fanciful or remote to which the clause could relate, other than loss or damage by fire caused by the defendant's negligence, the clause did not on its true construction extend to exempt the defendant from the consequences of negligence which caused the fire.

In *Casson v Ostley PJ Ltd,*[75] a quotation for plumbing work included the following clauses:

    2–027

"(a)   clause 6:
MATERIALS—the property in unfixed materials shall not pass until all materials shall have been paid for in full. All materials on the site fixed or unfixed are at the sole risk of the client and in the event of any of the same being damaged, destroyed or stolen, we shall be entitled to full payment therefore, and also for any work damaged, destroyed or lost, and the cost of replacing and of reinstating or restoring any such work shall be charged as an extra, provided that the client shall not be responsible for any loss occasioned solely by the negligence of our employees.

(b)   clause 15:
   works covered by this estimate, existing structures in which we shall be working, and unfixed materials shall be at the sole risk of the client as regards loss or damage by fire and the client shall maintain a proper policy of insurance against that risk in an adequate sum. If any loss or damage affecting the works is so occasioned by fire, the client shall pay to us the full value of all work and materials then executed and delivered."

The court had to decide preliminary issues as to whether the defendant was liable for fire damage to the property of the claimants at which building works were being carried out by the first defendant and its sub-contractors. It was assumed for the purposes of the preliminary issues that the cause of the fire was the negligence of the first defendant.

As Schiemann L.J. saw it, the "crucial question" was whether the words of cl.15 construed in context could not sensibly be construed other than as exempting the builder from liability for his own negligence. The High Court had held it so, but the Court of Appeal disagreed. Schiemann L.J. said that the interrelation of cll.6 and 15 was such that their effect could be reconciled only by either construing cl.15 in the way contended for by the claimants or by inserting words in cl.6 so as to add at the end after "any loss" some such words as "other than a loss caused by fire". Given what he called "that tension and resolving any

---

[73] [1982] 2 Lloyd's Rep. 42 at 49.
[74] (1990) 6 Const. L.J. 37. See para.2–015.
[75] [2001] EWCA Civ 1013.

doubt against the builder (whose clause it is) I do not regard the contract as expressly exempting him from the consequences of negligently causing a loss by fire".

The Lord Justice, moving on to stage 2 of Lord Morton's test, accepted that the words of cl.15 were wide enough to cover the consequences of the builder's negligence.

2–028 That took the court to stage 3. Schiemann L.J. accepted that there were a number of far from fanciful examples in which, without negligence, a builder might be held liable for a fire resulting from goods supplied and work done by him, and this meant that the application of the third of Lord Morton's tests was "fatal" to the builder's contentions.

He accepted that Lord Morton's tests were not to be applied as though they were contained in a statute, but they still:

> "embody the approach of the law and I do not regard the fact that in the present case there was an insurance aspect to the case as making them inapposite. Insurance provisions are primarily in a contract in order to provide a fund in the event of the risk eventuating. They are not there primarily for defining the obligations of one party to the other."

He explained that there were in this present case several "realistic reasons" why the builder might wish to ensure that the employer had a fund available in the event of a fire not caused by the builder's negligence. This meant that the clause "has a perfectly good commercial purpose even if it does not have the effect of exempting the builder from the consequences of his own negligence".

BREACH OF AN ABSOLUTE DUTY

2–029 Certain qualifications to the *Canada Steamship* case were expressed by the High Court in *HIH Casualty & General Insurance Ltd v Chase Manhattan Bank*.[76] The case involved allegations that various statements made prior to a contract of insurance involved fraudulent misrepresentations and non-disclosure by an agent of the assured.

The court said that the second and third rules of construction, set out in the earlier case, were intended to deal with cases where the exemption or indemnity clause wording had been deliberately drawn in a wide and general way. It was for that reason that its effect would appear equivocal and so the court would naturally ask: what did the parties actually intend to cover by these general words? The *Canada Steamship* case rules of construction were, it was said, not intended to apply to a particular clause that is specifically directed at exempting liability for the breach of a particular type of absolute duty, where the breach can be established whether or not negligence (or fraud) is proved. The duty of disclosure in insurance contracts is such an absolute duty in that it is infringed even if the non-disclosure was entirely inadvertent. The same is true of the duty not to misrepresent material facts. Having stated this, however, the court added that even if the clause in question was specifically directed at the consequences of non-disclosure or misrepresentation, that was not the end of the matter. Its task

---

[76] [2001] 1 Lloyd's Rep. 30.

was still to discern what the parties intended by the wording that they had agreed in the context of the particular type of contract under consideration:

> "Thus it seems to me that even if the *Canada Steamship* 'rules' of construction do not apply directly to a clause which specifically purports to exclude or limit a duty of utmost good faith or specifically purports to exclude or limit remedies for its breach, the Court still has to ask, objectively, what factual circumstances did the parties intend to cover by the wording that they have used? Thus, as an example, I think that a Court has to ask: does the contract wording cover a situation where there is a duty of disclosure, but the assured has failed to fulfil it as a result of its agent's negligence or deliberate concealment of facts?"

Stress was placed in the House of Lords on the fact that Lord Morton's test provided guidance and was not to be construed as a rule of law:

> "Lord Morton was expressing broad guidelines not prescribing rigid rules. It cannot be right mechanically to apply the guideline incorporated in his third paragraph so as to produce a result inconsistent with the commercial purpose of the contract in question. Given the commercial purpose of the Truth of Statement clause, namely, to insulate Chase from representations or nondisclosures by Heaths material to the effecting of the TVC insurance policy, it is impossible to conclude that the parties did not intend negligent representations or nondisclosures to be covered."[77]

JUDICIAL HOSTILITY FURTHER ILLUSTRATED

The lengths the courts will go to in finding that an exclusion clause does not extend to cover liability in negligence are nowhere better illustrated than in *Hollier v Rambler Motors Ltd*.[78] The contentious clause read: "The Company is not responsible for damage caused by fire to customers' cars on the premises". While the car was in the garage, a fire broke out as a result of the defendants' negligence which caused substantial damage to the car.

2–030

This clause had not, in fact, been incorporated into the contract.[79] The Court of Appeal proceeded, however, to interpret the clause, acknowledging that, as bailees, the defendants' liability could only ever sound in negligence. Salmon L.J. imagined that, faced with this particular clause, the ordinary man would say:

> " 'Well, what they are telling me is that if there is a fire due to any cause other than their own negligence they are not responsible for it.' To my mind, if the defendants were seeking to exclude their responsibility for a fire caused by their own negligence, they ought to have done so in far plainer language than the language here used. In my view, the words of the condition would be understood as being meant to be a warning to the customer that if a fire does occur at the garage which damages the car, and it is not caused by the negligence of the garage owner, then the garage owner is not responsible for damage."[80]

---

[77] [2003] UKHL 6, per Lord Scott. The approach taken in the House of Lords was approved in *Onego Shipping & Chartering BV v JSC Arcadia Shipping* [2010] EWHC 777 (Comm). For the position as to non-disclosure in consumer contracts, see now the Consumer Insurance (Disclosures and Representations) Act 2012.

[78] [1972] 1 All E.R. 399.

[79] See the discussion at para.1–035.

[80] [1972] 1 All E.R. 399 at 406.

Stamp L.J. regarded it as "settled" law that where there is an exclusion clause open to two constructions, one of which will make it applicable where there is no negligence, the other where there is, it:

"requires special words or special circumstances to make the clause exclude liability in case of negligence ... Similarly, I would hold that where the words relied on by the defendant are susceptible either to a construction under which they become a statement of fact in the nature of a warning or to a construction which will exempt the defendant from liability for negligence, the former construction is to be preferred."[81]

The clause in the instant case, he found, was capable of construction as a warning.[82]

Latey J. took the same approach. He rejected the argument that, because liability only sounds in negligence, "no sufficiently clear words are required". When this is the only source of liability, the law may more readily operate to give sanction to the exclusion clause, but "the law goes no further than that".[83]

This approach pushes the law to its limits. Indeed, some would say, beyond them. A reviewer has urged that:

"in principle it seems improbable that the defendants here, or indeed in any case, intended such a clause to be a warning that they were not liable in the absence of fault. This is the common sense justification for the well-established principle of construction now virtually discarded by the Court of Appeal."[84]

It is prudent not to place too strong a reliance on this part of the Court of Appeal's judgment. While it is not necessarily *obiter dicta* (being rather an alternative ground of judgment), it is permissible to regard it in that light.

2–031 It is, at any rate, reasonably clear that an exclusion clause is more likely to fulfil its intended role when negligence is the only ground for liability. In *Rutter v Palmer*,[85] the owner of a motor car deposited it for sale on commission with the owner of a garage upon the terms of a document containing the condition: "Customers' cars are driven by our staff at customers' sole risk". The car was sent out by the owner of a garage in the charge of one of his drivers to be shown to a prospective customer. The car was damaged owing to the negligence of the driver.

The Court of Appeal was unanimous in finding that the exclusion clause was effective. Bankes L.J. drew a distinction between those, such as common carriers, who are liable even in the absence of negligence, and other bailees whose liability lies in negligence alone. The former, when drafting an effective exclusion clause, must use words which will include those acts which are negligent: the latter may use more general words, since such words will generally cover negligent acts, although such acts are not specifically mentioned, because otherwise the words would have no effect.[86] In answer to the problem, Scrutton L.J. proposed what he

---

[81] [1972] 1 All E.R. 399 at 408.
[82] [1972] 1 All E.R. 399 at 408.
[83] [1972] 1 All E.R. 399 at 409.
[84] See *Barendt* (1972) 35 M.L.R. 644 at 646–647.
[85] [1922] 2 K.B. 87. See also *Robinson v Jones (Contractors) Ltd* [2010] EWHC 102 (TCC).
[86] [1922] 2 K.B. 87 at 90.

called a "rougher test". When construing exemption clauses, certain general rules apply. A clause will not exclude liability for negligence unless "adequate words are used". Next, the liability of the defendant apart from exempting words must be ascertained; then the particular clause must be considered. If the only liability is grounded in negligence, the clause "will more readily operate to exempt him".[87]

In *Hollier v Rambler Motors Ltd*,[88] Salmon L.J. accepted these statements by Scrutton L.J., observing only that the Lord Justice did not say, where liability obtained only in negligence, that the exclusion clause would "necessarily" exempt the negligent party from liability.[89]

The judgments were concurred in by Atkin L.J. who drew particular attention to *McCawley v Furness Railway Co.*[90] The crucial clause bore the words "at his [the passenger's] own risk". The carrier's liability lay in negligence alone. Atkin L.J. cited with approval the words of Cockburn C.J.:

> "The terms of the agreement under which the claimant became a passenger exclude everything for which the company would have been otherwise liable. They would have been liable for nothing but negligence... But it was agreed that the claimant should be carried at his own risk, which must be taken to exclude all liability on the part of the company for any negligence".[91]

Bankes and Scrutton L.JJ. were, however, careful to stress that the exclusion **2–032** clause, while effective in the present case, was nevertheless subject to limitation. The clause, which read "Customers' cars are driven by our staff at customers' sole risk", must be taken as referring to the regular driving staff.[92] Secondly, "driven" must mean "driven" for the purpose of the bailment.[93] The clause does not mean, Scrutton L.J. concluded, that "the garage keeper is to be free from liability if a member of his clerical staff takes the car out for pleasure".[94]

The principles to be deduced from this case were accepted and acted upon in *Alderslade v Hendon Laundry Ltd*.[95] The laundry lost certain articles received for laundering. Reliance was placed by the laundry on a clause which ran: "The maximum amount allowed for lost or damaged articles is 20 times the charge made for laundering". It was found that the only relevant liability lay in negligence. Given this, said Lord Greene M.R., to construe the clause as though it did not cover negligence would be to leave the clause "without any content at all".[96] MacKinnon L.J. agreed with this, adopting in its entirety the statement of principle given by Scrutton L.J. in *Rutter v Palmer*.[97]

It is necessary, perhaps, to express a word of caution as to this case. Lord Greene appeared to believe that the clause must be construed as covering liability

---

[87] [1922] 2 K.B. 87 at 92.
[88] [1972] 1 All E.R. 399.
[89] [1972] 1 All E.R. 399 at 405.
[90] [1872] L.R. 8 Q.B. 57.
[91] [1872] L.R. 8 Q.B. 57 at 61. See *Rutter v Palmer* [1922] 2 K.B. 87 at 94–95, per Atkin L.J.
[92] [1922] 2 K.B. 87, per Bankes L.J. at 91. See also Scrutton L.J. at 93.
[93] [1922] 2 K.B. 87 at 93, per Scrutton L.J.
[94] [1922] 2 K.B. 87.
[95] [1945] 1 All E.R. 244.
[96] [1945] 1 All E.R. 244 at 247.
[97] [1922] 2 K.B. 87.

for negligence,[98] an approach certainly endorsed by the Editorial Note.[99] This goes too far: as we have seen, Salmon L.J. has pointed out that Scrutton L.J. refrained from saying that, where negligence alone founds liability, an exclusion clause necessarily precludes liability.[100] It is rather the case that the clause will "more readily" have that effect. Exactly this point was made by May L.J. in the *Lamport & Holt* case.[101] In Lord Greene's speech, he said:

> "the word 'must' . . . should be read as 'should usually' or in some such way consistent with the guide to construction stated by Lord Justice Scrutton in *Rutter v Palmer*."[102]

2–033   In the end, whether or not the only ground for liability is negligence, the question whether an exclusion clause avoids there being liability for negligence is essentially a pure matter of construction. This was well illustrated by the decision in *Gillespie Bros & Co Ltd v Roy Bowles Transport Ltd*.[103] The clause in dispute was that one party agreed to indemnify the other "against all claims or demands whatsoever".[104] It was stated by Buckley L.J. to be "clearly settled" that liability for negligence may be excluded "provided that the language or the circumstances are such as to make it perfectly clear that this was the intention of the parties".[105] The Lord Justice stressed that the intention of the parties must be perfectly clear since it is "inherently improbable that one party to the contract should intend to absolve the other party from the consequences of the latter's own negligence".[106]

Since the clause under discussion failed to make express mention of negligence, the question to be decided was whether its language, given its ordinary meaning, was wide enough to cover negligence. If the answer to this were in the affirmative, the clause would effectively exclude liability for negligence if it was not intended to apply to claims derived otherwise than from negligence.[107]

There was no doubt in the Lord Justice's mind that the clause was effective. Buckley L.J. recognised that expressions sufficient to avoid liability for negligence were "however arising" and "from any cause whatsoever". Wherever, he continued, the relevant expression is "any loss" or "all claims and demands", it is rational to suppose that liability for negligence remained. The crucial factor here was that the exclusion clause contained the word "whatsoever". It must, Buckley L.J. concluded, have been intended to have some purpose and must be given effect to exclude liability for negligence.[108]

---

[98] [1922] 2 K.B. 87.
[99] Where liability rests on liability alone "the clause must be construed as extending to that head of damage": [1945] 1 All E.R. 244.
[100] See para.2–031.
[101] [1982] 2 Lloyd's Rep. 42.
[102] [1982] 2 Lloyd's Rep. 42 at 49.
[103] [1973] 1 All E.R. 193.
[104] Buckley L.J. noted that the principles for construing exclusion and indemnity clauses are the same: [1973] 1 All E.R. 193 at 204.
[105] [1973] 1 All E.R. 193 at 203.
[106] [1973] 1 All E.R. 193. See also *Lamport & Holt Lines Ltd v Coubro & Scrutton* [1982] 2 Lloyd's Rep. 42 at 51, per Stephenson L.J.; *Scottish and Newcastle Plc v GD Constructions (St Albans) Ltd* Unreported March 29, 2001 (HC).
[107] [1973] 1 All E.R. 193 at 204–205, per Buckley L.J.
[108] [1973] 1 All E.R. 193.

Some qualification was placed on the *Gillespie* case in *Smith v South Wales Switchgear Co Ltd*.[109] Factory owners engaged parties to perform an annual overhaul at the factory. The contract contained terms requiring the latter to indemnify the former against any liability, loss, claim or proceedings arising out of or in the course of the execution of the order. The House of Lords adopted the test put forward by Lord Morton in *Canada Steamship Lines Ltd v The King*.[110] They disagreed, however, with the view put forward by Buckley L.J. in the *Gillespie* case[111] that use of the word "whatsoever" was an express agreement to except liability for negligence: that required the word "negligence" or a synonym. The decision in that case, however, was accepted as correct.

The House of Lords held that the clause did not indemnify the factory owners for their own negligence because, on a proper reading, it only applied to liabilities incurred by the factory owners for the acts or omissions of the other parties in connection with the contract work. Furthermore, the clause could also be read as covering the far from fanciful liability of the factory owners in common law for the acts or omissions of the other parties, as occupiers of the factory or as employers. Even if the factory owners would have had a right of relief here, they were still entitled to rely on and use an express indemnity clause rather than raise an action of relief with its attendant hazards.

2–034

In *Motis Exports Ltd v Dampskibsselskabet AF 1912*,[112] it was said that the words "however caused" were very wide and could cover loss caused by negligence. They would cover theft by taking without consent, but they did not cover misdelivery even if obtained by fraud. In that case, the defendants had delivered goods at the discharge port against delivery orders issued by the defendants' agents to the holders of what turned out to be forged bills of lading. The Court of Appeal held that the defendants could not rely on a clause in the bill providing that the carrier should have no liability for any loss or damage to goods while in its actual or constructive possession after discharge over ship's rail "however caused". It was said that a court has to give the "natural" meaning to a clause in a bill of lading, particularly one that exempts or limits liability.[113]

In *Armitage v Nurse*,[114] a marriage settlement contained a trustee exemption clause in the following terms: "No trustee shall be liable for any loss or damage which may happen to P's fund or any part thereof or the income thereof at any time or from any cause whatsoever unless such loss or damage shall be caused by his own actual fraud". The court said that the meaning of the clause was plain and unambiguous. Under it, no trustee could be made liable for loss or damage to the capital or income of the trust property caused otherwise than by his own "actual fraud". Actual fraud meant what it said. It did not include "constructive fraud" or "equitable fraud". The clause excluded liability for all breaches of trust save for those committed with dishonest intent. "Dishonest intent" meant an intention on

---

[109] [1978] 1 All E.R. 18.

[110] See para.2–021.

[111] [1973] 1 All E.R. 193 at 205.

[112] [2000] 1 All E.R. (Comm) 91.

[113] This approach was approved by Aikens J. in *Trafigura Beheer BV v Mediterranean Shipping Company SA* [2007] EWHC 944 (Comm).

[114] [1998] Ch. 241. See also *Citibank NA v MBIA Assurance SA* [2006] EWHC 3215 (Ch); *Cavell USA Inc v Seaton Insurance Co* [2009] EWCA Civ 1363.

the part of the trustees to pursue a particular course of action, either knowing that it was contrary to the interests of the beneficiaries or being recklessly indifferent whether or not it was contrary to their interests. The court added that a party could exclude by contract liability for ordinary negligence, and that it would be very surprising if the law drew the line between liability for ordinary negligence and liability for gross negligence. English law draws a sharp distinction between negligence, however gross, on the one hand and fraud, bad faith and wilful misconduct on the other. But it regards the difference between negligence and gross negligence as merely one of degree.

In *Hinks v Fleet*,[115] the claimant entered into a contract with the defendant, who owned a caravan park, to take a semi-permanent pitch at the park for a season. That contract included the following clause:

> "LIABILITY. Vehicles and caravans are admitted on condition that the Park Owner shall not be liable for loss or damage to (a) any vehicle or caravan (b) anything in, on or about any vehicle or caravan however such loss or damage may be caused . . .".

2–035   Shortly before the end of the season, the caravan disappeared. The claimant claimed damages against the defendant for negligence, contending that the contract between himself and the defendant was a bailment so that the onus fell on the defendant to show that the caravan had disappeared without negligence on his part. Additionally or in the alternative, the claimant contended that there was to be implied into the contract a duty on the part of the defendant to take reasonable care of the caravan. The judge held in favour of the claimant on both issues, and found that the defendant had also failed to take reasonable care. He further held that the exclusion clause was not apt to exclude liability for loss arising through negligence, and in any event covered only loss "to" the caravan not loss "of" the caravan which was, in fact, what had occurred. On appeal, the Court of Appeal held that the contract between the claimant and the defendant was a licence only which did not contain an implied term requiring the defendant to take reasonable care in relation to the caravan. It also held that the only way in which the exclusion clause could be read sensibly so as to give effect to the clear intention of the parties was to insert the word "of" between the words "loss" and "or damage to", in which case the clause clearly covered the loss of the caravan. Furthermore, the wording of the clause, "however such loss or damage may be caused", was apt to cover loss or damage caused by negligence. Lloyd L.J. stated that the clause was effective "on high authority to exclude liability for negligence, even though the word 'negligence' is not used. This case thus comes within the first of the principles stated by Lord Morton in the *Canada Steamship* case".[116]

A clause which was upheld was contained in the *Lamport & Holt* case.[117] That clause ran:

---

[115] [1987] B.C.L.C. 289.
[116] [1987] B.C.L.C. 289 at 298.
[117] [1981] 2 Lloyd's Rep. 659; [1982] 2 Lloyd's Rep. 42.

"Except as stated herein we shall not be liable for any damage ... suffered by you ... and which may arise from or be in any way connected with any act ... of any person or corporation employed by us or by any subcontractors or engaged in any capacity herewith ...".

At first instance, Goff J. ruled that, on the ordinary meaning of these words, they were wide enough to cover negligence on the part of the servants of the defendants. This was the view also of the Court of Appeal. Donaldson L.J. agreed that there was no express reference to negligence, but held that the words "any act or omission" are "certainly wide enough to comprehend negligence", particularly when one bore in mind that in *Donoghue v Stevenson* itself, Lord Atkin had argued that reasonable care must be taken to "avoid acts or omissions which you can reasonably foresee would be likely to injure your neighbour".[118] When he interpreted the disputed clause, May L.J. was impressed by the fact that the opening words "[e]xcept as stated herein" admitted liability as accepted by the *proferens* in other clauses of the contract. This, of course, would predispose one towards accepting it as excluding liability more readily. He noted that the word "omission" would not of its own be sufficient to exclude liability for negligence, since, in many cases "the actual negligence giving rise to legal liability comprises a positive act, although the doing of it involves the necessary failure to take care".[119] On the other hand, he went on to say, the wider phrase "any act or omission" is "certainly wide enough on its ordinary meaning to cover negligence on the part of the respondents, their servants or agents".[120]

Another clause to survive challenge was that to be found in *Ailsa Craig Fishing Co Ltd v Malvern Fishing Co Ltd*.[121] A contract existed between Securicor and Aberdeen Fishing Vessel Owners Association whereby Securicor were to provide security cover in the harbour where the claimant's vessels were moored. As a result of negligence and breach of contract the claimant's vessels sunk. The relevant clause read:

"If ... any liability on the part of the company shall arise (whether under the express or implied terms of this contract or at common law, or in any other way) to the customer for any loss or damage of whatever nature arising out of or connected with the provision of, the services covered by this contract, such liability shall be limited to the payment by the company of the sum of £1,000 in respect of any claim arising from a duty assumed by them involving a service not related solely to the prevention or detection of fire or theft."

Unanimously, the House of Lords held that this clause was wide enough to cover **2–036** negligence.[122] Lord Wilberforce stressed that:

"Whether a clause limiting liability is effective or not is a question of construction of that clause in the context of the contract as a whole. If it is to exclude liability for negligence, it must be most clearly and unambiguously expressed ... But I venture to add at least one further

---

[118] [1982] 2 Lloyd's Rep. 42 at 45–46.
[119] [1982] 2 Lloyd's Rep. 42 at 48.
[120] [1982] 2 Lloyd's Rep. 42 at 48.
[121] [1982] S.L.T. 377.
[122] Upholding the decision reported at [1981] S.L.T. 130.

qualification or at least clarification: one must not strive to create ambiguities by strained construction... The relevant words must be given, if possible, their natural, plain meaning."[123]

Lord Fraser took the clear view that the clause in question:

"is sufficiently clear and unambiguous to receive effect in limiting the liability of Securicor for its own negligence or that of its employees ... It applies to any liability 'whether under the express or implied terms of this contract, or at common law, or in any other way'. Liability at common law is undoubtedly wide enough to cover liability, including the negligence of the *proferens* itself, so that even without relying on the final words 'any other way', I am clearly of opinion that the negligence of Securicor is covered."[124]

The same outcome is to be found in *Photo Production Ltd v Securicor Transport Ltd.*[125] In the Court of Appeal, Waller L.J. held that, even on a strict construction, cover was given against negligence on the part of the employees of the company by a clause which stated that: "Under no circumstances shall the company be responsible for any injurious act or default by any employee of the company ...".[126] A further clause which began: "If ... any liability on the part of the company shall arise (whether under the express or implied terms hereof or at common law)..." was so drafted, Waller L.J. ruled, that it "must cover negligence".[127] The House of Lords agreed that this was so, but little attention was given to this point, since other issues required attention.

In *Industrie Chimiche Italia Centrale v NEA Ninemia Shipping Co*,[128] a charterparty provided that a shipowner was to be exempt from repaying monies to the charterers if the ship were lost through "errors of navigation". A question arose as to whether this covered loss or damage brought about by negligent navigation.

According to the judge, the general conclusions which emerged from the cases were these. First, the court would not presume that a clause was intended to absolve a party from the consequences of his own negligence "unless the contrary was shown by clear words or implication". Secondly, statements which were made in one case, while they might assist in deciding another, could "not literally determine the decision. The court's task was one of construction in each case to ascertain the actual or implied intention of the parties".

2–037 The third conclusion which could be drawn from the cases was that, while the test was often what the ordinary literate and sensible person would make of the particular clause, the test would be that of the "reasonably informed practitioner" where the contract was made in a specialised business by two practitioners in that business. Finally, where the words used were wide enough to cover negligent as well as non-negligent acts or omissions, and the clause would lack "substance in practical terms if negligence were excluded", then the court might or might not

---

[123] [1982] S.L.T. 377 at 380. See also the endorsement of these words, and a similar finding, in *Amiri Flight Authority v BAE Systems Plc* [2002] EWHC 2481 (Comm). See too *Hirtenstein v Hill Dickinson LLP* [2014] EWHC 2711.
[124] [1982] S.L.T. 377 at 383.
[125] [1980] 1 All E.R. 556; [1978] 3 All E.R. 146.
[126] [1978] 3 All E.R. 146 at 160.
[127] [1978] 3 All E.R. 146 at 160.
[128] [1983] 1 All E.R. 686.

infer that the parties intended negligence to be covered, "depending on the proper inference to be drawn in the particular case".

In making his decision on this particular clause, Bingham J. declared that it did not matter that a carrier might be held to have no liability for errors of navigation unless he was negligent: "the important question was whether he could seek protection against the possibility of such liability". The clause itself contained no reference to negligence nor any synonym. That, said Bingham J., was "not fatal to the owners' argument, but it did mean that their task was a heavy one". He noted that "error" was essentially neutral and was not "primarily suggestive of negligence". However, he felt incapable of overlooking the fact that the form was amended to exclude the Hague Rules, which provided protection against negligent errors of navigation. It was also the case that the clause specified certain events, such as Act of God or restraint of princes, which were plainly inconsistent with negligence; and none of the specified events was clearly indicative of negligence (fire, dangers and accidents of the seas). The judge also took note of an earlier case where the use of the word "fire" was held not to cover fire caused by negligence.[129] Fire was a result whereas "errors of navigation" carried one into the minds of the owners. That made the lack of any express reference to negligence more striking. The inevitable conclusion, therefore, was that the clause was not apt to cover negligence liability.

The position established by these cases was clearly set out in *Stent Foundations Ltd v MJ Gleeson Group Plc*.[130] Clause 2.04 of the contract stated:

> "The Sub-Contractor shall be responsible for and indemnify the Contractor against any claims in respect of plant or tools of the Sub-Contractor or his workmen which may be lost or damaged by fire or any other cause and also be responsible for and indemnify the Contractor against any claims by the workmen of the Sub-Contractor in respect of the risks he is required to insure against under Clause 2.01 hereof."

Clause 2.01 of those terms read:

> "The Sub-Contractor shall maintain insurance and indemnify the Contractor against the risks commonly insured against arising out of the Sub-Contract Works in respect of workmen, third parties and adjoining property and shall maintain or procure the taking out of such insurance in respect of self-employed workmen brought in by the Sub-Contractor, and upon demand produce to the Contractor his policies of insurance and premium receipts, and the Contractor may register its interest with the insurance companies concerned, if he so desires, and in the event of failure by the Sub-Contractor to comply with the provision of this clause, the Contractor may himself insure and deduct the cost of the premiums so incurred from any monies becoming due to the Sub-Contractor."

After referring to the principles set out in cases such as *Canada Steamship Lines v The King*; *Industrie Chimiche v NEA Ninemia Shipping Co.*; and *ICS Ltd v West Bromwich Building Society*, the deputy judge concluded with the observation that:

2–038

> "In all projects, the allocation of the risks of negligence and the duty to insure against those risks is a matter to be considered. Clear allocation of risk may reduce the likelihood of litigation or arbitration. The decisions of the courts, including this decision, should not be read

---

[129] *Polemis and Furniss Withy and Co Ltd, Re* [1921] 3 K.B. 560.
[130] [2001] B.L.R. 134.

as being opposed to such allocation of risk. All that is being decided in this case, as in others, is that the parties should be clear and explicit in their contracts so that parties start a project with clear knowledge as to where the risks lie rather than disputing the allocation of risk when the project goes awry. There is so much guidance in the decided cases on this topic that it would be easy for any lawyer for a contracting party to draft clear words excluding liability, if that is what his client wants, and the other party could then decide with informed consent whether he wants to accept that exclusion."

He ruled that the clauses in the instant case could not be relied on since there was no express reference to negligence nor could they be fairly read as otherwise covering negligence.[131]

SOME SPECIAL EXCLUSION CLAUSES

"With all faults"

2–039   Where the phrase "with all faults" has been employed, or some equivalent, the view seems to be that this relates to merchantability (or satisfactory quality, in its latest formulation) or fitness for purpose, and does not offset the duty to supply goods which correspond with their description, this being the core of the contract. In *Shepherd v Kain*,[132] there was a sale of a "copper-fastened vessel", this being sold "with all faults, without allowance for any defect whatsoever". The court held that this did not suffice to protect the seller where what was delivered was not even a copper-fastened vessel.

The not dissimilar phrase "as is" fell for interpretation in *Choil Trading SA v Sahara Energy Resources Ltd*.[133] The claimant sought damages for breach of contract in respect of a cargo of naphtha purchased by him from the defendant FOB Port Harcourt in Nigeria. The cargo contained an abnormally high quantity of methyl tertiair buthyl ether (MTBE), a man-made substance which was not a by-product of the production of naphtha. The claimant relied on the contract term as to quality which provided: "Naphtha of normal running production as produced by Port Harcourt Refining Company . . ."; and the statutorily implied terms as to correspondence with description, satisfactory quality and fitness for purpose. The defendant contended that the parties had agreed an "as is" sale and thus the naphtha was sold without any warranty as to quality. The court rejected this defence. The background to the contract showed that the contract was to be on terms that the naphtha sold was to be of Port Harcourt naphtha quality, i.e. having characteristics within the range for naphtha normally produced by Port Harcourt. The court said that the expression "as is" was sufficient to indicate that the naphtha to be received would have whatever characteristics (within that range) the cargo supplied to Choil ex the port happened to have: "But, whatever might have been the position if the words 'as is' had stood alone, they cannot in context be taken to signify that the sellers could provide cargo which was not of

---

[131] In *Deepak Fertilisers & Petrochemical Corp Ltd v Davy McKee (London) Ltd* [1999] 1 All E.R. (Comm) 69, a clause provided that there was to be no liability "in tort". The High Court ruled that this covered negligence, but not liability for negligent misrepresentation. In this latter respect, the Court of Appeal said that the High Court was "clearly wrong".

[132] (1821) 5 B&Ald 240.

[133] [2010] EWHC 374 (Comm).

normal [Port Harcourt] quality for naphtha because of its very high MTBE". Much the same view was taken in *Dalmare SpA v Union Maritime L*.[134] No final decision was made, but the court said it was difficult to see how, in the absence of some customary meaning, the words "as is" could be said to be sufficiently clear and unequivocal to exclude the term as to satisfactory quality implied by the Sale of Goods Act 1979.

The actual phrase used in this case was that the vessel was to be delivered "as she was". The court ruled that those words recorded the obligation to deliver the vessel in the same condition as she was when inspected. They were part of a temporal obligation which arose because there would usually be a period of time of weeks or even months between inspection and delivery.

Excluding or limiting the damages recoverable

Where a clause provides for a precise sum to be recovered by way of damages in the event of a breach, that clause will be enforceable if it is a genuine pre-estimate of the likely loss; but it will be ineffective if it is a penalty clause and was inserted *in terrorem*, as an intended punishment in the event of breach.[135] On the other hand, a clause which places an upper limit on the damages recoverable (such as £1000 or 20 times the contract price) while still to be construed *contra proferentem* will not be construed quite as strictly as an exclusion clause properly so-called. This was made clear by the House of Lords in *Ailsa Craig Fishing Co Ltd v Malvern Fishing Co Ltd*.[136] According to Lord Wilberforce:

2–040

> "Clauses of limitation are not regarded by the courts with the same hostility as clauses of exclusion: this is because they must be related to other contractual terms, in particular to the risks to which the defending party may be exposed, the remuneration which he receives, and possibly also the opportunity of the other party to insure."[137]

Since it is not entirely clear why such considerations are not relevant when considering clauses of exclusion, perhaps more weight should be given to Lord Fraser's explanation for a more sympathetic view of limitation clauses. He argued that cases expounding principles of strict construction:

> "are not applicable when considering the effect of clauses merely limiting liability. Such clauses will of course be read *contra proferentem* and must be clearly expressed, but there is no reason why they should be judged by the specially exacting standards which are applied to exclusion and indemnity clauses. The reason for imposing such standards on these clauses is

---

[134] [2012] EWHC 3537. This case is valuable for the list of authorities cited and considered in relation to the phrase "as is". See too *Hirtenstein v Hill Dickinson LLP* [2014] EWHC 2711.

[135] See generally *Dunlop Pneumatic Tyre Co Ltd v New Garage & Motors Co Ltd* [1915] A.C. 79. For the most recent approach to distinguishing penalty clauses from liquidated damages clauses, see *Talal El Makdessi v (1) Cavendish Square Holdings BV (2) Team V&R Holdings Hong Kong Ltd* [2013] EWCA Civ 1539.

[136] [1982] S.L.T. 377.

[137] [1982] S.L.T. 377 at 380. See the doubts, however, of Lord Denning in *George Mitchell (Chesterhall) Ltd v Finney Lock Seeds Ltd* [1983] 1 All E.R. 108 at 116. Lord Wilberforce's dictum was approved in *South West Water Services Ltd v International Computers Ltd* [1999] B.L.R. 420; *BHP Petroleum v British Steel Plc* Unreported April 7, 2000 (CA); and in *Frank Maas (UK) Ltd v Samsung Electronics (UK) Ltd* [2004] EWHC 1502 (Comm).

the inherent improbability that the other party to a contract including such a clause intended to release the *proferens* from a liability that would otherwise fall upon him."[138]

In this case, there was also the special factor that, as a contract clause itself made clear, the potential losses which could derive from negligence were great in relation to the sum that could be charged by the *proferens* for its services.[139]

2–041 That such an approach is probably now outdated emerges from *Whitecap Leisure Ltd v John H Rundle Ltd.*[140] Referring to the argument that limitation clauses were to be judged less strictly than exclusion clauses, Moore-Bick L.J. said:

> "One can find in the authorities many statements to the effect that exclusion clauses must be clear and unambiguous if they are to operate effectively, many of which date from a period when courts took a more literal approach to the construction of commercial documents in general than is now generally the case. The modern approach to construction, which applies as much to exclusion and limitation clauses as to other contractual terms, is to ascertain the objective intention of the parties from the words used and the context in which they are found, including the document as a whole and the background to it: see *Mannai Investment Co Ltd v Eagle Star Life Assurance Co Ltd*,[141] and *Investors Compensation Scheme v West Bromwich Building Society*. However, in cases where there is uncertainty about the parties' intention, and therefore about the meaning of the clause, such uncertainty will be resolved against the person relying on the clause and the more significant the departure is said to be from what are accepted to be the obligations ordinarily assumed under a contract of the kind in question, the more difficult it will be to persuade the court that the parties intended that result."

Where the clause excludes any right to damages, the tendency is to restrict it, if possible, to minor matters, or to limiting its effect to forbidding rejection or to confining a buyer to claiming a return of the purchase price and nothing beyond. It does seem, however, that if the clause clearly applies to a contractual duty, it will be effective to deny a party any claim to damages.[142]

Consequential loss

2–042 Where there is in a contract an exclusion of liability for "consequential" loss or damage, the courts have held that it embraces only loss or damage not resulting directly or naturally from the breach of contract.[143] More specific guidance has been provided in *British Sugar Plc v NEI Power Projects Ltd*[144] where the relevant clause provided that:

---

[138] [1982] S.L.T. 377 at 382. See also the words of Burton J. in *Stocznia Gdynia SA v Gearbulk Holdings Ltd* [2008] EWHC 944 (Comm), when he said: "It is in any event difficult to see why the test in respect of clauses which exempt any liability should necessarily be less stringent than the test in respect of clauses which simply oust common law remedies".

[139] [1982] S.L.T. 377 at 382.

[140] [2008] EWCA Civ 429.

[141] [1997] A.C. 749.

[142] See *Wilkinson v Barclay* [1946] 2 All E.R. 337.

[143] See *Millar v Machinery Co Ltd v David Way & Son* (1935) 40 Com. Cas.204; *Croudace Contractors Ltd v Cawood Concrete Products Ltd* [1978] 2 Lloyd's Rep 55. See also *Civil and Maritime Slag Cement Ltd v Cambrian Stone Ltd* Unreported June 8, 2000; QBD.

[144] [1997] C.L.C. 622.

"The seller will be liable for any loss damage cost or expense incurred by the purchaser arising from the supply of any such faulty goods or materials or any goods or materials not being suitable for the purpose for which they are required save that the seller's liability for consequential loss is limited to the value of the contract."

The value of the contract was £106,000, while the damages claimed for breach topped £5 million. The court referred to the earlier cases and accepted them as holding that "consequential loss" must be taken to mean "such loss as the claimants may prove over and above that which arose as a direct result of such breaches". This decision was upheld by the Court of Appeal which added that, on its true construction, the clause simply limited NEI's liability for loss and damage not directly and naturally arising from the breach to an amount equal to the value of the contract.[145]

Much the same line was taken in *Deepak Fertilisers & Petrochemical Group v Davy McKee (London) Ltd*.[146] The defendants had supplied the claimants with a process licence, process design and know-how in relation to the proposed design, construction and maintenance of a methanol plant. Some time after the plant was commissioned, it exploded and caused a great deal of physical damage. The plant was rebuilt. A term of the contract provided that "in no event shall Davy by reason of its performance or obligation under this contract be liable ... for loss [of] anticipated profits, catalyst, raw material and products or for indirect or consequential damages".

The heads of claim put forward by Deepak were in respect of fixed costs and overheads referable solely to the methanol plant during the period from the explosion to the resumption of production, and loss arising from the fact that the plant, when back in action, used more catalyst per charge than the original. The High Court ruled that the direct loss contemplated was the cost of getting the plant right, not the indirect or consequential losses flowing from the plant being defective. It had, as a result, rejected the claims for fixed costs and overheads. The Court of Appeal, however, said that it was "unable to accept that conclusion". It said that the direct and natural result of the destruction of the plant caused by the explosion was that Deepak was left with a plant, the reconstruction of which would take time and money, losing the company production in the meantime. It said that the wasted overheads incurred during reconstruction were all one with the cost of reconstruction. Lost profits, though, were damages flowing directly from the breach. These could not be specifically recovered since this was expressly covered by the contract. As for the extra catalyst, the High Court had decided that this fell within the term "indirect or consequential damages". The Court of Appeal, accepting that this was not an easy question to resolve, held that:

"The extra cost claimed is the cost which has now become necessary in order to ensure and enable the plant safely to produce the methanol in those quantities which the plant was supposed to. In other words, we would hold that this extra cost is akin to any other cost (such

---

[145] [1997] EWCA Civ 2438.
[146] [1999] 1 Lloyds Rep 387. See too *McCain Foods GB Ltd v Eco-Tec (Europe) Ltd* [2011] EWHC 66.

as an additional piece of plant or part) which achieved the same result. This could not be categorised as an indirect or consequential loss or damage nor could its cost be categorised as constituting a loss of profit."

2–043   In *BHP Petroleum Ltd v British Steel Plc*,[147] a clause ran:

"Neither the supplier nor the purchaser shall bear any liability to the other (and each party hereby agrees to indemnify the party relying on this provision) for loss of production, loss of profits, loss of business or any other indirect losses or consequential damages arising during and/or as a result of the performance or non-performance of this contract regardless of the cause thereof but not limited to the negligence of the party seeking to rely on this provision."

The court ruled that the clause was to be interpreted as though it read "for loss of production, loss of profits, loss of business or indirect or consequential losses of any other kind". A defective pipeline had been supplied, and part of the claim related to deferral of production. The court said that such a claim was for loss of production or loss of profits or business and, as such, was excluded by the clause.

Broad approval was given to the above cases by the Court of Appeal in *Hotel Services Ltd v Hilton International Hotels (UK) Ltd*.[148] The exclusion clause in question ran:

"The Company will not in any circumstances be liable for any indirect or consequential loss, damage or liability arising from any defect in or failure of the System or any part thereof or the performance of this Agreement or any breach thereof by the Company or its employees."

The contract was for the supply of hotel minibars, which equipment had had to be removed because leaking ammonia corroded the equipment and created a risk of injury or fatality to guests. The court first noted that the use of "consequential" here was as a synonym of "indirect" since all recoverable loss is literally consequential. The court also gave attention to the so-called two rules in *Hadley v Baxendale*[149] whereby, in an action for breach of contract, the innocent party may:

(i)   recover for all such loss as should be fairly and reasonably considered as arising "naturally"; and

(ii)   for such loss as may reasonably be supposed to have been in the contemplation of both parties, at the time they made the contract, as the probable result of a breach.

2–044   The court in *Hotel Services Ltd* ruled that the clause was inapplicable, by holding that:

"if equipment rented out for selling drinks without defalcation turns out to be unusable and possibly dangerous, it requires no special mutually known fact to establish the immediacy both of the consequent cost of putting it where it can do no harm and—if when in use it was

---

[147] [1999] 2 All E.R. (Comm) 544.
[148] [2000] 1 All E.R. (Comm) 750 and see also *Civil and Marine Slag Cement Ltd v Cambrian Stone Ltd* Unreported June 8, 2000 (QBD).
[149] [1854] 9 Ex. 341. For the latest analysis of this case, see *John Grimes Partnership Ltd v Gubbins* [2013] EWCA Civ 37.

showing a direct profit—of the consequent loss of profit. Such losses are not embraced by the exclusion clause, read in its documentary and commercial context."

This was also the line taken in *Jewson Ltd v Kelly*.[150] The defendant had acquired a property which he wished to convert into flats. He discussed with the claimants the possibility of finding electric boilers to be used in the flats. Following a number of discussions and meetings, he purchased through them boilers manufactured by Amptec. The essence of the problem which later led to the litigation was that the boilers had an unsatisfactory Standard Assessment Procedure. This is designed to provide home energy ratings for domestic properties. It was held that the goods supplied were neither of satisfactory quality nor reasonably fit for their purpose.

The contract contained this clause:

"The Company shall not be liable for any consequential loss or indirect loss suffered by the Customer or any third party in relation to this contract (except personal injury directly attributable to the negligence of the Company) and the Customer shall hold the company fully and effectively indemnified against such losses whether arising from breach of a duty in contract or loss in any way including losses arising from the Company's negligence."

Referring to *Hadley v Baxendale*, the court said that, given that the claimant in this case had full knowledge of the intended purpose of the boilers, and of the possible consequences of an unsatisfactory SAP rating, the damage suffered by the defendant arose naturally from the breach and could not be regarded as consequential.

In *Leicester Circuits Ltd v Coates Bros Plc*,[151] a clause excluded liability for "consequential or incidental damage of any kind whatsoever... including without limitation any indirect loss or damage such as operating loss, loss of clientele...". This was held not to exclude liability for loss of profit since, in the circumstances of the case, this would have been within the reasonable contemplation of the parties and hence within the first limb of the rule in *Hadley v Baxendale*.[152]

2–045

Further guidance was provided in *Ferryways NV v Associated British Ports*.[153] This was an action brought by the claimant, a Belgian shipowner or operator against the defendant, an English port owner or operator. The claim arose out of the death at Immingham of the chief officer on board the vessel Humber Way. He

---

[150] [2003] EWCA Civ 1030.

[151] [2003] EWCA Civ 333.

[152] The court expressly approved *Croudace Construction Ltd v Cawoods Concrete Products Ltd* [1978] 2 Lloyd's Rep. 55. See also *The Simkins Partnership v Reeves Lund & Co Ltd* [2003] EWHC 1946 (QB); *Robertson Group (Construction) Ltd v Amey-Miller* [2005] CSOH 60. See also *Pegler Ltd v Wang (UK) Ltd* [2000] EWHC 137 (TCC), where a clause excluding liability "for any indirect, special or consequential loss, however arising, including... loss of anticipated profits... in connection with or arising out of the supply, functioning or use of (the goods or services supplied) was loss under the second limb of *Hadley v Baxendale* and hence did not cover loss whereas the loss claimed fell under the first limb. A claim for loss of profits was not within the clause since that clause only covered loss of profits falling within the second limb". A like decision was reached in *Glencore Energy UK Ltd v Cirrus Oil Services Ltd* [2014] EWHC 87.

[153] [2008] EWHC 225 (Comm). This case was approved in *Markerstudy Insurance Co Ltd v Endsleigh Insurance Services Ltd* [2010] EWHC 281 (Comm).

was supervising the loading and unloading operations when he was hit by a tugmaster vehicle driven by an employee of a sub-contractor of the defendant. Sums were paid by the North of England P&I Club (in which the vessel was entered) in respect of his death and of the cost of repatriating his body. The claimant, who was the demise charterer of the vessel and a member of the Club, sought to recover those sums from the defendant. The defendant resisted the claim. The terms on which the defendant provided its stevedoring services included the following:

> "9. Exclusion and Limitations of Liability
> (c)   Where the Company is in breach of its obligations in respect of the Services or under any Contract or any duties it may have as bailee of the Goods it shall have no liability to the Customer in contract, tort, negligence, breach of statutory duty or otherwise for any loss, damage, costs or expenses of any nature whatsoever incurred or suffered by the Customer which is of an indirect or consequential nature including without limitation the following: i) loss or deferment of profit; ii) loss or deferment of revenue; iii) loss of goodwill; iv) loss of business; v) loss or deferment of production or increased costs of production; vi) the liabilities of the Customer to any other party.
> (e)   Nothing in this Clause or Clause 10 shall exclude or limit the liability of the Company for death or personal injury resulting from the Company's negligence . . .".

The court said that, in interpreting this clause, in the light of the well-recognised meaning which has been accorded to it, and given the approach to clauses referring to "indirect" or "consequential" loss, it would "require very clear words indeed to indicate that the parties' intentions when using such words was to exclude losses which fall outside that well-recognised meaning. This is particularly so when 'indirect' is used as well as 'consequential'. The use of 'indirect' draws an implicit distinction with direct losses". The court said that the meaning which has been given to direct losses in the cases is "loss which flows naturally from the breach without other intervening cause and independently of special circumstances".

The court held that the words of the clause did not provide the sort of clear indication which was necessary for the defendant's argument. The parties, it said, were "merely identifying the type of losses (without limitation) which can fall within the exemption clause so long as the losses meet the prior requirement that they are 'of an indirect or consequential nature'". Had the parties intended that liability for losses which were the direct and natural result of the breach could be excluded "they would have hardly have described such losses as 'indirect or consequential'". The court concluded that the losses which were claimed in this case, liability for the death benefit and repatriation expenses, were losses which were the direct and natural result of the assumed breach of contract which caused the death. It was therefore held that liability for those losses has not been excluded by the terms of the stevedoring contract.

The general process of interpretation adopted in these cases was accepted in *Fujitsu Services Ltd v IBM United Kingdom Ltd*[154] X provided information technology services under a main contract and sub-contracted the day-to-day management to F, whilst retaining responsibility for other aspects of the contract. F brought a claim for loss of profit on the grounds that X had failed to provide it

---

[154] [2014] EWHC 752 (TCC).

with work in accordance with the sub-contract, failed to seek F's consent to material changes in the main contract, and to provide value for money services.

A clause in the contract ran thus:

"20.7 Neither Party shall be liable to the other under this Sub-Contract for loss of profits, revenue, business, goodwill, indirect or consequential loss or damage, although it is agreed that:

(a)   this Clause 20.7 shall not apply to exclude costs to PwC and other Participants of remedying failures and re-running activities, the cost of re-tendering, costs of engaging other providers in the case of Fujitsu failure, and cost of termination which would otherwise be recoverable from Fujitsu because they arose as a result of an event of default by Fujitsu (including its Sub-Contractors and Affiliates and their respective employees, servants and agents);

(b)   actual agreed revenue share may be recoverable to the extent expressly agreed between the parties;

(c)   loss of profits shall be recoverable only as specified in Schedule 13 (Finance) or as a basis which may be used for calculating damages payable for infringement of Intellectual Property Rights or breach of confidentiality claims; and

(d)   third party claims, including where a party has agreed to indemnify the other, shall be recoverable to the extent that the underlying third party claim results directly from a failure of the indemnifying Party, provided that this Clause 20.7(d) shall not be interpreted to make loss of profits recoverable in circumstances where under Clause 20.7(c), loss of profit would not be recoverable."

It was argued that this clause excluded or limited liability for "loss of profits, revenue, business, goodwill" only in so far as the same constituted indirect or consequential loss or damage and that that loss of revenue, business and goodwill were losses aiming at indirect or consequential, not direct, losses, and the reference to loss of profits was equivocal. Thus, the argument ran, the basic exclusion as a whole should be read as limited to indirect or consequential losses.

This was rejected by the court. The first point made was that given the obviousness of the point, the draftsman would have made it clear if the intention was only to exclude indirect loss of profit. The fact that losses of profit can be direct or indirect was, it said, "well-known" Second, and as the court saw it, "significantly", the construction advanced would be inconsistent with and render unnecessary the express exception provided for in clause 20.7(a) (which excluded what would be a claim for direct loss and damage, as probably did clause 20.7(b)). Third and last, the construction put forward would render otiose the words "loss of profits, revenue, business, goodwill".

Imposing time limits

Clauses which require proceedings to be commenced, or defects to be notified, within a certain time are interpreted strictly. In *Atlantic Shipping & Trading v Louis Dreyfus & Co*,[155] a clause in a charterparty required a claim to be made, and an arbitrator appointed, within three months of final discharge. This was held only to apply to the express terms of the contract and not to those implied by law. It has been maintained that there is:

2–046

---

[155] [1922] 2 A.C. 250.

"no reason why [such clauses] should not be drafted so as to apply to even the most serious breaches, for (unless the period is so short that they effectively bar a right altogether) they do not exclude liability, they simply require that buyers take vigilant steps to finalise the transaction."[156]

Excluding the right to reject

2–047 Where clauses purport to exclude an otherwise existing right to reject the goods, it is clear enough that they do not of themselves exclude the right to damages.[157] Since the right to reject does not exist in relation to a breach of warranty, it is supposed that the effect of such clauses is to indicate that the terms to which they apply are warranties, not conditions. This is supported by *Walkers, Winser & Hamm and Shaw, Re*[158] in which such a clause was said to prevent an implied condition arising, and to render it a warranty instead.

Relevance of contract description

2–048 It seems to be established that certain exclusion clauses only operate where goods of the contract description have been supplied. A clause excluding the right to reject the goods "herein specified" is effective only when the goods "herein specified" have in fact been supplied, but not when the goods do not conform with their description. In *J Aron & Co Inc v Comptoir Wegimont SA*,[159] the clause ran: "whatever the difference of the shipment may be in value from the grade, type or description specified, it is understood that any such question shall not entitle the buyer to reject the delivery...". It was held that the terms as to shipment were independent and not part of the description so that rejection was still allowed.

Arbitration

2–049 Section 89 of the Arbitration Act 1996, provides that the Consumer Rights Act 2014 shall apply to a term which constitutes an "arbitration agreement". This is a reference to "an agreement to submit to arbitration present or future disputes or differences (whether or not contractual)".[160] Section 91 of the Act says that an agreement is unfair for the purposes of the Act so far as it relates to a claim for a pecuniary remedy which does not exceed a specified amount, currently £5,000.[161]

---

[156] *Benjamin's Sale of Goods*, 8th edn (London: Sweet & Maxwell, 2010), para.13–039.
[157] *Benjamin's Sale of Goods*, 2010, para.13–033.
[158] [1904] 2 K.B. 152.
[159] [1921] 3 K.B. 435.
[160] Arbitration Act 1996 s.89(2). For the Consumer Rights Act, see Ch.10.
[161] Arbitration Act 1996 s.91; Unfair Arbitration Agreements (Specified Amount) Order 1999 (SI 1999/2167).

Acknowledgment and declarations of non-reliance

In *Lowe v Lombank*,[162] a clause in a hire purchase contract contained an acknowledgment that the goods were examined, found to be free of defects and to be of merchantable quality. It also contained an acknowledgment that the particular purpose for which the goods were wanted had not been revealed to the owner. Such clauses will not be conclusive, unless genuinely representing the intention of the parties. An estoppel might arise against the buyer or hirer, however, even where he had not examined the goods, provided the seller thought on reasonable grounds that he had.[163]

2–050

The precise use of estoppel in this context was made that much clearer in *Grimstead & Son Ltd v McGarrigan*.[164] The contract contained these terms:

> "2.5 The purchaser confirms that it has not relied on any warranty representation or undertaking of or on behalf of the vendors (or any of them) or of any other person in respect of the subject matter of this agreement save for any representation or warranty or undertaking expressly set out in the body of this agreement and for the avoidance of doubt no representation or warranty is given in respect of any of the matters contained in Schedule 2 save in respect of the facts and to the extent as expressly therein stated. . . .
>
> 8.1 This agreement sets out the entire agreement and understanding between each of the parties hereto in connection with the company and the sale and purchase of shares and no party hereto has entered into this agreement in reliance upon any representation, warranty or undertaking of any other party which is not set out or referred to in this agreement."

In considering the effect of these clauses, the court turned first to the remarks of Jacob J. in *Thomas Witter Ltd v TBP Industries Ltd*.[165] The judge had said, in relation to clauses indistinguishable from those in the present case, that:

> ". . . the point of exclusion from liability is not made explicit. It is perfectly possible to read the clause as doing no more than attempting to set out such representations as the purchaser thinks he is relying on at the time. He may have difficulty later in proof of any further representation, but if he can prove one, then his acknowledgment that there was no other may amount to no more than an acknowledgment of what he thought was the position at the time."

In the *Grimstead* case, Chadwick L.J. said that he found "difficulty in following that reasoning". What the judge had indicated to be the case did not seem to be the effect of the clause in the case before him, and was "plainly" not the effect of the two clauses in the case now before the Court of Appeal. It was not possible for a purchaser who has accepted that a representation was not relied on afterwards to say that that was no more than what he thought was the position at the time. He must be taken to know, at the time when he enters into an agreement, just what representations he is relying on:

> "Put another way, I reject the contention that it is open to a purchaser to assert both that he did not rely on a representation which was made to him and that he did rely upon that representation. He must be taken to know, at the time when he enters into the agreement, what representations he is relying on."

---

[162] [1960] 1 All E.R. 611.
[163] See also *Cremdean Properties Ltd v Nash* (1977) 244 E.G. 547; *Peart Stevenson Associates Ltd v Brian Holland* [2008] EWHC 1868 (QB).
[164] [1998] EWCA Civ 1523.
[165] [1996] 2 All E.R. 573 at 597.

Chadwick L.J. further explained that the clauses in question were capable of operating as an "evidential estoppel", apt to prevent the party giving the acknowledgment from asserting in subsequent litigation against the party to whom it has been given that it is not true.

2–051   The fact that the clause is capable of so acting, however, is not enough. The Court of Appeal said that the clause could operate as an evidentiary estoppel only if:

(i)   the statement in the disputed clauses was clear and unequivocal;

(ii)   the purchaser had intended the other party to act on the statements in the clauses; and

(iii) the other party must have believed the statements to be true and to have acted on them.

The Court of Appeal felt that the vendor failed in relation to this last requirement. In the absence of specific evidence, it would not be safe to conclude that the vendor had entered into the agreement on the basis that the purchaser was not relying on the relevant representations. If the representations were made as alleged, then that could only have been to persuade the purchaser to enter into the contract. In such a case, it would be open to hold that the vendor knew that the acknowledgment of non-reliance clauses did not reflect the true position. If that were the case, then the vendor could not rely on any estoppel which might otherwise have arisen. One can be forgiven for wondering if this finding will not always rule out the efficacy of non-reliance clauses.

It is, however, clear from subsequent cases that a distinction exists between an evidentiary estoppel and a contractual estoppel. As was said in *Trident Turboprop (Dublin) Ltd v First Flight Couriers Ltd*[166] "if the parties do agree a certain factual basis on which the contract is made, the contractual agreement is that neither party can subsequently deny that basis. Hence the phrase 'estoppel by contract' ". In that case, the relevant clause provided:

> "the Lessee ... also agrees and acknowledges that save as expressly stated in this Agreement and the other Transaction Documents to which the Lessor is a party, the Lessor has not and shall not be deemed to have made any warranties or representations, express or implied, about the Aircraft, including but not limited to the matters referred to above."

The court said that this clause differed from that in *Grimstead*. The relevant clause in that case was "to the effect that the purchaser confirmed that it had not relied on any representation by the vendors". The clause in the present case differed in that "the parties agree that no representation was made at all". It had been agreed that:

> "a state of affairs is the case, i.e. that there were no pre–contract (non–fraudulent) representations ... More importantly, the parties agree that this state of affairs is to form the

---

[166] [2008] EWHC 1686 (Comm). See also *Peekay Intermark Ltd v Australia & New Zealand Banking Group Ltd* [2006] 2 Lloyd's Rep. 511; *Warr v Cox* Unreported; 27 October 2010; and *FoodCo UK LLP v Henry Boot Developments Ltd* [2010] EWHC 358 (Ch). In this latter case, Lewison J. said that the relevant difference between estoppel by contract and evidential estoppel was that, in the case of a contractual estoppel, the party relying on the clause does not need to prove that he believed the truth of the acknowledgment of non-reliance. This case is discussed further at para.3–005.

basis of the transaction. Even if it was not in fact the case that there had been no representations, the parties are free to agree that it was so and base their contractual relations on that state of affairs".

In so deciding, the court expressly approved of the decision in *JP Morgan Chase Bank v Springwell Navigation Corp*.[167] The court in that case emphasised that ratio of the decision in *Lowe v Lombank* cannot:

"be regarded as authority for the far-reaching proposition that there can never be an agreement in a contract that the parties are conducting their dealings on the basis that a past event had not occurred, or that a particular fact was the case, although both parties know that, in reality, that past event had, or might have, occurred, or that the particular fact was not, or might not have been the case."

The court noted that, in that case, the written document recording a mere   **2–052** statement as to past facts could not as a matter of language amount to a contractual promise. But Diplock J. [in the *Lowe* case] himself drew a distinction between such a statement as to past facts and "a promise by the promisor to the promisee that acts will be done in the future or *that facts exist at the time of the promise or will exist in the future*".[168] The court thus decided that there was a contractual estoppel, but also held that the three criteria for an evidentiary estoppel referred to above had also been satisfied. It stated that the difference between the two categories of estoppel was that contractual estoppel does not require detrimental reliance to be shown.

The various authorities were considered by Christopher Clarke J. in *Raiffeisen Zentralbank Osterreich AG v Royal Bank of Scotland Plc*.[169] He referred to the words used by Diplock J. in the *Lowe* case and said:

"In circumstances where no reliance had been placed on estoppel in argument I decline to take the last phrase of that citation as a decision that a contractual estoppel (which may not be the same as a contractual promise or obligation) in relation to past facts can never arise".

He indeed went further and said that, if the court in that case had, however, so decided then the decision was wrong and decided *per incuriam* in the light of the relevant authorities.[170] He said that he was bound by *Lowe v Lombank* "to conclude that an agreement that no representations have been made or relied on (or as to any other past fact) can never amount to a contractual estoppel. There is no intrinsic reason why that should be so. There is good reason for allowing businessmen to agree with each other the basis of fact (including past fact) upon which they are to do business". He felt it better to follow the line of authority set out in such decisions as the *Springwell* and *Trident* cases.

An attempt to resolve what was agreed to be a case of conflicting authorities was made in *Morgan and Morgan v Pooley and Pooley*.[171] Edwards-Stuart J.

---

[167] [2008] EWHC 1186 (Comm); [2010] EWCA Civ 1221. See too *Avrora Fine Arts Investment Ltd v Christie, Manson & Woods Ltd* [2012] EWHC 2198.
[168] The emphasis was that of the judge in the *JP Morgan* case.
[169] [2010] EWHC 1392 (Comm).
[170] Aswell as the cases referred to in the text, the judge referred also to *Burroughs Adding Machine Ltd v Aspinall*(1925) 41 T.L.R. 276; *Colchester BC v Smith* [1992] Ch. 421.
[171] [2010] EWHC 2447.

perceived a difference between two types of situation. The first was where the non-reliance clause was one of many clauses in a long contract prepared by lawyers the parties to which may have had limited opportunity to read in detail beforehand. In that situation it might well be argued successfully that the party relying on the clause should not be allowed to do so because the clause falls with the contract when it is avoided for misrepresentation. The second type of situation is where the relevant clause was known to the relevant party, or their advisers, before the contract was made. The instant case satisfied this requirement where the contract was a short document and the conditions were printed in large type and were easily readable. This, taken together with the early notice that the sellers were entering into the transaction on the basis of the *William Sindall*clause,[172] led to the conclusion that in the circumstances of this case the non-reliance clause was to be given effect.

It would appear, furthermore, that clauses, such as acknowledgment clauses, will have no application to defects not patent at the time.[173]

WHETHER EXCLUSION CLAUSES ARE AVAILABLE TO THIRD PARTIES

2–053   Questions can arise as to whether an exclusion clause can operate to protect a person who is not a party to the contract. This is an issue which needs to be examined both in relation to the common law, and as the latter has been affected by the Contracts (Rights of Third Parties) Act 1999.

The common law

2–054   The basic rule is that the notion of privity of contract prevents non-parties from receiving any benefits or burdens which might be terms of an agreement made between others. In *Adler v Dickson*,[174] a ticket for a sea voyage contained terms exempting the shipping company from liability. One such term provided that "the company will not be responsible for any injury whatsoever . . . arising from or occasioned by the negligence of the company's servants". The claimant, having fallen from the gangway, brought an action against the master and boatswain. The Court of Appeal held that reliance could not be placed on the exclusion clause because, on its true construction, it did not purport to offer exemption to these parties. If the clause had on such a construction extended to the master and boatswain, a majority of the court were still prepared to hold it unavailing. The "company's servants", declared Jenkins L.J., are not parties to the contract.[175]

---

[172] The *Sindall* clause in the present case ran: "it is agreed and declared that the reply to any enquiry or information supplied in any property information form is given to the best knowledge, information and belief of the Seller, and that neither the Seller nor his legal representative has made any further enquiries into such matters (such as, but without limitation—conducting a site inspection or making specific enquiries of statutory authorities or utilities), and the replies are therefore given on that basis". See *William Sindall Plc v Cambridge CC* (1994) 3 All E.R. 932.

[173] See *Ormsby v H&H Factors Ltd* Unreported January 26, 1990 (CA). This was a point made in the county court and not commented upon in the Court of Appeal.

[174] [1954] 3 All E.R. 397.

[175] [1954] 3 All E.R. 397 at 403.

A similar finding was made in *Cosgrove v Horsfall*.[176] The claimant had a free pass for buses run by the London Passenger Transport Board, of which he was an employee. The terms of the pass were that neither the Board nor their servants were to be liable to the holder for injuries however caused. The claimant suffered personal injuries as the result of the negligence of the defendant bus driver whom he sued personally. The Court of Appeal held the driver liable. He could not claim the benefit of the exemption clause as he was not a party to the contract.

This strict view eventually received endorsement by the House of Lords in *Scruttons Ltd v Midland Silicones Ltd*.[177] A contract for the carriage of drum chemicals from the US to the UK contained a clause limiting the liability of the carriers. When the chemicals were being unloaded, they were damaged through the negligence of a firm of stevedores who were employed by the carriers. Lord Denning considered that the appellant stevedores could claim the benefit of the exclusion clause since the respondents, the consignees, had assented to the limitation of liability; but this was a dissenting judgment. The majority held that the appellants could not claim the benefit of an exclusion clause when they were not parties to the contract. Although "I may regret it," said Lord Reid:

> "I find it impossible to deny the existence of the general rule that a stranger to a contract cannot in a question with either of the contracting parties take advantage of provisions of the contract, even when it is clear from the contract that some provision in it was intended to benefit him."[178]

It has been suggested that there are two ways that the strictness of these decisions might be avoided and that these should be supported for this reason: between businessmen, the decisions denying third parties the right to the benefit of exclusion clauses can be inconvenient and cause uncertainty. They tend to falsify the assumptions on which the parties are contracting, with special regard to the decision as to the risks against which each should insure.

The first suggestion is that use be made of the concept of agency.[179] It is a **2–055** historical fact that railway companies in the 19th century issued tickets containing exclusion clauses which were held valid against other such companies because the particular company was agent for the other companies or was agent for the passenger.[180] The passenger thus had a direct relationship with the other companies. In *Scruttons*, where the House of Lords left open the question whether the stevedores could have been protected if the carriers had contracted as agents on their behalf, Lord Reid saw a possibility of an agency argument succeeding if:

> "(first) the bill of lading makes it clear that the stevedore is intended to be protected by the provisions in it which limits liability, (secondly) the bill of lading makes it clear that the carrier, in addition to contracting for these provisions on his own behalf, is also contracting as agent for the stevedore that these provisions should apply to the stevedore, (thirdly) the carrier

---

[176] [1945] 62 T.L.R. 140.
[177] [1962] 1 All E.R. 1.
[178] [1962] 1 All E.R. 1 at 10.
[179] *Anson's Law of Contract* (28th edn), p.647.
[180] *Anson's Law of Contract* (28th edn), p.647.

has authority from the stevedore to do that, or perhaps later ratification by the stevedore would suffice and (fourthly) that any difficulties about consideration moving from the stevedore were overcome."[181]

The second suggestion relates to an implied contract. The circumstances of the case may indicate that a contract is made with the third parties on the terms of that between the actual parties to the agreement. In *Pyrene Co v Scindia Navigation Co Ltd*,[182] the claimants in England sold goods to parties in India. The latter agreed with the defendants for the carriage of the goods to India. The contract of carriage limited liability to £200. The goods were damaged because of the defendants' negligence. The claimants sued the defendants for £900. Devlin J. held that the claimants were bound by the clause. Although not parties to the contract, they were entitled to its benefits and so must also accept its burdens. Viscount Simonds later said that the decision could be supported "only upon the facts of the case, which may well have justified the implication of a contract between the parties".[183] As Anson says, the implied contract was that all three parties intended the claimants to participate in the contract of carriage.[184]

In addition to such methods of avoiding the decision of the House of Lords, yet other authors have pointed to shortcomings in the judgment itself.[185] In particular, the Law Lords relied on overseas decisions which really rested on the basis that the clauses were inappropriately worded, rather than that the clauses did not extend to third parties.[186]

Most importantly, the decision, say these authors, is "not easy to reconcile with the earlier decision",[187] that in *Elder Dempster & Co Ltd v Patterson Zochonis & Co Ltd*.[188] Charterers had agreed to carry oil from West Africa to England. They chartered a vessel for this purpose. The bills of lading, made between the claimants and the charterers, contained a term purporting to protect both charterers and shipowners from claims arising out of bad stowage. When the oil was lost because of such stowage, the claimants sued both charterers and shipowners.

2–056   It was held by the House of Lords that both parties were protected by the clause. Precisely why the House thought this to be so is unclear. Indeed, in *Scruttons Ltd v Midland Silicones Ltd*, no attempt to uncover the ratio was made in view of its very obscurity.[189] Anson states that the most likely ratio appears to be that there was an implied contract between claimants and shipowners, the terms of which incorporated the exclusions and limitations contained in the bill of lading.[190]

---

[181] [1962] 1 All E.R. 1 at 10. *Anson's Law of Contract* (28th edn), pp.647–648. For an application of these principles, see *The Owners of the Ship "Borvigilant" v The Owners of the Ship "Romina G"* [2003] EWCA Civ 935.
[182] [1954] 2 All E.R. 158.
[183] See *Scruttons Ltd v Midland Silicones Ltd* [1962] 1 All E.R. 1 at 9.
[184] *Anson's Law of Contract* (28th edn), p.659.
[185] Cheshire, Fifoot and Furmston, *Law of Contract* (15th edn), pp.215–216.
[186] The cases are: *Krawill Machinery Corp v Herd* [1959] 1 Lloyd's Rep. 305 (USA); *Wilson v Darling Island Stevedoring* [1956] 1 Lloyd's Rep. 346 (Australia).
[187] Cheshire, Fifoot and Furmston, *Law of Contract* (15th edn), p.216.
[188] [1924] A.C. 522.
[189] [1962] 1 All E.R. 1 at 7, per Viscount Simonds.
[190] *Anson's Law of Contract* (28th edn), pp.658–659.

An alternative view was that of vicarious immunity, enunciated by Viscount Cave. This approach was to the effect that agents are entitled to any immunity conferred on their principals, and that this applied to the shipowners since they took possession on behalf of, and as agents of, the charterers.[191]Certainly, this line appealed to Scrutton L.J., not the least because he had enunciated this opinion in the Court of Appeal in this case,[192] and which he later repeated, citing the decision of the House of Lords, in *Mersey Shipping & Transport Co Ltd v Rea Ltd*.[193] Where there is a contract, he said, "which contains an exemption clause, the servants or agents who act under the contract have the benefit of the exemption clause . . . they can claim the protection of the contract made with their employers on whose behalf they are acting".[194]

This particular approach cannot be said to have survived *Scruttons Ltd v Midland Silicones Ltd*. Even so, it now appears that the courts will strive to bring third parties within exclusion clauses and so bring the law closer to the commercial realities of the situation.

This is well evidenced by the majority opinion of the Privy Council in *New Zealand Shipping Co Ltd v AM Satterthwaite & Co Ltd*.[195] The consignor loaded goods for carriage to the claimant consignee in New Zealand. Carriage was subject to a bill of lading issued by the carrier's agent which contained an exclusion clause purporting to operate, *inter alia*, for the benefit for the servants, agents and independent contractors of, and employed by, the carriers. After the claimant became holder of the bill of lading, the cargo was damaged through the negligence of the defendant stevedores, employed by the carriers to unload the goods in New Zealand. A bare majority of the Privy Council believed that the defendant was entitled to rely on the exclusion clause. The argument was that the exclusion was designed to cover the whole carriage from loading to discharge. The bill of lading brought a bargain into existence, initially unilateral, between the consignor and the defendant, made through the carrier as agent. That became a full contract when the defendant provided services by discharging the goods, for such performance for the consignor was the consideration for the agreement by the consignor that the defendant should have the benefit of the exclusion clause in the bill of lading. It did not matter that the defendant was already obliged to the carrier to perform those services, since the claimant thereby received the benefit of a direct obligation which he could enforce. Since Lord Reid had recognised that in this argument there was "a possibility of success of the agency argument",[196] the Privy Council opinion could be presented as in accord with existing precedent.

That this case is a move away from the spirit of *Scruttons Ltd v Midland Silicones Ltd* is, however, undoubted; and the movement was given further momentum by the decision of Donaldson J. in *Johnson Matthey & Co v Constantine Terminals and International Express Co*.[197] Very broadly, goods

---

[191] [1924] A.C. 522 at 534.
[192] [1923] 1 K.B. 420 at 441–442.
[193] [1925] 21 Ll. L. Rep. 375.
[194] [1925] 21 Ll. L. Rep. 375 at 378.
[195] [1974] 1 All E.R. 1015.
[196] *Scruttons Ltd v Midland Silicones Ltd* [1962] 1 All E.R. at 10.
[197] [1976] 2 Lloyd's Rep. 215.

were bailed by A to B who sub-bailed them to C. The goods were stolen. The question arose whether C could rely on the exclusion clause in the contract between himself and B when sued by A in negligence. There was no contractual nexus between A and C. It was accepted that if A could sue without alleging a bailment the decision in *Scruttons Ltd v Midland Silicones Ltd* would prevail; but that if C's duty arose only on the bailment, the whole contract of bailment, including the exclusion clause would prevail.

2–057   Donaldson J. found that C's duty to A arose solely out of the bailment and made it clear that the principle was limited to the special facts of the case. Strictly, therefore, the decision of the House of Lords is unaffected; but it is more truthful to recognise that it has been "undermined" since the doctrine of privity of contract was "basic to that decision".[198]

Further evidence of a movement away from the House of Lords is found in the Canadian decision in *Eisen und Metall AG v Ceres Stevedoring Co Ltd*.[199] P owned a container filled with scrap and arranged for its delivery to Montreal aboard a vessel owned by T under a bill of lading containing a clause protecting the carriers against the negligent acts and defaults of their servants or agents. The container was delivered to D, the terminal operators, who left it unguarded and exposed, so that it was stolen. D relied on the exclusion clause. Citing the view of Lord Wilberforce, that giving effect to "the clear intentions of a commercial document" meant giving effect to the exclusion clause, Owen J. found that the defendants in the case before him came within this reasoning and hence the clause prevailed.[200]

It is only fair to say, however, that this view has not gone unchecked. In *Herrick v Leonard & Dingley Ltd*,[201] McMullin J. distinguished the opinion of the Privy Council in that the document before him did not purport to include independent contractors, such as the defendant stevedores; and the stevedores had neither authorised nor ratified any attempt by the carrier to limit the former's liability to the claimant cargo owner. Again, in *The Suleyman Stalskiy*,[202] Schultz J. pointed out that in the case before the Privy Council the authority of the carrier to contract as agent of the stevedore was admitted, whereas it was not in the case before him. It has also been suggested that a stevedore who is ignorant of the terms of the bill of lading until after unloading the goods should not be capable of ratifying a contract made on its behalf by the carrier. In the Privy Council case, the stevedore received the bill two weeks prior to unloading: the stevedore was also the owner of the carrier and habitually did the latter's stevedoring work. A reviewer has thus argued that the opinion of the Privy Council was given on a case resting on an "occasional, and unusual, fact situation".[203] It is still thought the better view, however, to regard the wish of the courts to accord with commercial realities, and hence to give effect to exclusion clauses, as having the upper hand.

---

[198] [1977] 40 M.L.R. 706 at 708. See also *Haseldine v Daw & Son Ltd* [1941] 2 K.B. 343.
[199] [1977] 1 Lloyd's Rep. 665.
[200] [1977] 1 Lloyd's Rep. 665 at 671.
[201] [1975] 2 N.Z.L.R. 566.
[202] [1976] 2 Lloyd's Rep. 609.
[203] [1977] 40 M.L.R. 709 at 711.

In Scotland, as in England, the primary rule is that only a party to a contract can sue under it. There is an exception to this rule in the law of Scotland where it can be shown that the object of the contract is to benefit a third party. This is the *jus quaesitum tertio*.[204] No direct authority on the application of this principle in the context of exclusion clauses in Scotland exists. The absence of a doctrine of consideration in Scots Law would appear to remove one of the obstacles which may confront third parties seeking judicial support in England for claims to the benefit of exclusion clauses.

Statute law

The position above described has been considerably affected by the Contracts (Rights of Third Parties) Act 1999.[205] Section 1 provides that the Act applies in relation to a third party in two cases: where the contract itself expressly so provides; or the relevant term purports to confer a benefit on a third party. Section 1(2) further provides, however, that this latter will not apply if, on a true construction of the contract, it appears that the contracting parties did not intend the third party to have the right to enforce the term. Section 1(3) provides, as a condition for the Act to apply to third parties, that the third party must be expressly identified by name, class or description, but that the third party need not be in existence when the contract is made.[206] This could, for example, allow the Act to apply to a company yet to be incorporated.

2–058

Application to exclusion clauses   Thus far, the Act would not appear to apply to exclusion clauses, but this position is made good by s.1(6):

2–059

> "Where a term of a contract excludes or limits liability in relation to any matter references in this Act to the third party enforcing the term shall be construed as references to his availing himself of the exclusion or limitation."

This will, for instance, allow a term of a contract excluding or limiting liability for negligence, and which expressly states that the limitation or exclusion is for the benefit of the other party's "agents or servants or sub-contractors" to be enforced by such groups.

A third party cannot lose the rights otherwise made available by the Act, unless, in accordance with s.2, the contract is varied with his consent. This is subject to there being an express term in the contract to the effect that such consent is not needed, or that consent is to be required in specified circumstances different to those set out in s.2(1). This latter is a reference to the following:

---

[204] See T.B. Smith, *Short Commentaries on the Law of Scotland*, pp.177 and following.

[205] The Act implements, with some amendments, the recommendations of the Law Commission in its Report on *Privity of Contract: Contracts for the Benefit of Third Parties* (1996) Law Com. No.242.

[206] For authorities on the application of s.1, see *Nisshin Shipping Co Ltd v Cleaves & Co Ltd* [2004] 1 Lloyd's Rep. 38; *Laemthong International Lines Co Ltd v Abdullah Mohammed Fahem & Co* [2005] EWCA Civ 519. See too *Fortress Value Recovery Fund 1 LLC v Blue Skye Special Opportunities Fund LP (a firm)* [2013] EWCA Civ 367. In this case, it was held that as a matter of interpretation the language of a partnership deed was not sufficiently clear to bring about the result that the right of a third party to avail himself of an exclusion clause in the deed was in turn subject to an arbitration clause in the deed.

(a)   the third party has communicated his assent to the term to the promisor;

(b)   the promisor is aware that the third party has relied on the term; or

(c)   the promisor can reasonably be expected to have foreseen that the third party would rely on the term and the third party has in fact relied on it.

Section 3 of the Act enables the promisor, in any claim by a third party, to rely on any defence or set-off arising out of the contract and relevant to the particular term, which would have been available had the claim been made by the promisee. Section 3(6) makes it clear that this applies also when a third party seeks to rely on an exclusion or limitation clause, by providing that:

> "Where in any proceedings brought against him a third party seeks in reliance on section 1 to enforce a term of a contract (including, in particular, a term purporting to exclude or limit liability), he may not do so if he could not have done so (whether by reason of any particular circumstances relating to him or otherwise) had he been a party to the contract."

In *Prudential Assurance Co Ltd v Ayres and Grew*,[207] C had granted an underlease to D. D wished to assign the underlease to P. C agreed to the assignment by D to P. In the licence to assign D covenanted with and guaranteed to C that if P failed to pay rent then D would do so. By a separate supplemental deed between C and P it was agreed that the liability of P under the lease was limited to the partnership assets and did not extend to the personal assets of individual partners, and that any recovery by C against P or any previous tenant under the lease for any such default would be limited accordingly. P became insolvent leaving rent unpaid and C claimed against D. D argued that the effect of the supplemental deed in the events that had happened was wholly to exonerate D from liability to C. C argued that despite the supplemental deed the amount of rent due under the underlease remained unchanged and that any limitation on recoverability against P did not have as an inescapable consequence an alleviation of the burden on a previous tenant. It was held that D, although not party to the supplemental deed, could take advantage of the limitation of recovery against it by operation of the 1999 Act. The court held that the reference to "any previous tenant" was sufficient identification of the third party for the purposes of s.1(3) of the Act.

2–060   *Exclusions from the 1999 Act*   Section 6(1) says that the Act does not apply to a contract on a bill of exchange, promissory note or other negotiable instrument. There are also exemptions in relation to:

(a)   any contract binding on a company and its members under s.33 of the Companies Act 2006[208];

(b)   any term of a contract of employment against an employee;

(c)   any term of a worker's contract against a worker (including a home worker);

---

[207] [2007] EWHC 775 (Ch).

[208] This replaces the original reference to s.14 of the Companies Act 1985 which was repealed and replaced by the relevant provisions of the 2006 Act.

(d)   any term of a relevant contract against an "agency worker"[209]; or

(e)   any incorporation document of a limited liability partnership or any limited liability partnership agreement as defined in the Limited Liability Partnerships Regulations 2001.[210]

Application

The Act does not apply to Scotland.[211]   **2–061**

---

[209] This has the same meaning as in s.34(1) of the National Minimum Wage Act 1998.

[210] SI 2001/1090. For "limited liability partnership agreement", see reg.2.

[211] See s.10 of the Act, and refer also to *jus quaesitum tertio* considered at para.2–058.

CHAPTER 3

AVOIDANCE AND QUALIFICATION OF EXCLUSION CLAUSES

In this chapter, we discuss the methods by which the courts seek to avoid giving full effect to exclusion clauses, notwithstanding that the clause has been incorporated into the contract and is apt to cover the damage which has occurred.

3–001

ONUS OF PROOF

In *Levison v Patent Steam Carpet Cleaning Co*,[1] the terms of a contract for the cleaning of a carpet contained a clause reading: "All merchandise is expressly accepted at the owner's risk". The carpet was lost, presumably stolen. The defendants, pointing to the exclusion clause, argued that it clearly covered the case in hand because, on the balance of probabilities, the loss was due to their negligence: and that the burden of proof lay on the claimants to prove their case that the carpet had been lost because of a fundamental breach, the latter not being covered by the exclusion clause. The Court of Appeal held unanimously that the burden of proof in this case lay upon the defendants. A bailee, Lord Denning M.R. said, must prove all the circumstances in which the loss or damage occurred. If no explanation is forthcoming, then it is quite likely that the loss or damage was due to a fundamental breach of contract such as theft or delivery to the wrong address. The defendants were in the best position to provide an answer and the onus of proof, which they had failed to discharge, accordingly lay on them.[2]

3–002

In reaching this decision, the court had to face certain difficulties caused by the decision of an earlier Court of Appeal in *Hunt & Winterbotham v BRS Parcels*.[3] Goods which had been entrusted to a carrier were lost. It was held that the carrier could rely on a limitation clause without disproving fundamental breach. In *Woolmer v Delmer Price Ltd*,[4] on the other hand, the defendants had agreed to store a fur coat "at customer's risk". The coat was lost in a way not explained and the defendants were held liable as the duty was on them to show that the loss was not due to their fundamental breach.

Some doubt was cast on the correctness of Woolmer in the *Hunt & Winterbotham* case, although distinguished on the slender ground that it was a

---

[1] [1977] 3 All E.R. 498.
[2] [1977] 3 All E.R. 498. See Orr L.J. and Sir David Cairns at 506 and 508 respectively. See also *Matrix Europe Ltd v Uniserve Holdings Ltd* [2009] EWHC 919 (Comm).
[3] [1962] 1 All E.R. 111.
[4] [1955] 1 All E.R. 377.

case of deposit not carriage.[5] Furthermore, the court in *Hunt & Winterbotham* left open the possibility that where fundamental breach was specifically pleaded, as most significantly it was not in that case, the onus falls upon the bailee.[6] Sir David Cairns found this important in *Levison v Patent Steam Carpet Cleaning Co*,[7] while Lord Denning M.R. and Orr L.J. found nothing in the *Hunt & Winterbotham* case to prevent them finding as they did.

It is significant that Sir David Cairns drew attention to Lord Denning's remarks in *Spurling Ltd v Bradshaw*,[8] where he had said: "A bailor, by pleading and presenting his case properly, can always put the burden of proof on the bailee".[9] This, the best answer to the problem, is supported by Treitel: "It may be doubted whether a claimant can throw the burden of proof on the defendant by merely pleading fundamental breach. The burden might, however, pass to the defendant if the claimant could support his allegation by some evidence that the defendant might have been guilty of a fundamental breach".[10] This is just what happened in the *Levison* case.[11]

LIABILITY FOR FRAUD

3–003   In *S Pearson & Son Ltd v Dublin Corp*,[12] Lord Loreburn had said that "no one can escape liability for his own fraudulent statements by inserting in a contract a clause that the other party shall not rely on them",[13] Lord Halsbury agreed that "no craft or machinery in the form of contract can stop a person who complains that he has been defrauded from having that question of fact submitted to a jury",[14] Lord James adding that: "When the fraud succeeds, surely those who designed the fraudulent protection cannot take advantage of it ... As a general principle I incline to the view that an express term that fraud shall not vitiate a contract would be bad in law".[15]

In that case, an action had been brought against the corporation for deceit by its agent in misrepresenting the nature of the works to be undertaken under a particular contract. The Corporation had relied on a provision in the contract to the effect that the contractor should satisfy itself as to the nature of all existing works and all other matters relating to the contract works. The House of Lords concluded that the contract contemplated honesty on both sides, so that the clause relied on could not exclude liability for deceit.

---

[5] [1962] 1 All E.R. 111 at 115, per Lord Evershed M.R.
[6] [1962] 1 All E.R. 111 at 119, per Lord Evershed M.R.
[7] [1977] 3 All E.R. 498 at 508.
[8] [1956] 2 All E.R. 121.
[9] [1956] 2 All E.R. 121 at 125. See also [1977] 3 All E.R. 498.
[10] Treitel, *Law of Contract*, 4th edn (London: Sweet & Maxwell, 1975), p.193. This observation is not made in subsequent editions.
[11] The *Levison* case was accepted as correctly decided in *Euro Cellular (Distribution) Plc v Danzas Ltd* [2003] EWHC 3161 (Comm). See *too Waldon-Kelly v British Railways Board* Unreported March 17, 1981 (Stockport County Court).
[12] [1907] A.C. 351. See also *Boyd & Forrest v Glasgow & South Western Railway Co* [1915] S.C. (H.L.) 20.
[13] [1907] A.C. 351 at 353.
[14] [1907] A.C. 351 at 356.
[15] [1907] A.C. 351 at 362.

In *WRM Group Ltd v Wood*,[16] however, the Court of Appeal said that this case did not establish the proposition that it is not open to the parties to a contract to exclude the remedy of set off in relation to allegedly fraudulent misrepresentations. It pointed to *Society of Lloyd's v Leighs*[17] where Saville L.J. had said: "We know of no principle of law that should lead us to construe the words of the clause so as to exclude from its ambit any claim based or allegedly based on fraud".[18] In the *WRM* case itself, the disputed clause ran:

> "... the Purchaser shall not be entitled to set off against any amount otherwise payable to the Vendors under this Agreement (whether pursuant to the terms of the Retention Loan Notes or otherwise) or any other agreement or documents to be entered into by the Vendors or any of them in connection therewith, any amount which the Purchaser claims is due from the Vendors or any of them to the Purchaser ... under or by reason of any breach of the terms of this Agreement."

Morritt L.J. held that this clause was "clear and operates to exclude the possibility of set-off in respect of all sums claimed to be due because a warranty contained in the agreement was broken or because a representation made therein, whether innocently, carelessly or fraudulently, was false".[19]

The need for clarity was also expressed in *Satyam Computer Services Ltd v Upaid Systems Ltd*.[20] The court had been asked to determine preliminary issues relating to whether certain claims brought by the defendant company against the claimant company were excluded by the terms of a settlement agreement. U had developed software technology and had outsourced software development work to S. In order for U to patent its inventions in the United States, the parties made an agreement whereby S assigned to U all the relevant intellectual property rights. U submitted its patent application together with employee assignment forms from S and the assignment agreement annexed. Various disputes arose and the parties reached a settlement agreement to terminate the relationship. U later filed patent infringement proceedings against two companies that had obtained rights to the inventions from S's former employees. The employees denied signing employee assignment forms and S was unable to produce evidence capable of answering U's allegations of forgery. U alleged that, as a result of the alleged forgery, it was forced to settle the infringement proceedings on unfavourable terms. Flaux J. said that "where the claims in question are based on fraud or involve allegations of dishonesty, very clear and specific language in a settlement agreement will be required to settle such claims or exclude their subsequent pursuit, *a fortiori* if they are unknown at the time that the settlement agreement is entered into". In the Court of Appeal, Lawrence Collins L.J. said:

3–004

---

[16] [1998] C.L.C. 189. See also *Society of Lloyd's v Fraser* Unreported July 1, 1998.

[17] [1997] B.C.L.C. 1398.

[18] [1997] B.C.L.C. 1398 at 1407.

[19] Although the matter was not specifically considered, it is clear that Jacob J. accepted that in principle a clause could be drafted so as to exclude liability for fraud: *Witter Ltd v TBP Industries Ltd* [1996] 2 All E.R. 573 at 598. Morritt L.J.'s approach was endorsed by Popplewell J. in *FG Wilson (Engineering) Ltd v John Holt & Co (Liverpool) Ltd* [2012] EWHC 2477. An appeal was allowed in this case but not on a point relevant here: [2013] EWCA Civ 1232.

[20] [2008] EWHC 31 (Comm); [2008] EWCA Civ 487.

"If a party seeking a release asked the other party to confirm that it would apply to claims based on fraud, it would not, in most cases, be difficult to anticipate the answer . . . The true question is whether on its proper construction it applies to claims of the type made in the Texas proceedings, namely that, unknown to Upaid when the Settlement Agreement was entered into, Upaid was supplied by Satyam with forged assignments. To that question it seems to me that there is only one possible answer. In my judgment, express words would be necessary for such a release."

The *Pearson* case was subject to further critical analysis by the House of Lords in *HIH Casualty & General Insurance Ltd v Chase Manhattan Bank*.[21] Lord Bingham said this:

"It is clear that the law, on public policy grounds, does not permit a contracting party to exclude liability for his own fraud in inducing the making of the contract. The insurers have throughout contended for a similar rule in relation to the fraud of agents acting as such. After a very detailed examination of such authority as there is, both the judge . . . and the Court of Appeal . . . decided against the existence of such a rule. It is true that the ratio of the leading authority on the point, *S Pearson & Son Ltd v Dublin Corporation*, despite the distinction and numerical strength of the House which decided it, is not easy to discern. I do not however think that the question need be finally resolved in this case. For it is in my opinion plain beyond argument that if a party to a written contract seeks to exclude the ordinary consequences of fraudulent or dishonest misrepresentation or deceit by his agent, acting as such, inducing the making of the contract, such intention must be expressed in clear and unmistakable terms on the face of the contract."

Lord Wilberforce added: "There is no doubt that a party cannot contract that he shall not be liable for his own fraud".

3–005 This was followed in *FoodCo UK LLP v Henry Boot Development Ltd*.[22] The clause ran:

"This Agreement constitutes the entire agreement between the parties hereto and the Tenant acknowledges that it is entering into this Agreement on the basis of the terms hereof and not in reliance upon any representation or warranty whatsoever whether written or oral expressed or implied made by or on behalf of [Henry Boot] (save for written replies given by [Henry Boot's] solicitors to the enquiries raised by the Tenant's solicitors)."

In assessing this clause, Lewison J. referred to:

"the important principles that, as a matter of public policy, a contracting party cannot exclude liability for his own fraud; and that if he wishes to exclude liability for the fraud of his agent he must do so in clear and unmistakable terms on the face of the contract."

He cited here the observations made in the above case. The clause in the present case contained no clear words acknowledging non-reliance on fraudulent misrepresentations and this meant, the judge concluded that the clause covered innocent and negligent misrepresentations, but not fraudulent ones.

The same approach was taken in *Frank Maas (UK) Ltd v Samsung Electronics (UK) Ltd*.[23] The relevant clause provided: "Company's liability howsoever arising and notwithstanding that the cause of the loss or damage be unexplained shall not exceed . . .". Further clauses in the contract provided as follows:

---

[21] [2003] UKHL 6. For earlier reports see: [2001] EWCA Civ 1250; [2001] 1 All E.R. (Comm) 719.
[22] [2010] EWHC 358 (Ch).
[23] [2004] EWHC 1502 (Comm).

"24.   The company shall perform its duties with a reasonable degree of care, diligence, skill and judgment.

25.   The company shall be relieved of liability for any loss or damage if and to the extent that such loss is caused by:

(A)   strike, lock-out, stoppage or restraint of labour, the consequences whereof the Company is unable to avoid by the exercise of reasonable diligence;

(B)   any cause or event which the Company is unable to avoid and the consequences whereof the Company is unable to prevent by the exercise of reasonable diligence."

Clause 27A read, in part: "the Company's liability howsoever arising and notwithstanding that the cause of the loss or damage cannot be explained shall not exceed . . .".

The relevant goods were stolen from a warehouse by persons unknown.

Accepting that the clause had to be construed *contra proferentem*, the court pointed out that cl.27 covered not just negligence but also wilful default. It could not possibly be the case that the disputed clause did not have the effect of limiting any such liability. To argue the contrary would be "to render clause 27A inapplicable in an important, commonplace respect. As a matter of contractual scheme, that seems unlikely".   **3–006**

It had been argued that "howsoever arising" used in cl.27A amounted to "shorthand" for the bases of liability contemplated under cl.25. That approach was rejected by the court. Clause 25 contained an exhaustive statement as to when Maas would be relieved of liability. It did not deal with the basis of any liability. It was, the court said, understandable that Maas should be relieved of liability in certain limited circumstances. It did not follow from this, though, that that clause should be restricted likewise. As the court said, if the clause were co-extensive with cl.25, it would have no point. It saw the scheme of the contract as contemplating circumstances in which Maas would be unable to obtain relief under cl.25, but could then limit its liability under the clause in question.

The argument had been put to the court that, if the clause were interpreted as covering wilful default on the part of Maas's employees, then it would also cover fraud on the part of Maas itself. The court replied that, when it comes to personal fraud of a party, then, whether as a matter of public policy or construction, "fraud is indeed a thing apart". So far as concerns construction, even with regard to the invocation of a limitation clause in the course of the performance of an otherwise valid contract, the court said that the parties do not contemplate that one of them may take advantage of personal fraud. The various considerations already discussed (as to risk allocation, clarity of language and context) which point to the disputed clause extending to Maas' vicarious liability for wilful default, suggested a different conclusion where personal fraud on Mass's part was concerned.[24]

---

[24] See also *Granville Oil & Chemicals Ltd v Davis Turner & Co Ltd* [2003] EWCA Civ 570; [2003] 2 Lloyd's Rep. 356; *4Eng Ltd v (1) Roger Harper (2) Barry Simpson* [2007] EWHC 1568; *Regus (UK) Ltd v Epcot Solutions Ltd* [2008] EWCA Civ 361; *Rohlig (UK) Ltd v Rock Unique Ltd* [2011] EWCA Civ 18.

LIABILITY FOR BREACH OF FIDUCIARY DUTY

3–007 It is argued that any attempt by a person under a fiduciary duty to contract out of liability for a wilful default in that duty would be ineffective. This argument is based on the fact that the promoter of a company, who is under a fiduciary duty not to profit from the promotion without disclosing it, cannot contract out of that duty.[25] It was, however, held in *Armitage v Nurse*[26] that it was not contrary to public policy for a trustee to exclude liability for gross negligence.

LIABILITY FOR BREACH OF RULES OF NATURAL JUSTICE

3–008 Treitel also cites a number of *dicta* of Lord Denning to the effect that the rules of domestic tribunals purporting to oust the rules of natural justice would be ineffective.[27] Although Treitel offers no comment on these *dicta*, it is thought that Lord Denning's views are right.[28]

ORAL UNDERTAKINGS

3–009 This method of evading the full impact of exclusion clauses can be introduced by reference to *Couchman v Hill*.[29] The catalogue for a sale by auction described certain heifers as "unserved". The document also contained an exclusion clause, stipulating that "all lots must be taken subject to all faults or errors of description (if any) and no compensation will be paid for the same". Similar terms were contained in the conditions of sale exhibited at the auction rooms. The claimant orally requested the defendant to confirm that a particular heifer was unserved, which confirmation was duly given. After the sale, the heifer was found to be in calf and died as a result of carrying a calf too young. It was held that the oral declaration overrode the exclusion clause and that the claimant was entitled to damages.[30]

A similar decision was reached in *SS Ardennes (Cargo Owners) v Ardennes (Owners)*.[31] The claimants shipped cargo to England from Spain on the defendant's vessel. An oral promise was made by the latter to the effect that the voyage would be direct to England. The written terms of the bill of lading allowed the defendants to reach London "by any route and whether directly or indirectly". In fact, the vessel did not proceed directly to London, going instead via Antwerp. It was held that the oral promise was binding.

---

[25] See Treitel, *Law of Contract*, 4th edn, pp.192–193; Gower, *Modern Company Law*, 5th edn (London: Sweet & Maxwell, 1992), p.299; *Gluckstein v Barnes* [1900] A.C. 240.

[26] [1998] Ch. 241. See too *Cavell USA Inc v Seaton Insurance Co* [2009] EWCA Civ 1363; [2009] 2 C.L.C. 991 and *Halliwells LLP v Ian Dafydd Austin* [2012] EWHC 1194.

[27] Treitel, *Law of Contract*, 4th edn, p.193.

[28] See Lord Denning in *Lee v Showman's Guild* [1952] 1 All E.R. 1175; *Edwards v SOGAT* [1970] 3 All E.R. 689; *Enderby Town FC v The Football Association* [1971] 1 All E.R. 215.

[29] [1947] 1 All E.R. 103.

[30] [1947] 1 All E.R. 103 at 105, per Scott L.J.

[31] [1950] 2 All E.R. 517.

In both these cases, the oral promise directly contradicted the written exclusion clauses. It is clear, however, that the courts are still prepared to find that an exclusion clause has been overridden by an oral promise, even where that contradiction is not so glaring. A good example is *Mendelssohn v Normand*.[32] The claimant left his car at a garage owned by the defendants. An exclusion clause disclaimed liability for any loss, however caused: it was further provided that the terms of the agreement could only be varied if made in writing and signed by the management. On the relevant occasion, the attendant told him that the doors were not to be locked and that he, the attendant, would lock them himself. He did not and the luggage was stolen.

It was held that the attendant's promise was not within his actual authority: it nevertheless lay within his ostensible authority, and hence bound his employers, the garage owners.[33] It was held that this rendered the exclusion clauses ineffective. The reason was that:

3–010

> "the oral promise or representation has a decisive influence on the transaction—it is the very thing which induces the other to contract and it would be most unjust to allow the maker to go back on it. The printed condition is rejected because it is repugnant to the express oral promise or representation."[34]

Phillimore L.J. observed that the claimant "was clearly concerned about his luggage and ... was induced to leave the car there by the firm promise that it would be locked".[35] Hence, the printed clauses must fail "insofar as they are repugnant to the express undertaking".[36]

For all that these words are robustly put, the element of repugnance is not easily discernible, especially when a comparison is made with *Couchman v Hill*. This point emerges even more clearly in the decision of the Court of Appeal in *Evans & Son (Portsmouth) Ltd v Andrea Merzario Ltd*.[37] The claimants imported machines from Italy, habitually using the defendants as forwarding agents. Prior to 1967, transportation of the machines was always done below deck to avoid the problems of rust. In that year, the defendants proposed a changeover to containers. The claimants obtained an oral assurance that the machines would continue to be shipped below deck, and accordingly agreed to containerisation. In the present case, it appeared that, because of an oversight, the machines were shipped above deck and were lost overboard in a heavy swell.

The claimants sued upon the oral promise. The defendants countered that the printed terms of their agreement gave them the right to use whatever method of carriage they desired, that it excluded liability except for wilful neglect or default, and that the amount of damages was also limited by the printed terms. Lord Denning took the view that the oral agreement constituted a collateral contract, the consideration for this being the entry into the transportation contract.[38] There

---

[32] [1969] 2 All E.R. 1215.
[33] [1969] 2 All E.R. 1215 at 1218, per Lord Denning M.R.
[34] [1969] 2 All E.R. 1215 at 1218, per Lord Denning M.R.
[35] [1969] 2 All E.R. 1215 at 1219–1220.
[36] [1969] 2 All E.R. 1215 at 1220.
[37] [1976] 2 All E.R. 930.
[38] [1976] 2 All E.R. 930 at 933, citing *Heilbut v Buckleton* [1913] A.C. 30.

was a clear breach of this oral contract unless, he said, the printed exclusion clauses applied. Repeating what had been said in the previous case, that the printed condition is ineffective because repugnant to the oral promise, he found in favour of the claimants.

3–011   It is difficult entirely to accept this explanation. If the oral promise is a separate, albeit collateral contract, there should surely be no need to inspect the terms of the printed contract: this is relevant only insofar as it furnishes consideration for the oral promise. In any case, such repugnance as there is surely relates only to the printed term concerning the right of the forwarding agents to ship as they chose, and not to the exclusion and limitation clauses.

Roskill L.J., especially, and Geoffrey Lane L.J., rejected a solution based on a collateral contract. Roskill L.J. found there to be one entire contract, partly oral, partly written and partly a matter of conduct. Taken thus, the oral promise must be taken as overriding the exempting conditions, otherwise "the promise would be illusory".[39]

Geoffrey Lane L.J. regarded the oral agreement as a new term of the agreement. He held that this must override the clause as to the method of carriage as they "are logically inconsistent with each other" though this scarcely explains why it is the written term which is to be deleted.[40] As for the remaining clauses, they too were ineffective: any other conclusion "would be to destroy the business efficacy of the new agreement from the day it started".[41]

It is submitted that the arguments are wholly unconvincing since the two Courts of Appeal are dealing with clauses not wholly antithetical. What these cases in fact demonstrate is the determination of the courts to avoid the full impact of an exclusion clause.

It is also fair to say that doubt must be cast on the Evans case by the Court of Appeal ruling in *Daewoo Heavy Industries Ltd v Klipriver Shipping Ltd*.[42] In breach of contract, cargo was stowed above deck instead of below. A clause provided that: "Neither the carrier nor the ship shall in any event be or become liable for any loss or damage to or in connection with goods in an amount exceeding [£100]". Judge L.J. noted that the Evans case had been cited as offering the following proposition, that clauses: "which are clearly intended to protect the shipowner, provided he honours his contractual obligations to stow goods under deck, do not apply if he is in breach of that obligation. This rule is quite clearly based on contractual intention".[43] He said that that case did not support any such proposition: "the ultimate decision depends on the proper construction of the contract agreed by the parties". Judge L.J. disagreed with Hirst J. in the latter's view that as the limitation clause was "repugnant to and inconsistent with the obligation to stow below deck", it was "inapplicable".

3–012   Judge L.J. summarised the decision in Evans thus:

---

[39] [1976] 2 All E.R. 930 at 935.
[40] [1976] 2 All E.R. 930 at 936.
[41] [1976] 2 All E.R. 930 at 936.
[42] [2003] EWCA Civ 451.
[43] *The Chanda* [1989] 2 Lloyd's Rep. 494, per Hirst J.

"the limitation clause in *Evans* did not apply, either because it was not incorporated into the contract then under consideration (Geoffrey Lane L.J.) or because, looking at all the material, written and oral, or by way of inferences from conduct, in the contract under consideration, the exemption clauses did not avail the defendants (Roskill L.J.)."

That "it is ultimately a question of construction" was also the view taken by the Court of Appeal in *Thinc v Armstrong and Armstrong*[44] though no reference was made to the *Daewoo* case, the court referring instead to the *Evans* case and *Mendelssohn v Normand*.[45] In *Thinc*, Thinc carried on business in the financial services sector. The Armstrongs had an existing business and client base as independent financial advisers. Thinc was keen for them to bring those clients to it, with the prospect of recurring as well as new commission payments. Thinc entered into individual agreements with the Armstrongs and also a supplemental contract under which the latter received a "disturbance allowance" or "supplemental payment" based on 50 per cent of their last year's gross income. The supplemental contract provided that the supplemental payment would be repayable if a repayment event occurred within three years of payment. The repayment events included termination of the contracts with Thinc for whatever reason. Thinc had given notice within three years terminating the contracts. The judge upheld the Armstrong's contention that they had been assured by Thinc that the only condition for them to retain the supplemental payment was that they stayed with Thinc for three years so that Thinc would not be able to recover the supplemental payment unless the Armstrongs terminated their contracts. The judge held that those assurances were a collateral warranty which prevented Thinc from recovering the payment.

In the Court of Appeal, Thinc submitted that (1) the judge's decision was unfair because the collateral warranty was neither pleaded, nor the subject of evidence, nor the subject of submissions; (2) no such assurance was ever given or understood and therefore could not have been relied on; if any such assurance was given, it meant no more than the written contract between the parties provided, namely that the payment was repayable if Thinc served notice of termination without cause within three years.

The Court of Appeal ruled that the collateral warranty had been sufficiently pleaded and was the subject of evidence and argument.

It also held that the assurance that there were no other conditions relating to the supplemental repayment so long as the Armstrongs remained with Thinc for three years was clearly proved. The supplemental payment was a critical feature of the deal. Without it, the Armstrongs had not been interested in joining Thinc. With it, the deal became negotiable, but only if they could be satisfied that the money could not be reclaimed. They had pressed Thinc repeatedly on those features of the deal, and were repeatedly assured that there were no minimum performance requirements and no conditions which would permit recovery of the payment by Thinc provided that they stayed for three years. The judge was entitled to find that the proper interpretation of the "no other conditions" assurance was that the decision to go or stay was that of the Armstrongs. It would, the Court of Appeal said, "be illusory" for Thinc to give that assurance and then

---

[44] [2012] EWCA Civ 1227. See too *Mileform Ltd v Interserve Security Ltd* [2013] EWHC 3386.
[45] [1970] 1 Q.B. 177. See *supra* para.3–090.

for its printed contract to enable it to reclaim the money at will within that period by terminating the contract without cause: "That would be to impose a new condition for repayment".

MISREPRESENTING THE EFFECTS OF A TERM

3–013   Where the full effects of an exclusion clause have been misrepresented, that misrepresentation will be effective to qualify the terms of the clause as it originally stood.

The leading case is *Curtis v Chemical Cleaning & Dyeing Co.*[46] The claimant took to the defendants' shop a white satin wedding dress for cleaning. She was asked to sign a receipt which contained a clause exempting the defendants from all liability for damage to articles cleaned. She was given a document which she was asked to sign. She asked for an explanation of its contents and was told that it exempted the defendants from certain risks, and, in the present instance, from the risk of damage to the beads and sequins on the dress. The claimant then signed the document, which in fact contained a clause exempting the defendants from liability for "any damage, however caused". When the dress was returned, it was stained: in the subsequent action, the defendants placed reliance on this clause. The Court of Appeal held that the defendants were liable to damages, and that no regard could be placed on the exclusion clause. According to Somervell L.J., "owing to the misrepresentation the exception never became part of the contract between the parties".[47] Denning L.J. made the further point that it was quite irrelevant whether the misrepresentation was innocent or fraudulent.

The reasoning of this case was endorsed in *Jacques v Lloyd D George & Partners.*[48] The claimant wished to sell his cafe and orally agreed with the defendants, a firm of estate agents, to sell for £2,500 cash. The defendants told the claimant that if they found a purchaser and the deal went through, their commission would be £250. The claimant signed a printed contract which gave the defendants the right to their commission if the latter found a person "willing" to sign a contract to purchase. An introduction was made to a willing purchaser but the claimant's landlord, finding the references unsatisfactory, declined to proceed. The defendants, relying on the printed terms, claimed the commission. Finding against the defendants, Lord Denning M.R. remarked upon the principle that "an estate agent cannot rely on the printed form when his agent misrepresents the content or effect of the form".[49] Edmund Davies L.J. agreed, pointing to *Curtis v Chemical Cleaning and Dyeing Co.* The same approach could be applied here, he declared: "Their agent having misrepresented the position, it was not open to them to insist on payment".[50]

3–014   The decisions of these two Courts of Appeal represented acceptance of earlier dicta. In *L'Estrange v F Graucob Ltd*,[51] Scrutton L.J. had noted that a signed

---

[46] [1951] 1 All E.R. 631.
[47] [1951] 1 All E.R. 631 at 633.
[48] [1968] 2 All E.R. 187.
[49] [1968] 2 All E.R. 187 at 190.
[50] [1968] 2 All E.R. 187 at 192.
[51] [1934] 2 K.B. 394.

contract was binding on the signatory, regardless of whether he had read its terms or not. This, the Lord Justice said, applied provided there was no fraud or misrepresentation.[52] Furthermore, Denning L.J. had also argued in *Dennis Reed Ltd v Goody*[53] that if a clause in an estate agent's contract had been misconstrued to the signatory, the courts might well not enforce it.[54]

Predictably, Lord Denning also appears to have attempted considerably to advance the boundaries of this particular principle. In *Dennis Reed Ltd v Goody*, he appeared to take the view that if a person believes that a contract contains no exceptional clauses when it does, and the other party offers no explanation of the contract, this is tantamount to a misrepresentation of the terms.[55] In *Jacques v Lloyd D George & Partners*, Lord Denning made it clear that such indeed was his view. If an estate agent, he said, seeks to depart from ordinary and well-understood contractual terms, he must take care to explain the effect to the client. In the absence of such explanation, the estate agent would be precluded from enforcing a term which is "unreasonable or oppressive".[56]

It was held in *The Starsin*[57] that, where the typed entry on the face of bills of lading was inconsistent with the printed conditions on the back, the typed entry should prevail in determining whether bills were owners' or charterers' bills.

Illegal misleading practices

What now seems entirely possible, following the enactment of the Consumer Protection from Unfair Trading Regulations 2008[58] is that the matters dealt with above in relation to oral undertakings and misrepresenting the effects of a term, and other practices besides, can now give rise to a criminal offence in the case of consumer contracts. Overriding or misrepresenting an exclusion or limitation clause could easily be regarded as an unfair practice since it contravenes the requirements of professional diligence and induces a consumer to enter into a contract he would not otherwise have done. Again, such practices could well be misleading actions, and hence unfair under the Regulations. A practice is misleading if it induces a consumer to enter into a contract he would not otherwise have made, and "if it or its overall presentation in any way deceives or is likely to deceive the average consumer" in relation to any of certain listed matters, "even if the information is factually correct". The matters listed include any statement as to the extent of the trader's commitments; and any statement as

3–015

---

[52] [1934] 2 K.B. 394 at 403. This case is discussed in Ch.1 at para.1–044 If there has been a misrepresentation inducing a contract, the fact that the printed terms and conditions clarify the point does not alter the fact that the misrepresentation did induce the making of the contract nor affect the remedies available under the Misrepresentation Act 1967: *Peekay Intermark Ltd v Australia & New Zealand Banking Group Ltd* [2005] EWHC 830 (Comm).

[53] [1950] 1 All E.R. 919.

[54] [1950] 1 All E.R. 919 at 924.

[55] [1950] 1 All E.R. 919.

[56] [1968] 2 All E.R. 187. The question of reasonableness is discussed in greater detail in Ch.9. For a discussion of onerous or oppressive contract terms, see the cases discussed at para.1–019 and following.

[57] [2003] UKHL 12.

[58] SI 2008/1277 as amended by the Consumer Protection (Amendment) Regulations 2014 (SI 2014/870).

to the consumer's rights.[59] There are no equivalent provisions in the Business Protection from Misleading Marketing Regulations 2008,[60] so similar offences could not arise in the context of business to business contracts.

FUNDAMENTAL TERMS AND FUNDAMENTAL BREACH

3–016   For a number of years, what was virtually a substantive rule of law grew up to the effect that no exclusion clause was valid where a defendant was in fundamental breach of contract, or in breach of a fundamental term. In *Karsales (Harrow) Ltd v Wallis*,[61] Denning L.J. regarded it as:

> "now settled that exempting clauses of this kind, no matter how widely they are expressed, only avail the party when he is carrying out the contract in its essential respects ... They do not avail him when he is guilty of a breach which goes to the root of the contract ... If he has been guilty of a breach of those obligations in a respect which goes to the very root of the contract, he cannot rely on the exempting clauses."[62]

The effect of such cases, it was said, was that a person in fundamental breach of contract could not rely on an exemption clause inserted in the contract to protect him.[63] The House of Lords, however, attempted to reinterpret the doctrine of fundamental breach as one of construction, so that it should be viewed strictly as an application of the principle that an exclusion clause should not, in the absence of clear words, be construed as applying to breaches tending to defeat the main purpose of the contract. It was accepted, though, that, as a matter of drafting, there was no reason why a properly drafted exclusion clause should not apply to some instances of a fundamental breach.[64]

In subsequent cases, however, the Court of Appeal "behaved as if the House of Lords had never spoken at all"[65] and appeared to reinstate the proposition that, as a rule of law, no exclusion clause could offer protection against a fundamental breach of contract.[66]

The House of Lords, however, sought, and it would now appear successfully, to reimpose its view that everything depended on the construction of the clause in

---

[59] See regs 3 and 5.

[60] SI 2008/1276.

[61] [1956] 2 All E.R. 866.

[62] [1956] 2 All E.R. 866 at 868.

[63] Guest, "Fundamental Breach of Contract" [1961] 77 L.Q.R. 98. Other relevant cases include: *Yeoman Credit Ltd v Apps* [1961] 2 All E.R. 281; and *Charterhouse Credit Co Ltd v Tolly* [1963] 2 All E.R. 432.

[64] *Suisse Atlantique Société D'Armement Maritime SA v NV Rotterdamsche Kolen Centrale* [1966] 2 All E.R. 61 at 71, 89 and 93, respectively, per Lord Reid, Lord Upjohn and Lord Wilberforce (hereafter referred to as *Suisse Atlantique*). See also *UGS Finance v National Mortgage Bank of Greece SA* [1964] 1 Lloyd's Rep. 446 at 450, per Pearson L.J.

[65] Cheshire, Fifoot and Furmston, *Law of Contract*, 15th edn, p.229.

[66] See in particular *Mendelssohn v Normand* [1969] 2 All E.R. 1215; *Farnworth Finance Facilities Ltd v Attryde* [1970] 2 All E.R. 774; *Harbutt's "Plasticine" Ltd v Wayne Tank & Pump Co Ltd* [1970] 1 All E.R. 225. See also Donaldson J.'s attempt to reconcile these cases with the *Suisse Atlantique* decision in *Kenyon Ltd v Baxter Hoare & Co Ltd* [1971] 2 All E.R. 708.

dispute. *In Photo Production Ltd v Securicor Transport Ltd*,[67] Lord Wilberforce referred to Lord Denning's declaration that Suisse Atlantique had affirmed the view that:

> "when one side has been guilty of a fundamental breach of contract … and the other side accepts it so that the contract comes to an end … then the guilty party cannot rely on the exception or limitation clause to escape from liability for his breach."[68]

That case, Lord Wilberforce replied, was "directly opposed" to any such interpretation and the effect of the judgments in that case was "to repudiate it".[69] He declared that he had no:

3–017

> "second thoughts as to the main proposition that the question whether, and to what extent, an exclusion clause is to be applied to a fundamental breach, or to a breach of a fundamental term, or indeed to any breach of contract, is a matter of construction of the contract."[70]

These strictures appeared now to have had effect. In *Ormsby v H&H Factors Ltd*,[71] it was said that attempts had in the past been made to "circumvent exclusion clauses by the doctrine of fundamental breach. These attempts have been laid to rest by the House of Lords …".[72] In *George Mitchell (Chesterhall) Ltd v Finney Lock Seeds Ltd*,[73] the Court of Appeal accepted that the question as to whether an exclusion clause covered a fundamental breach was a matter of construction; and in *Edmund Murray Ltd v BSP International Foundations Ltd*,[74] the Court of Appeal specifically stated that:

> "It is always necessary when considering an exemption clause to decide whether as a matter of construction it extends to exclude or restrict the liability in question, but, if it does, it is no longer permissible at common law to reject or circumvent the clause by treating it as inapplicable to 'fundamental' breach."[75]

When any such decision has to be made, particularly strong and clear language is required when applying an exclusion clause to a deliberate act of wrongdoing. In *Internet Broadcasting Corp Ltd v MAR LLC*,[76] the contract contained an exclusion clause which stated that neither party would be liable to the other for any damage to software, damage to or loss of data, loss of profit, anticipated profit, revenues, anticipated savings, goodwill or business opportunity, or for any indirect or consequential loss or damage. The Deputy Judge, after a comprehensive review of the authorities, stated that the starting point was the:

---

[67] [1980] 1 All E.R. 556.
[68] *Harbutt's "Plasticine" Ltd v Wayne Tank & Pump Co Ltd* [1970] 1 All E.R. 225 at 235.
[69] [1980] 1 All E.R. 556 at 560.
[70] [1980] 1 All E.R. 556 at 561.
[71] Unreported January 26, 1990, CA.
[72] This was stated by the county court judge in remarks not commented on by the Court of Appeal.
[73] [1983] 1 All E.R. 108.
[74] (1992) 33 Con. L.R. 1.
[75] In *Carter v Emin* Unreported February 15, 2001 (Mayor's and City of London CC), the District Judge said that there had been a fundamental breach and that the particular exclusion clause would not protect the defendants. This appears to refer, however, to his finding that the clause was unreasonable, and not that it automatically failed to cover such a breach.
[76] [2009] EWHC 844 (Ch).

"rebuttable presumption that [the clause] was not intended to cover a deliberate repudiatory breach of contract. . . . There would have to be very clear, in the sense of strong, language to persuade a court that the parties intended the words to cover such a case. Pointing to a mere literal meaning was not enough."

3–018 The Deputy Judge took the view that the words used in the instant case contained "no strong language and no clear statement" that deliberate wrongdoing was intended to be covered, let alone deliberate personal and repudiatory wrongdoing. Any reasonable businessman, reading the words with an eye to an allocation of insurable risk, would understand that they did not extend to risks which were uninsurable or very unlikely to be insurable, such as losses flowing from a deliberate, personal, repudiatory breach: "The literal meaning in the instant case would defeat the main object of the contract". Interestingly, in view of the discussion above,[77] he also said that there was no question of repugnancy "but that did not answer the question as to the true construction of the clause and, in particular, whether it covered a deliberate personal repudiatory breach".

It is furthermore accepted that enactment of the Unfair Contract Terms Act 1977 has undermined the need for any separate doctrine relating to fundamental breach.[78] In what is almost a statutory reversal of the old rule of law approach, s.9 of the 1977 Act provides that, where the test of reasonableness is to be applied to any term, that term may be given effect whether or not the contract has been terminated; nor will affirmation of itself affect the applicability of that test.[79]

EXCLUDING THE OBLIGATION TO PERFORM

3–019 Such life as there might be in the now discredited approach to fundamental breach lies with those cases where a clause seeks to allow a party not to perform the contract at all. In *Suisse Atlantique*, Lord Wilberforce said that the parties to a contract cannot contemplate so wide an ambit to an exclusion clause as to deprive the contract of meaning so reducing it to a "mere declaration of intent". To that extent, he concluded, it may be "correct to say that there is a rule of law against the application of an exceptions clause to a particular type of breach".[80] Lord Diplock also took the view that the parties to a contract were free to modify their obligations to whatever degree they chose "within the limits that the agreement must contain the legal characteristics of a contract".[81]

This must be read subject to the provisions of the Unfair Contract Terms Act. Section 3, in certain circumstances[82] imposes the reasonableness test on clauses which seek to allow no performance at all. If the above observations were to apply to such cases, then the reasonableness test could never apply since the particular clause could never have effect anyway. The Act must, therefore, be

---

[77] See para.3–090 following.
[78] See [1980] 1 All E.R. 556 at 564, per Lord Wilberforce. See also *George Mitchell (Chesterhall) Ltd v Finney Lock Seeds Ltd* [1983] 2 All E.R. 737 at 739, per Lord Diplock.
[79] For application of the reasonableness test, see Ch.9.
[80] [1966] 2 All E.R. 61.
[81] [1980] 1 All E.R. 556 at 567. See too *A Turtle Offshore SA v Superior Trading Inc* [2008] EWHC 3034.
[82] See generally para.8–023 and following.

read as applying only to such terms as allow no performance in exceptional circumstances, but not to clauses which give an arbitrary right not to perform. Such clauses would be avoided under the principles stated above. The 1977 Act, following enactment of the Consumer Rights Act 2014, now applies only in the case of business to business contracts. The 2014 Act would though apply the fairness test to any such clause in a consumer contract and, if a court found such a clause to have any substance, would doubtless hold it unfair. Paragraph 2 of Sch.2 to the Act provides that a clause excluding liability for non-performance ranks as a term which may be regarded as unfair.

CHAPTER 4

HARSH AND UNCONSCIONABLE BARGAINS

There is a definite, if slender, line of authority (as far as English law is **4–001**
concerned) showing that an agreement fairly stigmatised as harsh and
unconscionable may well be declared unenforceable in the courts. Should this
prove too drastic in the individual case, there is nonetheless a degree of
precedent, founded principally on certain remarks by Lord Denning, that if an
individual clause (more often than not an exclusion clause) is unreasonable it will
be struck down. This is in addition to ss.140A, 140B of the Consumer Credit Act
1974 which permit the reopening of credit agreements where there is an unfair
relationship between the parties.

UNCONSCIONABLE BARGAINS

In the leading case of *Fry v Lane*[1] a claim was made that the sale of a **4–002**
reversionary interest should be set aside. Reviewing the earlier decisions, Kay J.
observed that three criteria had to be fulfilled before equity would set aside a
particular bargain. First, the victim must be "poor and ignorant"; secondly, the
sale must be at an undervalue; thirdly, the victim must have had no independent
advice.[2]

This was updated by the judgment of Megarry J. in *Cresswell v Potter*.[3] A
matrimonial home had been conveyed to a husband and wife as joint tenants, at
law and equity. The marriage broke down and the wife was handed a document to
execute, described as a conveyance. In fact, it released to the husband all the
wife's interest in the home. She received no consideration other than an
indemnity against the liabilities under a mortgage of the property. She had
believed that the document made it possible for the property to be sold without
her rights being affected.

The judge assessed the case against the three criteria laid down by Kay J.
There was no doubt but that the disposition had been at an undervalue. It was also
a fact that the wife had received no independent legal advice. As for the final
requirement, that the claimant be "poor and ignorant", Megarry J. gave this a
modern tone. More appropriate terms, he said, would now be "member of the

---

[1] (1889) L.R. 40 Ch.D. 312.
[2] (1889) L.R. 40 Ch.D. 312 at 322. Among the previous authorities were: *Evans v Llewellin* [1787] 1
Cox Eq. Cas. 333; *Anderson v Elsworth* (1861) 3 Giff. 154; *Clarke v Malpas* [1862] 31 Beav. 801;
[1862] 4 De G.F. & J. 401. See generally Lawson, "The Law Relating to Improvident Bargains"
[1973] 24 N.I.L.Q. 171.
[3] [1978] 1 W.L.R. 255. See Ross-Martin [1971] 121 N.L.J. at 1160.

lower income group" and "less highly educated". Furthermore, this latter was to be construed in a relative sense: while the wife needed alertness in her career as a telephonist, in the context of property transactions she could fairly be described as "ignorant". This updating of *Fry v Lane* "demonstrates that the jurisdiction is in good heart and capable of adaptation to different transactions entered into in changing circumstances".[4]

This approach to the third condition clearly gives the courts considerable scope. While the better-off may obtain independent legal advice, they are as capable as the impoverished of believing independent legal advice to be unnecessary.

4–003   Although no reference was made to the above cases in *Jones v Morgan*,[5] the formulation there adopted was broadly to the same effect. The judge in the lower court had referred to the three elements which the High Court had identified, in *Alec Lobb (Garages) Ltd v Total Oil Great Britain Ltd*,[6] as characteristic of a case in which the court would interfere to relieve a party of a bargain on the ground of unconscionability: (i) that one party was at a serious disadvantage to the other, "whether through poverty or ignorance or lack of advice or otherwise", so that circumstances existed of which unfair advantage could be taken; (ii) that the weakness of the one party had been exploited by the other in some morally culpable manner; and (iii) that the resulting transaction has been, not merely hard and improvident, but overreaching and oppressive. The lower court had also referred to the observations in *Multiservice Bookbinding Ltd v Marden*[7] where it had been said that "a bargain cannot be unfair and unconscionable unless one of the parties to it has imposed the objectionable terms in a morally reprehensible manner, that is to say in a way which affects his conscience".[8]

In the instant case, the court said that the law on unconscionable bargains was not "in dispute". It agreed with what had been said in the *Marden* case, adding that the observations in that case had been approved in *Alec Lobb (Garages) Ltd v Total Oil Great Britain Ltd* where it had also been said that:

> "there must ... be some impropriety, both in the conduct of the stronger party and in the terms of the transaction itself (though the former may often be inferred from the latter in the absence of an innocent explanation) which in the traditional phrase 'shocks the conscience of the court', and makes it against equity and good conscience for the stronger party to retain the benefit of a transaction he has unfairly obtained."[9]

This was further refined in *Ruddick v Ormston*,[10] where it was said that a transaction could only stand if it could be shown to be objectively fair, just and reasonable. Inequality of bargaining power did not make the use of such power

---

[4]   *Portman Building Society v Dusangh* [2000] EWCA Civ 142, per Simon Brown L.J.
[5]   [2001] EWCA Civ 995.
[6]   [1983] 1 W.L.R. 87.
[7]   [1979] Ch. 84 at 110, per Browne-Wilkinson J.
[8]   See also *Greenwood Forest Products (UK) Ltd v Roberts* Unreported March 12, 2010 (HC).
[9]   [1983] 1 W.L.R. 87 at 95, per Millett L.J.
[10]   [2005] EWHC 2547 (Ch).

unconscionable. There had to be conduct that on any reasonable view involved the conscious and unfair exploitation or oppression of the weaker party. It was not enough that the contract was unfair.[11]

That the law is not confined to the impoverished is readily deducible from those early cases where reversioners of no small means were relieved from the consequences of their improvident agreements.[12] It is better, then, to read the expression "poor and ignorant" as now meaning "incapable of coping with the individual transaction without independent legal advice".[13]

Although making no formal decision to that effect, the High Court in *Liddle v Cree*[14] dealt with the argument that a mental incapacity could result in an unenforceable contract on the grounds that it was harsh and unconscionable. The parties had been the joint legal and beneficial owners of a farm that had a barn with planning permission for residential development. They executed Land Registry transfers partitioning the property into two titles; one of them the house and five acres of land, registered in Cree's sole name, the other the barn with 13 acres of land in Liddle's name. It was common ground that there was a disparity of £75,000 in value in Cree's favour for which no compensation was paid to Liddle. They had had a personal and business relationship for over 15 years, but the business had been wound up, and after the partition Liddle lived in the barn and Cree in the house.

4–004

Liddle had bipolar disorder and developed other illnesses shortly before and after the partition. Shortly after it, Cree wrote to social services describing Liddle's condition as one in which he would not be able to look after himself or make responsible decisions. Liddle's case was that he had come under Cree's domination while mentally debilitated and not understanding the disadvantageous nature and consequences of the partition. He submitted that his participation in the implementation of the partition was no more than the signing of documents which he was led to believe related merely to the winding-up of the partnership business. He argued that the transaction was a harsh and unconscionable bargain, completed when he was in a position of serious bargaining weakness, and that even if he and Cree had originally agreed in unobjectionable circumstances, Cree had taken unconscionable advantage in proceeding with it despite his declining health.

The argument that the court could interfere with a contract on the ground that it was harsh and unconscionable, was said by counsel to require proof of three requirements: (1) that the partition had become for Mr Liddle a harsh and oppressive bargain; (2) that it was completed at a time when he was suffering from a serious bargaining weakness; and (3) that even if it had been informally

---

[11] In *Boustany v Piggott* [1993] N.P.C. 75, it was said that, for a contract to be set aside in equity as unconscionable, the behaviour of the stronger party must be characterised by some moral culpability or impropriety. He must be guilty of some actual or constructive fraud. It is not enough to prove that a bargain is harsh, unreasonable or foolish. This is consonant with the requirement that the agreement be unconscionable.

[12] See, for example, *Everitt v Everitt* [1870] L.R. 10 Eq. 405.

[13] In *O'Rorke v Bolingbroke,* Lord Hatherley referred simply to "uneducated ignorant persons": [1877] L.R. 2 App. Cas. 814 at 823.

[14] [2011] EWHC 3294.

agreed under unobjectionable circumstances, Cree took unconscionable advantage of him in proceeding with it despite his declining health.

4–005   Briggs J. noted that Chitty had referred to the "doubtful general equitable principle that the court will interfere with freedom of contract on the ground that it is, in all the circumstances of the case, a harsh and unconscionable bargain".[15] Without deciding this issue one way or the other, he said that the criteria put forward by counsel had been met only in relation to the second of the above-described criteria.

A strong boost to the belief that grossly inequitable contracts are unenforceable was provided by the House of Lords in *Schroeder Music Publishing Co Ltd v Macaulay*.[16] The contract was one whereby a young and unknown songwriter entered into an agreement with a music publishing company, whereby the latter engaged his services exclusively for a period of five years. Such was the stringency of the contract in favour of the publishers (they were, for example, under no obligation even to publish any of the songwriter's publications) that it was urged that the contract was void for being an unreasonable restraint of trade. Lord Reid stressed that this particular contract, one cast in standard form, was not made freely by parties bargaining on equal terms, nor moulded under the pressures of negotiation, competition and public opinion.[17] This being so, he held the agreement unenforceable. Lord Diplock took a robust line. In such cases, he declared, the court intervenes to protect those "whose power is weak against being forced by those whose bargaining power is stronger to enter into bargains which are unconscionable".[18] His Lordship continued by dividing standard form contracts into two categories. One such category related to contracts moulded and produced by parties of equal bargaining power. Here a strong presumption is raised that the contract is fair and reasonable. Such contracts include bills of lading and policies of insurance.[19]

This presumption, Lord Diplock maintained, does not apply to the more modern category of standard contracts of which the nineteenth-century ticket cases are probably the best examples. These have not been subject to negotiation between the parties. They have been imposed by parties whose bargaining power enables them to say: "If you want these goods or services at all, these are the only terms on which they are obtainable. Take it or leave it".[20]

Such cases raise no presumption of unconscionability, but the court must consider all the terms of the agreement to determine the issue of enforceability.[21]The vital factor to note was that, although this was a case involving an alleged restraint of trade, Lord Diplock pushed the discussion beyond such confines. His clear belief was that any standard form contract imposed upon a party of weaker bargaining power could be void for unconscionability, regardless of the nature of the contract. Indeed, there is no reason to suppose that Lord Diplock would confine himself to standard term

---

[15] Chitty on Contracts, 30th edn, para.7–132.
[16] [1974] 3 All E.R. 616.
[17] [1974] 3 All E.R. 616 at 622.
[18] [1974] 3 All E.R. 616 at 623.
[19] [1974] 3 All E.R. 616 at 623.
[20] [1974] 3 All E.R. 616 at 624.
[21] [1974] 3 All E.R. 616 at 623 and 624.

contracts. A verbal contract, or a written contract produced for the particular occasion only, can equally be imposed on weaker parties.

This decision of the House of Lords was applied in the not dissimilar case of **4–006** *Clifford Davis Management Ltd v WEA Records Ltd*.[22] Composers of popular songs signed publishing agreements with music publishers. Among the terms of the agreements were clauses assigning copyright in the songs to the publishers and giving the publishers the right to reject any work without payment. Even when a work was retained, the publishers were under no obligation to exploit it. The present action was for an interlocutory injunction to prevent the composers from breaking the agreement. Since this was the nature of the action, no firm rule of law was required or given. Lord Denning, however, was quick to point to the words of Lord Diplock in the House of Lords. He found it clear on the evidence that the composers had received no independent legal advice: it may well be said that "there was such inequality of bargaining power that the agreement should not be enforced . . .".[23] Certainly, the balance of convenience was that the injunction ought to be discharged.[24]

The Court of Appeal had enunciated similar principles in *Lloyds Bank Ltd v Bundy*.[25] The owner of land had mortgaged his property to support a business venture of his son's. The bank had foreclosed and sought possession of the land. The evidence showed that the owner was an elderly man not well versed in business affairs. Nor did he receive any independent advice. Reviewing the cases, including *Fry v Lane*, Lord Denning found the principle to be that relief is given to one:

> "who, without independent advice, enters into a contract on terms which are very unfair or transfers property for a consideration which is grossly inadequate, when his bargaining power is grievously impaired by reason of his own needs or desires, or by his own ignorance or infirmity, coupled with undue influences or pressures brought to bear on him by or for the benefit of another."[26]

Sir Eric Sachs was only concerned with the fact that the bank, by failing to ensure that the mortgagor had independent advice, was in breach of its duty to take fiduciary care.[27]

---

[22] [1975] 1 All E.R. 237.
[23] [1975] 1 All E.R. 237 at 240.
[24] [1975] 1 All E.R. 237 at 240.
[25] [1974] 3 All E.R. 757.
[26] [1974] 3 All E.R. 757 at 765.
[27] [1974] 3 All E.R. 757 at 770. See also *National Westminster Bank Plc v Morgan* [1985] 1 All E.R. 821; *Kings North Trust Ltd v Bell* [1986] 1 All E.R. 423; *Midland Bank Plc v Shepherd* [1988] B.T.L.C. 395; *Zang Tumb Tumb Records v Holly Johnson* Unreported, 26 July 1989; CA; *Barclays Bank v O'Brien* [1993] 4 All E.R. 417; *CIBC Mortgages Plc v Pitt* [1993] 4 All E.R. 433; *Cheese v Thomas* [1994] 1 All E.R. 35; *Dunbar Bank Plc v Nadeem* [1998] 3 All E.R. 876; *Bank of Cyprus (London) Ltd v Markou* [1999] 2 All E.R. 707; *Royal Bank of Scotland v Etridge (No.2)* [2001] 4 All E.R. 449; *Lloyds TSB Plc v Holdgate* [2002] EWCA Civ 1543; *Thomson v Royal Bank of Scotland Plc* [2003] ScotCS 284; *Royal Bank of Scotland Plc v Chandra* [2010] EWCA Civ 105; *Proactive Sports Management Ltd v (1) Wayne Rooney (2) Coleen Rooney (formerly Mcloughlin) (3) Stoneygate 48 Ltd (4) Speed 9849 Ltd* [2011] EWCA Civ 1444.

This particular case is extraordinarily close to one which it did not cite, the decision of Crisp J. in *Harrison v National Bank of Australasia Ltd.*[28] An elderly woman, without legal advice, gave a bank security over land. The money was to aid her son-in-law in a business venture. She knew that she would be liable should the business fail, although she was completely ignorant of business matters. Crisp J. set the agreement aside, noting that the court will set aside a bargain entered into "without due deliberation, without independent advice and not knowing its true effect".[29]

4–007   In *Lloyds Bank v Bundy*, Lord Denning recognised that not "every transaction is saved by independent advice".[30] This had already been attested to in *Grealish v Murphy*.[31] A settlement of land and money was made by a person suffering from some degree of backwardness. He received independent legal advice, but the solicitor neither knew all the facts nor gave the settlor a complete explanation of the nature and effect of the settlement. The solicitor was also unaware of the full extent of the settlor's backwardness. In such circumstances, and despite the independent advice, the court set the agreement aside.[32]

These cases indicate a willingness to accept that contracts may become unenforceable if harsh and unconscionable, particularly where independent advice has not been obtained.[33] While exclusion clauses were not an issue in any of these cases, it still seems safe to say that the measure and extent of any exclusion clause can be a relevant factor in determining whether a contract may be so inequitable as to be unenforceable. Although a decision has never yet had to be cast in such terms, it must be possible that a consumer contract or a business contract for the hire of a television, the purchase of goods, or the leasing of equipment, will be declared void, not least because of the stringency of the exclusion clauses.

REASONABLENESS

4–008   As far back as *Parker v South Eastern Railway Co*,[34] there have been obiter asserting a right in the courts to ignore as void those exclusion clauses which are unreasonable. Bramwell L.J. asked himself: "what if there was some unreasonable condition, for instance, to forfeit £1,000 if the goods were not removed within 24 hours?" The Lord Justice argued against the clause being binding if the particular individual was told that the conditions were there to be read, but did not in fact read them. I think, he said, that:

---

[28] (1928) 23 Tas. L.R. 1.
[29] (1928) 23 Tas. L.R. 1 at 8.
[30] [1974] 3 All E.R. 757 at 765.
[31] [1946] I.R. 35.
[32] Accepted as correct, but distinguished in *Haverty v Brooks* [1970] I.R. 214.
[33] Except where the advice was refused: *Harrison v Guest* (1855) 6 De G.M. & G. 426; (1860) 8 H.L.C. 481.
[34] (1877) L.R. 2 C.P.D. 416.

"there is an implied understanding that there is no condition unreasonable to the knowledge of the party tendering the document and not insisting on its being read—no condition not relevant to the matter in hand."[35]

It appears that if the contract had been read (or, perhaps, if the one contracting party had ignored the other's insistence on the condition being read) or if the unreasonable terms were relevant to the matter in hand, then the term would have been effective. This, though, is perhaps to go too far since, in *Thompson v London, Midland Co & Scottish Railway*,[36] Lawrence L.J. expressly endorsed the view of Bramwell L.J., saying:

"If there were a condition which was unreasonable to the knowledge of the company tendering the ticket I do not think the passenger would be bound."[37]

This seems to mean that the mere unreasonableness of a clause invalidates it, read or not by the other side. Sankey L.J. too thought that a "ridiculous condition" would not be binding: nor, he added, would conditions printed in Chinese.[38] The most vigorous modern proponent of this view, not unexpectedly, has been Lord Denning. In *John Lee & Son (Grantham) Ltd v Railway Executive*,[39] he expressed an opinion that an unreasonably onerous term in a standard form contract would not be enforced in the courts, for "there is the vigilance of the common law which, while allowing freedom of contract, watches to see that it is not abused".[40] In *Thornton v Shoe Lane Parking Ltd*,[41] Lord Denning, when judging a particular clause, did not "pause to enquire whether the exempting condition is void for unreasonableness",[42] clearly believing there were circumstances where this could be so.

Yet a further example is *Gillespie Bros & Co Ltd v Roy Bowles Transport Ltd*,[43] where Lord Denning restated the views first expressed in *John Lee & Son (Grantham) Ltd v Railway Executive*: the common law "will not allow a party to exempt himself from his liability at common law when it would be quite unconscionable for him to do so".[44]

These various observations are all, however, obiter dicta[45]: more than that, they have on occasions been actively contradicted. In *Grand Trunk Railway Company of Canada v Robinson*,[46] Viscount Haldane, referring to the implied duty of care

4–009

---

[35] (1877) L.R. 2 C.P.D. 416 at 428.
[36] [1930] 1 K.B. 41.
[37] [1930] 1 K.B. 41 at 53.
[38] [1930] 1 K.B. 41 at 56.
[39] [1949] 2 All E.R. 581.
[40] [1949] 2 All E.R. 581 at 584.
[41] [1971] 1 All E.R. 686.
[42] [1971] 1 All E.R. 686 at 690.
[43] [1973] 1 All E.R. 193.
[44] [1973] 1 All E.R. 193 at 200. See also *Foley Motors Ltd v McGhee* [1970] N.Z.L.R. 649 at 652, per Richmond J.
[45] In *Watkins v Rymill* (1882–83) L.R. 10 Q.B.D. 178 at 189, Stephen J., referring to the statement of Bramwell L.J., said "there is no absolute decision on this point".
[46] [1915] A.C. 740.

incumbent on a railway company, observed that this duty can be superseded by a specific contract which may enlarge, diminish or exclude it. Such a contract, if authorised by the law:

"cannot be pronounced to be unreasonable ... The specific contract, with its incidents either expressed or attached by law, becomes in such a case the only measure of the duties between the parties, and the claimant cannot by any device of form [sic] get more than the contract allows him."[47]

This was accepted as a statement of general principle by the Privy Council in *Ludditt v Ginger Coote Airways*.[48]

A more robust dissent came in the *Gillespie* case itself. It is not, said Buckley L.J., the "function of a court of construction to fashion a contract in such a way as to produce a result which the court considers that it would have been fair or reasonable for the parties to have intended", although he allowed that, in the event of two possible interpretations, the court should adopt the more reasonable.[49]

An even more substantial blow to the proponents of Lord Denning's view came in *Suisse Atlantique*.[50] There is no indication, said Lord Reid, "that the courts are to consider whether the exemption is fair in all the circumstances or is harsh and unconscionable or whether it was freely agreed by the customer ... it appears to me that its solution should be left to Parliament".[51] This was approved by Donaldson J. in *Kenyon, Son & Craven v Baxter Hoare & Co*.[52]

Undaunted, Lord Denning restated his beliefs in *Levison v Patent Steam Carpet Cleaning Co*.[53] His view was that the exclusion clause was unreasonable, and this was one of his grounds for finding against the defendants.[54] He also held that the doctrine of fundamental breach applies to standard form contracts where there has been an inequality of bargaining power. Where the superior party has imposed an exclusion clause on the weaker party, it will not be valid where he has been guilty of a breach going to the root of the contract.[55] None of the other Lord Justices discussed the point.

4–010   Lord Denning gave his final summing-up on the common law and the test of reasonableness in *Photo Production Ltd v Securicor Transport Ltd*.[56] The point we have now reached, he felt, and one which "lies behind all our striving" is that:

"the court will not allow a party to rely on an exemption or limitation clause in circumstances in which it would not be fair or reasonable to allow reliance on it; and, in considering whether

---

[47] [1915] A.C. 740 at 747.
[48] [1947] 1 All E.R. 328 at 331, per Lord Wright.
[49] [1973] 1 All E.R. 193 at 205.
[50] [1966] 2 All E.R. 61.
[51] [1966] 2 All E.R. 61 at 76.
[52] [1971] 2 All E.R. 708 at 720.
[53] [1977] 3 All E.R. 498.
[54] [1977] 3 All E.R. 498 at 503.
[55] [1977] 3 All E.R. 498 at 504.
[56] [1978] 3 All E.R. 146. He repeated his views in *George Mitchell (Chesterhall) Ltd v Finney Lock Seeds Ltd* [1983] 1 All E.R. 108 at 115.

it is fair and reasonable, the court will consider whether it was in a standard form, whether there was equality of bargaining power, the nature of the breach and so forth."[57]

He acknowledged that this was to follow the lead provided by Parliament in the Supply of Goods (Implied Terms) Act 1973, and in the Unfair Contract Terms Act 1977.[58] The judge below had found that the exclusion clause in this case was reasonable. Lord Denning, however, judged that it was not fair and reasonable to allow Securicor to rely on the disputed clause when it was their own patrolman whose deliberate act burned down the factory.[59] Yet again, it has to be reported that none of the other Lord Justices discussed the point. In the House of Lords, no discussion was given to whether there was an independent common law doctrine of reasonableness to be applied to exclusion clauses. Lord Wilberforce did say, though, that he found the clause to be a reasonable allocation of the risk.[60]

In the *Photo Production* case, Lord Denning had switched from the reasonableness of the clause to the different question as to whether the clause (which could well be reasonable) was one on which it would be fair and reasonable to allow reliance. Either way, however, Lord Denning's views (even after conceding that he has not been altogether alone in what he has had to say) must be treated with considerable circumspection. Indeed, the very existence of the Unfair Contract Terms Act 1977, and its requirement of reasonableness, indicates an omission in the common law. Yet considerable sympathy must still extend to this view, particularly in the form in which it was expressed in *Gibaud v Great Eastern Railway Co.*[61] If, said Bray J., a condition is so "irrelevant or extravagant" that it must have been known that the recipient never intended to be so bound, his assent to the contract would be deemed to have been obtained by fraud. The mere fact of a condition being unreasonable would not of itself, however, show fraud. Indeed, he held that the county court judge erred when holding that the claimant was not bound because the clause was unreasonable.[62] Sankey J. went slightly further, saying that an extravagant condition (such as having to claim the goods in five minutes) is tantamount to fraud, while irrelevant ones (such as requiring the depositor of goods to become a shareholder in the bailee company) are for that reason not binding.[63] There is much to be said for such a view, which falls short of eliminating clauses that are merely unreasonable. It still remains, however, for the matter to be decided authoritatively.[64]

---

[57] [1978] 3 All E.R. 146 at 153.
[58] [1978] 3 All E.R. 146 at 153.
[59] [1978] 3 All E.R. 146 at 154.
[60] [1980] 1 All E.R. 556 at 564.
[61] [1920] 3 K.B. 689.
[62] [1920] 3 K.B. 689 at 699–700.
[63] [1920] 3 K.B. 689 at 703.
[64] The case was affirmed on appeal, but the present matters were not discussed: [1921] 2 K.B. 426.

PART 2

LEGISLATIVE CONTROL

CHAPTER 5

UNLAWFUL EXCLUSION CLAUSES

PRELIMINARY

The question whether exclusion or limitation clauses are illegal raises questions as to the interpretation of the Consumer Protection from Unfair Trading Regulations 2008.[1]

5–001

UNFAIR COMMERCIAL PRACTICES

Regulation 3(1) prohibits unfair commercial practices. Regulation 3(3) states that a commercial practice is unfair if it:

5–002

(a) contravenes the requirements of professional diligence; and
(b) it materially distorts or is likely to distort the economic behaviour of the average consumer with regard to the product.

RELEVANT DEFINITIONS

Regulation 2(1), as so amended, defines "product" to mean (a) goods, (b) a service, (c) digital content, (d) immoveable property, (e) rights or obligations. A "product" can also be the demand by a trader. In such a case the product that the trader offers to supply comprises the full or partial settlement of those liabilities or purported liabilities. for a full or partial settlement of liabilities owed or purported to be owed by a consumer. "Goods" means "any tangible moveable items, but that includes water, gas and electricity if and only if they are put up for sale in a limited volume or set quantity." "Professional diligence" means the standard of special skill and care which a trader may reasonably be expected to exercise towards consumers which is commensurate with either:

5–003

(a) honest market practice in the trader's field of activity; or
(b) the general principle of good faith in the trader's field of activity.[2]

---

[1] SI 2008/1277 as amended by the Consumer Protection (Amendment) Regulations 2014 (SI 2014/870).
[2] "It is interesting to see that the relatively unfamiliar concepts of 'honest market practice' and 'the general principle of good faith', which are both relevant to the concept of 'professional diligence' . . . are construed in such a way that a breach may be found even in the absence of dishonesty as it is traditionally understood in domestic jurisprudence": *Tiscali UK Ltd v British Telecommunications Plc* [2008] EWHC 3129 (QB), per Eady J.

An activity materially distorts the economic behaviour of a consumer, in relation to the average consumer, if it appreciably impairs such consumer's ability to make an informed decision, thereby causing him to take a transactional decision he would not have taken otherwise. Finally, a "transactional decision" means any decision, whether it is to act or not to act, in relation to:

(a)   whether, how and on what terms to purchase, make payment in whole or in part for, retain or dispose of the product; or
(b)   whether, how and on what terms to exercise a contractual right in relation to a product.

When considering the effect of a practice on an "average consumer", reg.2(2) requires account to be taken of the material characteristics of such a consumer "including his being reasonably well informed, reasonably observant and circumspect".

POSSIBLE APPLICATION TO EXCLUSION CLAUSES

5–004   It may well be that a trader makes use of an exclusion clause which is so drafted as to exclude liability in a comprehensive way, even drafted with sufficient clarity and precision to exclude liability for negligence. A consumer seeing such a clause might well be prompted not to enter into the proffered contract. The average consumer would probably be unaware of his rights to challenge such a clause under the Unfair Contract Terms Act 1977 or the Consumer Rights Act 2014. Indeed, this reasoning is valid in relation to any exclusion or limitation clause, since the average consumer cannot be expected to be aware of his rights under those enactments. Thus, the commercial practice of including an exclusion or limitation clause in a contract could arguably be said to impair the average consumer's ability to make an informed decision as to the making of a transactional decision. It may well be that the effect of the Regulations in such a case is to ensure that the trader complies with the requirements of professional diligence only if the contract also advises the consumer of his rights to challenge the relevant clause under either or both of these enactments. The use of clauses rendered void by the Unfair Contract Terms Act (and now in relation to consumer contracts by the 2014 Act)[3] was originally an offence under the now repealed 1976 Order.[4] The use of such clauses would undoubtedly give rise to a breach of professional diligence and, in line with the foregoing arguments, could well constitute an unfair commercial practice, and hence be illegal under the Regulations.

---

[3] See para.10–012.
[4] This being a reference to the Consumer Transactions (Restrictions on Statements) Order 1976 (SI 1976/1813) which was repealed by the 2008 Regulations.

MISLEADING ACTIONS

The argument for the possible illegality of exclusion clauses under the **5–005**
Regulations gains perhaps greater support from the application of those
Regulations to misleading actions. These also constitute an unfair, and hence
illegal, commercial practice if the action falls within the definition set out in reg.5
as applied by reg.3(4)(a). A practice will be a misleading action if it contains false
information and is therefore untruthful in relation to any of a number of matters,
and if it causes or is likely to cause a consumer to take a transactional decision he
would not otherwise have made. It is also misleading if, in its overall
presentation, it deceives or is likely to deceive the consumer in relation to any of
the listed matters. The listed matters include:

(a)   the extent of the trader's commitments; and
(b)   the consumer's rights.

A contract containing a clause rendered void by the 2014 Act could easily be
subsumed under either of these headings and, since the presence of such clauses
could well deter a consumer from making a purchase, the clause would thus
become illegal. Similarly, clauses rendered void by other enactments could, if
they involved contracts which would fall within these Regulations, amount to
illegal clauses.[5]

Again, a trader who makes use of clauses which are not automatically void,
but which may become so under the 2014 Act, may well be guilty of a misleading
action. The trader who fails to spell out that such clauses could be challenged
could be said to be falsely stating the extent of his commitments, in that he is
inferring that he has no commitment in relation to the relevant exclusions, when
this is not necessarily so, given the possible impact of the Act.

The Regulations also state that the "consumer's rights" referred to in the relevant   **5–006**
list includes his rights under Pt 5A of the Sale of Goods Act 1979 and Pt 1B of the
Supply of Goods and Services Act 1982. These refer to the rights of the consumer
buyer, when goods do not conform to the contract, to seek a repair or replacement
of the goods, or to a reduction in the price.[6]

The listed items also refer to an indication of the trader's rights. These are as
defined by reg.5(6), and it can be accepted that none of the items listed within
that definition (identity, assets, qualifications, status, approval, affiliations or
connections, ownership of industrial, commercial or intellectual property; awards
and distinctions) have any bearing on exclusion clauses. The definition, however,
is stated to be inclusive not exhaustive. Accordingly, it is arguable that using
clauses automatically void, or which are subject to challenge under the 2014 Act,
is a false statement as to the trader's rights since, in the first case, using void
clauses is a clear mis-statement as to the trader's rights (to deny redress in certain
cases); or, in the second, the use of clauses subject to challenge on grounds of

---

[5] See Ch.6.
[6] These provisions were inserted by the Sale and Supply of Goods to Consumers Regulations 2002
(SI 2002/3045).

fairness or reasonableness could amount to a false statement of the trader's right automatically to rely on the particular clause.

MISLEADING OMISSIONS

5–007 Regulation 6 provides that a commercial practice constituters a misleading omission (and hence becomes an illegal unfair practice under reg.3(4)(b)) in the following cases:

(a)   the commercial practice omits material information;
(b)   the commercial practice hides material information; and
(c)   the commercial practice provides material information in a manner which is unclear, unintelligible, ambiguous or untimely.

In all cases, the further qualification is that the omission must have caused, or be likely to cause, the average consumer to take a transactional decision he would not have taken otherwise. "Material information" is defined by reg.6(3) as meaning "the information which the average consumer needs, according to the context, to take an informed transactional decision". This clearly embraces important matters such as exclusion clauses. It is also expressly stated to cover any information requirement applied by virtue of an obligation arising from UK membership of the European Union.

OMITTING MATERIAL INFORMATION

5–008 The trader who uses an exclusion clause which is automatically void, without pointing out the invalidity of such a clause (which is not that likely) is surely omitting material information. Again, the trader who fails to warn that a clause can be challenged under the 2014 Act could clearly be said to be omitting material information.

It can also be said that the trader whose contract says "subject to terms and conditions", without immediately disclosing that those terms and conditions contain an exclusion clause, is also omitting material information.

HIDING MATERIAL INFORMATION

5–009 It is not clear just what is meant in this context by "hiding". It seems fairly clear that it could cover the case of a trader who, perhaps even inadvertently, obliterates an exclusion clause. Thus, a trader who presents a contractual document with the relevant clause wholly or substantially obliterated, or with the contract folded so as to cover up the exclusion clause, could now be said to be guilty of hiding material information.[7]

---

[7] See *Richardson Spence & Co Ltd v Rowntree* [1894] A.C. 217, discussed at para.1–010.

It is also highly arguable that material information is hidden if, for example, the colour or the size of the print, or even perhaps the use of a foreign language, renders the contract terms unreadable.

UNCLEAR, ETC.

In the context of exclusion clauses, much greater attention should perhaps be given to reg.6(3)(c) which refers to the provision of material information "in a manner which is unclear, unintelligible, ambiguous or untimely". It can hardly be doubted that many contract terms, whether or not exclusion or limitation clauses, will fall foul of the first three of these categories. An untimely clause could be one presented when the consumer is already committed to a transaction and has no realistic chance of withdrawing from the contract, as when a ticket from a parking barrier is revealed only when the barrier is activated.[8] Failure to provide the relevant terms earlier in the procedure can be said to have induced a transactional decision which would not otherwise have been made.

5–010

THE CONTEXT OF THE OMISSION

In deciding whether an omission is misleading, reg.6(1) requires certain matters to be taken into account. These are: all the features and circumstances of the commercial practice; the limitations of the medium used to communicate the commercial practice (including limitations of space or time); where the practice does impose these latter limitations, account must be taken of measures adopted by the trader to make the information available by other means. Online advertising might direct consumers on how to buy without providing a proper opportunity to see the terms and conditions on which a purchase is to be made, particularly if a time constraint is imposed on the consumer. It would appear from reg.6 that the display must be such that a consumer must be given the chance to see a full set of terms and conditions before he is committed to the purchase.[9] It would be enough for the first page to show those terms, or at least to be given advice as to where those terms can be inspected, before any commitment is made by him to purchase. This view is strengthened by reg.6(4) which, in the context of an invitation to purchase, lists certain items which constitute material information (that list not being relevant here) but which is stated to be in addition to "material information" as defined above.[10]

5–011

It was noted above that one of the factors to be taken into account when determining if an omission was unfair was "the limitations of the medium used to communicate the commercial practice". It is not clear if this is to be read in favour of the trader or the consumer. If the trader, it could allow a trader who uses a deliberately impractical way of communicating the information to escape the charge of providing a misleading omission. Given that the Regulations are a measure of consumer protection, it is more likely that this will be read in favour

---

[8] See the discussion of *Thornton v Shoe Lane Parking Ltd* [1971] 2 Q.B. 163 at para.1–018.
[9] See *Motor Depot Ltd v Kingston upon Hull City Council* [2012] EWHC 3257.
[10] See para.5–007.

of the consumer, thus accepting that an offence may arise where the trader chooses an impractical measure if appropriate measures are not taken to overcome the problems posed. This is supported by the fact that, when the limitations are of time or space, reg.6(3)(c) does expressly state that account must be taken of any measures taken to overcome the problems caused.

AGGRESSIVE COMMERCIAL PRACTICES

5–012   Subject to the usual requirement that the practice must cause a consumer to take a transactional decision he would not have taken otherwise, reg.7 bans practices which significantly impair the average consumer's freedom of choice through the use of harassment, coercion or undue influence. As a practical matter, "coercion" (defined in reg.7(3)(a) to include physical force) can be discounted. Regulation 7(3)(b) defines "undue influence" as meaning the exploitation of a "position of power in relation to the consumer so as to apply pressure, even without using or threatening to use physical force, in a way which significantly limits or reduces the consumer's ability to make an informed decision". One of the matters to be taken into account, as spelled out in reg.7(2)(d) is the "onerous or disproportion-ate, non-contractual barrier imposed by the trader where a consumer wishes to exercise rights under the contract, including the rights to terminate a contract...". If then, a utility excludes or limits liability for any breach on its part, and then threatens immediately to disconnect the consumer should the latter wish, for example, to challenge the clause under the 2014 Act, and thus sue for breach, then this would amount to unlawful aggressive behaviour. It should be recalled that the definition of "transactional decision" contained in reg.2(1) refers to any decision taken by a consumer "whether, how and on what terms to exercise a contractual right".

It could also be maintained that, if a powerful organisation stipulates that it will not accept a contract without an exclusion clause, or that it will not negotiate around an existing clause placed before the consumer, that too is undue influence. The list of factors to be taken into account by reg.7(2) refers to nothing of this kind, but there is no stipulation that reg.7(2) is exhaustive. It is thus permissible to say that all matters can be taken into account when deciding if a practice is aggressive, not just the items listed.

Harassment is not defined. It is thus permissible to argue that a trader who is constantly chivvying a consumer to sign a contract containing an exclusion clause is guilty of an aggressive trade practice.

OFFENCES

5–013   Regulation 8 provides that a trader[11] is guilty of an offence if he knowingly or recklessly engages in a commercial practice which contravenes the requirements of professional diligence under reg.3(3)(a), and the practice materially distorts or is likely to materially distort the economic behaviour of the average consumer

---

[11] For guidance on who can constitute a trader under the Regulations, see *R. v Scottish and Southern Energy Plc* [2012] EWCA Crim 539.

with regard to the product under reg.3(3)(b).[12] A trader is reckless if he engages in a commercial practice without regard to whether the practice contravenes the requirements of professional diligence and shall be deemed recklessly to engage in the practice, whether or not the trader has reason for believing that the practice might contravene those requirements. This is therefore not an offence of strict liability. In contrast, the offences relating to misleading actions, misleading omission and aggressive trade practices are strict liability offences,[13] as is a breach of the 31 prohibited practices[14] (with the exception of those listed in paras 11 and 28, which are not offences at all, though they could be subject to enforcement action under the Enterprise Act 2002). Similarly, no offence arises where the misleading action is one of failure to observe a code of practice, but again action could be taken under the 2002 Act.

The penalty on summary conviction is a fine not exceeding £5,000. On indictment, the penalty is a fine, a sentence not exceeding two years, or a combination of the two.[15]

ENFORCEMENT

The Regulations are enforced by the Competition and Markets Authority and local weights and measures authorities. Regulations 20–25 provide for: power to make test purchases; power of entry and investigation, etc.; power to enter premises with a warrant; obstruction of authorised officers; notice of test and intended proceedings; and compensation.[16] An amendment was made to the Enterprise Act 2002 (Pt 8 Community Infringements Specified UK Laws) Order 2003[17] to include a reference to the Regulations. This will allow injunctions and undertakings to be obtained under the Act against offending traders.

5–014

DEFENCES

Regulation 17 provides for the due diligence defence. A person is entitled to an acquittal if he can show that the offences were due to (i) a mistake; (ii) reliance on information supplied to him by another person; (iii) the act or default of another person; (iv) an accident; or (v) another cause beyond his control; and that he took all reasonable precautions and exercised all due diligence to avoid the commission of such an offence by himself or any person under his control.[18]

5–015

---

[12] For examples of offences (none though concerning exclusion or limitation clauses), see *R. v Parking Control Services Ltd* [2012] EWCA Crim 1560; *R. v Williams* [2012] EWCA Crim 1483; *Secretary of State for Business, Innovation and Skills v Anti-Marketing Ltd* [2013] EWHC 3626; *R. v Scott King* [2014] EWCA Crim 62.

[13] See *R. v Stone (Rodney)* [2012] EWCA Crim 186 and *Price v East Cheshire Borough Council* [2012] EWHC 2927.

[14] See para 5–021.

[15] See *R. v Connors* [2012] EWCA Crim 2106.

[16] See *R. v Brent Magistrates' Court* [2012] EWHC 2140.

[17] SI 2003/1374.

[18] Illustrative cases on the due diligence defence, which appears in several enactments, notably the Trade Descriptions Act 1968, now repealed, include: *Sherratt v Gerald's The American Jewellers Ltd* (1970) 68 L.G.R. 256; *Hicks v S.D. Sullam Ltd* (1983) 147 J.P. 488; *Taylor v Lawrence Frazer*

Regulation 18 provides for the innocent publication of an advertisement. In any proceedings against a person for an offence committed by the publication of an advertisement it shall be a defence for a person to prove that: (a) he is a person whose business it is to publish or to arrange for the publication of advertisements; (b) he received the advertisement for publication in the ordinary course of business; and (c) he did not know and had no reason to suspect that its publication would amount to an offence under the regulation to which the proceedings relate. This is a defence available to the media but not to advertising agencies since they would not receive an advertisement for publication within (b) above.

THE BY-PASS PROVISION

5–016   Regulation 16 provides that, where an offence arises, and such offence arises because of the act or default of another, then that other can be prosecuted under the Regulations even if that other is not a trader or engaged in a commercial practice. That other person can be prosecuted whether or not proceedings are brought against the party actually committing the offence.[19]

TIME LIMIT

5–017   Regulation 14 provides that no proceedings for an offence under these Regulations shall be commenced after: (a) the end of the period of three years beginning with the date of the commission of the offence, or (b) the end of the period of one year beginning with the date of discovery of the offence by the prosecutor, whichever is earlier.

(Bristol) Ltd (1977) 121 S.J. 157; *Riley v Webb* [1987] C.C.L.R. 65; *Rotherham Metropolitan Borough Council v Raysun (UK) Ltd* [1989] C.C.L.R. 1; *Hurley v Martinez* [1991] C.C.L.R. 1; *P&M Supplies (Essex) Ltd v Devon CC* [1991] C.C.L.R. 71; *Robert Gale v Dixon's Stores Group* (1994) 158 J.P.N. 256; *Berkshire CC v Olympic Holidays Ltd* (1994) 158 J.P.N. 337; *Carrick District Council v Taunton Vale Meat Traders Ltd* (1994) 158 J.P.N. 319; *Westminster City Council v Pierglow* Unreported February 8, 1994; *London Borough of Sutton v David Halsall* (1995) 159 J.P.N. 431; *Warwickshire CC v Verco* Unreported June 28, 1994; *Coventry City Council v Ackerman Group Plc* [1995] Crim L.R. 140; *Bury MBC v United Norwest Co-Operatives Ltd* Unreported November 14, 1994; *South Tyneside Metropolitan Borough Council v Gill* Unreported November 28, 1994; *Coventry City Council v Lazarus* (1996) 160 J.P. 188; *Alan Balding v Leeways Ltd* Unreported February 21, 1995; *R. v F&M Dobson Ltd* Unreported March 2, 1995; *Tesco Stores Ltd v North Norfolk DC* (1999) 78 P. & C.R. 359; *Kilhey Court Hotels Ltd v Wigan MBC* [2004] EWHC 2890 Admin; *Davies v Carmarthenshire CC* [2005] EWHC 464 Admin.

[19] See for example *Padgett Bros (A–Z) Ltd v Coventry City Council* (1998) 162 J.P. 673. The case was heard under the General Product Safety Regulations 1994 (SI 1994/2328), since replaced by the General Product Safety Regulations 2005 (SI 2005/1803).

RIGHT OF REDRESS

Where a trader has been guilty of an aggressive or misleading trade practice contrary to the Regulations, the consumer has a right of redress which can be the right to unwind the relevant contract or to obtain a discount.[20]

5–017A

BUSINESS PROTECTION

The foregoing provisions do, of course, apply only to traders when dealing with consumers. The scope of the Business Protection from Misleading Marketing Regulations 2008[21] is much less wide. Regulation 3(1) creates the sole offence under the Regulations, that of misleading advertising, and reg.2(1) defines "advertising" as "any form of representation which is made in connection with a trade, business, craft or profession in order to promote the supply or transfer of a product". In turn, reg.3(2) defines advertising as being "misleading" if, in any way, including its presentation, it "deceives or is likely to deceive the traders to whom it is addressed or whom it reaches; and by reason of its deceptive nature, is likely to affect their economic behaviour; or ... for those reasons, injures or is likely to injure a competitor".

5–018

The precise terms of a contract will hardly, if ever, come under the definition of "advertising". On the other hand, the trader who advertises certain terms of the contract, perhaps free delivery, a price claim, or perhaps that "we guarantee the quality of our goods", but who does not also mention the presence of exclusion clauses could well be guilty of misleading advertising. This is supported by reg.3(3)(c) which says that, when determining if an advertisement is misleading, account is to be taken of the conditions on which the product is supplied or provided.

OFFENCES, ETC.

The provisions discussed above as to offences, defences, the due diligence defence, the by-pass provision, time limits and enforcement have their exact counterparts in these Regulations.[22]

5–019

COMMERCIAL PRACTICES WHICH ARE IN ALL CIRCUMSTANCES CONSIDERED UNFAIR

1. Claiming to be a signatory to a code of conduct when the trader is not.
2. Displaying a trust mark, quality mark or equivalent without having obtained the necessary authorisation.
3. Claiming that a code of conduct has an endorsement from a public or other body which it does not have.

5–020

---

[20] See Pt 4A of the 2008 Regulations as inserted by the Consumer Protection (Amendment) Regulations 2014 (SI 2014/870).
[21] SI 2008/1276.
[22] See Pts 2 and 3 of the Regulations. See *R. v York Magistrates' Court* [2012] EWHC 3636.

4. Claiming that a trader (including his commercial practices) or a product has been approved, endorsed or authorised by a public or private body when the trader, the commercial practices or the product have not; or making such a claim without complying with the terms of the approval, endorsement or authorisation.

5. Making an invitation to purchase products at a specified price without disclosing the existence of any reasonable grounds the trader may have for believing that he will not be able to offer for supply, or to procure another trader to supply, those products or equivalent products at that price for a period that is, and in quantities that are, reasonable having regard to the product, the scale of advertising of the product and the price offered (bait advertising).

6. Making an invitation to purchase products at a specified price and then:
   (a) refusing to show the advertised item to consumers;
   (b) refusing to take orders for it or deliver it within a reasonable time; or
   (c) demonstrating a defective sample of it with the intention of promoting a different product (bait and switch).

7. Falsely stating that a product will only be available for a very limited time, or that it will only be available on particular terms for a very limited time, in order to elicit an immediate decision and deprive consumers of sufficient opportunity or time to make an informed choice.

8. Undertaking to provide after-sales service to consumers with whom the trader has communicated prior to a transaction, in a language which is not an official language of the EEA State where the trader is located, and then making such service available only in another language without clearly disclosing this to the consumer before the consumer is committed to the transaction.

9. Stating or otherwise creating the impression that a product can legally be sold when it cannot.

10. Presenting rights given to consumers in law as a distinctive feature of the trader's offer.

11. Using editorial content in the media to promote a product where a trader has paid for the promotion without making that clear in the content or by images or sounds clearly identifiable by the consumer (advertorial).

12. Making a materially inaccurate claim concerning the nature and extent of the risk to the personal security of the consumer or his family if the consumer does not purchase the product.

13. Promoting a product similar to a product made by a particular manufacturer in such a manner as deliberately to mislead the consumer into believing that the product is made by that same manufacturer when it is not.

14. Establishing, operating or promoting a pyramid promotional scheme where a consumer gives consideration for the opportunity to receive compensation that is derived primarily from the introduction of other consumers into the scheme rather than from the sale or consumption of products.

15. Claiming that the trader is about to cease trading or move premises when he is not.

16. Claiming that products are able to facilitate winning in games of chance.

17. Falsely claiming that a product is able to cure illnesses, dysfunction or malformations.
18. Passing on materially inaccurate information on market conditions or on the possibility of finding the product with the intention of inducing the consumer to acquire the product at conditions less favourable than normal market conditions.
19. Claiming in a commercial practice to offer a competition or prize promotion without awarding the prizes described or a reasonable equivalent.
20. Describing a product as "gratis", "free", "without charge" or similar if the consumer has to pay anything other than the unavoidable cost of responding to the commercial practice and collecting or paying for delivery of the item.
21. Including in marketing material an invoice or similar document seeking payment which gives the consumer the impression that he has already ordered the marketed product when he has not.
22. Falsely claiming or creating the impression that the trader is not acting for purposes relating to his trade, business, craft or profession, or falsely representing oneself as a consumer.
23. Creating the false impression that after-sales service in relation to a product is available in an EEA State other than the one in which the product is sold.
24. Creating the impression that the consumer cannot leave the premises until a contract is formed.
25. Conducting personal visits to the consumer's home ignoring the consumer's request to leave or not to return, except in circumstances and to the extent justified to enforce a contractual obligation.
26. Making persistent and unwanted solicitations by telephone, fax, e-mail or other remote media except in circumstances, and to the extent justified, to enforce a contractual obligation.
27. Requiring a consumer who wishes to claim on an insurance policy to produce documents which could not reasonably be considered relevant as to whether the claim was valid, or failing systematically to respond to pertinent correspondence, in order to dissuade a consumer from exercising his contractual rights.
28. Including in an advertisement a direct exhortation to children to buy advertised products or persuade their parents or other adults to buy advertised products for them.
29. Explicitly informing a consumer that if he does not buy the product or service, the trader's job or livelihood will be in jeopardy.
30. Creating the false impression that the consumer has already won, will win, or will on doing a particular act win, a prize or other equivalent benefit, when in fact either—
    (a) there is no prize or other equivalent benefit; or

(b)   taking any action in relation to claiming the prize or other equivalent benefit is subject to the consumer paying money or incurring a cost.[23]

---

[23] Consumer Protection from Unfair Trading Regulations 2008 (SI 2008/1277) Sch.1 amended by the Consumer Contracts (Information, Cancellation and Additional Charges) Regulations 2013 (SI 2103/3134). For an important ruling on the meaning of para.31, see *Purely Creative v Office of Fair Trading* (C-428/11) [2013] Bus. L.R. 985. For the preceding domestic cases, see [2011] EWHC 106 and [2012] EWHC 3636.

CHAPTER 6

VOID AND INEFFECTIVE EXCLUSION CLAUSES

In certain cases, Parliament has provided that certain exclusion and limitation **6–001** clauses are to be void and of no effect. It must be realised that such legislation does not render the continued use of such clauses unlawful. It merely means that they have no legal validity. For reasons argued earlier, the continued use of such clauses could, however, be illegal under the provisions of the Consumer Protection from Unfair Trading Regulations.[1]

We turn now to consider those exclusion clauses which various enactments have in specific instances rendered void and of no effect.

CONSUMER CREDIT

The Consumer Credit Act 1974 contains a considerable number of provisions **6–002** which can fairly be regarded as inserted into the Act for the protection of the debtor (where the contract relates to the provision of credit) or the hirer (where the contract is one of rental or hire). Section 173(1) of the Act provides that any term in a regulated agreement or linked transaction is void if, and to the extent that, it is inconsistent with a provision "for the protection of the debtor or hirer or his relative or any surety contained in the Act or in any regulation made under this Act". It may be usefully noted here that a regulated agreement, by virtue of ss.8 and 15, may be broadly construed as one where the credit or rental payments are of any amount, subject to exceptions in relation to high net worth individuals or business agreements where the relevant sums exceed £25,000.[2] A "linked transaction", as defined in s.19, is impossible to summarise briefly. The classic example of such a transaction is the maintenance contract which must be entered into under the terms of a television rental agreement.

The subsection bites not only on exclusion clauses contained in regulated or linked agreements. It applies also to clauses in "any other agreement relating to an actual or prospective regulated agreement or linked transaction". This appears to be essentially an anti-avoidance device. It means that a separate contract, one which is not itself a regulated agreement, cannot provide that such protective measures as are inserted into the agreement by the Consumer Credit Act 1974 are themselves to be excluded. Were it otherwise, the relevant terms of the Consumer Credit Act 1974 could easily be avoided.

---

[1] See Ch.5.
[2] See Consumer Credit Act 1974 ss.8 and 15 as amended by the Consumer Credit Act 2006 ss.16A and 16B as so inserted.

Section 173(2) takes the matter further by recognising that a provision of the Act may, in certain circumstances, impose duties or liabilities upon a debtor or hirer, or his relative, or any surety. Where this is so, subs.(2) continues, a term is inconsistent with that provision if it purports "to impose, directly or indirectly, an additional duty or liability on him in those circumstances". This is not drafting at its best, since the Act fails to state that, because of such inconsistency, the inconsistent term is void. This is, however, the plain intent of the Act and it will be so interpreted. It may also be taken that the words "directly or indirectly" are apt to be construed as an anti-avoidance device in the manner just discussed.

6–003 The ineffectiveness of clauses to avoid the various provisions of the Consumer Credit Act 1974, while absolute, is not without a degree of qualification. Section 173(3) provides that, notwithstanding s.173(1), nothing in the Act operates to prevent a person consenting to a thing being done which could otherwise only be done on an order of the court or the Financial Conduct Authority. The person's consent, according to subs.(3), must be given at the time the particular thing is to be done. This seemingly abstruse provision means that, for example, a person can consent at the time of repossession, to the repossession of protected goods. The repossessing party is thus relieved of the obligation otherwise imposed on him by s.90 of first obtaining an order of the court. The result is that a clause in the agreement excluding s.90 would be void; but consent to repossession without a court order is effective. Such consent, it must be stressed, is valid only if given at the time of the intended act; repossession, in our example. Consent written into the contract itself, therefore, will be of no effect.

There is nothing specific in the 1974 Act regarding the use of unfair terms in consumer credit agreements. Such matters are dealt with by the general law (notably the Consumer Rights Act) and also by the power of the FCA to take account of contract terms in the course of its deciding whether to grant, withhold or revoke the licence required by consumer credit and consumer hire businesses. The Act also provides that the FCA can, in its oversight of consumer credit and consumer hire businesses, take account of any business practice,[3] and order the business to do or to cease doing something. This could easily embrace the use of exclusion or limitation clauses.[4] Failure to comply with a requirement from the FCA could lead to a civil penalty not exceeding £50,000.[5] Again, the court is empowered to rewrite credit agreements where it determines the existence of an "unfair relationship", a matter which will depend on the terms and conditions of the contract. This too could cover the use of exclusion or limitation clauses.[6]

---

[3] From April 1, 2014, the supervisory powers of the Office of Fair Trading were transferred to the Financial Conduct Authority under the provisions of the Financial Services Act 2012.
[4] Consumer Credit Act 1974 s.33A as inserted by the Consumer Credit Act 2006.
[5] Consumer Credit Act 1974 s.39 as so inserted.
[6] Consumer Credit Act 1974 s.140A as so inserted.

TRANSPORT

Any antecedent agreement or understanding between the user of a motor vehicle **6–004** and his passenger(s) which purports to restrict the driver's liability to that passenger in respect of risks for which compulsory insurance cover is required (as to which, see s.143 of the Road Traffic Act 1988) is void under s.149(2) of that Act.

Section 29 of the Public Passenger Vehicles Act 1981 invalidates a provision contained in a contract for the carriage of a passenger in a public service vehicle where that provision purports to restrict the liability of a person in respect of a claim which may be made against that person in respect of the death or personal injury to a passenger while being carried in, or who is entering or is alighting from the vehicle, or which purports to impose any conditions as to the enforcement of such liability.[7]

The Carriage by Air Acts (Implementation of the Montreal Convention 1999) Order 2002,[8] under the heading "Liability of the Carrier and Extent of Compensation for Damage", provides that any provision tending to relieve the carrier of liability or to fix a lower limit than that which is laid down in the Convention shall be null and void. An identical provision also applies in relation to combined carriage (that is carriage partly by air and partly by some other mode). The limit is currently approximately €1134.71. A passenger can increase this by making an advance declaration and paying a supplementary fee.

HOUSING

Section 11 of the Landlord and Tenant Act 1985 implies into certain leases **6–005** covenants by the landlord to repair. By virtue of s.12, these terms can be excluded, but only by court order made with the consent of the parties.

The Defective Premises Act 1972 imposes a liability on local authorities, their builders, sub-contractors and architects if they fail to build in a professional or workmanlike manner (as the case may be) with proper materials, or fail to ensure that the dwelling is fit for human habitation. By s.6(3) of the Act, it is not possible to exclude or restrict the operation of such provisions by any agreement.

Section 25 of the Landlord and Tenant (Covenants) Act 1995 states that any agreement which has the effect of excluding, modifying or frustrating the operation of the Act is void. There is, however, nothing in this provision to suggest that the statute was intended to exclude the parties' ability to limit their liability under their covenants from the outset in whatever way they agreed.[9]

---

[7] See *Gore v Van der Lann* [1967] 2 Q.B. 31.
[8] SI 2002/263. The Order amends the Carriage by Air Act 1961, and disapplies s.1 of that Act in relation to Community carriers to the extent that Council Regulation 2027/97 has the force of law in the United Kingdom. The Convention entered into force in the European Union on June 28, 2004. The Convention itself came into force on November 3, 2003. For a list of signatory countries, see *http://legacy.icao.int/icao/en/leb/mtl99.pdf* [Accessed March 20, 2014]. The term "damage" in the Montreal Convention includes both material and non-material damage: *Axel Walz v Clickair SA* (C-63/09) May 6, 2010 (ECJ). See too *Dawson v Thomson Airways Ltd* [2014] EWCA Civ 845.
[9] *Avonridge Property Co Ltd v London Diocesan Fund* [2005] UKHL 70; *K\S Victoria St v House of Fraser (Stores Management) Ltd* [2011] EWCA Civ 904.

Section 179 of the Housing Act 1985 provides for the unenforceability of provisions affecting the right to buy.

Sections 24–28 of the Landlord and Tenant Act 1954 provide, in certain circumstances, for security of tenure. Originally, a clause providing for contracting out was valid only if authorised by court order. The new procedure requires a landlord to serve a prescribed notice on the tenant at least 14 days before the parties enter into such an agreement. The tenant must sign a simple declaration that he has received and accepted the consequences of the notice. If the parties wish to waive the 14-day period, the tenant will have to sign a statutory declaration, rather than a simple declaration, that he has received and accepted the consequences of the notice. In the case of an agreement to exclude security of tenure, the declaration must be made before the tenant enters into the tenancy or becomes contractually bound to do so. In the case of an agreement to surrender, the declaration must be made before entering into the agreement.[10]

SEEDS

6–006   The warranties arising from the statutory statements required under regulations made under the Plant Varieties and Seeds Act 1964 ss.16 and 17, in relation to seeds cannot be excluded.[11]

FEEDING STUFFS

6–007   Section 72(3) of the Agriculture Act 1970 provides that the warranty of fitness of animal feeding stuffs implied by the Act has effect regardless of any contract or notice to the contrary. Similarly, the warranties arising from the statutory statements required to be given by the Act cannot be excluded.

CONSUMER SAFETY

6–008   Parts I and II of the Consumer Protection Act 1987 deal with product liability and consumer safety, respectively. Section 2 of the Act provides that the producer of a defective product is liable for the damage which it causes. Section 7 provides that liability cannot be limited or excluded by any contract term, by any notice or by any other provision. Part II of the 1987 Act makes provision for the enactment of safety regulations. Section 41(1) provides that a person affected by breach of a safety regulation will have a right to bring an action as on a breach of statutory duty. Subsection (4) provides that, except as may be provided by the relevant safety regulation, the rights granted by subs.(1) cannot be limited or excluded by

---

[10] See the Regulatory Reform(Business Tenancies) (England and Wales) Order 2003 (SI 2003/3096).
[11] Current Regulations are: Seeds England Seed Marketing Regulations (SI 2011/463); Seeds England, Seed Marketing (Amendment) Regulations (SI 2011/2992) and Seeds England, Seed Marketing (Amendment) Regulations (SI 2012/3035), and corresponding Regulations for Northern Ireland, Scotland and Wales.

any contract term, by any notice or by any other provision. Safety regulations made under the Consumer Protection Act 1961 are deemed to be made under the Consumer Protection Act 1987.[12]

DISABILITY DISCRIMINATION

Part 10 of the Equality Act prevents contracting out of the duty imposed by the Act to make reasonable adjustments to ensure that a disabled person is not discriminated against.[13]

6–009

SOCIAL SECURITY

Section 91 of the Pensions Act 1995 provides for the inalienability of certain rights under an occupational pension scheme and provides that an agreement contravening such inalienability shall be unenforceable.[14]

6–010

SOLICITOR AND CLIENT

Section 60(5) of the Solicitors Act 1974 provides that a term in an agreement in relation to contentious business to the effect that a solicitor shall not be liable for negligence, or that he shall be relieved from any responsibility to which he would as a solicitor otherwise be subject, is void.

6–011

EMPLOYMENT

Section 1(3) of the Law Reform (Personal Injuries) Act 1948 invalidates any provision contained in a contract of employment or apprenticeship, or in any collateral agreement, in so far as it has the effect of excluding or limiting any liability of the employer in respect of personal injuries caused to the particular person by the negligence of persons in common employment with that person.

Section 203 of the Employment Rights Act 1996 contains a general restriction on contracting out of the Act's provisions. Section 14 of the Employment Relations Act 1999 applies broadly similar controls in relation to those of its provisions dealing with the right to be accompanied at disciplinary and grievance proceedings.

Section 49 of the National Minimum Wage Act 1998 provides that any attempt to contract out of the provisions of the Act has no legal effect, nor is it possible to preclude a person from bringing proceedings under the Act before an employment tribunal. The two exceptions to this are where an agreement has

6–012

---

[12] Details of current safety regulations can be obtained from the Department of Business, Innovation and Skills: *https://www.gov.uk/product-safety-for-manufacturers*; Tel: + 44 20 7215 5000.
[13] The relevant provisions of the 2010 Act came into force on October 1, 2010 under the provisions of the Equality Act 2010 (Commencement No.4, Savings, Consequential, Transitional, Transitory and Incidental Provisions and Revocation) (SI 2010/2317).
[14] See also Pension Schemes Act 1993 ss.77–80.

been arrived at in circumstances where a conciliation officer has taken action under the 1996 Act; and where a compromise agreement has been agreed between the parties.

Regulation 35 of the Working Time Regulations 1998[15] provides that any provision in an agreement (whether a contract of employment or not) is void in so far as it purports:

(a)   to exclude or limit the operation of any provision of these Regulations, save in so far as these Regulations provide for an agreement to have that effect; or

(b)   to preclude a person from bringing proceedings under these Regulations before an employment tribunal.[16]

The Transfer of Undertakings (Protection of Employment) Regulations 2006[17] are designed to protect the rights of employees on a change of employer. Regulation 18 provides that any agreement which is designed to exclude or limit the operation of the Regulations is invalid.

LATE PAYMENT

6–013   The Late Payment of Commercial Debts (Interest) Act 1998 provides for interest at 8 per cent above base rate to be added to qualifying debts which are paid late. Section 14 of the Act applies s.3(2)(b) of the Unfair Contract Terms Act 1977[18] to any contract term which purports to have the effect of postponing the time at which a qualifying debt would otherwise be created. This is stated to be the case whether or not the relevant contract is on written standard terms, and will thus have the effect of applying the reasonableness test to all such contract terms.[19] Identical provisions apply in relation to the sums which a supplier can claim in addition to the interest as compensation for the late payment.[20]

In *Yuanda (UK) Co Ltd v WW Gear Construction Ltd*,[21] it was a term of the contract that interest on late payment should be paid at 0.5 per cent above base rate. The Act allows for a contract term to exclude the statutory rate so long as the contract itself provide a "substantial contractual remedy" for late payment. Section 8(1) of the 1998 Act provides that a term displacing the statutory rate will not be regarded as providing a substantial remedy for late payment if:

---

[15] SI 1998/1833.

[16] Certain exceptions are given in reg.35(2).

[17] SI 2006/246.

[18] See para.8–020 and following.

[19] The 1988 Act applies to all commercial contracts for the supply of goods and services, regardless of the size of the relevant enterprise: see The Late Payment of Commercial Debts (Interest) Act 1998 (Commencement No.5) Order 2002 (SI 2002/1673).

[20] Section 5A(4) of the Late Payment of Commercial Debts (Interest) Act as inserted by the Late Payment of Commercial Debts (Interest) Regulations (SI 2013/395). For the sums payable, see s.5A(2) of the Act. For the application of the Act to charterparties providing for English law and London arbitration but otherwise having no "significant connection" to the UK, see *Martrade Shipping and Transport GMBH v United Enterprises Corp.* [2014] EWHC 1884.

[21] [2010] EWHC 720 (TCC).

"(a)   the remedy is insufficient either for the purpose of compensating the supplier for late payment or for deterring late payment; and

(b)   it would not be fair or reasonable to allow the remedy to be relied on to oust or (as the case may be) to vary the right to statutory interest that would otherwise apply in relation to the debt."

The Act goes on to say that regard shall be had to "all the relevant circumstances at the time the terms in question are agreed". The Act also says that regard must be had when deciding this issue to:

(a)   the benefits of commercial certainty;

(b)   the strength of the bargaining positions of the parties relative to each other;

(c)   whether the term was imposed by one party to the detriment of the other (whether by the use of standard terms or otherwise); and

(d)   whether the supplier received an inducement to agree to the term.

It was the view of the court that it was not the intention of the Act to treat a contractual rate of interest for late payment as not meeting the "substantial remedy" test simply because it was materially lower than the statutory rate. The court then applied the criteria referred to above. As to the benefits of "commercial certainty", the court took this to mean that, where the rate is not obviously unreasonable and appears to have been the product of genuine consensual agreement, "it should not be set aside lightly". As for the relative strength of the bargaining positions of the parties, the court thought that there was not much to choose between the parties. It did say that as time went on, Yuanda's bargaining position would have improved since it would become increasingly difficult for Gear to find another curtain walling trade contractor within the required time frame. It was also noted that this was not a case where Yuanda received an inducement to agree to the term.

The court pointed to the fact that, in the standard printed form of JCT Trade Contract, the rate was 5 per cent over base, (which had been amended to 0.5 per cent in the present contract) which might suggest that this was thought by those responsible for drafting the contract to be a fair rate of interest for late payment in the context of the construction industry. Given this, when taken together with the other considerations referred to above, the court said it could see no reason why 5 per cent over base should not be regarded as a substantial remedy within the meaning of the Act, even though 3 per cent less than the statutory rate. It went on to say that a case could be made for saying that 3 to 4 per cent would provide a substantial remedy for late payment, particularly if the rate had been specifically discussed and agreed between the parties. In the present case, though, Yuanda's rate, was much lower at 0.5 per cent over base. What appeared to have happened was that the rate was effectively imposed on Yuanda, although it did have the chance to protest about it had it noticed the provision and wished to do so. This told "marginally" in favour of Yuanda. The court's verdict was that the rate of 0.5 per cent could not be regarded as a substantial remedy within the meaning of the Act in the absence of special circumstances relating to the parties and the making of the contract. There were, the court said, no such circumstances here. Ultimately, there was no reason why it would be fair or reasonable to allow Gear to oust the statutory rate. It would not be "fair or reasonable to allow Gear to take advantage of the fact that during the pre-contract negotiations Yuanda failed to spot the amendment in the rate of interest". The result was that the statutory rate of interest at 8 per cent above base rate was to be substituted for the contractual rate of 0.5 per cent.

CANCELLATION AND INFORMATION RIGHTS

6–014   Various duties as to the provision of information to consumers and their rights to cancel certain contracts are set out in the Consumer Contracts (Information, Cancellation and Additional Charges) Regulations 2013.[22] Although there is no specific provision barring the exclusion or, limitation of these rights, reg.18 has the same effect by providing that every contract is presumed to contain a term asserting that the trader has complied with the relevant requirements.

ELECTRONIC COMMUNICATIONS

6–015   The Privacy and Electronic Communications (EC Directive) Regulations 2003[23] impose certain obligations in relation to electronic communications. Regulation 27 provides that any contract term between subscriber and the provider of a public electronic communications service or, between the provider of such a service and the product of an electronic communications network, inconsistent with any such right, shall be void.

HOLIDAY ACCOMMODATION CONTRACTS

6–016   A term in a holiday accommodation contract is void if it allows a consumer to waive rights conferred by the Regulations.[24]

Insurance

6–017   Section 17 of the Third Parties (Rights against Insurers) Act 2010 provides that a contract of insurance to which the section applies is of no effect in so far as it purports, whether directly or indirectly, to avoid or terminate the contract or alter the rights of the parties under it in the event of the insured—

(a)   becoming a relevant person; or
(b)   dying insolvent (within the meaning given by s.5(2)).

---

[22] SI 2013/3134.
[23] SI 2003/2426.
[24] The Timeshare, Holiday Products, Resale and Exchange Contracts Regulations (SI 2010/2960) reg.19.

A contract of insurance is one to which this section applies if the insured's rights under it are capable of being transferred under s.1. A "relevant person" is one who incurs a liability against which that person is insured under a contract of insurance.

Section 10 of the Consumer Insurance Act 2012 provides that a term of a consumer insurance contract, or of any other contract, which would put the consumer in a worse position as respects the matters mentioned in subs.(2) than the consumer would be in by virtue of the provisions of this Act is to that extent of no effect. Section 10(2) lists those matters as:

(a)   disclosure and representations by the consumer to the insurer before the contract is entered into or varied; and
(b)   any remedies for qualifying misrepresentations (these are set out in Sch.1).

This section does not apply in relation to a contract for the settlement of a claim arising under a consumer insurance contract.

A "consumer insurance contract" means a contract of insurance between an individual who enters into the contract wholly or mainly for purposes unrelated to the individual's trade, business or profession, and a person who carries on the business of insurance and who becomes a party to the contract by way of that business (whether or not in accordance with permission for the purposes of the Financial Services and Markets Act 2000).

CHAPTER 7

THE UNFAIR CONTRACT TERMS ACT 1977: SOME PRELIMINARY POINTS

THE ANTI-AVOIDANCE PROVISIONS

The marginal note to s.10[1] of the Unfair Contract Terms Act 1977 refers to **7–001** "evasion by means of secondary contract". It is stated that, where the Act itself prevents a party from excluding rights arising under, or in connection with, the performance of one contract, no other contract will be effective in prejudicing or taking away those rights. In other words, no term in contract B can operate to affect the rights of a party under contract A which the Act prevents another party from excluding or restricting.[2] If, for example, a party leases goods and takes out an associated contract of maintenance with a third party, nothing in the latter would be allowed to affect rights in the former which are safeguarded by the Act.

It was held in *Tudor Grange Holdings Ltd v Citibank NA*[3] that s.10 did not apply to a contract to settle disputes which had arisen concerning the performance of an earlier contract. It was further held that s.10 did not apply where the parties to both contracts were the same, the reasoning being that if the same parties entered into two contracts, it would make no difference if the relevant clause was contained in a different contract from that under which, for example, goods were supplied. The relevant sections of the Act would themselves apply the test of reasonableness: "Why then should Parliament have thought that in s.10 there was some possibility of evasion in such circumstances?"[4]

The section refers to those rights which the Act "prevents" a party from excluding. It has been argued from this[5] that the section does not apply where an exclusion clause is subject only to the test of reasonableness and is not automatically void.[6] Not only would this be contrary to the intention of Parliament, but it seems to ignore the effect of the Act itself which is to prevent a party excluding liability if a term fails the test of reasonableness where this is to be imposed.

It has also been held that there is "no substantial reason of policy for distinguishing between compromises of claims already made and compromises of claims which may in the future be made arising out of past acts or omissions, and

---

[1] In relation to Scotland, see s.23.
[2] As to what these rights are, see para.8–004 and following.
[3] [1991] 4 All E.R. 1.
[4] [1991] 4 All E.R. 1 at 13–14, per Brown-Wilkinson V.C.
[5] See Cheshire, Fifoot and Furmston, *Law of Contract*, 14th edn, p.210, though not repeated in subsequent editions.
[6] See further paras 8–018 to 8–027.

rendering the latter wholly ineffective". Accordingly, the Act did not apply to compromises of all other future claims arising out of past acts or omissions.[7]

VARIETIES OF EXEMPTION CLAUSE

7–002   Not every clause which seeks to exclude or restrict liability will be phrased in such direct terms. To cater for clauses which seek to achieve this effect, albeit indirectly, s.13(1) of the 1977 Act[8] states that, where a provision of the Act prevents the exclusion or restriction of liability, it also prevents:

(a)   making the liability or its enforcement subject to restrictive or onerous conditions;

(b)   excluding or restricting any right or remedy in respect of the liability; and

(c)   excluding or restricting rules of evidence or procedure.

The subsection goes on to say that, to that extent, the Act will also apply to terms and notices which exclude or restrict the relevant obligation or duty.[9] This is, however, stated not to apply to s.3,[10] the reason presumably being that this provision relates solely to contracts where the parties themselves spell out the nature of the bargain, and where, therefore, there can be nothing to exclude or restrict any duty implied by law.

These further restrictions imposed by the Act would cover such clauses as those requiring a claim to be notified within a particular time before it will be entertained; requiring several copies of a claim; requiring it to be attested to by one or more persons; restricting particular remedies, such as the right of rejection; or reversing the burden of proof.

An illustration of the operation of these provisions is found in *Smith v Eric S Bush*; *Harris v Wyre Forest DC*.[11] A disclaimer of liability stated that no valuation would be obtained save on terms that the valuer was under no obligation to take reasonable care or exercise reasonable skill. This was held by the Court of Appeal to remove the duty of care.[12] The House of Lords said that such a construction "would not give effect to the manifest intention of the 1977 Act but would emasculate the Act". The construction would provide no control over standard form exemption clauses which individual members of the public are obliged to accept. A party to a contract or a tortfeasor could opt out of the 1977 Act by declining "... to recognise their 'own answerability to the claimants in making

---

[7] *Cape Plc, Re* [2006] EWHC 1316 (Ch).

[8] In relation to Scotland, see s.25(3).

[9] In relation to Scotland, see s.25(5). A scheme of arrangement sanctioned under Companies Act 1985 s.425 (now Pt 26 of the Companies Act 2006) is not a contract or notice within the meaning of s.2(1) of the 1977 Act. Although it may bind the parties to the same extent as if they had made a contract, it is a statutory procedure involving the proposal of the scheme, its approval by the statutory majorities of creditors and its sanction by the court: see *Cape Plc, Re* [2006] EWHC 1316 (Ch).

[10] As to which, see para.8–019 and following.

[11] [1989] 2 All E.R. 514.

[12] [1988] 1 All E.R. 691.

the valuation'".[13] Lord Griffiths said that he regarded the Act as "introducing a 'but for' test in relation to a notice excluding liability. [Its provisions] indicate that the existence of a common law duty to take reasonable care ... is to be judged by considering whether it would exist 'but for' the notice excluding liability".[14]

The view that it was the effect of the relevant term which had to be considered **7–003** was approved in *Johnstone v Bloomsbury Health Authority*.[15] A clause in the employment contract of a senior house officer ran thus:

> "Your hours of duty will be the standard working week of 10 units of Medical Time (40 hours) and in addition you will be available for Class A UMTs ... on average a week ...".

It was agreed that this could mean an average working week of 88 hours, with some weeks in excess of that. It was felt arguable (the matter did not fall for definite decision) that this clause could be construed as ineffective by virtue of the Act because it could be regarded as a voluntary assumption of the risk of damage or because its operation was to restrict or limit the ambit and scope of the employer's duty of care. If that were the correct analysis, then the substance and effect of the clause, though not its form, was such that it could properly be said to be a term seeking to exclude or restrict liability for negligence resulting in death or personal injury.[16]

In *Anthony Snookes v Jani-King (GB) Ltd*,[17] the applicant company applied to strike out or stay a claim brought against it by the respondent franchisee on the ground that Swansea District Registry, where the proceedings had been commenced, did not have jurisdiction to hear the claim. The parties had entered into a franchise agreement, one clause of which stated that proceedings arising in connection with the agreement should be "brought in a court of competent jurisdiction in London". The respondent lived and worked in the Midlands. It was contended that this clause fell within s.13(1) as making "enforcement [of the claimant's contractual rights] subject to restrictive or onerous conditions".

In addressing this question, the court noted that the process of issuing proceedings could at all times be achieved in London comparatively easily by the claimants' Swansea solicitors either through agents in London or by sending all the relevant documents by post to London. It said that no cogent evidence has been adduced by the claimants explaining how and why the clause "would be restrictive or onerous". The court said that, even if this clause did require all proceedings up to and including trial to be brought in London, there was no evidence for concluding that the clause imposed a requirement which was in any way "onerous or restrictive" for the claimants, who did not live in Swansea where this claim was brought, but resided in Birmingham. Their only connection with Swansea was that the claimants had instructed solicitors who practiced there, but who had instructed London-based counsel. The claimants had filed "carefully

---

[13] [1989] 2 All E.R. 514 at 523. The words quoted are those of Nourse L.J. at [1988] 1 All E.R. 691 at 697.

[14] [1989] 2 All E.R. 514 at 530.

[15] [1991] 2 All E.R. 293.

[16] See [1991] 2 All E.R. 293 at 301, per Stuart-Smith L.J.

[17] [2006] EWHC 289 (QB).

drafted and lengthy witness statements but significantly they fail to explain in them why clause 27.14 is 'restrictive or onerous' for them".

It had been contended that s.13 applies to clauses limiting the time in which litigation may be commenced. In *BHP Petroleum Ltd v British Steel Plc*,[18] the court noted that it had received no submissions that a time-limitation clause, which limited the period during which a party was to be liable for a breach, did not fall within s.13(1) when it considered that it did.

7–004   In *Granville Oil & Chemicals Ltd v Davies Turner & Co Ltd*,[19] the Court of Appeal proceeded on the basis that a similar time-limitation clause fell within s.13(1)(a) of the 1977 Act.

The court in the instant case found there to be "fundamental differences" between time-limitation clauses and the clause in the present case. The court accepted that if an agreement between two North European companies contained a provision that it could only be enforced in a particular court in South America, then s.13(1)(a) might well have applied. That, though, would not be the case if the clause had said only that the contract could be enforced anywhere but in that particular court in South America. In the present case, the court found there to be no good evidence to the effect that by requiring proceedings to be brought in London, the disputed clause was "restrictive or onerous" either for reason of cost or for any other.

It had also been argued that s.13 could still be invoked because the clause had the effect of "excluding or restricting rules of evidence or procedure". The court, however, said that the clause did not have such effect when it specified where proceedings were to be brought; nor did it exclude or restrict any "rules of evidence" in the way that an arbitration clause might. The court also ruled that, even if s.13 applied, it would ultimately be of no avail since the clause would be upheld as reasonable.

Defining the liability accepted

7–005   It was said by Gloster J. in *JP Morgan Chase Bank v Springwell Navigation Corp*[20] that:

"There is a clear distinction between clauses which exclude liability and clauses which define the terms upon which the parties are conducting their business; in other words, clauses which prevent an obligation from arising in the first place."

The court went on to say that:

"terms which simply define the basis upon which services will be rendered and confirm the basis upon which parties are transacting business are not subject to section 2 of UCTA. Otherwise, every contract which contains contractual terms defining the extent of each party's obligations would have to satisfy the requirement of reasonableness."

---

[18] [1999] 2 Lloyd's Rep. 583.
[19] [2003] 2 Lloyd's Rep. 356.
[20] [2008] EWHC 1186 (Comm).

The court in this case approved the approach taken in *IFE v Goldman Sachs*.[21] The contract between the parties included these terms:

> "The information contained in this Memorandum has been obtained from the Sponsors [various identified financial institutions], Auto Distribution, Finelist, professional consultants and/or public sources. The Sponsors have approved the information obtained from them and its inclusion in this Memorandum and have authorised the distribution of this Memorandum. None of this Memorandum, the information contained in it or any other information supplied in connection with the Facilities shall form the basis of any contract...
>
> i) The Arranger [Goldman Sachs] has not independently verified the information set out in this Memorandum. Accordingly, no representation, warranty or undertaking, express or implied, is made and no responsibility is accepted by Goldman Sachs International ... as to or in relation to the accuracy or completeness or otherwise of this Memorandum or as to the reasonableness of any assumption contained therein or any other information made available in connection with the Facilities (whether in writing or orally) to any interested party (or its advisors) ...
>
> ii) Neither the arranger nor any of its respective directors ... shall be liable for any direct, indirect or consequential loss or damage suffered by any person as a result of relying on any statement contained in this Memorandum or any such other information.
>
> iii) This Memorandum contains only summary information and does not purport to be comprehensive ...
>
> iv) The information contained in this Memorandum should not be assumed to have been updated at any time subsequent to the date shown on the cover hereof and the distribution of this Memorandum does not constitute a representation by any person that such information will be updated at any time after the date of this Memorandum. The arranger expressly does not undertake to review the financial condition, status or affairs of Autodistribution, Finelist or any of their affiliates or any obligor in respect of the facilities, at any time or to advise any potential or actual participant in the Facilities of any information coming to the attention of the Arranger."

Toulson J. dismissed the argument that these provisions in any way constituted exclusion clauses. Such clauses, he said, "went to the scope of the representations being made and cannot properly be characterised for the purposes of [the Misrepresentation Act 1967 or the Unfair Contract Terms Act 1977] as attempts to exclude liability for misrepresentation". It had been argued in the alternative that there had been a duty of care in negligence, based not on negligent misstatement but on a duty of care to provide information. The court rejected this argument saying that the foregoing reasoning applied here too. Toulson J. said that the contract terms were: **7–006**

> "not ... to be characterised in substance as a notice excluding or restricting a liability for negligence, but more fundamentally as going to the issue whether there was a relationship between the parties (amounting to or equivalent to that of professional adviser and advisee) such as to make it just and reasonable to impose the alleged duty of care."[22]

It does appear, however, that the more recent tendency is to take the view that the Act is more likely to apply than not, and, in that sense, there is something of a move away from the view expressed in the two cases above. Consider first the observations made in *Raiffeisen Zentralbank Osterreich AG v The Royal Bank of Scotland Plc*.[23] One of the issues Christopher Clarke J. had to consider in that

---

[21] [2006] EWHC 2887 (Comm). See also *Titan Steel Wheels Ltd v Royal Bank of Scotland Plc* [2010] EWHC 211 (Comm).

[22] The judge's approach was approved of by the Court of Appeal: [2007] EWCA Civ 811.

[23] [2010] EWHC 1392.

case was whether certain provisions fell within s.3 of the Misrepresentation Act. In the course of doing so, he referred to the above passage from the judgment of Gloster J. The judge agreed that it was desirable for contracting parties of equal bargaining strength to be able to set out their respective duties without having to satisfy the reasonableness test, but at the same time there was the worry that the ingenuity of the draftsman "will insert into a myriad of contracts a clause to the effect that the basis upon which the parties are contracting is that no representations have been made, are intended to be relied on or have been relied on, as a means of evading liability which is intended to be impregnable". Christopher Clarke J. then considered the position of sophisticated commercial parties who can distinguish between statements that are meant to be relied on and those which are not, and who should be allowed to agree into which category a statement should fall. They were to be contrasted with the man on the street who is told that the car he is buying is in perfect condition, but who is then told that no representations as to the car have been made. The "key question", he summarised, was "whether the clause attempts to rewrite history or parts company with reality". The judge's view was endorsed when the *Springwell* case reached the Court of Appeal.[24]

These cases were given detailed consideration in *Avrora Fine Arts Investment Ltd v Christie, Manson & Woods Ltd*.[25] A term In the defendants' contract with the claimant provided that all statements made were statements of opinion; that, subject to the limited warranty, the defendants would not be responsible for errors and omissions in the catalogue. Referring to the rival approaches, Newey J. said that there was "surely scope for argument as to what distinguishes the two situations". This seems to imply that the distinction perhaps cannot be sustained. Although the *Springwell* case had involved the Misrepresentation Act 1967, Newey J. felt it of value in relation to the Unfair Contract terms Act. Adopting the phrase that the conditions did "part company with reality", the judge noted that the reality was that the defendants had taken responsibility for authorship of the piece they were selling: they had given a warranty to that effect and had pointed to the research they had done; and they were to charge a substantial premium. It could not be decisive that they had not wanted to assume liability.

Since it was not specifically ruled that a draftsman could never avoid the Act by the use of such clauses, it must be assumed that that remains possible. The "part with reality" test seems to be that, if parties can sit down and settle on the precise terms of the contract, then the properly drafted clause can remove any assumption of liability in the first place. Having said that, if the test were not satisfied in the *Avrora* case, it is difficult to see just when it will be.

Set-off

7–007   It has been accepted for some time that, providing the language is appropriate, the right to set off can be excluded by the terms of a contract.[26]

---

[24] [2010] EWCA Civ 1221, per Aikens L.J.

[25] [2012] EWHC 2198.

[26] See *Gilbert-Ash (Northern) Ltd v Modern Engineering (Bristol) Ltd* [1974] A.C. 689 at 717, per Lord Diplock; *Coca-Cola Financial Corp v Finsat International Ltd* [1996] 3 W.L.R. 849; *BOC*

In *Stewart Gill Ltd v Horatio Myer & Co Ltd*,[27] it was held that a term excluding a right of set-off came within the provisions of s.13(1)(b) and (c) because the term excluded the right to set-off claims against the supplier's claim for the price and further excluded the remedy which would otherwise have been available to allow enforcement of claims against the suppliers by means of set-off; and because it also excluded or restricted the procedural rules as to set-off.[28]

This was followed in *Esso Petroleum Co Ltd v Milton*.[29] The relevant clause ran:

> "The licensee agrees that he will not for any reasons withhold payment of any amount properly due to Esso under this licence whatsoever … Esso may set off any payment due to the licensee hereunder against any unpaid debts of the licensee to Esso."

The Court of Appeal referred to the *Gill* case and accepted that the instant term came within s.13. Lord Donaldson said that it was "quite clear" that the contract term excluded the right to set-off and excluded the remedy which the defendants would otherwise have had of being able to enforce a claim against the claimants by means of set-off. He further felt that the term also excluded or restricted the procedural rules as to set-off.[30]

In *Granby Village (Manchester) Management Co Ltd v Unchained Growth III Plc*,[31] a contract term provided that a maintenance charge was to be paid "without any deduction (whether by way of set-off lien charge or otherwise) whatsoever". The High Court judge rejected a submission on behalf of the appellants that that provision was subject to the Unfair Contract Terms Act 1977 and that it was caught by s.13 of the Act. This decision, which was noted without comment in the Court of Appeal, does not appear consistent with the above decisions. At the same time, in *Society of Lloyd's v Leighs*,[32] the Court of Appeal said that it was "far from persuaded" that a set-off clause should be treated as an exceptions clause. The-relevant clause ran:

Group Plc v Centeon LLC [1999] 1 All E.R. (Comm) 970; *Petrotrade Inc v Texaco Ltd* Unreported December 21, 1999 (CC). For further developments in this case, where issues as to set-off were not raised, see [2001] 4 All E.R. 853. For a set-off bar in a loan agreement to be effective, the set-off has to impugn the claim itself. It would not be effective where the set-off arose out of actions taken by the lender, after repayment had become due, to enforce his rights and to ensure that he did not lose any security: *Crastvell Trading Ltd v Bozel SA* [2010] EWHC 0166 (Comm). See too: *Skipskredittforeningen v Emperor Navigation* [1997] C.L.C. 1151; *Deutsche Bank (Suisse) SA v Gulzar Ahmed Khan* [2013] EWHC 482.

[27] [1992] 2 All E.R. 257. See also Axa *Sun Life Services Plc v Campbell Martin Ltd* [2011] EWCA Civ 133 and *United Trust Bank Ltd v Dalmit Singh Dohil* [2011] EWHC 3302.

[28] [1992] 2 All E.R. 257 at 260, per Lord Donaldson M.R. See also Stuart-Smith L.J. at 262. See also *Bank of Scotland v Singh* Unreported June 17, 2005 (HC).

[29] [1997] 1 W.L.R. 938.

[30] In *Overland Shoes Ltd v Schenkers Ltd* [1998] 1 Lloyd's Rep. 498, it was said that it was established in the *Gill* case that the effect of s.13 was to apply the Act to set-off clauses. See also *WRM Group v Wood* [1998] C.L.C. 189 and *Rohlig (UK) Ltd v Rock Unique Ltd* [2011] EWCA Civ 18.

[31] [2000] 1 W.L.R. 739.

[32] [1997] EWCA Civ 2283.

> "5.5 Each name shall be obliged to and shall pay his Name's Premium in all respects free and clear from any set-off, counterclaim or other deduction on any account whatsoever including in each case, without prejudice to the generality of the foregoing, in respect of any claim against ERL, the Substitute Agent, any Managing Agent, his Members' Agent, Lloyd's or any other person whatsoever and:
>
> (a) in connection with any proceedings which may be brought to enforce the Name's obligation to pay his Name's Premium, the Name hereby waives any claim to any stay of execution and consents to the immediate enforcement of any judgment obtained;
>
> (b) the Name shall not be entitled to issue proceedings and no cause of action shall arise or accrue in connection with his obligation to pay his Name's Premium unless the liability for his Name's Premium has been discharged in full; and
>
> (c) the Name shall not seek injunctive or any other relief for the purpose, or which would have the result, of preventing. ERL, or any assignee of ERL, from enforcing the Name's obligation to pay his Name's Premium."

Referring to this, the Court of Appeal said: "It does not purport to exclude or limit liability for claims of the Names, but merely to regulate their effect on a claim for the premium made on the Names". It may be, however, that the argument was more one of interpretation of the clause rather than an attack on the notion that s.13 did not apply to set-off clauses.[33] That s.13 does apply was accepted without question by Field J. in *Barclays Bank Plc v Alfons Kufner*.[34]

In the *Gill* case, Lord Donaldson, obiter, indicated that the references in s.13 to the exclusion or restriction of a relevant obligation or duty appeared to be intended to cover "an exclusion or restriction of liability not by contract but by reference to notices or terms of business which are not incorporated in a contract".[35] This seems unlikely, since the particular words are used in relation to sections of the Act which deal with contractual liability, and where any non-contractual provision would not in any event have force. It is more likely that this particular provision refers generally to further types of clause which, whether in a contractual or tortious context, seek to overcome direct exclusion or restriction by purporting instead to eliminate the relevant obligation or duty.

IMPOSING TIME LIMITS

7–008   In *Thomas Witter Ltd v TBP Industries Ltd*,[36] a contract contained the following clause:

> "Notwithstanding anything in this agreement to the contrary the vendor shall not be liable (by way of damage or otherwise) in respect of a breach of this agreement or claim by the purchaser in respect of a warranty unless the vendor shall have been given written notice of such breach or claim on or prior to January 1, 1992. Such notice shall be in writing and shall contain the purchaser's then best estimate of the amount claimed and the basis on which such estimate is made. Any liability in respect of a breach or claim of which notice is given as aforesaid shall cease unless proceedings in respect of such breach or claim are issued and served within six months of the date of the written notice (unless liability has been agreed in the interim)."

---

[33] See *Acsim (Southern) Limited v Danish Contracting and Development Co Ltd* (1989) 47 BLR 55; *Totsa Total Oil Trading SA v Bharat Petroleum Corporation Ltd* [2005] EWHC 1641.
[34] [2008] EWHC 2319 (Comm).
[35] See [1992] 2 All E.R. 257 at 260. This was not commented upon in the other judgments.
[36] [1996] 2 All E.R. 573.

This was, as the judge accepted, a "contractual limitation clause". No attack was made on the clause under the 1977 Act, the judge saying:

> "I was a little surprised by this because I would have thought that to the extent to which the clause prevents a claim based on what in the law of limitation is called 'concealed fraud' it might be unreasonable."[37]

In *Sargant v CIT (England)*,[38] the claimant booked a holiday with the defendant tour operators. The defendants, in their booking conditions, accepted responsibility for the injury caused by their own negligence or that of their suppliers, including hotels. They also required customers with a complaint to bring it to the attention of the local representative, and to write in with the complaint within 28 days of returning home. The claimant was injured and brought her injury to the attention of the representative. She did not, however, bring the claim against the defendants for five months.

The court ruled that the limitation clause was effective. The liability undertaken by the defendants was wider than the definition of "negligence" in the Act[39] and the clause passed the reasonableness test because delay caused prejudice to the defendants' chance of defending the claim and the Code of Practice for Tour Operators of the Association of British Travel Agents permitted a time limit on complaints of not less than 28 days. Furthermore, such restrictions were permitted by the Package Travel, Package Holidays and Package Tours Regulations 1992 although not in force at the relevant time.[40]

ARBITRATION AGREEMENTS

It is expressly provided that an agreement in writing to submit present or future differences to arbitration is not to be treated as excluding or restricting any liability.[41] In *Kaye v Nu Skin UK Ltd*,[42] the relevant clause was as follows:

7–009

> "Any dispute or claim arising from this Agreement not resolved by the above procedure, or disputes between Distributors arising out of business relationships as Nu Skin independent contractors, shall be submitted to mediation in Utah, USA and failing a satisfactory result from mediation a continuing dispute shall be settled by binding arbitration in the same location."

It had been argued that the subsection was limited to the term which contained the arbitration agreement and did not apply to other terms relating to the conduct of the arbitration and, in particular, any additional agreement as to the seat of the arbitration. This was rejected by Kitchen J.:

---

[37] [1996] 2 All E.R. 573 at 599, per Jacob J.
[38] Unreported June 6, 1994 (Croydon CC).
[39] Section 1(1) of which provides that negligence means the breach of any obligation, arising from the terms of the contract, to take reasonable care or exercise reasonable skill; of any common law duty to take reasonable care or exercise reasonable skill, but not any stricter duty; or of the common duty of care imposed by the Occupiers' Liability Act 1957.
[40] SI 1992/3288.
[41] Unfair Contract Terms Act 1977 s.13(2).
[42] [2009] EWHC 3509 (Ch).

"The arbitration clause in issue must be considered as a whole, and it is an agreement in writing to submit present or future differences to arbitration. Section 13(2) is mandatory and clearly ousts the agreement from the provisions of UCTA."

INTERNATIONAL SUPPLY CONTRACTS

7–010   In certain circumstances, the limits imposed by the 1977 Act on the extent to which a person may use a contract term to exclude or restrict liability are not to apply[43] and the requirement of reasonableness imposed by ss.3 and 4 will in those circumstances be inapplicable.[44]

The relevant circumstances where the foregoing exemptions from the Act apply are where the contract is one of sale, or one under or in pursuance of which possession or ownership passes, and the contract is made between parties whose places of business (if not their habitual residences) are in the territories of different states.[45] Furthermore, the contract must also fall into one of the following categories:

(a)   At the time of the conclusion of the contract, the goods were in the course of carriage, or were to be carried, from one state to another.

(b)   The acts constituting offer and acceptance were effected in the territories of different states.

(c)   The contract provides for the goods to be delivered to the territory of a state other than that in whose territory the acts of offer and acceptance were effected.[46]

In *Amiri Flight Authority v BAE Systems Plc*,[47] the parties' place of business or habitual residence were in the territories of different states. The acts constituting offer and acceptance had been done in the territory of the same state, Abu Dhabi in the UAE. The contract was a contract for the sale of goods, and it provided for the goods to be delivered to the territory of a state, the UK, other than that within whose territory the acts of offer and acceptance were done. It had been argued that the language of the Act, which speaks of delivery "to" a territory, rather than "in" a territory, connotes the goods being taken from one territory to another. The Court of Appeal ruled that the words "delivered to" in s.26(4)(c) required the goods to be moved from one state to another and did not cover the case of goods simply delivered "in" the UK, as in this case. Section 26(4)(c) required international movement of goods to a state other than that of the contract.

The effect of these provisions was further explained in *Trident Turboprop (Dublin) Ltd v First Flight Couriers Ltd*.[48] The respondents leased aircraft to the appellants, an Indian courier company. F said that the aircraft were unreliable and

---

[43]   Unfair Contract Terms Act 1977 s.26(1).
[44]   Unfair Contract Terms Act 1977 s.26(2). For ss.3 and 4, see paras 8–019 and following and 8–033 respectively.
[45]   Unfair Contract Terms Act 1977 s.26(3). The Channel Islands and the Isle of Man are expressly stated to be different states; Unfair Contract Terms Act 1977 s.26(3)(b).
[46]   Unfair Contract Terms Act 1977 s.26(4).
[47]   [2003] EWCA Civ 1447; reversing [2002] EWHC 2481 (Comm).
[48]   [2009] EWCA Civ 290; [2008] EWHC 1686 (Comm).

suffered from various defects. In the subsequent action, the High Court held that exclusion clauses in the leases fell within the scope of the Misrepresentation Act 1967 s.3 (as substituted by s.8 of the 1977 Act and which prescribes that clauses seeking to exclude or restrict liability for misrepresentation are subject to the reasonableness test) but were in fact not subject to the requirement of reasonableness in the Unfair Contract Terms Act 1977 because the lease agreements were international supply contracts within s.26 of the 1977 Act. Section 26(3)(b) of the 1977 Act was satisfied because the parties' places of business were in different states and s.26(4)(a) of the 1977 Act was satisfied because the two aircraft were to be carried from the states where they were delivered, Sweden and the United Kingdom, to India. Accordingly, the clauses were effective to exclude the appellant's right to rely on the alleged misrepresentations in order to rescind the agreements.

On appeal, the appellant submitted that s.26 of the 1977 Act did not apply because it referred to the "limits imposed by this Act" meaning the 1977 Act whereas the limits on a party's ability to restrict liability for misrepresentation were not imposed by the 1977 Act but by s.3 of the 1967 Act; and that any liability for misrepresentation in the instant case was not a liability arising "under a contract" within the meaning of s.26. It was further submitted that the leases were not within s.26 because they did not make provision for the aircraft to be transported to another country.   **7–011**

The Court of Appeal held that when s.26 of the 1977 Act spoke of "the limits imposed by this Act" it was referring to the requirement of reasonableness embodied in the Act and, by operation of s.8 of the 1977 Act, to terms excluding liability for misrepresentation. That interpretation was to be preferred as giving effect to the policy of excluding international supply contracts from the statutory control of exclusion clauses. The Court of Appeal said that it would create an anomaly to treat s.3 of the 1967 Act as independent of the Unfair Contract Terms Act "and frustrate the intention of Parliament to exclude international supply contracts from the statutory controls". Since s.3 of the 1967 Act was worded in terms which rendered an exclusion clause ineffective unless it complied with the controls set out in the Unfair Contract Terms Act, it made the latter the controlling instrument. As for the statutory expression "liability arising under such a contract", the purpose of s.26 as a whole was to exclude international supply contracts from the statutory regime governing exclusion clauses, and this meant that "there was every reason" to interpret the expression as extending both to liability for damages for misrepresentation and to the right of the injured party to rescind the contract where that remained possible.

It was further held that s.26(4)(a) appeared to be directed to any case in which the parties contemplated at the time of entering into the contract that the goods in question would be transported across national boundaries, not necessarily in order to fulfil the terms of the contract, but in order to achieve its commercial object. If a person who carried on business abroad hired equipment from a supplier in the UK in circumstances where both knew that the intention was for it to be used abroad, the lease was one pursuant to which the goods would be carried from the territory of one state to the territory of another within the meaning of s.26(4)(a) and could sensibly be described as an international supply contract. The Court of

Appeal held that, in the instant case, although the aircraft were to be delivered in the UK, both parties were well aware that they were being leased for use in India. Since s.26(4)(a) was not limited to contracts under which goods had to be carried across national boundaries in order to fulfil a contractual obligation, the contracts fell within it. The aircraft were to be "carried" from the UK to India within the meaning of s.26(4)(a) even though they were to be flown there under their own power. It followed that the leases were within s.26 and therefore excluded from the operation of the 1977 Act.

Further clarification on the application of s.26, particularly In relation to issues of offer and acceptance, was given in *Air Transworld Ltd v Bombardier Inc*.[49] The claimant C was a Gibraltar company controlled by an individual (M) resident in Angola. The aircraft was to be M's private jet and C became the purchaser under the aircraft purchase agreement (APA) by virtue of an assignment agreement. The terms of the APA were negotiated between the parties at meetings in Portugal and London. The APA was then faxed to Canada for execution by B. It provided that it was to be effective as of the date of its acceptance and execution by B. The APA provided that the warranty, obligations and liabilities of the seller and the rights and remedies of the buyer in the agreement were exclusive and were in lieu of, and the buyer waived and released, all other warranties, obligations, representations or liabilities, express or implied, arising by law, in contract, civil liability or in tort, or otherwise including but not limited to any implied warranty of merchantability or of fitness for a particular purpose. B submitted that the APA was an international supply contract so that the above exclusion clause was not subject to the test of reasonableness.

7–012   Cooke J. ruled that s.26 of the Act, when referring to "the acts constituting the offer and acceptance", was referring to the totality of the acts which constituted the offer and acceptance, including both the making and receiving of each. Section 26(4)(b) was intended to exclude cases where there was an international element in the formation of the contract, so that all elements of the offer and acceptance had to occur in the same state if the provisions of the 1977 Act were to apply. That interpretation avoided the application of technical rules of English law about the location of communicated offers and communicated acceptances and the differences which arose in relation to different means of communication. On that basis the acts constituting the offer and acceptance in respect of the APA and the assignment agreement were done in different states. The assignment agreement, as the contract on which C sued, was the relevant contract for the purpose of determining whether the 1977 Act applied. If the APA had not been an international supply contract but the assignment agreement was, then the Act would not apply. Alternatively, if the two agreements had to be considered together, they would fall outside the Act.

The court also ruled that, at the time of the conclusion of the APA and the assignment agreement, the aircraft was, in the contemplation of the parties, to be "carried" from the territory of one state to the territory of another within

---

[49] [2012] EWHC 243.

s.26(4)(a), since delivery was to take place in Canada and the aircraft was to be exported straight away and registered abroad. Both agreements were international supply contracts.

In *Ocean Chemical Transport and Ocean Ships Inc v Exnor Craggs Ltd*,[50] a contract for the supply of oil was made between suppliers based in the UK and buyers based in Delaware. The contract had been made on behalf of the buyers by agents based in the UK. The Court of Appeal ruled that this was an international supply contract which therefore was not regulated by the Act.

The contract had been made by parties whose places of business were in different states. The court also held that the word "party" meant "party to the contract", namely someone who accepted liability as principal. The party to the contract was the supplier and not their UK-based agent. The court further agreed that "place of business" meant the particular party's place of business and not the place where an agent from time to time appointed by him happened to carry out business.[51]

CHOICE OF LAW CLAUSES

Where the proper law of a contract is the law of any part of the UK, but only because the parties have so chosen, then ss.2–7[52] do not operate as part of that proper law.[53]

7–013

This was illustrated in *Deutsche Bank (Suisse) SA v Gulzar Ahmed Khan*.[54] The parties had chosen English law as the applicable law when otherwise Swiss law would have applied. Under the provisions of the Rome Convention, as implemented by the Contracts (Applicable Law) Act 1990, a contract is, in the absence of a choice of law clause, to be governed by the law of the country with which it is most closely connected. The court decided that, on the evidence, that country was Switzerland. As a result, the choice of law clause was given effect and the Act was held not to apply.

CARRIAGE CONTRACTS

Section 28 of the Act had had the effect of giving effect to the Athens Convention relating to the Carriage of Passengers and their Luggage by Sea. This section ceased to have effect when the relevant provisions of the Merchant Shipping Act 1979 were brought into force.[55]

7–014

The provisions implementing the Convention are now found in ss.183–186, and Sch.6 of the Merchant Shipping Act 1995. The extent of liability set out in the Convention covers death or injury or loss of luggage. Luggage claims require

---

[50] [2000] 1 All E.R. (Comm) 519.
[51] See also *Balmoral Group Ltd v Borealis (UK) Ltd* [2006] EWHC 1900 (Comm).
[52] Or, in relation to Scotland, ss.16–21.
[53] Unfair Contract Terms Act 1977 s.27(1).
[54] [2013] EWHC 482.
[55] See the Merchant Shipping Act 1979 (Commencement No.11) Order 1987 (SI 1987/635). The relevant provisions are now contained in the Merchant Shipping Act 1995. For limitations in relation to air travel, see para.6–004.

notice of loss to be given, and there is an exclusion for valuables unless they are deposited with the carrier.[56] Carriers are required to give passengers notice of the limits.[57]

Exclusion of liability

7–015 Section 186 of the 1995 Act provides that the owner of a UK ship[58] is not liable for any loss or damage where:

(a)   any property is lost or damaged by reason of fire; or
(b)   any gold, silver, watches, jewels or precious stones are lost or damaged by reason of theft, robbery or other dishonest conduct and their nature and value were not at the time of shipment declared by owner or shipper to the owner or master of the ship in writing.

Section 186(2) further provides that, where the loss or damage arises from anything done or not done by any person in his capacity of master or member of the crew or as a servant of the shipowner, the above provisions will also exclude the liability of the master, member or servant and, where the master or member is the servant of a person whose liability is not excluded by the above provisions, the person whose servant he is.

None of the foregoing provisions of s.186 exclude the liability of any person for any loss or damage resulting from a personal act or omission, committed with the intent to cause such loss, or recklessly and with knowledge that such loss would probably result.[59] Nothing in s.186 will operate to relieve a person of any liability imposed on him by the Convention.[60]

TERMS AUTHORISED OR REQUIRED

7–016 Nothing in the Unfair Contract Terms Act affects any contract term which is authorised or required, expressly or by implication, by any enactment.[61] This has particular relevance to a number of enactments concerned with international carriage. These are: Carriage by Air Act 1961, as amended; Carriage by Air (Supplementary Provisions) Act 1962; Carriage of Goods by Road Act 1965; Carriage by Air Acts (Application of Provisions) Order 2004[62]; Carriage of

---

[56] See the Carriage of Passengers and their Luggage by Sea (United Kingdom Carriers) Order 1998 (SI 1998/2917). Details of the relevant sums can be found by reference to the Athens Convention relating to the Carriage of Passengers and their Luggage by Sea, and the attached protocols.

[57] Carriage of Passengers and their Luggage by Sea (Notice) Order 1987 (SI 1987/703).

[58] For "United Kingdom ship", see Merchant Shipping Act 1995 ss.1(3), 313(1).

[59] Merchant Shipping Act 1995 s.186(3), Sch.7 Pt I.

[60] Merchant Shipping Act 1995 Sch.6 Pt II para.13.

[61] Unfair Contract Terms Act 1977 s.29(1)(a). "Enactment" means any legislation, including subordinate legislation, of the UK or Northern Ireland and any instrument which has effect by virtue of such legislation; Unfair Contract Terms Act 1977 s.29(3).

[62] SI 2004/1899. A contract of carriage made and to be performed wholly within the territory of a foreign state or between two foreign states is outside the Order: *Holmes v Bangladesh Biman Corp* [1989] 1 All E.R. 852.

Goods by Sea Act 1971; Railways (Convention on International Carriage by Rail) Regulations 2005[63]; Carriage of Passengers and their Luggage by Sea (Domestic Carriage) Order 1987[64]; Carriage of Passengers and their Luggage by Sea (United Kingdom Carriers) Order 1998[65]; Carriage by Air and Road Act 1979; and Merchant Shipping Act 1995.

The Act further provides that it does not affect any contract term which derives from an international agreement to which the UK is party, provided that the particular term is not more restrictive than provided in that agreement.[66] Once more, this has particular relevance to international contracts of carriage. The Convention concerning International Carriage by Rail of May 9, 1980 is used by the railways in their international contracts of carriage.[67]

It is also provided that the reasonableness test will be taken to be satisfied where the relevant term is incorporated or approved by, or incorporated pursuant to a decision or ruling of, a competent authority[68] acting in the exercise of any statutory jurisdiction or function, provided always that that authority is not itself a party to the contract.[69] The Defective Premises Act 1972 allows a builder to opt out of the duties imposed by that Act[70] if he assumes other obligations prescribed in an approved scheme.[71]

In *Timeload Ltd v British Telecommunications Plc*,[72] the dispute centred on a clause in a contract used by BT.[73] The Court of Appeal accepted that the regulatory body, the Office of Telecommunications (now the Office of Communications), had seen and not objected to the clause, and so could be said "in a general way" to have approved all the terms and conditions of that contract. Even so, the Master of the Rolls said that he had "grave doubts" as to whether Oftel could be said to have approved the terms and conditions in the exercise of any statutory function or jurisdiction: "Oftel has no such jurisdiction or function to approve terms and conditions as such", and his "provisional view" was that these provisions of the Act would not save the clause. No formal decision was reached, this being an interlocutory hearing, though the Court of Appeal did grant the requested injunction since *Timeload's* case was arguable.

---

[63] SI 2005/2092. See also the limitation on liability for lost luggage imposed by cl.50 the National Rail Conditions of Carriage (2011 version).

[64] SI 1987/670.

[65] SI 1998/2917.

[66] Unfair Contract Terms Act s.29(1)(b).

[67] Details can be accessed at *http://www.otif.org/index.php?id=142&L=2*.

[68] Defined as a court, arbitrator or arbiter, government department or public authority; 1977 Act s.29(3).

[69] 1977 Act s.29(2). "Statutory" means conferred by an enactment as defined in fn.56; 1977 Act s.29(3).

[70] That is to perform work in a "workmanlike or . . . professional manner, with proper materials and so that as regards that work the dwelling will be fit for habitation . . .", Defective Premises Act 1972 s.1.

[71] Since March 31, 1979, NHBC's Buildmark scheme has not been approved for the purposes of s.2 of the Defective Premises Act 1972. The question whether contract terms limiting protection to that conferred by the NHBC Agreement were reasonable was considered in *Robinson v PE Jones (Contractors) Ltd* [2011] EWCA Civ 9.

[72] [1995] E.M.L.R. 459.

[73] See para.8–020.

SPECIFIED EXCLUSIONS

7–017   Schedule 1 to the Unfair Contract Terms Act 1977 provides that ss.2, 3 and 7[74] do not extend to contracts of insurance; contracts relating to the creation, transfer or termination of an interest in intellectual property; contracts relating to the formation or dissolution of a company, to its constitution, or the rights or obligations of its members; any contract relating to the creation or transfer of securities or of any right or interest in securities; or contracts relating to the creation, transfer or termination of an interest in land.

SECURITIES

7–018   In *Micklefield v SAC Technology Ltd*,[75] the claimant was entitled to participate in a share option scheme run by the defendant company. An issue arose as to whether the terms of the scheme excluding or restricting the company's liability was within the 1977 Act. The court ruled that, although the relevant provisions were contained in the contract of employment, the wording of the exclusion in the Act referred to any contract, "so far as it relates to" the creation or transfer of securities, and that was enough to bring the relevant term within the exclusion.[76]

In *Philip Alexander Securities and Futures Ltd v Werner Bamberger*[77] a customer agreement referred to:

> "General investment advisory and dealing services and related research in the following investments, and the effecting of margined transactions thereon:
> (a)   futures on any commodity, security, interest rate instrument of other indices, precious metals or any currency and forward foreign exchange transactions;
> (b)   contracts for differences, e.g. contracts based on the FTSE 100 or S&P 500 stock indices;
> (c)   options to acquire or dispose of any of the instruments specified in (a) and (b) above, any securities, any currency or gold, palladium, platinum or silver;
> (d)   securities where the transaction in question is ancillary to a transaction in any of the foregoing; and
> (e)   units in collective investment schemes which are not regulated."

It was argued that this agreement "related to" the transfer of securities or at the least a right or interest in securities.

Noting that the Act contained no definition of "securities", the Court of Appeal said that it could not be defined by reference to subsequent events such as the enactment of the Financial Services Act, 1986 (since repealed). Although the court recognised that a comprehensive definition of the term was probably not possible:

> "for present purposes it is in our view sufficient to indicate that it refers to the financial assets represented by certificates attesting ownership of stocks and shares and the like. Futures and options, even when concerned with securities so defined, are to be distinguished from securities themselves."

---

[74] For discussions of these sections, see paras 8–004 and 8–026.
[75] [1991] 1 All E.R. 275.
[76] [1991] 1 All E.R. 275 at 281.
[77] Unreported July 12, 1996 (CA).

The Court of Appeal also said that the agreement in this case would not normally relate to rights or interests in securities either. The usual option or futures contract would be one which if exercised or matured would lead to a contract for sale by description. Such a contract would not confer any right or interest in specific securities until securities answering the description had been appropriated to the contract. It further said that the words "relate to" could not cover the contracts in this case. They do not relate to the creation or transfer of the securities or of any right or interest in such securities. The performance of the contract may lead to such a contract but is not a contract of that description itself.

INTERESTS IN LAND

This exclusion was considered in *Electricity Supply Nominees Ltd v IAF Group Ltd*.[78] A landlord brought an action against a tenant for non-payment of rent and for interest on late payment. The terms of the lease included a covenant by the tenant "to pay the rent and all other sums payable under this lease . . . without any deduction or set-off whatsoever". The tenant's defence relied on a counterclaim and set-off for alleged breaches under the repairing covenant. The tenant contended that, notwithstanding the exemption in the 1977 Act for a contract "so far as it relates to the creation or transfer of an interest in land", these provisions fell within the Act. He argued that the Act only excluded that part of the lease which created the interest in land itself, i.e. the actual demise, so that it would not extend to those provisions relating to the rights and duties of the parties during the term which had been created by the lease.

7–019

The judge considered the *Micklefield* case was correctly decided, though consistent with both sets of arguments presented in the present case, but "more in line with the landlord's case than the tenant's case".[79] Concluding that the landlord's argument was to be preferred, the judge explained that the demise was made in consideration of the payment of rent, and that the covenants to pay rent, additional rent and other sums were "an integral part of the creation of the interest in land by the demise. The repairing covenant is also an integral part of the creation of the interest in land".[80] He held that the statutory words were wide enough to cover the covenant to pay rent and other sums as well as the set-off clause, adding that:

> "all the covenants that are integral to the lease which creates the interest in the land 'relate to' the creation of that interest in land. What is taken out of the exemption provided [by the Act] would be provisions which are not integral to the lease, but constitute a transaction of a different kind, included in the same document as the lease."[81]

In *Star Rider v Inntrepreneur Pub Co*,[82] the claimant had been allowed into possession as licensee on the terms of a draft lease. Under the terms of the draft lease the claimant was obliged to pay rent and to purchase all its beer from the

---

[78] [1993] 3 All E.R. 372.
[79] [1993] 3 All E.R. 372 at 376.
[80] [1993] 3 All E.R. 372 at 376.
[81] [1993] 3 All E.R. 372 at 376–377.
[82] [1998] 1 E.G.L.R. 53.

defendant or its nominee. The draft lease provided that the rent, or the licence fee, was to be paid "without any deduction or set-off whatsoever".

The claimant fell into arrears with payment of licence fees and ceased purchasing beer from the defendant. In the action the claimant challenged the beer tie as being contrary to art.85 (now art.101) of the Treaty on the Functioning of the European Union and claimed damages on that basis. The defendant landlords served notice to quit and counterclaimed for possession, arrears of licence fees and mesne profits. The claimant in his defence to the counterclaim claimed set-off in respect of his damages claim. The defendant landlord sought summary judgment on its counterclaim relying on the *Electricity Supply Nominees* case to defeat the defence of set-off. The judge followed the earlier ruling, saying:

> "The set-off provision is contained in the tenant's covenant to pay rent. It is concerned with the amount of rent that the tenant must pay. It, no less than the covenant of which it forms part, is integral to the agreement by Inntrepreneur to grant a lease of the premises in that the rent payment is part of the consideration for the agreement to grant the lease. The grant of a lease involves the creation of an interest in land. An agreement for the grant of a lease is a contract for the creation of an interest in land. It is therefore directly within paragraph 1(b). It is none the less a contract within paragraph 1(b) where, as here, under the terms of the agreement, no interest in land is to arise until the lease is actually granted."[83]

7–020   The two cases above were approved by the Court of Appeal in *Granby Village (Manchester) Management Co Ltd v Unchained Growth III Plc*.[84] The clause, in a contract between tenant and management company read thus:

> "To pay to the Company the Yearly Rent and to the Management Company the Maintenance Charge on the days and in the manner herein provided without any deduction (whether by way of set-off lien charge or otherwise) whatsoever."

Jonathan Parker J. held that:

> "In my judgment, both these cases were correctly decided. The obligation to pay a service charge to a management company charged with responsibility for the maintenance and management of a development of which the demised property forms part is, in my judgment, plainly a provision which 'relates to' the creation of the leasehold interest. It is an integral part of the lease, providing the administrative mechanism for the enjoyment of the leasehold interest in common with, and for the benefit of, the other tenants of the development. To conclude that it did not 'relate to' the creation of the leasehold interest would, in my judgment, be to lose sight of commercial reality."

INTELLECTUAL PROPERTY

7–021   The reasoning adopted in the *Micklefield* case was also followed in *Salvage Association v CAP Financial Services Ltd*.[85] The contracts concerned related to the installation of computer software. Schedule 1 to the 1977 Act excludes any contract "so far as it relates to the creation or transfer of any interest in . . . intellectual property". It was argued that, since all the issues in the case related to

---

[83] [1998] 1 E.G.L.R. 53 at 55.
[84] [2000] 1 W.L.R. 739.
[85] [1995] F.S.R. 654.

such matters, the action was within the provisions of the Schedule. Referring to the *Micklefield* case, the official referee rejected this argument.

The provisions of the Schedule, he ruled, apply only to those provisions of a contract which deal with the creation or transfer of a right or interest in the relevant intellectual property:

> "It does not extend generally to all the terms of a contract simply because the contract is concerned overall with the provision of a service, performance of which will result in a product to which the law affords the protection of one or more of the specified intellectual property rights."

He agreed that the Schedule would apply to any term concerned with the creation or transfer of a right or interest in intellectual property; but if a term was one concerned with other aspects of the contract, then the Schedule would not apply. The official referee pointed to the difference in wording between the provision under consideration and that part providing that the Act does not extend "to any contract of insurance", which would exclude the entire contract, and not just individual terms. It is not at all clear that this is consistent with the line of reasoning approved by the Court of Appeal in the *Granby Village* case, but it nonetheless appears attractive.

MARINE CONTRACTS

The Schedule also offers limited exclusion from the Act for contracts of marine salvage or towage, charterparties of ships or hovercraft. In such cases, the provisions of s.2(1) will apply,[86] but those of ss.2(2), 3 and 7, as appropriate, will not apply.

7–022

EMPLOYMENT

The provisions of s.2 do not apply to contracts of employment except in favour of the employee. Furthermore, s.2(1) does not affect the validity of any discharge and indemnity given in connection with an award of compensation in respect of pneumoconiosis contracted in the coal industry.[87] This means that, although liability for any negligence which might have been involved in the contraction of the disease cannot be excluded or limited, a person receiving an award as compensation is restricted to the amount of that award.

7–023

---

[86] See para.8–005.
[87] Scottish law goes further. Section 15(1) of the 1977 Act states that nothing in the Act as applied to Scotland alone affects the validity of any discharge or indemnity given in consideration of the receipt of compensation in settlement of any claim.

CHAPTER 8

THE UNFAIR CONTRACT TERMS ACT: AREAS OF APPLICATION

CONTRACTS WITH CONSUMERS

Following enactment of the Consumer Rights Act 2014, the Unfair Contract Terms Act ceased to apply to contacts with a consumer. Many of its provisions, along with certain additional provisions, are, however, carried on under the 2014 Act, and these are discussed in Ch.10.

8–001

BUSINESS LIABILITY

For the most part, the provisions of the 1977 Act apply only in relation to "business liability", that is to say:

8–002

(a) things done or to be done by a person in the course of his or another's business (this latter ensures that the Act covers vicarious liability); and
(b) the occupation of premises used for business purposes of the occupier. The subsection further provides that the liability of an occupier for breach of duty or obligation towards a person obtaining access to the premises for educational or recreational purposes, being a liability or damage suffered by reason of the dangerous state of the premises, is not to be treated as a business liability unless granting the particular person access falls within the business purposes of the occupier.[1]

This was qualified by the Occupiers' Liability Act 1984 which added this provision:

> "but liability of an occupier of premises for breach of an obligation or duty towards a person obtaining access to the premises for recreational or educational purposes, being liability for loss or damage suffered by reason of the dangerous state of the premises, is not a business liability of the occupier unless granting that person such access for the purposes concerned falls within the business purposes of the occupier."[2]

The purpose of the 1984 amendment, as expressed in the long title, was to amend the 1977 Act "in relation to persons obtaining access to premises for

---

[1] Unfair Contract Terms Act 1977 s.1(3).
[2] The 1984 Act does not apply to Scotland but was extended to Northern Ireland by the Occupiers' Liability (Northern Ireland) Order 1987 (SI 1987/1280).

recreational or educational purposes". The restriction of the Act to business liability is, however, expressly excluded in the case of contracts within s.6(4).[3]

The supremacy of statutory provisions

8–003   In *Anderson v HMRC*,[4] X had taken out life insurance policies issued by an Irish company whilst not resident in the United Kingdom, but became a UK resident for the relevant tax years. Over the life of the policies X had made a loss, but because of the rules under the Income Tax (Trading and Other Income) Act 2005 relating to taxation of part surrenders, and because one of the polices was classified as a personal portfolio bond, X was treated as having an additional income tax liability of £33,000. X did not dispute that the additional tax liability was in accordance with the applicable legislation, but argued that the legislation led to a result that was so unfair in his case that it should not be applied to him. In particular, X argued that the legislation breached the Unfair Contract Terms Act.

The Tribunal said that this argument must fail, "for the simple reason that the applicable legislative provisions are contained in an Act of Parliament. The Tribunal cannot review the provisions of primary legislation in the manner suggested. An Act of Parliament is not a contract for purposes of the Unfair Contract Terms Act 1977".

NEGLIGENCE LIABILITY

8–004   Section 2 deals with liability arising from negligence, an expression defined in s.1(1)[5] to mean the breach of any obligation to take or exercise reasonable care or skill in the performance of a contract, where that obligation arises from its express or implied terms. Negligence is also defined as the breach of any common law duty to take or exercise reasonable care and skill, but not of any stricter duty. Since this definition is phrased independently of any contractual connection, it extends to the activities of those providing services under the National Health Service or state education (it is impossible to locate a contract in such a context), and to those providing free services, such as some car parks. Equally, this definition will cover the tort of negligence, and so extends to producers and manufacturers who negligently put defective goods into circulation. "Negligence" is also defined to cover any breach of the duty of care imposed by the Occupiers' Liability Act 1957, or the equivalent legislation in Scotland and Northern Ireland.

---

[3] See para.8–025.
[4] [2013] UKFTT 126.
[5] In relation to Scotland, see s.25(1).

DEATH OR PERSONAL INJURY

Section 2(1) of the Unfair Contract Terms Act 1977[6] provides that no person, by **8–005** reference to any contract term or notice, can "exclude or restrict his liability for death or personal injury resulting from negligence". This is stated to be so whether or not such notice is given to "persons generally or to particular persons". "Notice" is defined in s.14 as including (so the definition is not exhaustive) "an announcement, whether or not in writing, and any other communication or pretended communication". This last phrase is designed to cover notices which, for whatever reason, are not brought to the attention of the relevant party.[7] It is also important to note that s.14 defines "personal injury" to include (so again the definition is not exhaustive) any disease and any impairment of physical or mental condition.

Section 1(4)[8] states that, in determining whether there has been a breach of duty or obligation, no account is to be taken of whether the breach was inadvertent or intentional, or whether liability for any breach arose directly or indirectly. Employers are thus prevented from using exclusion clauses to safeguard themselves from the consequences of an employee's liability. The reference to intention is presumably to ensure that, while the deliberate infliction of physical injury or death might not constitute negligence outside the Act, it is nevertheless so treated for the purposes of the Act.

The result of these provisions is therefore this: where death or personal injury, as above defined, results from negligence, also as above defined, then no clause, whether a contractual term or notice, will have any effect to exclude or restrict liability.[9]

NEGLIGENCE HAVING OTHER CONSEQUENCES

Section 2(2) further restricts exclusion clauses relating to liability in negligence. **8–006** It provides that in the case of loss other than death or personal injury, liability cannot be excluded or restricted "except so far as the term or notice satisfies the requirement of reasonableness".[10]

It should not be supposed that this other loss or damage means only physical loss or damage, since it can also extend to pure economic loss in so far as this is recoverable at law. It must be remembered, though, that nothing in the Act creates

---

[6] Or s.16 in relation to Scotland. This section also contains provisions equivalent to s.1(3), though no amendment was made to this section corresponding to that made to s.1(3) by the Occupiers' Liability Act 1984.

[7] A trustee exemption clause is not a form of notice. See *Derinda Baker Personal Representative of Victor Arthur Baker (Deceased) v JE Clark & Co (Transport) UK Ltd* [2006] EWCA Civ 464.

[8] In Scotland, s.25(1).

[9] Cases such as *Bennett v Pontins* (Unreported 1973) cannot recur. In that case, damages were refused when, even though negligence was proved, a widow failed to recover for the death of her husband since the matter was covered by an appropriate exclusion clause.

[10] For full consideration of the reasonableness test, see Ch.9.

any right to sue for economic loss where none exists outside the Act. It merely gives greater, or potentially greater, impact to such rights as already exist.[11]

The scope of the above provisions was considered in *Phillips Products Ltd v Hyland*[12] and *Thompson v T Lohan (Plant Hire) Ltd*.[13] In the former, the second defendants (Hamstead) let an excavator out on hire to the claimants and the first defendant, a driver, for use in certain building work. Condition 8 of the contract of hire provided that where drivers and plant were supplied by the owner, they were: "... for all purposes in connection with [their] employment in the working of the plant to be regarded as the servants or agents of the hirer ... who alone shall be responsible for all claims arising in connection with the operation of the plant by the said drivers or operators". The claimants sued for damage caused by the driver's negligence. The second defendants argued that they were protected from liability by virtue of the above condition.

The Court of Appeal, agreeing with the Divisional Court, held that the effect of the disputed condition, if it were to be given effect, would be to negative a liability which would otherwise fall on the owner of the plant. Stressing that it was not relevant to decide whether a clause could be called an "exclusion" or "restriction" clause, the court said that the effect and substance of that clause had to be considered to determine if it were in fact a clause excluding liability: "The effect here is beyond doubt. Hamstead does most certainly purport to exclude its liability by reference to condition 8".[14] Since the clause had been determined by the Divisional Court as failing the reasonableness test, it was therefore ineffective.

In the latter case, the first defendants hired out to the third party an excavator and driver. The terms of hire included the above condition 8 and a further condition providing that the hirer was to "fully and completely indemnify the owner in respect of all claims by any person whatsoever for injury to person or property caused by or in connection with or arising out of use of the plant". The claimant's husband was killed in an accident involving the excavator while it was driven by the driver supplied by the first defendants.

8–007   The Court of Appeal held that, where the wording of a clause indicated a clear intention for the parties, as between themselves, to transfer liability in the event of negligence from one to the other, that would be effective at common law. Section 2(1) of the 1977 Act, it was said, was intended to prevent restriction or exclusion of liability; it was not concerned with arrangements made by a tortfeasor with others for sharing or transferring the burden of compensating the victim. Section 2(1) could not therefore apply to strike down condition 8 since the only relevant liability under the subsection was that owed to the claimant which could be enforced against the first defendants and which was not affected by the

---

[11] For the recovery of economic loss, see *Hedley Byrne & Co Ltd v Heller & Partners Ltd* [1964] A.C. 465; *Junior Books Ltd v Veitchi Co Ltd* [1982] 3 All E.R. 201; *DoE v Thomas Bates & Sons Ltd* [1990] 2 All E.R. 943; *Nitrigin Eireann Teoranta v Ince Alloys Ltd* [1992] 1 All E.R. 854; *Lancashire & Cheshire Association of Baptist Churches Inc v Howard & Seddon Partnership* [1993] 3 All E.R. 467; *White v Jones* [1995] 2 A.C. 207; *Shell UK Ltd v Total UK Ltd* [2010] EWCA Civ 180.
[12] [1987] 2 All E.R. 620.
[13] [1987] 2 All E.R. 631.
[14] [1987] 2 All E.R. 620 at 626, per Slade L.J.

operation of that condition. That condition therefore transferred liability for the driver's negligence to the third party who was required to indemnify the first defendants under the further clause.

The Court of Appeal, noting that it made no difference that this case was heard under s.2(1) while the earlier was heard under s.2(2), distinguished the cases in that, in the earlier, there was liability in negligence by Hamstead to Phillips, which was sought to be excluded; whereas, in the later case, no exclusion of liability was sought to be attained by reliance on the relevant terms. It was pointed out that the claimant in the later case had a judgment which could not be prejudiced by those terms. All that had happened was that the first defendants and the third party had agreed as to who was to bear the consequences of a negligent act. It was observed that the liability to the claimant:

> "is the only relevant liability in the case ... and that liability is still in existence and will continue until discharge by payment to the claimant. Nothing is excluded in relation to the liability, and the liability is not restricted in any way whatever. The liability of Lohan to the claimant remains intact. The liability of Hamstead to Phillips was sought to be excluded."[15]

ASSUMPTION OF RISK

It is settled law that, where a person accepts the risk of injury, he cannot subsequently bring an action in relation to that risk, the so-called doctrine of *volenti non fit injuria*.[16] Knowledge of danger, however, is only evidence of acceptance of risk, nothing more.[17] This has been recognised in s.2(3)[18] which provides that agreement to, or awareness of, an exclusion clause is not "of itself to be taken as indicating [the injured party's voluntary acceptance of the risk]". The subsection, of course, does not obliterate the *volenti* doctrine: it only states that an exclusion clause will not "of itself" suffice to bring it into play.

8–008

THE APPLICATION OF SECTION 3: WRITTEN STANDARD TERM CONTRACTS

Section 3 of the Unfair Contract Terms Act 1977[19] applies where one party enters a contract on the basis of "the other's written standard terms of business".[20] The burden of proof lies upon the party seeking to show that the Act applies.[21]

No definition is provided of this phrase. Since every business has a beginning, it may be supposed that any terms drawn up to act as a party's terms of contract may suffice, even if the particular contract is being used for the first time.

8–009

---

[15] [1987] 2 All E.R. 631 at 638–639, per Fox L.J. See too *Halliday v Lyall Scott Ltd (Kennings Ltd (third party))* Unreported November 3, 1994 (Outer House).
[16] See, for example, *Salmond and Heuston on the Law of Torts*, 20th edn (London: Sweet & Maxwell, 1992), pp.485–494.
[17] *Smith v Charles Baker & Sons* [1891] A.C. 325.
[18] Section 16(3) in Scotland.
[19] Its previous application to consumer contracts was removed by the Consumer Rights Act 2014.
[20] The relevant section in the case of Scotland is s.17. The phrase used in relation to Scotland is "standard form contracts" (see s.17(1)).
[21] *British Fermentation Products Ltd v Compair Reavell Ltd* [1999] 2 All E.R. (Comm) 389.

There are, however, some questions which are less straightforward. If a contract is produced for a specific party, is this contract on written standard terms? It may be supposed that it is if it is presented as "take it or leave it". In *Oval Ltd v Aegon Insurance Co (UK) Ltd*,[22] the court said that if an organisation, such as in the instant case, a firm of insurers, prepared a printed form, or a series of printed forms, on the basis of which it offers to undertake a particular class of business, it did so on the basis of written standard terms.

Again, should all the terms of the written contract be standard? There will no doubt be some terms of a written contract which will always be standard; such as those dealing with the passing of property or risk. There will, however, also be others which will differ from contract to contract, such as dates and place of delivery, details of payment. Then again, it may be asked whether it is necessary for the contract to be exclusively on written standard terms; that is to say whether any agreement is still within the Act if it contains implied terms, or is supplemented by an oral agreement. The answer must surely be that it is, since the Act would be easily evaded, indeed rendered nugatory if it were, otherwise since virtually all agreements will contain certain implied terms. The same considerations, it is suggested, mean that only part of a contract entirely in writing need be on standard terms. In *St Albans City and District Council v International Computers Ltd*,[23] for example, Scott Baker J. said that it was his view that the Act did not require all the terms to be fixed in advance by the supplier, since in many contracts there will be negotiations relating to such matters as quality or price. In the case before him, there had been some pre-contract negotiations but the contract proceeded on the basis of standard terms which were acknowledged by both parties as being accepted by over 250 local authorities. Those prior negotiations had left the standard terms "effectively untouched".

8–010   In the Court of Appeal, it was argued that one person cannot be said to deal on another's standard terms of business if, as in the present case, there were negotiations with the other party over the terms before the contract was made. This was regarded as an "impossible construction" to place on the Act for two reasons: first:

> "... as a matter of plain English 'deals' means 'makes a deal' irrespective of any negotiations that may have preceded it; secondly, section 12(1)(a) equates the expression 'deals as consumer' with 'makes the contract'. Thus it is clear that in order that one of the contracting parties may deal on the other's written standard terms of business within section 3(1) it is only necessary for him to enter into the contract on those terms."[24]

Further support for the argument that terms can be standard, even though altered in part, is to be found in *McCrone v Boots Farm Sales Ltd*.[25] Lord Dunpark thought it plain that:

---

[22] (1997) 85 B.L.R. 97.
[23] [1995] F.S.R. 686.
[24] [1996] 4 All E.R. 481 at 491, per Nourse L.J. Since enactment of the Consumer Rights Act 2014, there is no longer any reference to "deals as consumer," but this does not affect the court's argument.
[25] [1981] S.L.T. 103. While s.17(1) refers to "standard form contracts", s.17(2) also refers to a "customer" under such a contract as one "who deals on the basis of written standard terms of

"the section is designed to prevent one party to a contract from having his contractual rights, against a party who is in breach of contract, excluded or restricted by a term or condition, which is one of a number of fixed terms or conditions invariably incorporated in contracts of the kind in question by the party in breach, and which have been incorporated in the particular contract in circumstances in which it would be unfair and unreasonable for the other party to have his rights excluded or restricted. If the section is to achieve its purpose, the phrase 'standard form contract' cannot be confined to written contracts in which both parties use standard forms. It is, in my opinion, wide enough to include any contract, whether wholly written or partly oral, which includes a set of fixed terms or conditions which the proponent applies, without material variation, to contracts of the kind in question."[26]

This was also the line adopted in *Salvage Association v CAP Financial Services Ltd.*[27] A contract was still regarded as on written standard terms even though the recipient of those terms negotiated and agreed certain important matters and details. The official referee explained that the one party had said that, while it had briefly read and considered the other side's terms, which had been written and produced in advance as a suitable set of terms for use in future contracts, it did not attempt any negotiation with regard to those conditions nor consider it appropriate to do so.

Where, however, there are negotiations, and a number of alterations made to standard terms so as to fit the particular circumstances of the other party's case, s.3 will not apply.[28] This point was re-emphasised in the *Salvage Association* case.[29] A further, separate, contract between the parties was based on and closely followed a set of standard conditions, and they were used as the starting point for negotiating and agreeing the precise terms of this particular contract. The official referee stated that, in such a case, it will be a "question of fact and degree to be decided in all the circumstances of the case" whether it will be correct to describe the terms eventually agreed as the standard terms of the party who originally put them forward. He then laid down some guidelines for resolving this issue, though he was careful to say that these were not exhaustive. The following should, however, be considered:

(1) The degree to which the "standard terms" are considered by the other party as part of the process of agreeing the terms of the contract.
(2) The degree to which the "standard terms" are imposed on the other party by the party putting them forward.
(3) The relative bargaining power of the parties.
(4) The degree to which the party putting forward the "standard terms" is prepared to entertain negotiations with regard to the terms of the contract generally and the "standard terms" in particular.
(5) The extent and nature of any agreed alterations to the "standard terms" made as a result of the negotiations between the parties.
(6) The extent and duration of the negotiations.

---

business". There is therefore no material difference between ss.3 and 17. Following enactment of the Consumer Rights Act, these provisions are disapplied in the case of consumer contracts.
[26] [1981] S.L.T. 103 at 105. Lord Dunpark's dicta were followed in *Chester Grosvenor Hotel Co v Alfred McAlpine Management* [1993] 7 C.L. 71.
[27] [1995] F.S.R. 654.
[28] *Flamar Interocean Ltd v Denmac Ltd* [1990] 1 Lloyd's Rep. 434.
[29] [1995] F.S.R. 654.

8–011   In this case, the party presented with the terms had taken legal and other advice on all the proposed terms in order to decide on the alterations it desired. To the extent that changes were largely agreed to, the official referee declared himself satisfied that the terms of this contract were not imposed on the recipient of the original standard terms and that the party proposing them was "prepared to engage in a meaningful process of negotiation ... as to those terms". He added that the process of negotiation had taken place over a considerable period of time.

Ultimately, it will be a question of assessing the degree and significance of any changes made to prospective standard terms when it comes to determining whether or not a contract has been made on written standard terms. This was so stated by Scott Baker J. in the *St Albans* case and acceded to in the Court of Appeal.

The point was further emphasised in *Yuanda (UK) Co Ltd v WW Gear Construction Ltd.*[30] Gear prepared a standard package of contract documents that were to be issued to each trade contractor involved in the project, some 30 or so. The package was based on the JCT Trade Contract with a substantial number of amendments which were set out in a separate Schedule of Amendments. Edwards-Stuart J. pointed to the six factors listed above, and said that:

> "I agree that factors (1), (2) and (4) of those identified in the *Salvage Association* case may be relevant in deciding whether or not a particular set of terms may constitute a party's standard terms of business, at least when they are proffered, but I do not consider that the existence of negotiations is itself a relevant consideration: the *St Albans* case held that it was not. In my view, the only important factor of those listed in the *Salvage Association* case is (5). If there is any significant difference between the terms proffered and the terms of the contract actually made, then the contract will not have been made on one party's written standard terms of business."

In the case before him, he held that the contract had not been made on written standard terms. He said that there were:

> "at least two reasons for this, both of which are fatal to Yuanda's case. First, Yuanda itself negotiated some material alterations to the proffered 'standard' terms and this means that it did not deal on the 'standard' terms. As the decision in *St Albans City and District Council v International Computers Ltd* ... makes clear, the reference to dealing in section 3 of UCTA is to the making of the contract, not to its negotiation."[31]

8–012   In *SoftLanding Systems Inc v KDP Software Ltd,*[32] the evidence was that the defendants in an action for breach of contract had never had any standard agreements at the time that the agreement was concluded. The relevant agreement was the first such agreement that they entered into. Such licence agreements that they afterwards concluded contained provisions that were significantly different as to risk and liability. The agreement was based on one of SoftLanding's distributorship agreements retyped internally by the defendants and suitably amended to substitute KDP Software Ltd as licensor and SoftLanding Systems Inc as the distributor. Evidence was led as to how the typist had retyped the

---

[30] [2010] EWHC 720 (TCC).
[31] See also *Hadley Design Associates Ltd v Westminster LBC* [2003] All E.R. (D) 164 (Jul) and *Ferryways NV v Associated British Ports* [2008] EWHC 225 (Comm).
[32] [2010] EWHC 326 (TCC).

original SoftLanding agreement, suitably adapting it and amending it as the basis of the written agreement between the parties. The judge considered the correspondence between the parties at this time and felt it was:

> "clear beyond a doubt that this was a collaborative process conducted by letter and email. The sage contribution of [the claimants' principal owner] is to be found in the drafting of Addendum A and the amendments respectively to paragraph 1 of section 8 and the third paragraph of section 10 of the original draft agreement."

The court accordingly rejected the submission that the agreement was a standard agreement drafted and used by the defendant. It held that the principal source for the draft content of the agreement was furnished by that the principal owner.

Crucially, it has also been held that, even if only the exclusion and limitation clauses are the standard non-negotiable terms in the contract, the contract is on written standard terms for the purposes of the Act.[33]

NEGOTIATING THE EXCLUSION CLAUSE

It appears from Lord Dunpark's observation that the exclusion clause must itself **8–013** be one of the fixed terms, which was no doubt what Parliament intended. Scott Baker J. in the *St Albans* case also said that, while there may be negotiations on a number of terms, there might be none on the "crucial exempting clauses". On the other hand, the wording of the Act simply refers to contracts on written standard terms, and leaves it open for the exclusion clauses to be one of the negotiated conditions. It is of course the case that, if the exclusion or limitation clause is one of those subjects to individual negotiation, it is likely to pass the reasonableness test.

In the *Salvage Association* case,[34] the official referee, after finding that the contract was on written standard terms even though some "important" matters had been negotiated, stated as a consequence that, in so far as the presenter of the terms sought to rely on any exclusion or limitation clause in the contract, that clause was within the Act. At first sight, this appears to mean that even an exclusion clause, or limitation clause separately negotiated, would be subject to the test of reasonableness, but this point was not directly in consideration and, in any event, the relevant clauses were among those which had been drafted in advance. The issue therefore remains awaiting a specific ruling.

In *Fillite (Runcorn) Ltd v APV Pasilac Ltd*,[35] the evidence was that APV were willing to negotiate terms as to price, specification and delivery, but were not willing to negotiate such terms as related to exclusion of liability for consequential loss. APV argued that, since some of the terms were negotiable, the contract was thus deprived of "the quality of being standard". Fillite had successfully negotiated in relation to the price, payment, the timing of retentions, and the period and extent of the warranties and the indemnity clause. The exclusion clause had not been varied and had been presented on a "take it or leave

---

[33] *Pegler Ltd v Wang (UK) Ltd* [2000] EWHC 137 (TCC).
[34] [1995] F.S.R. 654.
[35] *The Buyer*, July 1995 (CA).

it" basis. The Court of Appeal duly concluded that "the terms in question in this appeal were written standard terms of business".

USING OUT-OF-DATE TERMS

8–014   The parties in the *St Albans* case had contracted on the basis of the defendants' 1985 General Conditions, even though these had been superseded by General Conditions adopted in 1988. This appeared to have been done in error. Scott Baker J. dismissed the argument that this meant that the contract had not taken place on the defendants' written standard terms. He thought that the "practical way of looking at it is that the claimants were dealing on the defendants' written standard terms albeit the 1985 edition".

CONTRACTS ON TRADE ASSOCIATION TERMS

8–015   It is to be noted that the above provisions apply when one party deals "on the other's terms". Where the latter prepared his own set of terms, this is clear enough. There will, however, be cases where those terms are in fact prepared by some such body as a trade association for use by its members. If those terms are adopted by one side to the contract, then the other can be fairly said to be contracting on the first party's terms and conditions. If, however, both parties, perhaps being members of the same association, agree that the particular terms will be used by them, it is difficult to say that one is contracting on the other's terms and conditions. It may be that this is a situation which is not within the Act, not least because there would be no argument of one party attempting to exercise superiority over the other. If, however, this argument is not accepted, then presumably the answer is that the contract is on the basis of the terms of that party whose offer was the one finally accepted.

Considerable guidance has been given on this issue by the decision in *British Fermentation Products Ltd v Compair Reavell Ltd*.[36] The relevant terms, which essentially dealt with issues arising if the particular goods were defective, and which replaced the implied warranties and conditions, were contained in a contract drawn up by the Institutions of Mechanical Engineers Model Form of General Conditions of Contract. It was the defendants' argument that, since the terms and conditions were those produced by a third party, they were not on the other's written standard terms of business. In resolving the issue, the court took note of the approach adopted by the Law Commissions in formulating the recommendations which had led to the 1977 Act.[37] The Commissions had accepted that there were standard terms and conditions drafted by parties to a contract, and those, as in the present case, which are drafted by third parties. While it was the former which had come in for most criticism, the Commissions thought that the two categories shared much in common in that neither were drafted with consideration of the individual contract in mind. The conclusion then reached by the Commissions was that:

---

[36] [1999] 2 All E.R. (Comm) 389.
[37] Law Com. No.69; Scot. Law Com. No.39, paras 151–157.

"We think that the courts are well able to recognise standard terms used by persons in the course of their business... We have not, therefore, attempted to formulate a statutory description of a standard form of contract."

The court found that "one essential" for the application of the Act in cases such as the present was proof that the model contract was "invariably or least usually" used by the party in question. It would need to be shown that the relevant party, by practice or express statement, had adopted a model form as its standard terms of business. The court did add, though, that the presence of such proof did not necessarily mean that the Act would apply, rather the Act could not apply in the absence of such proof.

In the instant case, there was nothing to show that the defendants invariably or usually used the Model Form. There had been correspondence between the parties as to whether the IME terms had superseded the terms and conditions which had been printed on the reverse of the claimants' order form. In one letter, the defendants had said that they made "extensive" use of the IME terms, but, the court said, this was not to say that these terms were the only, or even the usual, terms on which the defendants contracted. The defendants had not said that they were prepared to contract only on the IME terms, and it was possible, on the evidence, that they would have been prepared to negotiate as to whether these terms, or some others, would have formed the basis of the agreement. The burden of proof had not been satisfied, and it was held that the contract had not been made on written standard terms.

That it will be difficult to apply the Act when trade terms are used is well illustrated in *Langstane Housing Association Ltd v Riverside Construction (Aberdeen) Ltd.*[38] In an action for damages by a housing association against consulting engineers for breach of contract following the collapse of part of the former's building which the latter were involved in renovating, a preliminary proof was heard to determine what terms were incorporated into the contract and the extent to which Riverside were entitled to rely thereon. The engineers had been appointed to the association's panel of consultants by letter which stated that the appointment would be on the basis of the current ACE Conditions of Engagement. The court held that there had been no dealing on another's party's standard terms, and this was for two reasons:

8–016

"First, the ACE Conditions are not the second defenders' standard terms of business. They are drafted and promulgated by the Association of Consulting Engineers and used... widely within the profession. Secondly, it is by no means clear that, in the context of the relationship between the parties as a whole, it was the second defenders rather than the pursuers who put forward the ACE Conditions. It would be wrong, in my opinion, simply to take the letter of 15 March 2001 and deduce from that that it was the second defenders who were relying on the ACE Conditions. One has to look also at the letter of appointment to the Panel of Consultants on 16 May 1995, in terms of which it was the pursuers who put forward the ACE Conditions."

The letter of March 15 was one in which the second defenders had set out their fee proposals and the proposed basis of their engagement. The letter of May 16 was one in which the pursuers had reiterated the terms of engagement.

---

[38] [2009] CSOH 52.

In the *St Albans* case, Scott Baker J., noting that standard terms drawn up by trade associations take conflicting interests into account, hinted, and perhaps no more than that, that exclusion or limitation clauses contained in such terms would of necessity be reasonable. In the *Compair* case, the judge, obiter, upheld the clause as reasonable.

THE OTHER PARTY'S "BUSINESS"

8–017   For s.3 to apply, the contract must be made on the other party's standard terms of business. The fact that the terms might be standard terms is not of itself enough. In *Commerzbank AG v James Keen*,[39] it was held that s.3 did not extend to a contract of employment since the employee could not be regarded as dealing as consumer.[40]

THE APPLICABILITY OF SECTION 3: IN THE EVENT OF BREACH

8–018   Given that a contract is on written standard terms, the Act then applies where the party whose terms they are is in breach.[41] In such a case, no exclusion clause will be valid, unless reasonable, in relation to that breach. The nature of the breach is not spelled out and is irrelevant. It does not matter that the breach was innocent, wilful, based on negligence or whatever.

THE APPLICABILITY OF SECTION 3: NON-BREACH CASES—VARIATIONS IN PERFORMANCE

8–019   Subject once more to the test of reasonableness, the 1977 Act provides that no clause in a contract on written standard terms is valid if it allows the relevant party to render a performance substantially different from what was reasonably expected of him.[42]

The use of the phrase "reasonably expected" causes problems. What matters is reasonable expectations; that is to say the objective standards of the reasonable person, not the perhaps unreasonable expectations of a particular individual. Furthermore, it is difficult to see how a person can have his reasonable expectations disappointed when a contract contains the particular term, even more so when, as might be the case, that term is somehow highlighted. Unlike the case in relation to negligence liability, where, as we have seen,[43] the Act carefully spelled out the position as to acceptance of risk, no equivalent precaution is taken

---

[39] [2006] EWCA Civ 1536, thus overruling *Brigden v American Express Bank Ltd* [2000] I.R/L.R 94. Since the Consumer Rights Act 2014 has disapplied the reference to "consumer" in this context, the *Commerzbank* case now stands only as authority for the approach which the courts are prepared to adopt as to the meaning of the other party's "business".

[40] See also *Chapman v Aberdeen Construction Group Plc* [1991] I.R.L.R. 505; *Peninsula Business Services Ltd v Sweeney* [2004] I.R.L.R. 49.

[41] See s.3(2)(a); s.17(1)(a) in Scotland.

[42] See s.3(2)(b)(i); s.17(1)(b) in Scotland.

[43] See para.8–008.

here. Presumably, the disputed clause has to be isolated from the rest of the contract, and it is on the basis of the latter that reasonable expectations have to be judged.

Considerable assistance in the interpretation of these provisions was given by High Court in *Zockoll Group Ltd v Mercury Communications Ltd*.[44] The case was concerned with the free call number 0500 FLIGHTS. When tapped out on an alphanumeric keypad, this would give the number 0500 354 448, the addition of the final S being irrelevant since the final number 7 would not affect the dialling of what in fact was a six digit number. Zockoll acquired 53 numbers from Mercury, including the FLIGHTS number. That agreement contained a number of clauses, cl.8.1 reading:

> "It is hereby acknowledged that the telephone number(s) allocated by Mercury to the Customer as part of the Agreement do not belong to the Customer and Mercury shall be entitled at its sole discretion at any time to withdraw or change any telephone number used by the Customer on giving the Customer reasonable notice in writing. The Customer accepts that it shall acquire no rights whatsoever in any telephone number allocated by Mercury and the Customer shall make no attempt to apply for registration of the same as a trade or service mark, whether on its own or in conjunction with some other words or trading style."

Mercury invoked this clause when they decided that the number was better allocated to a firm called Manchester Flights. In response, Zockoll maintained that the clause was subject to the provisions of s.3, in that it purported to entitle Mercury to provide a performance of the contract which was substantially different from what was reasonably expected. Blackburne J. said that a broad view of the Act had to be taken: "So regarded, it seems to me that the contractual performance reasonably expected of Mercury was to provide 53 numbers (of which 50 were apparently random) for use as free call numbers". If that approach were adopted, the judge said, it would then become impossible to contend that a withdrawal, in reliance on cl.8.1, coupled with the offer of a substitute, was "to render a contractual performance *substantially different* from that which was reasonably expected". The point was, he said, that the other 49 random numbers remained with Zockoll, as well as what the judge called "three golden numbers". The fact that the number which was withdrawn could be converted to FLIGHTS was "irrelevant". This was because, when the agreement was made, Mercury simply did not know of the attributes of the apparently random numbers which it was providing: "A condition of what was reasonably expected of [Mercury] by way of contractual performance, cannot . . . be coloured by Mercury's subsequent knowledge of the attributes of the disputed number". He added that, even if the contractual performance reasonably expected of Mercury was that no number would be withdrawn without good reason, Zockoll were no more able to show that Mercury was claiming, by its reliance on cl.8.1, to be entitled to render a contractual performance which was "*substantially different*" from that expectation.

---

[44] [1998] F.S.R. 354.

8–020   A not dissimilar issue had arisen in *Timeload Ltd v British Telecommunications Plc.*[45] BT agreed to make available to Timeload the number 0800 192 192 and did so subject to a contract containing this provision:

> "Termination of service by notice. At any time after service has been provided this contract or the provision of any service or facility under it can be ended:
> (1) by one month's notice by us; or
> (2) by seven days' notice by you."

It was put before the Court of Appeal that this was a clause which allowed BT to offer a service which was substantially different from that which was reasonably expected. The Master of the Rolls said that this part of the Act was not entirely clear, but added that:

> "If a customer reasonably expects a service to continue until BT has substantial reasons to terminate it, it seems to me at least arguable that a clause purporting to authorise BT to terminate without reason purports to permit partial or different performance from that which the customer expected."

No formal decision was reached since the case was an interlocutory hearing, but the court did grant the injunction since it felt that *Timeload's* case was arguable.

In *Durabella Ltd v J Jarvis & Sons Ltd*,[46] it appears to have been accepted, though the case is not entirely clear on this point, that a "pay when paid" clause did fall within the Act.

In the *Oval* case,[47] a performance bond was entered into, which, in its relevant parts, stated:

> "The Contractors and the Surety are held and firmly bound to the Employer in the above Sum for due payment of which sum the Contractors bind themselves... THIS BOND is executed by the Surety upon the following conditions which shall be conditions precedent to the right of the Employer to recover hereunder...".

The court rejected an argument that s.3(2)(b) applied to this clause:

> "By its defence the Defendant does not... claim to be entitled to render a contractual performance substantially different from that which was reasonably expected of it nor does it claim to render no performance at all. By its defence the Defendant does no more than rely upon the claimant's failure to give the written notice required by an expressly agreed condition precedent. As I have previously indicated an express agreement, as part of a guarantee contract, that one party will provide to the other information concerning the performance of the underlying contract is a term upon which the parties are entitled to agree if they wish. The information to be provided has actual or potential commercial significance to a guarantor and, having contracted on the basis that liability was to depend upon such information being supplied... it was entitled to refuse payment if the requisite information was not in fact supplied."

---

[45] [1995] E.M.L.R. 459.
[46] (2001) 83 Con.L.R. 145.
[47] (1997) 85 B.L.R. 97.

In *Barclays Mercantile Business Finance Ltd v Marsh and Soundalive Ltd*,[48] a **8–021** company sought to enforce a guarantee and indemnity clause. The court said that this did not fall within the Act since it did not require any contractual performance at all. In *Do-Buy 925 Ltd v National Westminster Bank Plc*,[49] a jeweller had an agreement with the bank by which the jeweller accepted credit cards and the bank acted as merchant acquirer. A clause in the contract read: "You agree that as between You and Us it is Your responsibility to prove to Our Satisfaction that the debit of a cardholder's account was authorised by the genuine cardholder". The court said that the Act was not engaged by this clause because it neither proposed a substantially different performance nor no performance at all: "On the contrary [the bank's] contractual obligation, and the performance that could be reasonably expected of it, was to pay for authorised transactions".

In *Ilanchelian v Esso Petroleum Co Ltd*,[50] a clause ran thus:

> "8.2 Payment in lieu of notice.
> 8.2.1 Upon written notification to the agent Esso may elect to pay a sum to the agent for the period of notice set out in clause 8.1 in lieu of the agent acting as Esso's agent during the notice period . . .
> 8.2.2 . . . the sum to be paid by Esso to the agent pursuant to clause 8.2.1 shall be £2000 save for where, immediately prior to the giving of notice, the agent shall have completed a continuous period of two years as Esso's agent or licensee, in which event the sum shall be £6000."

Clause 8.1 dealt with the procedure for termination on notice. In response to the argument that this clause provided for a substantially different performance than that which was reasonably expected, Rimer J. felt that there was no basis for any such contention. He said that there was, for example, no evidence to suggest that there was any case for saying that it was reasonably expected of Esso that it would invoke cl.8.1 and would not invoke cl.8.2: "There is, in particular, no suggestion that Esso ever made any representations to the claimant to that effect".

In contrast, it was said that there was a "genuine triable issue" to the effect that the following clause, in a contract for spread betting, was a clause seeking to allow a substantially different performance from that which was reasonably expected: one giving the defendants the right "to close any or all, in whole or in part, of your open bets (including those held on a joint account with others) on the basis of City Index's current (or next available) market quotations . . .". The court appeared to indicate that the evidentiary burden of showing that the relevant provisions of the Act did not apply lay on the party who sought to uphold the clause when it said that: "In the absence of such evidence it seems to me to be impossible to conclude that the case is not within section 3(1)(b)".[51]

In *Harrison v Shepherd Homes*,[52] the judge when faced with the following clauses, said only that the relevant party, would be in breach of an implied contractual duty and/or "seeking to exclude or restrict liability or be claiming to

---

[48] [2002] EWCA Civ 948.
[49] [2010] EWHC 2862 (QB).
[50] [1998] EWCA Civ 1535.
[51] *City Index Ltd v Stephenson* Unreported November 6, 2001.
[52] [2011] EWHC 1811. The case went on appeal but the 1977 Act was not in issue: [2012] EWCA Civ 904.

be entitled to render a contractual performance substantially different from that which was reasonably expected of it or in respect of the whole or any part of its contractual obligation, to render no performance at all". Such terms were these:

"The Works shall be completed by the Seller in a good and workmanlike manner and shall be so completed and made ready for occupation with all reasonable despatch after the Agreement Date This clause will not merge on completion...

This Agreement and the 'Buildmark' Offer of Cover constitute the entire contract between the parties and shall be only varied or modified... in writing under the hands of the parties and any terms, undertakings, promises or agreements not set out in this Agreement are released by both parties and shall have no effect. The buyer acknowledges that save as to such of the written statements of the Seller's Solicitors prior to the Agreement Date as were not susceptible of independent verification by inspection and search and enquiry of any local or other public authority (and whether or not such inspection search and enquiry has been made) the Buyer has not entered into this Agreement in reliance wholly or partly on any statement or representation made to him.

Any obligation of this Agreement or of the Buildmark Offer of Cover which *is* expressed as or which implies any obligation which will remain to be performed or observed after the completion of the sale and purchase and the Lease or Transfer of the Property to the Buyer shall remain in full force and effect after such completion."

8–022   A restrictive approach to the interpretation of the Act was adopted in the *Brigden* case.[53] The disputed clause, contained in an employment contract, provided that "an employee may be dismissed by notice and/or payment in lieu of notice during the first two years of employment, without implementation of the disciplinary procedure". The court held that this clause, while expressed in negative terms, was neither a term excluding or restricting liability for breach or one which entitled the defendants to render a contractual performance substantially different from what was reasonably expected.

There is an argument for saying that a retention of title clause comes within the Act.[54] If such a clause stipulates that a buyer does not become full owner of the goods until all debts with the seller have been cleared, whether under the particular contract or some other between the same parties, then there is room for saying that the buyer is being offered a performance substantially different from that which he was reasonably expecting. The contra-argument is that the Act, when speaking of performance, is referring to the core of the agreement, namely that which was to be supplied or tendered, and not to matters which might be regarded as annexed issues to that essential performance.

THE APPLICABILITY OF SECTION 3: NON-BREACH CASES—TOTAL
NON-PERFORMANCE

8–023   The Unfair Contract Terms Act 1977 also provides that, subject to the test of reasonableness, no clause in a written standard term contract can purport to allow no performance at all of a party's "contractual obligation".[55] This is perhaps more difficult to interpret than the problems raised above. Since the Act does refer to

---

[53] This aspect to the case is unaffected by the decision in the *Commerzbank* case, see para.8–017.
[54] Such clauses first achieved prominence in *Aluminium Industrie Vaassen BV v Romalpa Aluminium Ltd* [1976] 1 W.L.R. 676.
[55] See s.3(2)(b)(ii); s.17(1)(b) in Scotland.

the "contractual obligation", it is to the contract that one must turn to determine just what that obligation is. It is, however, the contract itself that contains the terms permitting non-performance. The contractual obligation therefore consists in part of the right not to perform, and hence making use of the particular term is, in a contractual sense, a performance of the contract. This, however, would be to defeat the plain intention of Parliament which is that the disputed term should be judged separately from the remaining terms of the contract.

There has so far been no relevant litigation, although it was held in the *Brigden* case[56] that the clause involved there was not one which provided for no performance at all, with no specific reasoning applied to this ruling. It may be supposed, however, that a force majeure clause is an example of the type of clause which falls into the "no performance" provisions. Typically, a force majeure clause will specify that, in certain circumstances (such as fire, lockouts, flooding or outbreak of war) the relevant party will not be liable for any failure to perform his obligations under the contract. A clause which went further, and gave that party an unfettered right not to perform at all, with no reference to any qualifying circumstances, would almost certainly be of itself ineffective since it would reduce the contract to the level of a mere declaration of intent, something that the courts would seek to deny.[57]

THE RELEVANT PERFORMANCE

Section 3(2)(b) of the Act refers to a substantially different "contractual performance" and to the right to render no "performance". The question raised in *Paragon Finance Plc v Staunton*[58] was which party's performance was relevant to the application of the Act. The case concerned the following clause in a consumer credit contract:

8–024

> "Interest shall be charged at such rate as the Company shall from time to time apply to the category of business to which the Company shall consider the Mortgage belongs and may accordingly be increased or decreased by the Company at any time and with effect from such date or dates as the Company shall determine . . .".

It was submitted on behalf of the borrowers that they were reasonably entitled to expect that, in performing its side of the bargain, the lender would not apply rates which were substantially out of line with rates applied by comparable lenders to borrowers in comparable situations to the present borrowers. It was contended that the setting of interest rates was "contractual performance" within the meaning of s.3(2)(b) of the 1977 Act.

The Court of Appeal rejected this argument. Distinguishing the *Timeload* and *Zockoll* cases,[59] Dyson L.J. said that, in the present case, there was no relevant obligation on the lender, and therefore nothing that could qualify as "contractual performance" for the purposes of s.3(2)(b)(i):

---

[56] See p.8–017. This aspect to the decision is unaffected by the *Commerzbank* case, see *ibid*.
[57] See para.3–016 and following.
[58] [2001] 2 All E.R. (Comm) 1025.
[59] See para.8–019 and following.

"Even if that is wrong, by fixing the rate of interest at a particular level the [lender] is not altering the performance of any obligation assumed by it under the contract. Rather, it is altering the performance required of the appellants."

This was followed in *Nautch Ltd v Mortgage Express Ltd*.[60] A term in a mortgage agreement provided for the full amount of the loan to be repayable if "you are late paying money under the agreement and the amount overdue is equal to at least two monthly payments". Rejecting the argument that s 3(2)(b) applied, the court said:

"ME did not assume an obligation to leave the loan outstanding for three years, or any further period. Had the borrower in each case made the monthly payments due, ME's right to repayment of the whole ahead of the expiry of the mortgage term, and its right to appoint a receiver, would not have arisen. Not having a right to early payment is not the same as being under an obligation not to seek early payment. Had ME sought repayment in the absence of the relevant two months' arrears, it would have rightly been rebuffed. That would not be because ME would be in breach of any obligation, but because it would on that hypothesis have no right to demand payment of the mortgage debt or to appoint a receiver. As it was, there were in a number of cases two months' arrears and ME's enforcement rights were thereby engaged. The whole of the mortgage debt fell due and ME could appoint receivers in consequence. That remained the position in those cases where the arrears were paid off in whole or in part, whether before or after the appointment of receivers. I would also add that I would, if necessary, regard a standard clause providing for payment of the whole to fall due on two months' default as reasonable, though, strictly, this point does not arise."

EXCLUDING TERMS AS TO TITLE

8–025 A quite separate regime applies in relation to terms which seek to exclude the conditions and warranties as to title implied by the Supply of Goods (Implied Terms) Act 1973 and the Sale of Goods Act 1979.[61] Where a clause seeks to restrict these obligations, then any such clause is void and of no effect.[62] The above provisions apply to all contracts of sale or hire-purchase, whether or not the seller or supplier is acting in the course of a business.[63]

Where the ownership of goods passes under a contract which is neither one of sale nor of hire purchase, such as a contract for work and materials or for the installation of equipment, the terms as to title implied by s.2 of the Supply of Goods and Services Act 1982 cannot be excluded.[64]

Where ownership or possession passes under any contract not subject to that section, such as a contract for the lease of goods, then liability in respect of the right to transfer possession or ownership of the goods, or any assurance of quiet possession given to the person taking the goods, cannot be excluded except where the relevant clause can be shown to be reasonable.[65] Nothing is said as to any

---

[60] [2012] EWHC 4136.
[61] See ss.8–11 and 12–15, respectively, of those Acts.
[62] See the Unfair Contract Terms Act 1977 s.6(1); s.20(1) in relation to Scotland.
[63] Unfair Contract Terms Act 1977 s.6(4). There is no equivalent covering Scotland, but this is because those provisions of the Act relating to Scotland were not subject to the provisions of s.1(3) (applicability of 1977 Act to business liability) in the first place.
[64] Unfair Contract Terms Act 1977 s.7(3A). The 1982 Act does not apply to Scotland, so there is no equivalent to s.7(3A).
[65] Unfair Contract Terms Act s.7(4).

warranty as to freedom from encumbrances, which means, if such a term is implied in the first place,[66] that it can be excluded or restricted unimpeded by the provisions of the Unfair Contract Terms Act 1977.[67]

EXCLUDING TERMS AS TO DESCRIPTION, QUALITY, ETC.

Section 6(3) of the Unfair Contract Terms Act[68] states that the terms implied into contracts as to description, quality and fitness by the 1973 and 1979 Acts cannot be excluded or limited in contracts with businesses except where the particular exclusion clause is reasonable. In relation to contracts other than those of sale or hire purchase, where ownership or possession passes, the position is identical; that is to say, those implied terms as to description, sample, quality and fitness cannot be excluded unless the relevant term is reasonable.[69]

8–026

There will inevitably be cases where the contract is one of sale or hire-purchase and is also made on the other's written standard terms. It seems that the matter can be dealt with either under s.3 or under the present provisions. The question as to which provision takes precedence was raised but not decided in *Sovereign Finance Ltd v Silver Crest Furniture Ltd*,[70] but the correct position would seem to be that the claimant could make use of both.

MISREPRESENTATION

Section 3 of the Misrepresentation Act 1967, which does not apply to Scotland, provides that if a contract contains a term excluding or restricting:

8–027

> "(a) any liability to which a party to a contract may be subject by reason of any misrepresentation made by him before the contract was made; or
> (b) any remedy available to another party to the contract by reason of such a misrepresentation,[71]
> that term shall be of no effect except so far as it satisfies the requirement of reasonableness as stated in section 11(1) of the Unfair Contract Terms Act 1977."

In *WRM Group Ltd v Wood*,[72] cl.5.7 of a contract read:

> "The purchaser shall (without prejudice to its other rights hereunder ... or to any right or remedy that it may have in law or equity) be entitled to set off... against any amount otherwise payable to the Warrantors in respect of the retention Loan Notes up to a maximum aggregate of £300,000 ... which the Purchaser claims by written notice to the Warrantors is

---

[66] There is no such term implied by statute.

[67] In Scotland, the reasonableness test will apply where the contract is one for the transfer of ownership or possession of goods: see Unfair Contract Terms Act 1977 ss.15(2)(a), 21(1)(b), (2) and 3(b). These provisions do not apply to contracts of sale or hire. The provisions relating to Scotland refer to the implied terms as to the right to transfer possession or ownership and the enjoyment of quiet possession.

[68] In relation to Scotland, s.20(2)(b).

[69] Unfair Contract Terms Act 1977 s.7(3) or, in relation to Scotland, s.21(1)(b).

[70] [1997] C.C.L.R. 76.

[71] For the Misrepresentation Act to be invoked, there must first be a reliance on the representation: *Fleet Mobile Tyres Ltd v Stone* [2006] EWHC 1947 (QB).

[72] [1998] C.L.C. 189. See also *Barclays Bank Plc v Alfons Kufner* [2008] EWHC 2319 (Comm).

properly due from the Warrantors or any of them to the Purchaser . . . under or by reason of any breach of the terms of the Warranties . . . Such right of set-off shall be limited to the right of cancellation of up to £300,000 by nominal value of Retention Loan Notes issued . . . in accordance with the conditions endorsed thereon . . . and shall cease if no written notice of a claim in accordance with Clause 6.3 has been made by July 31, 1996."

Clause 5.8 provided that:

"Save as provided by Clause 5.7 the Purchaser shall not be entitled to set off against any amount otherwise payable to the Vendors under the Agreement (whether pursuant to the terms of the Retention Loan Notes or otherwise) or any other agreements or documents to be entered into by the Vendors or any of them in connection therewith, any amount which the Purchaser claims is due from the Vendors or any of them to the Purchaser . . . under or by reason of any breach of the terms of this Agreement."

Morritt L.J. said that the clauses operated "to exclude the possibility of set-off in respect of all sums claimed to be due because a warranty contained in the Agreement was broken or because a representation made therein, whether innocently, carelessly or fraudulently, was false". Counsel accepted that, following the ruling in *Stewart Gill Ltd v Horatio Myer & Co Ltd*,[73] cl.5 was clearly a clause which sought to exclude or restrict a remedy available to the other party, but reserved his position on whether the clause excluded or restricted any liability.

Instead of directly excluding liability for misrepresentation, a different approach, but seeking the same ends, is occasionally tried. In *Cremdean Properties Ltd v Nash*,[74] the defendants against whom it was alleged that a misrepresentation had been made relied on a clause reading:

"These particulars are prepared for the convenience of an intending purchaser or tenant and although they are believed to be correct their accuracy is not guaranteed and any error, omission or misdescription shall not annul the sale or the grounds on which compensation may be claimed and neither do they constitute any part of an offer of a contract. Any intending purchaser or tenant must satisfy himself by inspection or otherwise as to the correctness of each of the statements contained in these particulars."

8–028 Bridge L.J. paraphrased the argument of the defendants in these words: "the footnote is effective . . . to bring about a situation in law as if no representations at all have even been made".[75] In the more robust wording of Scarman L.J., the defendants were arguing thus:

"a statement is not a representation unless it is also a statement that what is stated is true. If in context a statement contains no assertion, express or implied, that its content is accurate, there is no representation. Ergo, there can be no misrepresentation; ergo, the Misrepresentation Act 1967 cannot apply to it."[76]

The Court of Appeal was unanimous in finding that this argument was untenable.[77] The language of the exclusion clause, said Bridge L.J. "simply does

---

[73] [1992] 2 All E.R. 257. See the discussion of this case at para.7–007.
[74] [1977] 244 E.G. 547.
[75] [1977] 244 E.G. 547 at 549.
[76] [1977] 244 E.G. 547 at 551.
[77] Thus upholding the decision of Fox J.: [1977] 241 E.G. 837.

not, on its true interpretation, have the effect contended for".[78] Scarman L.J. found that, fairly construed, the exclusion clause was a warning to the would-be purchaser to check the facts. Such a warning:

> "does not destroy the representation; indeed, it is wholly consistent with the statement being a representation. It is because the statement contains the representation that the warning is given. Since the statement was false, there was a false representation; the Act therefore applies."[79]

Bridge L.J. took the matter further. While finding against the defendants in that the clause could not bear the construction sought to be placed upon it, he felt "extremely doubtful whether the court" would ever allow s.3 to be thus evaded. Supposing, he said, an exclusion clause was drafted to read: "notwithstanding any statement of fact included in these particulars the vendor shall be conclusively deemed to have made no representation within the meaning of the Misrepresentation Act 1967".[80] It was his opinion that "this was only a form of words the intended and actual effect of which was to exclude or restrict liability, and I should not have thought that the courts would have been ready to allow such ingenuity in forms of language to defeat the plain purpose at which section 3 is aimed".[81] This is surely right: a misrepresentation cannot change its character by simply saying that it is not what it is.[82]

The Court of Appeal, through Bridge L.J., supported in this by Scarman L.J., rejected the idea that for the purposes of the Misrepresentation Act there was a distinction between a "representation" and statements of opinion, belief or information. The word itself, said Bridge L.J. is:

> "an extremely wide term; I cannot see why one should not be making a representation when giving information or when stating one's opinion or belief... it would be a retrograde step if the court were to give the word 'representation' where it appears in the Misrepresentation Act 1967, any narrow or limited construction less wide than the perfectly natural meaning of the word."[83]

The court left undecided the issue whether or not the clause was reasonable. That was a matter for consideration at the trial. The only issue here was whether the Misrepresentation Act 1967 applied at all.

---

[78] [1977] 244 E.G. 547 at 551.

[79] [1977] 244 E.G. 547 at 551. It was assumed for the purposes of the action that a misrepresentation had been made.

[80] [1977] 244 E.G. at 551.

[81] *ibid.*

[82] But the court agreed with *Overbrooke Estates v Glencombe Properties* [1974] 1 W.L.R. 1335 that s.3 does not qualify the right of a principal to limit his agent's authority: [1977] 244 E.G. 547 at 549, per Bridge L.J. The *Overbrooke* case was also endorsed by the Court of Appeal in *Collins v Howell-Jones* (1980) 259 E.G. 331 and the High Court in *HIH Casualty & General Insurance Ltd v Chase Manhattan Bank* [2001] 1 Lloyd's Rep. 30.

[83] [1977] 244 E.G. 547 at 551. The same approach was adopted in *BG Plc v Nelson Group Services (Maintenance) Ltd* [2002] EWCA Civ 547. That court did not approve of the contrary view taken by the High Court in *Lancaster CC v Unique Group Ltd* Unreported December 15, 1995, noting that *Cremdean* had not been cited in that case. See also *Nicholas St John Fordy v Richard Cecil Harwood* Unreported March 30, 1999 (CA).

The court also left over until trial the possible impact of the final part of the clause which required intending purchasers or tenants to satisfy themselves as to the correctness of the particulars. This part of the clause, said Bridge L.J., "may have considerable importance ... as bearing upon the question of fact ... as to whether the claimants relied upon any misrepresentation".[84]

8–029 In *Walker v Boyle*,[85] Dillon J. referred to the small print which appeared above replies on the form of preliminary enquiries: "These replies on behalf of the vendor are believed to be correct but accuracy is not guaranteed and they do not obviate the need to make appropriate searches, enquiries and inspections". He concluded that words such as these cannot negative any representation which may in fact have been made.[86]

Despite the observations made in these cases, it does remain possible so to draft a provision of which the effect is to avoid there being a misrepresentation at all. The following provision was considered in *IFE Fund SA v Goldman Sachs International*[87]:

> "The Arranger [Goldman Sachs] has not independently verified the information set out in this Memorandum. Accordingly, no representation, warranty or undertaking, express or implied, is made and no responsibility is accepted by Goldman Sachs International ... as to or in relation to the accuracy or completeness or otherwise of this Memorandum or as to the reasonableness of any assumption contained therein or any other information made available in connection with the Facilities (whether in writing or orally) to any interested party (or its advisors). ... Neither the arranger nor any of its respective directors ... shall be liable for any direct, indirect or consequential loss or damage suffered by any person as a result of relying on any statement contained in this Memorandum or any such other information."

In distinguishing this case from *Cremdean,* the judge considered these two hypothetical examples.

> "If a seller of a car said to a buyer 'I have serviced the car since it was new, it has had only one owner and the clock reading is accurate', those statements would be representations, and they would still have that character even if the seller added the words 'but those statements are not representations on which you can rely'."

That was to be contrasted with the seller who said: "The clock reading is 20,000 miles, but I have no knowledge whether the reading is true or false". The judge said that this latter was different because the qualifying words could not fairly be regarded as an attempt to exclude liability for a false representation arising from the first half of the sentence. The slender difference between this case and the two cited above appears to be that in each of these two the statement said that the information was believed to be correct.

8–030 The *Cremdean* approach is not the only possible approach to non-reliance clauses. In *Peart Stevenson Associates Ltd v Brian Holland*,[88] the relevant clause ran thus:

---

[84] [1977] 244 E.G. 547 at 549.

[85] [1982] 1 All E.R. 634.

[86] [1982] 1 All E.R. 634 at 640.

[87] [2006] EWHC 2887 (Comm). See too *Titan Steel Wheels Ltd v Royal Bank of Scotland Plc* [2010] EWHC 211.

[88] [2008] EWHC 1868.

"The Franchisee acknowledges that this Agreement contain [sic] the whole agreement between the parties and it has not relied upon any oral or written representation made to it by the Franchisor or its employees or agents and has made its own independent investigations into all matters relevant to the Business."

The court said that it could approach the issue based on the *Cremdean* approach or it could apply the principles set out in *Lowe v Lombank*.[89] The latter approach did not contemplate a non-reliance clause having a free rein, but rather, as the court put it, "potentially crashing into a different set of buffers", these being the requirements set out in the *Lowe* case. If those requirements were met, there was no need to consider the requirement of reasonableness. If those requirements were not met, there was also no need or opportunity to consider the requirements of reasonableness—the provision was of no effect. In the end, the court declined to choose between these approaches, saying instead that the non-reliance clause was, in this case, ineffective, because it did not apply to the fraudulent representations which the court found had been made in this case.

Entire agreement clauses

It has been held that the provisions of s.3 have no application to a term in a contract stating that that contract contains the entire terms of the contract. In *Inntrepreneur Pub Co Ltd v East Crown Ltd*,[90] the clause in question read as follows:

8–031

"14.1 Any variations of this Agreement which are agreed in correspondence shall be incorporated in this Agreement where that correspondence makes express reference to this Clause and the parties acknowledge that this Agreement (with the incorporation of any such variations) constitutes the entire Agreement between the parties."

According to Lightman J. entire agreement clauses were designed to prevent parties to a written contract from "threshing through the undergrowth and finding in the course of negotiations some (chance) remark or statement . . . on which to found a claim . . . such as . . . to the existence of a collateral warranty". In the judge's view, an entire agreement clause constituted a binding agreement between the parties that the full contractual terms were to be found in the contractual document and not elsewhere.[91]

Lightman J. recognised that entire agreement clauses come in many different forms. He adopted the approach of Rix J. and the Court of Appeal in *Deepak v ICI*[92] by focusing on the wording of the clause. In *Deepak*, the clause read:

---

[89] See para.2–050.
[90] [2000] 2 Lloyd's Rep. 611. See also *Cheverney Consulting Ltd v Whitehead Man Ltd* [2007] EWHC 3130; *Ravennavi SpA v New Century Shipbuilding Co Ltd* [2007] 2 Lloyd's Rep 24; *Axa Sun Life Services Plc v Campbell Martin Ltd* [2011] EWCA Civ 133; and *Theodoulos Papanicola (Liquidator of Atlantic Fashions Ltd) v Bulbinder Singh Sandhu* [2011] EWHC 1431.
[91] See also *McGrath v Shah* (1989) 57 P. & C.R. 452, distinguished in *Fulton Motors Ltd v Toyota (GB) Ltd* [1999] EWCA Civ 1776. This must be read subject to the requirements of evidentiary estoppel; see para.2–051.
[92] [1999] 1 Lloyd's Rep. 387.

> "This contract comprises the entire agreement between the parties ... and there are not any agreements, understandings, promises or conditions, oral or written, express or implied, concerning the subject matter which are not merged into this contract and superseded thereby ...".

This was held to be wide enough to exclude all liability for collateral warranties, but not misrepresentations.

Lightman J. also considered *Alman & Benson v Associated Newspapers Group Ltd*[93] in which it was provided that a contract "constituted the entire agreement and understanding between the parties with respect to all matters therein referred to". In the latter case, the court held that the language was apt to exclude all liability for a collateral warranty. An alternative approach, designed to achieve the same end, is to reduce the clause to an acknowledgment by the parties that the agreement constitutes the entire agreement between them. That formula was used by *Inntrepreneur* in cl.14.1 of the agreement for lease. Lightman J. considered that this form of clause was also sufficient to constitute an agreement that "the full contractual terms to which the parties agreed to bind themselves are to be found in the agreement and nowhere else".

8–032 Lightman J. also held that an entire agreements clause did not itself preclude a claim in misrepresentation. The denial of contractual force to a particular statement could not affect the status of that statement as a representation. A further clause in the case before him did set out to exclude liability for misrepresentation and breach of duty. The effectiveness of this clause could depend on its reasonableness.[94]

That a purported entire agreements clause must be carefully drafted is well attested by *BSkyB Ltd v HP Enterprise Services UK Ltd*[95] The relevant clause was as follows:

> "Subject to Clause 1.3.2, this Agreement and the Schedules shall together represent the entire understanding and constitute the whole agreement between the parties in relation to its subject matter and supersede any previous discussions, correspondence, representations or agreement between the parties with respect thereto notwithstanding the existence of any provision of any such prior agreement that any rights or provisions of such prior agreement shall survive its termination. The term 'this Agreement' shall be construed accordingly. This clause does not exclude liability of either party for fraudulent misrepresentation."

Ramsey J. pointed to the following words as being the crucial part of the clause under consideration:

> "... this Agreement and the Schedules shall together represent the entire understanding and constitute the whole agreement between the parties in relation to its subject matter and supersede any previous discussions, correspondence, representations or agreement between the parties with respect thereto ...".

He had no doubt about it: those words "do not, in my judgment, amount to an agreement that representations are withdrawn, overridden or of no legal effect so

---

[93] Unreported June 20, 1980.
[94] *Government of Zanzibar v British Aerospace (Lancaster House) Ltd* [2000] 1 W.L.R. 2333. See also the *Fleet Mobile* case at para.8–027.
[95] [2010] EWHC 86 (TCC).

far as any liability for misrepresentation may be concerned". He explained that the clause was concerned with the terms of the agreement. It provided that the agreement was to represent the entire understanding and constituted the whole agreement. He stressed that it was in that context that the agreement had the effect of superseding any previous representations: "That is, representations are superseded and do not become terms of the agreement unless they are included in the agreement". Had it been intended to withdraw representations for all purposes, "then the language would, in my judgment, have had to go further".

In this case the statement that the agreement superseded any previous discussions, correspondence, representations or agreement between the parties with respect to the subject matter of the agreement prevented other terms of the agreement or collateral contracts from having contractual effect. It did not, though, supersede those matters so far as there might be any liability for misrepresentation based on them.[96]

In *Ryanair Ltd v SR Technics Ireland Ltd*,[97] Gray J. gave effect to a collateral contract, despite the existence of an entire agreement clause. He did so, on the basis that both parties proceeded on the common assumption that the collateral contract would be honoured, despite the existence of the entire agreement clause. The entire agreement clause did not prevent the contention that the entire agreement was found partly in the formal contract and partly in the collateral contract. In words endorsed by the court in *Mileform Ltd v Interserve Security Ltd*,[98] it has been said that "[i]t may be thought that this decision undermines the general purpose of an entire agreement clause."[99] Accordingly, this case must be considered of doubtful validity.

Indemnities and guarantees

The provisions in the Act dealing with indemnities and guarantees were repealed by the Consumer Rights Act. Section 4 provided that a consumer was liable under an indemnity for a third party's negligence or breach of contract only to the extent that such provision was reasonable. Section 5 provided that no term in a guarantee could exclude or restrict liability for negligence on the part of the manufacturer or distributor. This latter did not apply to guarantees provided by the actual supplier to the consumer, hence only to what are generally called "manufacturers' guarantees". Neither of these provisions are repeated in the 2014 Act, presumably because such terms would fail the fairness test, or at least be subject to it.

8–033

---

[96] See also *Man Nutzfahrzeuge AG v Freightliner Ltd* [2005] EWHC 2347 (Comm).
[97] [2007] EWHC 3089.
[98] [2013] EWHC 3386.
[99] The words being those of Lewison in *Interpretation of Contracts*, 5th edn (London: Sweet & Maxwell, 2011).

CHAPTER 9

THE REASONABLENESS TEST

When the test of reasonableness is applied to a contract term, the Unfair Contract Terms Act 1977 provides that that term "shall have been a fair and reasonable one to be included having regard to the circumstances which were, or ought reasonably to have been, known to or in the contemplation of the parties when the contract was made".[1] *In Shared Network Services Ltd v Nextiraone UK Ltd*,[2] a contract provided that, regardless of the form of action, any liability to the claimant for damages for breach of contract or tort would be limited to 50 per cent of the service charges paid by it during the preceding 12 months. The claimant began proceedings for breach of contract and sought damages of approximately €1.75 million for alleged wasted expenditure said to have been caused by the defendant severing a virtual private network. The defendant sought summary judgment, contending that as the claimant had not paid any service charges in the 12 months preceding the claim, the limitation clause rendered the value of its claim nil.

9–001

The claimant accepted that the clause had appeared to be reasonable at the time of the agreement, as it had expected to earn a substantial income as a result of the agreement. However, it argued that the clause was unreasonable in the circumstances because the defendant's deliberate failure to perform its contractual obligations meant that it had been prevented from earning any income.

The court stressed that it had to decide the issue on the pleaded case before it, which did not contain an allegation of deliberate breach. In any event, under the Act the time for assessing reasonableness of a clause was when the contract was made, and at that time the claimant had considered the clause to be reasonable.

Where that test is to be applied to a notice not having contractual effect, the requirement of reasonableness is that it should be fair and reasonable to allow reliance on it, having regard to all the circumstances obtaining when the liability arose or would have arisen but for the notice.[3]

The burden of proof is on the party seeking to uphold the clause.[4] Thus, it has been said that "[i]f a party wishes to rely upon clauses, which are caught by the Act and in respect of which he has to discharge a burden of proof of reasonableness, he has to make a positive case and prove whatever is necessary by way of factual background and other commercial considerations that he says suffice to establish the reasonableness of the clause".[5] Where a bank sought to

---

[1] Unfair Contract Terms Act 1977 s.11(1); or s.24(1) in relation to Scotland.
[2] [2012] EWCA Civ 1171.
[3] Unfair Contract Terms Act 1977 s.11(3). There is no equivalent provision in relation to Scotland.
[4] Unfair Contract Terms Act 1977 ss.11(5) and 24(4).
[5] *AEG (UK) v Logic Resource Ltd* [1996] CLC 265 at 278, per Hobhouse L.J.

rely on an exemption clause, it failed to establish its reasonableness when it did not call evidence directed to establishing the reasonableness of the terms.[6]

THE STATUTORY GUIDELINES

9–002   If the contract is one for the sale or supply of goods,[7] then the issue of reasonableness is to be determined after consideration of the matters specified in Sch.2 to the Act.[8] These are as follows:

(1)   The strength of the bargaining position of the parties relative to each other, taking into account (among other things) alternative means by which the customer's requirements could have been met.

(2)   Whether the customer received an inducement to agree to the term, or in accepting it had an opportunity of entering into a similar contract with other persons, but without having to accept a similar term.

(3)   Whether the customer knew or ought reasonably to have known of the existence and extent of the term (having regard, among other things, to any custom of the trade and any previous course of dealing between the parties).

(4)   Where the term excludes or restricts any relevant liability if some condition is not complied with, whether it was reasonable at the time of the contract to expect that compliance with the condition would be practicable.

(5)   Whether the goods were manufactured, processed or adapted to the special order of the customer.

Such matters are, however, no more than those that a court would take into account, whether they are required to do so by the terms of the Act or not. In *Woodman v Photo Trade Processing Ltd*,[9] the Registrar, although not required by the Act to refer to Sch.2, adopted its contents when considering the question of reasonableness since the guidelines contained in the Schedule "would be among the matters necessarily needing consideration in this case". Scott Baker J. in *St Albans City and District Council v International Computers Ltd*[10] also said that the guidelines could be applied when considering s.3 of the 1977 Act and were

---

[6] *Jayesh Shah v HSBC Private Bank (UK) Ltd* [2012] EWHC 1283.
[7] i.e. one covered by ss.6 and 7, or, in relation to Scotland, ss.20 and 21.
[8] Unfair Contract Terms Act 1977 s.12(2) or, in relation to Scotland, s.24(2).
[9] Unreported April 3, 1981 (Exeter CC).
[10] [1995] F.S.R. 686.

not in practice confined to ss.6 and 7.[11] The same point was made by Popplewell J. in *FG Wilson (Engineering) Ltd v John Holt & Company (Liverpool) Ltd*[12] when saying:

> "Schedule 2 to UCTA contains guidelines for the application of the reasonableness test. They are not made applicable to the present contracts by the statute because they are directed to sections other than s. 3, but they identify matters that are likely to be of relevance when determining whether the term is reasonable for the purposes of s. 3 and should be taken into account for that purpose".

It is furthermore to be noted that, when the guidelines in Sch.2 are required to be considered, the court is not confined to those factors listed in the Schedule, since they are not to be treated as exhaustive of the matters to be considered when determining if a term is reasonable.[13]

It is also provided that, when Sch.2 does fall to be considered, nothing is to prevent the court from holding that the particular term is not a part of the contract.[14] This is a curious provision, not least because there is nothing in the Act, nor this subsection in particular, which would prevent the court from so holding. This is accentuated by the fact that no similar provision exists where the test of reasonableness is to be applied without reference to Sch.2.

PLEADING THE ACT

In *Sheffield v Pickfords Ltd*,[15] it was held that in a case which may be affected by the 1977 Act, it is for the party who relies on standard form conditions to plead the matters on which it relies if it seeks to contend that its conditions are reasonable. This was followed in *Lacey's Footwear Ltd v Bowler*.[16]   **9–003**

LIABILITY LIMITED TO A SPECIFIED SUM

Where a contract term limits liability to a specified sum, the court is also required (in addition to considering Sch.2, should that be applicable), to take note of the following factors: **9–004**

---

[11] See also *Flamar Interocean Ltd v Denmac Ltd* [1990] 1 Lloyd's Rep. 434 at 438–439, per Potter J; *Salvage Association v CAP Financial Services Ltd* [1995] F.S.R. 654; *Oval Ltd v Aegon Insurance Co (UK) Ltd* (1997) 85 B.L.R. 97; *Overland Shoes Ltd v Schenkers Ltd* [1998] 1 Lloyd's Rep. 498; *Moores v Yakeley Associates Ltd* Unreported October 28, 1998; *Overseas Medical Supplies Ltd v Orient Transport Services Ltd* [1999] 1 All E.R. (Comm) 981; *Granville Oil & Chemicals Ltd v Davis Turner & Co Ltd* [2003] EWCA Civ 570; *Bank of Scotland v Singh* Unreported June 17, 2005; *Snookes v Jani-King (GB) Ltd* [2006] EWHC 289 (QB); *Shepherd Homes Ltd v Encia Remedies Ltd* [2007] EWHC 70 (TCC); *Barclays Bank Plc v Alfons Kufner* [2008] EWHC 2319 (Comm); and *Yuanda (UK) Co Ltd v WW Gear Construction Ltd* [2010] EWHC 720 (TCC); *United Trust Bank Ltd v Dohil* [2011] EWHC 3302; *Levantine Full Circle Ltd v AMEC Earth Environmental (UK) Ltd* [2013] EWHC 1643; *Marex Financial Ltd v Creative Finance Ltd* [2013] EWHC 2155.
[12] [2012] EWHC 2477 (Comm).
[13] *W Photoprint Ltd v Forward Trust Group Ltd* (1993) 12 Tr. L.R. 146.
[14] Unfair Contract Terms Act 1977 s.11(2) or, in relation to Scotland, s.24(2).
[15] [1997] C.L.C. 648.
[16] [1997] 2 Lloyd's Rep. 369.

(1)   The resources which the relevant party could expect to be available for the purpose of meeting the liability should it arise; and
(2)   How far it was open to him to obtain insurance cover.[17] Although the Act does not specify what is meant by a "specified sum", it is thought that it covers both those cases where a precise amount is mentioned and where the application of a formula provided by the term would produce a specific sum, as where damages are limited to so many times the contract price.

Considerable guidance on the application of these provisions was given in *Overseas Medical Supplies Ltd v Orient Transport Services Ltd.*[18] A contract of carriage contained terms which limited liability for loss or damage to approximately £600. The contract also said that, by special agreement in writing, the carrier would accept a greater degree of liability "upon the customer agreeing to pay the company's additional charges for accepting such increased liability. Details of the company's additional charges will be provided on request". There was also a clause which provided for insurance cover to be effected if written instructions were given by the customer, and that, when effecting such insurance, the carrier would act as agent for the customer using its best endeavours to arrange such insurance. Instructions were given, but ignored, to take out insurance.

The county court had ruled that the limitation clause was unreasonable, a ruling upheld by the Court of Appeal. It accepted in full the following points on which the lower court had based its decision:

(a)   The actions of the carriers, in their capacity of arrangers of insurance, in contrast to their position as handlers and carriers of goods, had to be considered separately as far as their terms and conditions of contract were concerned. This was because, in those circumstances where the defendants failed in breach of instructions to effect a contract of insurance, the effects of the insurance clause would be that a customer would lose both his goods and the very insurance designed to make good his loss, rather than just suffer the £600 limit imposed by the contract.
(b)   The judge had found that, in the circumstances of the case, there was no equality of bargaining power. This was because there was "no realistic likelihood" that the claimants would do anything other than entrust the arrangements as to insurance to the defendants. In reality, it was "neither practicable nor convenient for them to go elsewhere".
(c)   The judge had said that the terms and conditions of the contract had failed to make it clear that the £600 limit would apply if the defendants failed to take out the agreed contract of insurance. There was, in other words, "no 'reality of consent' to the effect of the clause".
(d)   The final point made by the judge was that the standard limit of £600 was "derisory". It had struck him that the defendants were offering the services of carriage and insurance, yet were offering a limit of liability in each case.

---

[17] Unfair Contract Terms Act 1977 s.11(4) or, in relation to Scotland, s.24(3). See further the discussion of *Salvage Association v CAP Financial Services Ltd*, para.8–010.
[18] [1999] 1 All E.R. (Comm) 981.

While there might well be cases involving package deals where a broad brush approach to the limitation of liability might be reasonable, this was "unjust and inappropriate" in the present case.

In *South West Water Services Ltd v International Computers Ltd*,[19] a clause read:

> "if the customer (being legally entitled to do so) rejects the entire system or any part thereof, after having given the company reasonable opportunity to modify the system or relevant part thereof and resubmit the same for Acceptance [damages payable] are limited to the sum of all monies paid by the customer for the system."

The court said that there was no evidence of any arm's length discussion between the parties, nor evidence that the contract was subject to detailed discussion. The defendants, whose clause this was, argued that it meant that, if the goods failed the acceptance test, then monies would be returned: if, however, the goods did not get as far as such test, then it could keep any monies paid subject to a possible return of £250,000 under another provision in the contract. SWW had in fact paid more than £2 million.

9–005

The court accepted that, in some cases, such a clause might be reasonable as a way of reflecting the risks of a development project, but there was no evidence of that in this case. It held that the limitation clause was "manifestly unreasonable".

Every case where a limitation clause is in issue must, of course, be judged on its individual facts, and such clauses have on occasion been upheld.

In *Hi-Flyers Ltd v Linde Gas UK Ltd*,[20] the relevant clause stated that:

> "The Company shall have no liability whatsoever (howsoever arising) in relation to any loss suffered by the Customer or any third party arising from the supply of the Products and in particular the Company shall not be liable for any loss of profit or any other consequential loss by the Customer howsoever arising above and beyond that level which the Company has insured itself for consequential loss claim full details of which will be made available to the Customer from time to time upon written request and the Customer hereby acknowledges and agrees that such limitation in respect of consequential loss is reasonable and that the amount of insurance obtained by the Company in respect of such consequential loss liability is a reasonable amount and is the most that the Company could be expected to obtain at the reasonable cost."

This clause was upheld. Negotiations over the contract had proceeded over several weeks and the terms and conditions discussed and agreed. The claimant had been subject to no form of pressure to accept the contract containing such clause, and had received quotes from alternative sources of supply. The clause was clearly printed in the section headed "Limitations of Liability". The sale agreement, signed by the claimants, showed that the contract had been signed subject to the terms and conditions "as described overleaf", and the contract also provided that full details of the defendants' insurance cover could have been obtained on written request. More generally, the court said that given the defendants' potentially indeterminate liability, and the cost of insurance to cover

9–006

---

[19] (1999) B.L.R. 420.
[20] [2004] EWHC 105 (QB).

this, it was reasonable of them to seek to limit liability for what was purely economic loss by a clause setting a reasonable level of limitation.

Another such example is *Regus (UK) Ltd v Epcot Solutions Ltd*,[21] a series of exclusion clauses was followed by this clause:

> "We will be liable: without limit for personal injury or death; up to a maximum of £1 million (for any one event or series of connected events) for damage to your personal property; up to a maximum equal to 125% of the total fees paid under your agreement up to the date on which the claim in question arises or £50,000 (whichever is the higher), in respect of all other losses, damages, expenses or claims."

The court upheld this term, finding the relevant *maxima* "generous".

Generosity also seemed to be the reason why the court felt that any challenge to the following clause had no real prospect of success:

> "[Defendant's] total liability to Service Reseller [the Claimant] for damages under this Agreement will not exceed fifty percent (50%) of the service charges paid by Service Reseller during the twelve months preceding any claim. This limitation will apply regardless of the form of action (i.e. whether the law suit is in contract or in tort, including negligence). But it will not apply to Service Reseller's claims for bodily injury or damage to real or tangible personal property for which [defendant] is solely liable."

For one thing, the relevant party had indicated in advance that he thought the clause reasonable. More pertinently, the clause was a limitation clause and not a clause which excluded liability altogether. It was a clause under the terms of which, for example, if there were bodily injury or damage or damage to property, then the defendant would remain totally liable for that. It was only limiting certain categories of claim, whether in contract or in tort, and in any event, in the areas where it bit, it was not an absolute exclusion clause, because it operated by reference to 50 per cent of the service charges paid. The clause was one which not only encouraged the prompt bringing of claims within 12 months of any breach, but also had the effect of increasing the level of any cap under the clause on damages in proportion to the amount of business carried out by the claimant. In other words, as the business increased, so the service charges increased, and the recoverable damages would follow suit. The court felt that those consequences were not in any sense unreasonable and "this form of limitation of liability by reference to an amount received under a contract by a party seeking to limit liability is, in my experience, quite common under various types of commercial contract, and there is nothing inherently unreasonable in this form of limitation".[22]

The availability of insurance

9–007   In *Flamar Interocean Ltd v Denmac Ltd*,[23] the owners of vessels claimed damages for breach of contract against the technical managers of the vessels, and applied to obtain further discovery of the documents relating to the latter's

[21] [2008] EWCA Civ 361.
[22] *Shared Network Services Ltd v Nextiraone UK Ltd* [2011] EWHC 3845.
[23] [1990] 1 Lloyd's Rep. 434.

insurance position. It was held that a court would, when determining the reasonableness of a contract term, assume that the parties contracted on the basis of the insurance which was available. A court would not assume that it was or ought reasonably to have been known to or in the contemplation of the parties what the actual insurance arrangements were in circumstances in which neither of them alleged that the existence or extent of insurance cover of one of them was discussed in the pre-contract negotiations or that the terms of the contract were based on that cover. It followed that the defendants' insurance documents did not relate to any matter in question between the parties.

In *Moores v Yakeley*,[24] a clause in an architect's contract provided:

"6.1   The Architect's liability for loss or damage shall be limited to such sum as the Architect ought reasonably to pay having regard to his responsibility for the same on the basis that all other consultants, Specialists and the contractor, shall where appointed, be deemed to have provided to the Client contractual undertakings in respect of their services and shall be deemed to have paid to the Client such contribution as may be appropriate having regard to the extent of their responsibility for such loss or damage.

6.2   6.2 The liability of the Architect for any loss or damage arising out of any action or proceedings referred to in clause 5 shall notwithstanding the provisions of clause 6.1 in any event be limited to a sum not exceeding £250,000.

6.3   For the avoidance of doubt, the Architect's liability shall never exceed the lower of the sum calculated in accordance with clause 6.1 above and the sum provided for in clause 6.2."

Applying both the provisions of s.11(4) and the Guidelines in Sch.2,[25] the court upheld the clause for the following reasons:

(i)   The £250,000 limit was not an arbitrary figure. It was based on Mr Yakeley's assessment of the likely cost of the works. His opinion that £250,000 was a reasonable estimate of the likely construction cost was not challenged in evidence, which the court accepted as a reasonable figure. As such, the court said that it was to be contrasted with *Salvage Association v CAP Financial Services Ltd*[26] where the party relying on the limitation did not provide any rational explanation for it. It would, the court said:

"take some quite exceptional circumstances beyond the reasonable contemplation of the parties, to give rise to a liability for damages in a sum greater than the total estimated cost of the project itself."

(ii)   It was "significant" that, when cross-examined, the claimant accepted that if the limitation of damages clause was roughly sufficient to cover the total building cost, that would be "fair enough".

(iii)   The fees that it was envisaged in March that Mr Yakeley would earn from the commission were of the order of £20,000, with more fees being dependent on the scope of the contract being enlarged to include certain further specified stages. The ceiling on damages was therefore, as the court

---

[24] Unreported October 28, 1998.
[25] For their general applicability, see para.9–002.
[26] [1995] F.S.R. 654.

pointed out, more than 10 times the amount of the fee income that would necessarily be generated by the contract.

(iv)   The claimant was in a stronger bargaining position than the defendant. He could have instructed any architect and had indeed approached another architect. There was a severe recession in the construction industry at the time and architects were chasing work. The claimant was in no particular hurry to enter into this contract with the defendant, and had a solicitor to protect his interests in the negotiations with the defendant.

(v)   Both the claimant and his solicitor were aware of the existence of cl.6. They both had ample opportunity to object to it. Instead, they both said that they were "happy" with the proposed agreement.

(vi)   A comparison of their respective resources showed that the defendant company had none whereas the claimant was a very wealthy man. The defendant did, however, have in place insurance cover of £500,000 in respect of each and every claim.

The court said that, under s.11(4), it was obliged to have particular regard to the question how far it was open to a defendant to cover itself by insurance. In this case, the defendant actually did cover itself in a sum substantially in excess of the ceiling figure. That was a factor which the court said had to be taken into account in deciding the issue of reasonableness. It further said, however, that the fact that the insurance cover was in excess of the ceiling figure could not be decisive. An architect might have insurance cover of £10 million, and be engaged to carry out a small project with an estimated contract value of £10,000. It would be "absurd" in such a case to say that any ceiling figure lower than £10 million would be unreasonable. When asked why he had not inserted a figure of £500,000 in cl.6.2, the defendant said that (i) he considered the figure he inserted to be reasonable having regard to the estimated cost of the project; and (ii) he was concerned to leave some allowance in case he had to meet any legal costs. The reasonableness of this second point was not tested, and the policy was not produced to the court. Even so, it regarded his first explanation alone as a reasonable one.

It was said in *SAM Business Systems Ltd v Hedley & Co*,[27] where the suppliers of a software system had made no effort to obtain insurance cover, that this was a factor which the court regarded as "entirely neutral". As it went on to say, it was "not unlikely that they did not try to obtain insurance because they considered that, having regard to the terms of the contract, it was an unnecessary expense to do so". There was no evidence as to whether the other party had asked if there was insurance cover but, had it done so, the court said that that would have made no difference. SAM would be insured only against the risks it took, and these were defined by the particular exclusion and limitation clauses. It said that the real question was as to the extent to which SAM could have obtained insurance without such clauses, or some of them, as to which there was no evidence. The court also said that there was no reason why it should have been for the purchasers to insure against SAM failing to do what was expected of them.

---

[27] [2003] 1 All E.R. (Comm) 465.

In *Horace Holman Group Ltd v Sherwood International*,[28] the defendant 9–008
suppliers argued that a clause was reasonable, having regard to the ability of the
purchasers to obtain insurance against any defect arising from the goods. The
court said that the availability of insurance was just one factor to be taken into
account when deciding the issue of reasonableness. In fact, the suppliers were in
a better position to obtain insurance and that, coupled with the difficulty
experienced by the purchasers of obtaining the goods on better terms, or at all,
outweighed the fact that the latter had negotiated the relevant terms with eyes
open. The clause was accordingly unreasonable.

It is also the case that advising customers to take out insurance can indicate
that a particular clause is reasonable. In the *Regus*[29] case, the claimant was a
supplier of office accommodation. An exclusion clause recommended that
customers take out insurance. The Court of Appeal upheld the clause, stressing
that it would be better business sense for the customers to take out insurance than
for the claimant to so.

REASONABLENESS: THE APPROACH OF THE COURTS

In *Photo Production Ltd v Securicor Transport Ltd*,[30] Lord Diplock said that: 9–009

> "In commercial contracts negotiated between businessmen capable of looking after their own
> interests and of deciding how risks inherent in the performance of various kinds of contract
> can be most economically borne [generally by insurance] it is . . . wrong to place a strained
> construction on words in an exclusion clause which are clear and fairly susceptible of one
> meaning . . .".

Lord Wilberforce said that, in the light of the 1977 Act:

> "in commercial matters generally, when the parties are not of unequal bargaining power, and
> when risks are normally borne by insurance, not only is the case of judicial intervention
> undemonstrated, but there is everything to be said . . . for leaving the parties free to apportion
> the risks as they think fit and for respecting their decisions."[31]

This has been an approach which has been alluded to on a number of
occasions. In *White Cross Equipment Ltd v Farrell*,[32] the deputy judge made
specific reference to the earlier observations when holding that an exclusion
clause in a contract "between two commercial parties of equal bargaining

---

[28] Unreported April 12, 2000 (TCC).
[29] See para.9–006.
[30] [1980] 1 All E.R. 556.
[31] [1980] 1 All E.R. 556 at 568 and 561 respectively. These words were cited with approval in *JP Morgan Chase Bank v Springwell Navigation Corp* [2008] EWHC 1186 (Comm), which was itself cited with approval in *Titan Steel Wheels Ltd v Royal Bank of Scotland Plc* [2010] EWHC 211 (Comm). See also *Tradigrain SA v Intertek Testing Services (ITS) Canada Ltd* [2007] EWCA Civ 154; *Whitecap Leisure Ltd v John H Rundle Ltd* [2008] 2 Lloyd's Rep 216; *Stocznia Gdynia SA v Gearbulk Holdings Ltd* [2009] 1 Lloyd's Rep 461. *Raiffeisen Zentralbank Osterreich AG v Royal Bank of Scotland Plc* [2010] EWHC 1392 (Comm); *Sucden Financial Ltd v Fluxo-Cane Overseas Ltd* [2010] EWHC 2133 (Comm) *Bikam Ood (2) Central Investment Group SA v Adria Cable SARL* [2012] EWHC 621 and *Fujitsu Services Ltd v IBM United Kingdom Ltd* [2014] EWHC 752.
[32] [1983] 2 Tr. L.R. 21.

strength" was a reasonable one on which to allow reliance. This did of course relate to the differently worded test contained in the Supply of Goods (Implied Terms) Act 1973, but, given not least the fact that the court made reference to guidelines contained in Sch.2 to the 1977 Act, it seems clear that it would also have found that the clause was a fair and reasonable one to incorporate into the contract.

In *Oval Ltd v Aegon Insurance Co (UK) Ltd*,[33] the court had to determine the reasonableness of a clause in a performance bond entered into between an insurance company and a limited liability company owned by the University of Bristol.[34] The bond was in the following terms:

> "The Contractors and the Surety are held and firmly bound to the Employer in the above Sum for due payment of which sum the Contractors bind themselves, their heirs, executors and administrators or their successors and assigns and the Surety binds itself its successors and assigns jointly and severally by this Bond. Whereas the Contractors have entered into a Contract for the work with the Employer which Contract with all its covenants and conditions shall be regarded as being incorporated herein. If the Contractors shall fully comply with all the terms covenants and conditions of the Contract on their part to be kept and performed according to the Contract or if on default by the Contractors the Surety shall satisfy and discharge the damages sustained by the Employer thereby up to the amount of this Bond then this obligation shall be null and void otherwise it shall remain in full force.
>
> THIS BOND is executed by the Surety upon the following conditions which shall be conditions precedent to the right of the Employer to recover hereunder.
>
> The Surety shall be notified by the Employer in writing of any non-performance or non-observance on the part of the contractors of any of the stipulations or provisions contained in the said Contract and on their part to be performed and observed within one month after such non-performance or non-observance shall have come to the knowledge of the Employer or his authorised representative(s) having supervision of the said Contract and the Employer shall in so far as it may be lawful permit the Surety to perform the stipulations or provisions of the said Contract which the Contractors shall have failed to perform or observe. If any suits at law or proceedings in equity are to be brought against the Surety to recover any claim hereunder the same must be served within six months after the expiry of the maintenance period stated in the Contract."

9–010 The court first noted that the disputed clause had a "discernable commercial purpose". The court also considered it important that "temporary disconformities" would not constitute either non-performance or non-observance of the terms of the construction contract. In general, it would only be if the contractor refused to acknowledge that the work in question was unsatisfactory (and *a fortiori* if the contractor refused to comply with a specific formal instruction issued in respect of that work) that a notifiable non-performance or non-observance would arise.

The court also referred to the Sch.2 Guidelines.

(a) These contracting parties are to be regarded as having relatively equal bargaining positions. Neither party adduced evidence of the wording or cost of surety bonds which might have been obtained from other financial institutions in 1993.

---

[33] (1997) 85 B.L.R. 97.
[34] The contract was held to be a contract made in the course of a business since the claimant "obviously contracted with this Defendant in the ordinary mainstream course of the business which it had been established to undertake".

(b)   No evidence was adduced of any inducement to the claimant to agree to the retention of the condition precedent which was shown on the face of the copy of the earlier bond which was sent by way of a draft in January 1993. No evidence was adduced of the claimant's exploring the possibility of negotiating with the defendant to amend the draft wording or of entering into a similar contract with some other financial institution without the condition precedent.

(c)   The claimant clearly knew of the existence of the term because it was very prominently positioned on the face of a one-page document, a draft of which had been submitted some seven months before the contract came to be made. If the claimant did not in fact appreciate "the extent of the term", it ought reasonably to have done so by the time the contract came to be made. The claimant (or the University) had ample time and the necessary resources to enable it to obtain legal or other professional advice on performance bonding generally and/or the wording of this proposed bond in particular.

(d)   As at August 1993 or January 1994 it was indeed reasonable to expect that compliance with the first part of the first condition precedent would be practicable. In the light of these factors, the clause was adjudged reasonable.

The remarks made in the *Photo Production* case were also raised in *W Photoprint Ltd v Forward Trust Group Ltd; Hope Industries UK Ltd*.[35] The claimants entered into a hire purchase agreement with the first defendant in relation to a print processing machine supplied by the second defendant. The machine was unsatisfactory and the claimants brought an action against the first defendants for damages for breach of the hire purchase agreement. The agreement contained a term to the effect that the customer had examined the goods and declared that "they are in every respect satisfactory and suitable for the purpose for which they are required and that he has relied on his own skill and judgment in choosing the goods". The agreement also stated that, subject to the requirement of reasonableness, the first defendants did "not let the goods subject to any undertaking express or implied whether statutory or otherwise save the condition as to title . . .".

The court understood the House of Lords' judgment to mean that, where parties are of equal bargaining power, then the courts should "not be astute either to cut down the clear effect of exclusion clauses or to change the balance and assumptions of risk provided for in such a contract".

The deputy judge, however, was more concerned to apply the guidelines contained in Sch.2 to the 1977 Act. He regarded (1) as of doubtful application since it seemed more concerned with the question of whether another source of the goods was available. He did find, however, that the parties were of equal strength and "well able to look after themselves". He did not think that the comparative size of the parties was of great importance.

---

[35] [1993] 12 Tr. L.R. 146.

9–011   In relation to guideline (2), the deputy judge noted that the claimants could have made the contract with another party who could have undertaken to give them the benefit of any rights that party might have against the seller. It also appeared possible that the first defendant could have deleted the clause and charged customers generally for the cost of appropriate insurance cover. These points, the deputy judge indicated, tended to support the claimants' arguments.

As to (3), he indicated that the claimants probably did know of the clause. Their attention was drawn to it immediately above the provision for signature of the agreement. It was also the case that eight of the previous 13 agreements between the parties contained similar clauses. The claimants accepted that they should have known of the existence of the clause, but not of its meaning or effect.

The other relevant guideline was (5). These goods had not been manufactured, processed or adapted to the claimants' order, which would appear to place this guideline in their favour, but the deputy judge noted as of "relevance" the first defendant's submission that the claimants had looked at this particular machine and others on the market, and that it had actually been installed and had developed problems before the claimants signed the agreement and sent it to the first defendant.

Following consideration of the guidelines, the deputy judge had regard to the overriding requirement of the 1977 Act that the term was fair and reasonable bearing in mind the "circumstances which were, or ought reasonably to have been, known to or in the contemplation of the parties when the contract was made". Here, the deputy judge listed the following factors:

(1)   The claimants (as noted above) were very familiar with such agreements.

(2)   There was no question of them being hived off by a dealer to a captive hire purchase company, since they had a large credit facility with the first defendant.

(3)   The claimants had relied solely on their own evaluation of the machine.

(4)   They had also argued that the quality of the machine could not be ascertained until it had been up and running for at least a couple of weeks, and that it would be unfair to allow the first defendant to exclude liability at a time when they were unable to determine the question of merchantability and when they did not have the benefit of the first defendant's rights against the second defendant. The deputy judge ruled, however, that this argument could not be relied on since the fact relied on, as to when the quality of the goods could be assessed, was not one known to or contemplated by the first defendant at the time.

(5)   The claimants could probably have financed the acquisition of the machine in some other way, as for example by lease, a bank loan or the use of retained profits. The first defendant would have been aware of this since the credit facility accorded to the claimants was based on their rating of their financial situation. The overall conclusion was that, in these circumstances, the first defendant had discharged the burden of proof and had shown that the clause was a fair and reasonable one to include in the contract.

A very similar approach, with reference to the statutory guidelines, was taken in **9–012**
Granville Oil & Chemicals Ltd v Davies Turner & Co Ltd.[36] DT was an
international freight forwarder. GOC made and exported paint. In 1999, DT
agreed to carry a return consignment of paint from Kuwait to GOC's warehouse
near Rotherham. The contract was subject to the British International Freight
Association standard trading conditions (1989 edition) which by cl.30(A)
required a claim to be made in writing within 14 days and by cl.30(B) required
suit to be brought within nine months. DT agreed to arrange insurance of the
consignment against all risks in transit under Institute Cargo Clauses (A). GOC
claimed that the paint had been damaged in transit and made a claim against DT
within 14 days. DT made a claim on the insurance on GOC's behalf. The
underwriters told DT that there was no cover on March 31, 2000 and again, for a
different reason, on June 27, 2000. DT did not tell GOC that the insurance claim
had been rejected until August 22, 2000, the day before the nine-month period in
cl.30(B) expired. GOC brought proceedings only in November 2001 alleging
breach of contract by DT in damaging the goods and by failing to insure against
all risks. On a trial of preliminary issues the judge held that the cl.30(B) time bar
was ineffective to bar GOC's claim because it failed the test of reasonableness
under the Unfair Contract Terms Act 1977. DT appealed.

In allowing the appeal, the Court of Appeal said that the clause would not bar
a claim for fraud or a claim which had been fraudulently concealed by the
conduct of the freight forwarder. The judge had erred in thinking that the clause
applied to such a claim. The term in question was reasonable as between the
parties to the contract at the time when the contract was made. The parties were
of equal bargaining strength. This was a commercial contract between
commercial parties where GOC might have been able to contract other than on
BIFA conditions or to make its own insurance arrangements had it wished. GOC
ought reasonably to have known of the time-bar. The judge held that the
conditions had been sufficiently brought to GOC's attention. Compliance with the
nine-month time limit was practicable. A freight forwarder, who usually was not
the carrier, needed a time limit of nine months to enable it to make a claim over
against the responsible carrier before that claim became time-barred (frequently
within one year). Nine months was a reasonable time limit for a claim for loss of
or damage to goods in transit. The loss or damage could be ascertained on
delivery. Nine months was ample time for the customer to decide whether to
bring suit. In this case DT also faced a claim for failure to insure. GOC would
have had ample time to claim against DT within the nine-month time limit for
failure to insure if it had been told by DT when and why the underwriters had
declined liability. There was no question of the information being deliberately
withheld. DT acted as GOC's agent in pursuing the insurance claim. DT was in
breach of duty in failing to tell GOC until August 22 that it had no cover and
GOC would have had nine months from that date to make a claim based on
breach of that duty. It did not do so. It was fair and reasonable to fix the same
time limit for a claim based on failure to insure the goods as was fixed for the

---

[36] [2003] 1 All E.R. (Comm) 819. See also, for its discussion of this case, *Rohlig (UK) Ltd v Rock
Unique Ltd* [2011] EWCA Civ 18.

claim for damage to those goods. The judge was wrong and cl.30(B) of the BIFA conditions was effective to bar GOC's claims. Tuckey L.J. said this:

> "The 1977 Act obviously plays a very important role in protecting vulnerable consumers from the effects of draconian contract terms. But I am less enthusiastic about its intrusion into contracts between commercial parties of equal bargaining strength, who should generally be considered capable of being able to make contracts of their choosing and expect to be bound by their terms."[37]

The same view, albeit obiter, was taken in relation to the following clause in *British Fermentation Products Ltd v Compair Reavell Ltd*[38]:

> "(i)   If within 12 months after delivery there shall appear in the goods any defect which shall arise under proper use from faulty materials, workmanship, or design (other than a design made, furnished, or specified by the purchaser for which the vendor had disclaimed responsibility), and the purchaser shall give notice thereof in writing to the vendor, the vendor, shall, provided that the defective goods or defective parts thereof have been returned to the vendor if he shall have so required, make good the defects either by repair or, at the option of the vendor, by the supply of a replacement. The vendor shall refund the cost of carriage on the return of the defective goods or parts and shall deliver any repaired or replacement goods or parts as if [the contract terms as to delivery] applied.
>
> (ii)   The vendor's liability under this Condition or under Condition 5 (Rejection and Replacement) shall be accepted by the purchaser in lieu of any warranty or condition implied by law as to the quality or fitness for any particular purpose of the goods and save as provided in this Condition the Vendor shall not be under any liability to the purchaser (whether in contract, tort or otherwise) for any defects in the goods or for any damage, loss, death or injury (other than death or personal injury caused by the negligence of the vendor as defined in section 1 of the Unfair Contract Terms Act 1977) resulting from such defects or from any work done in connection therewith."

In finding these terms reasonable, the court referred to their "good business sense". It was the case that, in the absence of the clause, the defendants might have wished to revise the price quoted to take account of their increased risk: "When considering reasonableness one has to consider reasonableness for the vendor as well as reasonableness for the purchaser". It was also the case that had the compressor, which was the subject of the contract, not been as promised, the claimants would not be without a remedy. Had the goods been rejected, and opportunity not taken up by the claimants, they would have recovered the purchase price and the defendants would have paid the reasonable costs of a replacement. The choice made by the claimants to continue with a less efficient working for the life of the compressor was, the court felt, foreseeable when the contract was made, and thus was one of the circumstances known, or which reasonably should have been known, when the contract was made.

9–013   The clause in dispute in *Do-Buy 925 Ltd v National Westminster Bank Plc*,[39] in a contract between a retailer and a merchant operator, ran: "You agree that as between You and Us it is Your responsibility to prove to Our satisfaction that the debit of a cardholder's account was authorised by the genuine cardholder". After

---

[37] These words were endorsed in *Frank Maas (UK) Ltd v Samsung Electronics (UK) Ltd* [2004] EWHC 1502 (Comm) and in *Sterling Hydraulics Ltd v Dichtomatik Ltd* [2006] EWHC 2004 (QB).
[38] [1999] 2 All E.R. (Comm) 389.
[39] [2010] EWHC 2862 (QB).

holding that this clause was not in fact subject to the reasonableness test,[40] the court nonetheless went on to say that the clause was reasonable for the following reasons:

(1) While it might at first sight appear reasonable to allow the merchant to rely on the fact of authorisation as his part in avoiding fraudulent use of cards, the literature which formed the contractual documentation made clear that authorisation does no more than identify whether the card has been reported lost or stolen and whether there is sufficient credit; it is no guarantee of payment, and the system of chargebacks contemplates that payment will be refused or reversed if there is unauthorised use of the card, a fact which is specifically pointed out in the Merchant Operating Instructions. In this case Do-Buy ran a case of estoppel or collateral contract based on allegations that at the initial meeting and again during the second authorisation telephone conversation Do-Buy had been assured that payment was guaranteed if the authorisation was given and goods could then safely be released. Those allegations were not made good on the evidence and not pursued at the conclusion of the hearing. In the absence of any specific assurances, the merchant is fairly and squarely on notice that authorisation does not guarantee payment. Indeed it is a factor in favour of the reasonableness of the term that it was fairly and squarely brought to the attention of Do-Buy in the Merchant Operating Instructions.
(2) The clause reflected the allocation of risk which is imposed on all merchants by the Scheme Operators who enable the merchants to take payment by card. The merchants benefit from the ability to sell goods and services by taking payment by card. The clause no more than allocates to Do-Buy the same risk as applies to all merchants who use these cards as a form of payment, and which is an essential part of the scheme which enables it to take the benefit of payment by card.
(3) In allocating the risk of fraud to the customer, the clause reflected the allocation of risk which arises in most if not all other forms of payment, which in the case of cash and cheques rests on the merchant.
(4) The merchant acquirer is in no better position to assess whether a customer is the genuine cardholder than the merchant; indeed he is usually in a worse position. The merchant acquirer in most cases has no more information before processing the transaction than information from the card issuer as to whether the card has been reported lost or stolen and whether there is sufficient credit for the transaction. Unless he happens also to be the card issuer he has no control over the issue of the card to the customer or what the customer does with it. By contrast the merchant is in a position to assess the customer by reference to the transaction in question and to ask questions of him. It had been argued that the claimant was dependant on the bank for access to the real cardholder and information about his account, but this was to conflate the happenstance that in this case the bank was also the card issuer. The merchant acquirer acting in his capacity as such had no such preferential access to information. More important was the fact that

---

[40] See para.8–021.

the merchant had the ability to mitigate the risks of identity fraud by imposing delivery terms which optimised the chance of indisputable payment before delivery, or ultimately to decline to complete the sale.

(5)   Conversely, it would not be reasonable to require a merchant acquirer to assume the risk of identity fraud. That would:

(a)   bind it to process transactions notwithstanding that it had no opportunity to investigate whether the transactions were authorised by the cardholder;

(b)   bind it to take the financial reputational and regulatory risk of a fraudulent transaction which it would be in no better position to assess as fraudulent or genuine than the merchant (unless it happened also to be the card issuer);

(c)   bind it to process transactions even if it knew or suspected that the transaction was not genuinely authorised;

(d)   oblige it to breach the obligations (for itself and for its merchants) under the Scheme Rules to ensure that only valid transactions with the bona fide cardholder are submitted; and would import the risk of sanctions for the merchant acquirer, including fines and ultimately suspension of its membership, under the Scheme Rules.

(6)   It had also been submitted that factors pointing to the unreasonableness of the clause included the dominant position of the bank as one of only a handful of merchant acquirers and the weak bargaining position of Do-Buy. This approach was rejected by the court. It was not the bank or any of the other merchant acquirers who imposed this term, but MasterCard who insisted on this as a part of the basis for conferring the benefit on merchants of being able to take payments by card. In fact, it was Do-Buy who had the option not to use cards in payment; but if they wished to do so, the bank had no option but to insist on the allocation of risk in the disputed clause. The bank was not in a bargaining position of any kind vis-à-vis Do-Buy in relation to the clause. Nor was it itself in a dominant position: it was merely the facilitator of a scheme by MasterCard which had this allocation of risk as one of its ingredients. The present was not a case of a stronger party imposing an onerous term on a weaker party. The bank was contractually obliged to impose the term if it were to supply the service at all; and the term was one which all merchants who use cards must be subjected to. It was accurately described by the bank as an "industry standard clause".

(7)   A further argument was that the clause was unreasonable because it would allow the bank to refuse payment in cases where it was at fault in facilitating or not preventing the fraud. Certain criticisms had been made in argument of the bank's conduct in this case, but it had been accepted that there was no ground for asking the court to find that the bank had been negligent because the allegation had not been pleaded and there had been no cross examination in this regard of the bank's witnesses. The court said that it was, though, sufficient for this argument on this part of the case to posit a hypothetical case in which the bank might have been negligent and to argue that the clause was unreasonable in allocating the risk to the merchant even in such cases. Referring to the *Canada Steamship Lines v*

The King line of authorities[41] the court said that it may bethat in such a case the merchant would be protected by a construction of the clause which did not exempt from the consequences of the bank's own negligence; or by a duty of care, an implied term or an estoppel. The court, however, had not been addressed on those arguments which did not arise on the facts of this case and accordingly no opinion was expressed. It was sufficient for present purposes to record the view that, even if the clause would operate to allocate the risk to the merchant in the case of negligent failure on the part of the bank to detect the fraud, that would not be sufficient to outweigh the other factors which make it reasonable.

(8) Reliance had also been placed on other clauses which imposed an obligation on the merchant to accept payments by card if desired by the customer if they fell within the terms of the contractual agreement. This, though, was not an obligation to take card payment in cases of known or suspected fraud and it left untouched the merchant's ability in other cases to impose protective delivery terms or simply not to proceed with the transaction. It took the argument little further in deciding the reasonableness of allocation of risk in cases where the fraud was undetected.

Lord Wilberforce's approach was much echoed in *Watford Electronics Ltd v Sanderson CFL Ltd*.[42] The purchasers had bought a software package which contained this provision:

> "The company and the customer agree to indemnify each other against any liability arising in respect of injury (including death) to any person or loss or damage to property which results from the act, default or negligence of itself, its employees, agents or subcontractors."

The contract also provided: 9–014

> "Neither the company nor the customer shall be liable to the other for any claims for indirect or consequential losses whether arising from negligence or otherwise. In no event shall the company's liability under the contract exceed the price paid by the customer to the company for the equipment connected with any claim."

An addendum to the conditions secured by the purchasers provided:

> "In addition to the above clause, Sanderson CFL Ltd commit to their best endeavours in allocating appropriate resources to the project to minimise any losses that may arise from the contract."

There was also an entire agreement clause, as follows:

> "The parties agree that these terms and conditions (together with any other terms and conditions expressly incorporated in the contract) represent the entire agreement between the parties relating to the sale and purchase of the equipment and that no statements or representations made by either party have been relied on by the other in agreeing to enter into this contract."

---

[41] See para.2–021 and following.
[42] [2001] EWCA Civ 317. See too *Deutsche Bank AG v Sebastian Holdings Inc* [2013] EWHC 3463.

Problems arose with the system purchased and attempts at repair failed. Eventually, Watford purchased a different system from alternative suppliers. In the proceedings which followed, the High Court found that the disputed clauses were not reasonable. The judge said:

> "The clause is not justified by any particular onerous or unusual liabilities that Sanderson might encounter, nor by any difficulties in obtaining insurance nor by any particular features of either the negotiations or the parties. Watford would have had considerable difficulties in obtaining the relevant software elsewhere without such a clause since it was a common feature of the software supply industry at the time. The effect of the clause is to deprive Watford of the opportunity of recovering any damages in circumstances in which... there have been significant failures to represent the features of the software and to comply with the contractual requirements as to merchantability and quality."

The Court of Appeal referred to the words of Lord Bridge setting out the principles to be applied when deciding appeals on the question of reasonableness[43] and stated that, when considering if this was one of the necessarily rare cases where a lower court's ruling should be overturned, the precise effect of the disputed term had first to be determined. In its relevant part, the clause had run: "Neither the company nor the customer shall be liable... for any claims for indirect or consequential losses... In no event shall the company's liability exceed the price paid...". The Court of Appeal held that each sentence of this clause was to have separate effect, and disagreed with the High Court's decision to the contrary. The second sentence imposed a limit on the quantum of liability; the first was intended to exclude a loss which did not arise in the ordinary course of things. The High Court had been wrong to say that the first sentence went beyond contract claims and had sought to exclude liability for misrepresentation.

9–015 The Court of Appeal also said that the disputed clause had to be judged in the light of the entire agreement clause. The High Court, in a passage the Court of Appeal had "some difficulty in following", had said that the clause excluded liability as opposed to preventing liability from arising in the first place. The Court of Appeal read that clause as preventing a person to whom a misrepresentation had been made from asserting that he had relied on it. An entire agreement clause was not an exclusion clause, and it was wrong to disregard it when determining if an exclusion or limitation clause was reasonable. Given the intent of this clause, there was no reason why the parties should have intended the first sentence of the disputed clause to exclude liability for misrepresentation:

> "Where both parties... have acknowledged, in the document itself, that they have not relied upon any pre-contract representation, it would be bizarre (unless compelled to do so by the words which they have used) to attribute to them an intention to exclude a liability which they thought would never arise."

Bearing in mind that a lower court's ruling was to be reversed only exceptionally, the Court of Appeal identified three respects in which the lower court had erred.

The first was the failure properly to identify the scope and effect of the limitation clause. It had sought to exclude liability for one category of loss and to

---

[43] See para.9–049.

limit to the contract price any liability for the other category of loss. Contrary to what the High Court said, it did not seek to avoid liability for misrepresentation.

Second, the High Court had found to be "meaningless" the addendum negotiated by Watford that Sanderson would "commit to their best endeavours". Instead, the Court of Appeal stressed that this superimposed obligations on Sanderson over and above the obligations imposed on them by the relevant standard terms and conditions. Thus, unless that company could "show that it did use its best endeavours to allocate appropriate resources to ensure that the software performs the specified functions", it could not rely on the clause excluding claims for indirect and consequential loss.

Third, and perhaps the most interesting finding, the Court of Appeal specifically disagreed with the High Court's finding that Watford's own standard terms of business could not be taken into account when deciding if Sanderson's standard terms were reasonable. Watford's own terms imposed strict limitations on their liability, and this indicated that they clearly understood the commercial considerations which could lead suppliers such as themselves and Sanderson to include exclusion clauses in their contracts.

The Court of Appeal then turned to deciding whether that part of the term which **9–016** excluded liability for indirect and consequential loss was reasonable. The key points in deciding the issue were stated to be these:

(i)   there was a "significant risk" that a non-standard software product, "customised" to meet the particular marketing, accounting or record-keeping needs of a substantial and relatively complex business, such as that carried on by Watford, might not perform to the customer's satisfaction;

(ii)   if the products did not perform, there would be a further "significant risk" that the customer might not achieve the profits or savings it hoped to make, and may also incur consequential losses from the failure to perform;

(iii)   such risks were, or at any rate should have been, known to both parties when the contract was made;

(iv)   Sanderson was in the better position to assess the risk that the product would fail to perform;

(v)   Watford was in the better position to assess the amount of the potential loss if the product did fail to perform;

(vi)   the risk of loss was likely to be such as could be covered by insurance, at a cost;

(vii)   both the parties would have known, or ought reasonably to have known, at the time the contract was made, that the identity of the party who was to bear the risk of loss, or the cost of insurance, was a factor which would be taken into account when working out the price at which the customer was willing to purchase.

The Court of Appeal said that it was reasonable to expect the contract to make provision for the risk of such loss to fall on one party or the other. Where parties of equal bargaining power negotiate a price for the supply of a product under a contract providing for such risk "the court should be very cautious before reaching the conclusion that the agreement reached is not a fair and reasonable one". It then went on to say, in words closely approximating those of Lord Wilberforce, that:

> "Where experienced businessmen, representing substantial companies of equal bargaining power negotiate an agreement, they may be taken to have had regard to the matters known to them. They should... be taken to be the best judge of the commercial fairness of the agreement which they have made, including the fairness of each of the terms in that agreement. They should be taken to be the best judge of the question whether the terms of the agreement are reasonable."

These remarks have added force given that the Court of Appeal disagreed with the lower court's finding that the disputed term was unreasonable. It should be added that the Court of Appeal also disagreed with that court's finding as to the unreasonableness as to the limitation of liability to a specific sum.

Where a clause is in common use, and is well known in the trade following comprehensive discussions between reputable and representative bodies "mindful of the considerations involved, the likelihood is that a clause will be held to be reasonable". This will be because the clause "reflects a general view as to what is reasonable in the trade concerned".[44] Similarly, it was said in *Expo Fabrics (UK) Ltd v Naughty Clothing Co Ltd*,[45] where a clause in a contract for the supply of cloth contained a clause requiring complaints as to defects to be made within 20 days, that it would not be right to declare unreasonable a provision which was a standard provision in the trade. It had been argued that the clause was unreasonable because there was a possibility of a skin allergy or defect in washing, in relation to which the court had no evidence.[46]

Summary rulings

9–017   While acknowledging that issues as to fairness are "fact sensitive", the court in *Macquarie Internationale Investments Ltd v Glencore (UK) Ltd*[47] was still prepared to make a summary judgment that, in the particular case, a clause was reasonable, and that there was no need to await disclosure and witness evidence at trial. It was said that the matters relied on as showing that the clause was unreasonable were "obviously inadequate". The disputed clause formed part of a "carefully calibrated commercial agreement" on which Glencore had expert legal and financial advice. There was no suggestion that it was under any unusual commercial pressure to enter into the agreement, and the resources available to it were far greater than those available to the defendants.

---

[44] *Overland Shoes Ltd v Schenkers Ltd* [1998] 1 Lloyd's Rep. 498.
[45] Unreported July 21, 2003 (CA).
[46] For further examples of clauses being upheld as reasonable in business contracts; see *Robinson v PE Jones (Contractors) Ltd* [2011] EWCA Civ 9; *Allen Fabrications Ltd v ASD Ltd* [2012] EWHC 2213; *FG Wilson (Engineering) Ltd v John Holt & Co (Liverpool) Ltd* [2012] EWHC 2477.
[47] [2008] EWHC 1716 (Comm).

Unreasonable terms in business contracts

It has become increasingly evident, as case law progresses, that Lord **9–018** Wilberforce's views, while remaining valid, will never preclude a decision that, even where both parties are businesses, a particular clause will fail to pass the reasonableness test. Even in such contracts, the burden placed by the Act still falls on the party seeking to uphold the clause. Thus, in *Salvage Association v CAP Financial Services Ltd*,[48] each of two contracts relating to the supply of computer software between the parties contained a limitation clause putting an upper limit of liability at £25,000. The facts disclosed that the respective parties were of equal bargaining power, that the contracts were freely negotiable and that there were other software houses to whom the relevant party could have gone and that the terms of one of the contracts were subject to considerable negotiation. It was also the case in regard to this particular contract, that advice had been sought from solicitors, accountants and insurance brokers. If these were all the relevant facts, the official referee acknowledged that he would have upheld the limitation clauses, noting the position of a party: "well able to look after itself [which] enters into a commercial contract, [and which] willingly accepts the terms of the contract which provide for apportionment of the financial risks …".

There were, however, other circumstances which led to an opposite conclusion. The figure of £25,000 was entirely arbitrary and bore no relationship to company turnover, the level of insurance cover available, the value of the contract or the financial risk to which the other side was exposed and for which it could not obtain insurance cover. It had also been accepted that the upper limit of £25,000 should be increased to £1 million, and no reason was ever given as to why this had not been applied to these particular contracts.

These factors alone were held enough to justify a finding that the limitation clauses could not be shown to be reasonable. The official referee, however, thought that other factors could be taken into account as supporting this decision. To begin with, there had never been any suggestion by the party seeking to rely on the limitation clauses that it would fail to perform the contractual task. This task was not exceptionally demanding and it was well within the relevant party's range of skills. It was generally believed that the software system would be satisfactorily completed within a very short period of time. It was also the case that the party receiving the services under the contract was unable to obtain insurance against non-performance by the other side at anything like a reasonable cost, if at all. The official referee did add, however, that given the relatively straightforward nature of the task, there was no reason for any particular concern to be felt over the lack of insurance cover. In addition, the party providing the service had the resources to meet its possible liability. It also had insurance cover of £5 million with an excess of £500,000. These several factors reaffirmed the official referee's view that the limitation clauses in question did not satisfy the requirement of reasonableness.

---

[48] [1995] F.S.R. 654.

9–019   In *Edmund Murray Ltd v BSP International Foundations Ltd*,[49] a contract for the supply of a rig was subject to a term providing that, while the supplier would make available to the buyer any rights afforded by his own supplier, this was to be in place of

> "any other conditions, guarantees, liabilities or warranties expressed or implied statutory or otherwise and in no event shall the sellers be liable for any loss, injury or damage however caused . . .".

There followed an exception for death or personal injury, reflecting no doubt that liability for such matters cannot be restricted or excluded.[50]

The High Court ruled that this term was reasonable. The Court of Appeal noted the observations in the *Photo Production* case, but decided the issue by particular reference to Sch.2 to the 1977 Act. The parties were roughly of equal strength and the buyers knew of the disputed terms. Even so, it was held that, since the problem with the rig lay in the failure of the suppliers to provide one which was fit for the purpose disclosed to the suppliers upon whom Edmund Murray Ltd relied, and which complied with the agreed specifications, the clause was invalid notwithstanding the fact that the suppliers would repair or replace goods which were defective "by reason solely of faulty materials or workmanship supplied or performed . . .". It was stressed that the Act required reasonableness to be judged by reference to the "circumstances which were, or ought reasonably to have been, known to or in the contemplation of the parties when the contract was made". These circumstances, it was said, were to be viewed through the eyes of both parties and were these: the rig was specially ordered; the specification contained precise details of the desired technical standards; and EML made known the precise reasons and purpose for which the rig was wanted.

The Court of Appeal also said that matters had to be considered in the light of what both parties knew. This meant that the fact that EML had a solicitor on the board who could have been approached was irrelevant since this was not a matter known to both sides. It also meant that the High Court had been wrong to enquire whether EML understood the condition to exclude a particular category of claim.

A further clause excluded liability for loss of profit or for any other category of loss however caused, and it also provided that the suppliers were not to be liable for damage which arose from any "stoppage or breakdown of the goods or in any other way from the performance of the goods in operation or any damage to the plant". This had also been upheld by the High Court as reasonable. The Court of Appeal accepted that a term excluding consequential loss would appear to be fair and reasonable between parties who were contracting at arm's length. This clause, though, went further in that it extended to a breach of the agreed specifications or the implied term as to fitness for purpose. It was therefore unreasonable. The Court of Appeal left open the question whether the objectionable bits of this particular clause could be severed from those which were not objectionable, regarding this as a matter to be decided by the judge at the later hearing.[51]

---

[49] (1992) 33 Con. L.R. 1.
[50] See para.8–005.
[51] See para.9–053.

The provision in the contract whereby the suppliers agreed to repair or replace the **9–020** goods was made subject to certain conditions such as notification to the suppliers and to the return of the:

> "defective goods or part or parts thereof... satisfactorily packed, at the risk of the buyers, carriage paid, to the sellers' works, or to such other place as the sellers may direct."

The High Court and the Court of Appeal agreed that the provision relating to the return of the goods was unreasonable, but no firm ruling was needed by the Court of Appeal since it ruled that the limited obligation undertaken by the suppliers did not cover the problems which had arisen in this case.

In *Motours Ltd v Euroball (West Kent) Ltd*,[52] the claimant, a travel agency, sought damages in respect of the interruption of a telephone service provided by the defendant, as a result of which it suffered a significant downturn in turnover and a consequent loss of profit. The contract contained a clause excluding liability for any consequential loss arising from a breach of contract. It excluded liability even if the loss were caused by negligence, recklessness or failure to take reasonable care. At the time the contract was made, the defendants knew of the "crucial importance" to the claimants of their telephone system; that the claimants needed a certain number of incoming lines; that the claimant would probably suffer loss of business and profit if these lines were not provided; and that the claimant was entirely dependent on the defendants to provide the particular services. The parties would also have known that this was a competitive business and that there would be some limitation of liability so that the defendants could protect their commercial interests. The claimant, however, would never have known or contemplated that the defendants would exclude all liability for all consequential loss, particularly if caused by negligence. The fact that the claimant had little choice and that the clause in question was common did not mean that the reasonableness test had been met. The defendants did not encourage or expect a customer to discuss or negotiate the terms on the back of the order form, which in any case were difficult to read. The defendants were large providers of telephone services and had substantial resources. In approaching the claimant with a financial incentive, the defendants had the financial strength and the superior bargaining position. They had therefore failed to establish that the exclusion clause was a reasonable one.

Again, in *Northern Electric Ltd v Econofreight Heavy Transport Ltd*,[53] the relevant clause sought to discharge the defendant in any event "from all liability whatsoever in respect of the goods unless the suit is brought within one year of the delivery date". The court ruled that this was wide enough to cover liability for negligence and claims for breach of duty of a bailee. Applying the Sch.2 guidelines, the court held that the clause was unreasonable.

Specific reference was made in *Kingsway Hall Hotel Ltd v Red Sky IT (Hounslow) Ltd*,[54] to Chadwick L.J.'s observations in *Watford* of the general

---

[52] [2003] EWHC 614 (QB).
[53] [2001] EWCA Civ 286.
[54] [2010] EWHC 965 (TCC). As also in *Levantine Full Circle Ltd v AMEC Earth & Environmental (UK) Ltd* [2013] EWHC 1191.

desirability of not interfering in business contracts. Even so, the court, applying the statutory guidelines, held the relevant clause to be unreasonable.

SUPPLIER'S LIABILITY FOR MANUFACTURER'S DEFAULT

9–021 That Lord Wilberforce's observations do no more than raise a presumption is well-evidenced by the *Benzene* cases. These cases also seem to indicate that, even though a supplier is not responsible for defects in goods supplied to him by the manufacturer, there will be no assumption that this makes it reasonable for the former to limit or exclude liability in such circumstances.

Britvic Soft Drinks Ltd v Messer UK Ltd[55]

9–022 Terra manufactured carbon dioxide at its Bristol chemical plant, and the cause of contamination was a leak, which enabled benzene to by-pass the reforming section of the plant where it would normally have been removed. Terra supplied Messer, which resold to various customers. After some period during which the contamination went undetected, its discovery led to extensive recalling and destruction of finished drinks supplied to wholesalers and others. Benzene in sufficiently high quantities is a carcinogen, but in the quantities in which it was present in the finished drinks, it presented no health hazard. Public concern and the need to protect business made recall necessary. The proceedings related to the purchase of carbon dioxide for incorporation into light alcoholic drinks. THP acquired the carbon dioxide from Messer under a contract subject to Messer's standard terms, and incorporated it with water into bottled and packaged drinks using alcoholic concentrate, bottles, caps, labelling and printed trays supplied by Bacardi-Martini Ltd.

It was stated in the contract that the carbon dioxide would conform to British Standard 4105. The exclusion clause provided that:

> "Messer warrants that the purity of the gas is not less than that laid down in the Standard. All other implied warranties and conditions as to quality or description are excluded except to the extent that such exclusion is governed by law. It is the customer's responsibility to satisfy itself that the gas is suitable for the purpose for which the customer intends to use it. Recommendations relating to the use of the gas made by Messer, in writing or otherwise, are given in good faith but no warranty is given as to the suitability of the gas for any particular purpose."

The High Court held that this clause was unreasonable, rejecting the argument that it was reasonable for a supplier, but not a manufacturer, to limit liability to compliance with the Standard on the basis that this represented contemporary understanding of the required purity. It said that it was:

> "wholly unreasonable for the supplier of a bulk commodity such as CO_2 for a food application to seek to exclude liability for the commodity not being of satisfactory quality or being unfit for its purpose where that has come about as a result of a breakdown in the manufacturing process allowing the inadvertent introduction of a redundant carcinogen."

---

[55] [2002] EWCA Civ 548.

The High Court had referred to the Guidelines in the 1977 Act and had held that the parties were of equal bargaining power and that other suppliers were available. It also said that the buyer must be taken to be "cognisant of [the] existence and effect" of the contract terms.[56] In rejecting the argument that the clause was reasonable, the judge had said:

> "I suspect that if the parties had been asked when they were contracting on whom should the risk be of a breakdown in the manufacturing process permitting the unexpected introduction into the CO_2 of a redundant carcinogen in quantities which, whilst not injurious to health would render products made using the CO_2 unsaleable, they would have unhesitatingly replied that of course the risk should be borne by the supplier ... it is wholly unreasonable for the supplier of a bulk commodity such as CO_2 for a food application to seek to exclude liability for the commodity not being of satisfactory quality or being unfit for its purpose where that has come about as a result of a breakdown in the manufacturing process allowing the inadvertent introduction of a redundant carcinogen."

On appeal, Messer argued that the High Court's finding was based on hindsight, **9–023** with the court knowing what had actually happened and the particular consequences, instead of asking whether the disputed terms were fair and reasonable to include having regard to the circumstances which were, or ought reasonably to have been, in the contemplation of the parties when the contract was made.

The Court of Appeal, however, felt that the High Court had been right to reject the submission that it was reasonable for a supplier, and not a manufacturer, to limit its liability to compliance with the British Standard, on the basis that this represented "the contemporary understanding" of the required purity. The authors of the Standard had been concerned to regulate the quantities of, and methods of testing for, elements which carbon dioxide might be expected to contain. They had not identified or regulated other elements, not because such understanding was that carbon dioxide might contain them, but because the presence of an extraneous or deleterious substance was wholly unexpected, and could only occur due to some understanding or mishap:

> "If one asks whether it was reasonable to limit Messer's liability to compliance with BS 4105, the answers seems ... therefore, to be that it ought to have been appreciated that compliance with BS 4105 would not, by itself, necessarily mean that the carbon dioxide was suitable for use."

The Standard assumed that the process of manufacture and supply would exclude the introduction of extraneous elements and so did not actually address such matters. The exclusion clauses were unreasonable because they contradicted a:

> "fundamental assumption that all parties would have made in this respect. Since it is accepted that there was no basis on which the buyers ... could have expected to test for extraneous components which they had no reason to consider would be present, and since their presence

---

[56] In this regard, the Court of Appeal slightly qualified the judge's finding by saying that it seems "quite legitimate to consider and take account of the actual extent and quality of the knowledge of a party, however much he or it, under ordinary contractual principles, have become contractually bound by the particular term(s)".

could only arise from some mishap in manufacture or supply, responsibility should rest on the supplier... who would be expected to be able to pass it on, where appropriate to the manufacturer ...".

Bacardi-Martini Beverages Ltd v Thomas Hardy Packaging Ltd[57]

9–024   These proceedings were brought by Bacardi against THP, by THP against Messer and by Messer against Terra, in each case in contract. They led to claims by THP against Terra in tort and for contribution under the Civil Liability (Contribution) Act 1978, on the basis that, if THP were liable to Bacardi, THP as manufacturer was also liable to Bacardi in respect of the same damage.

The first step in the contractual claim was determined by the judgment which the Court of Appeal had given in the *Britvic* proceedings. Messer's supplies of the carbon dioxide to THP were subject to implied undertakings as to the quality and fitness for purpose of the carbon dioxide, which, it was common ground, had been broken. The next step required examination of cll.12.1 and 12.2 of Messer's standard terms and conditions which had been incorporated into the contract with THP. These terms were:

> "12.0   Limitation of Liability
> 12.1   Subject to any other limitation or exclusion of liability expressed elsewhere in this Contract, the liability of Messer, its employees and Agents to the Customer in respect of personal injury or direct physical damage to property (and losses, costs and expenses directly arising from such injury or damage), whether through negligence or otherwise, shall be limited to £500,000 in respect of any one incident, except that nothing in this Contract shall restrict Messer's liability to an injured person or his personal representatives for personal injury or death resulting from negligence.
> 12.2   Messer, its employees and Agents shall have no liability whatsoever in respect of losses, costs or expenses of a purely financial or economic nature (including, but not limited to, loss of profits, loss of use or other consequential loss), or any other loss or damage not covered in Clause 12.1, unless such loss, cost, expense or damage be caused by Messer supplying Gas that is not of the purity warranted or by failure to deliver or by late delivery of Gas by Messer and unless such defective or late delivery or failure to deliver is notified within five days of the delivery or failure to deliver is notified within five days of the delivery or intended delivery, in which case Messer's liability shall be limited to the value of the quantity of Gas concerned (at Messer's selling price)."

The High Court, in a decision against which there was no appeal, had ruled that cl.12.1 was reasonable, but that cl.12.2 was not. It was argued before the Court of Appeal that the judge's conclusion that cl.12.1 was not unreasonable could not be squared with his further conclusion that cl.12.2 was not shown to be reasonable. It was argued that he had failed in the latter context to identify or place any or sufficient weight on the effective equality of bargaining power and on the availability (although THP chose not to take this out until late 1999) of product recall insurance, both of which factors influenced him in the former context. As the Court of Appeal pointed out, however, the judge was considering the reasonableness of cl.12.1 on a hypothesis which he (and also the Court of Appeal) rejected, namely that it offered at least the prospect of recovery of up to £500,000 in respect of any one incident of "damage" arising from the

---

57   [2002] EWCA Civ 549.

contamination of any end product into which defective carbon dioxide was added. Clause 12.2 by contrast operated as a blanket exemption, both in respect of losses of a "purely financial or economic nature" and in respect of "any other loss or damage not covered in Clause 12.1".

The argument advanced for reversing the High Court stressed the preservation of **9–025** liability in respect of supplies of gas "not of the purity warranted", referring to failure to meet the requirements of BS 4105 which, it was argued, represented the only type of deficiency that the parties could have foreseen. Reference was also made to another contract term which provided for the customer to determine suitability, so that any claim could be put forward within the five-day period specified in the exception to cl.12.2. The limitation of liability under the concluding part of that exception to the value of the quantity of gas concerned on this submission also corresponded with the amount of loss that the parties could foresee, if the contract operated as provided.

The Court of Appeal pointed to one difficulty with these submissions which was that they did not correspond with the reality of the parties' expected behaviour. The carbon dioxide supplied by Messer to THP was supplied into equipment (storage vessels with associated vaporising and/or other equipment) which Messer provided to THP under a separate agreement. Those tanks were never allowed to be less than 40 per cent full. Accordingly, any defective carbon dioxide supplied would necessarily contaminate a considerably greater quantity of carbon dioxide, quite apart from any effect as and when gas from the relevant tank was later mixed with Bacardi concentrate. The Court of Appeal went on to say that no one in reality ever expected THP to test the quality of carbon dioxide supplied into such tanks, whether for compliance with BS 4105, which Messer warranted, or for absence of other contaminating substances, which Terra's manufacturing and Messer's delivery process should have avoided. The High Court had found, in the light of the process of delivery and admixture, that "compliance with the five-day notice period would be impractical and to all intents and purposes impossible"; but, even if one simply describes such compliance as "unrealistic" and "not to be expected", the implications for the reasonableness of cl.12.2 seemed, as the Court of Appeal judged matters, to be the same.

It was also argued that no one would have foreseen that carbon dioxide matching the requirements of BS 4105 would be contaminated by some other substance, not mentioned in that standard, so that it was reasonable to include cl.12.2. It was accordingly maintained that, because the drafters could not have had such contamination in mind, cl.12.2 or at least its five-day notice requirement could not apply in such a case at all. What the Court of Appeal saw to be the difficulty about this argument was that cl.12.2 was in absolute terms. The exception only applied to loss, etc. caused by supplying "[g]as that is not of the purity warranted", which must in turn refer back to Messer's standard and so to BS 4105. As the Court of Appeal said, once it had been concluded, as it had been in the *Britvic* proceedings, that neither Messer's standard conditions nor BS 4105 contained any express undertaking regarding freedom from contamination by other substances not specified by BS 4105, it followed that cl.12.2 purported to exclude all liability for any such other contamination. The fact that no one would have conceived of other contamination by some entirely extraneous elements (whether benzene or a poison) was because all concerned would have assumed that Terra's manufacturing process (and, so far as material, Messer's delivery service) would have been operated efficiently in such a way as to make it impossible. The Court of Appeal concluded that, far from justifying an exclusion of responsibility if extraneous contamination occurred, this demonstrated the unreasonableness of any clause purporting to exempt Messer from liability in respect of such contamination.

CONSIDERATION OF UNLIKELY CIRCUMSTANCES

9–026   In the case just discussed, the clause was found to be unreasonable in the very circumstances which had arisen. The High Court had also said that, even if the clause was likely to be unreasonable even in exceptional circumstances, that would make it unreasonable for all circumstances.[58] In *Skipskredittforeningen v Emperor Navigation*,[59] Mance L.J. had said that if the clause as a whole was to be judged either valid or invalid, then courts "should not be too ready to focus on remote possibilities or to accept that a clause fails the test by reference to relatively uncommon or unlikely situations".[60] In the *THP* case, he stressed that he had been speaking in the context of an exclusion of set-off which would in terms cover any cross-claim for alleged fraud:

> "I stand by the warning, but I do not consider that the exemption provided by the terms of cl.12.2, viewed as a whole, can in any way be regarded as referring only to relatively uncommon or unlikely situations. The delivery of gas complying with BS 4105 and of suitable quality is one of the main subjects that it covers. An exemption that would, in practice (since no-one expected THP to test even for compliance with BS 4105), operate as a blanket exemption in respect of matters which the parties would have regarded as fundamental to each supply is a quite different exemption to that which I was addressing in *Skipskredittforeningen*."

SPECIAL BUSINESS AREAS

Surveyors

9–027   In *Smith v Eric S Bush; Harris v Wyre Forest DC*,[61] the House of Lords heard two cases where the question was whether a surveyor, who was instructed by a mortgagee to value a house, owed to the purchaser a duty of care in tort and whether a disclaimer of liability for negligence by or on behalf of the surveyor was effective. The House of Lords ruled that there was such a duty. In relation to the reasonableness of the clause, Lord Griffiths said that in such cases, though it was not possible to draw an exhaustive list of factors to be taken into account, the following should always be considered:

---

[58] The judge had referred to *Stewart Gill Ltd v Horatio Myer & Co Ltd* [1992] Q.B. 600 at 608–609, per Stuart-Smith L.J.
[59] [1998] 1 Lloyd's Rep. 66; cited with approval in *Deutsche Bank (Suisse) SA v Khan* [2013] EWHC 482.
[60] [1998] 1 Lloyd's Rep. 66 at 75.
[61] [1989] 2 All E.R. 514.

(1) Were the parties of equal bargaining power? If they were and the court was dealing with a one-off situation, then the reasonableness test would be more easily satisfied than in such a case as the present where the purchaser had no effective power to resist the imposition of the clause.

(2) In the case of advice, would it have been reasonably practicable to obtain the advice from an alternative source taking account of costs and time? The purchasers in this case had argued that obtaining a report of their own would have meant extra expense, and that this could strain the finances of young first-time buyers.

(3) How difficult is the task being undertaken for which liability is being excluded? To report on visible defects is, Lord Griffiths indicated, at the lower end of the surveyor's field of professional expertise.

(4) What are the practical consequences of the decision on the question of reasonableness?

As regards (4), above, Lord Griffiths stressed that this raised the question of insurance which had to be considered when determining who should carry the particular loss. Placing that liability on the surveyor would not, given his insurance cover, place undue liability on him, whereas placing it on the purchaser could leave the latter with a valueless property. Any increase in insurance premiums could be spread out among other customers. Lord Griffiths did, however, indicate that, where the sums involved were high, so that insurance cover was not available, it would be possible to provide advice on the basis of no liability or on the basis of liability limited to the extent of such insurance cover as was available.[62] The clause in this case failed the reasonableness test.

It was this latter observation which was relied on by the Court of Appeal in *Omega Trust Co Ltd v Wright Son & Pepper*.[63] A valuer had provided a valuation over certain property on behalf of a clearing bank. The valuer was later approached by a separate bank (the first claimant) for a valuation over the same properties. This second bank unknown to the valuer would provide the loan in conjunction with a third bank (the second claimant). This valuation, like the one first made, was subject to this provision:

> "This report shall be for private and confidential use of the clients for whom the report is undertaken and should not be reproduced in whole or in part or relied upon by third parties for any use whatsoever without the express written authority of the surveyors."

The securities, contrary to the report, proved valueless and the claimants sought damages.

It was held that the disclaimer could not avail the second claimant, since that party was not a client of the surveyor. This left for consideration whether, in relation to the first claimant, it was fair and reasonable to allow reliance on the disclaimer.

The High Court had held that it was not. It was a fact that the parties were of equal bargaining power, and that it had been open to the first claimant to obtain an independent valuation:

---

[62] [1989] 2 All E.R. 514 at 532.
[63] [1997] P.N.L.R. 424.

> "It would have been the easiest thing in the world either to go and get their own independent advice, or to do what the disclaimer would, in the ordinary course of business, prompt them to do, that is to say, to get in touch with the valuer and ask the valuer as to whether they too could rely on the valuation given."

9–028   It was also the case that no issues of cost or speed would impede such further valuation, a valuation which was in itself straightforward.

Section 11(3) of the 1977 Act, which refers to a notice not itself a term of a contract, requires the issue of reasonableness to be determined having regard to all the circumstances obtaining when the liability arose or, but for the disclaimer, would have arisen. In what the Court of Appeal considered an "important point", it was said that, at that time, the valuers would have discovered for the first time that there was a second lender, and that that lender had taken responsibility for 60 per cent of the loan without either getting in touch with them or anyone notifying them or seeking their permission, or making any payment to them. Were it not for that lender appearing on the scene, the valuer's liability if negligent would have been to the first claimant alone, but that liability would have been for the same sum of money whether there was one lender or two. The Court of Appeal said that the "first and obvious purpose" of the disclaimer, as obtained by construction of the document, was to limit the assumption of responsibility to the first claimant and to no one else. It was entered into "to assure clarity, to assure transparency and to assure certainty". The Court of Appeal regarded the valuer as entitled to do all that could be done to prevent himself having to fight a difficult law suit as to whether he owed a duty to an unknown lender. If his disclaimer had been complied with by either claimant, that would have been the position. If his document had been complied with and consent from him had been sought, he could, had he wished, have declined to assume the additional responsibility. As the Court of Appeal said:

> "It can, in certain circumstances, be more onerous in fact to face potential claims from two claimants who may be separately represented, and in relation to whom there may be two measures of damage appropriate, than to face claims from one, though that point pales into insignificance beside the point that what he had been deprived of was a position where everything would have been clear and certain and he had, through no fault of his own, a position where he could only rely on the terms of the disclaimer after fighting a difficult law suit in relation to it."

In response to this, the second claimant argued that this was simply an "uncovenanted benefit" to the valuer, and it would be unreasonable to let him rely on the clause, because, had in fact they asked permission of him, he probably would have granted permission. As the Court of Appeal said, however, that was something which would never be known. It was, though, clear that no fee was paid to the valuer and that he would have been entitled to a fee had permission been sought of him. The court said that a professional valuer, valuing expensive properties in a commercial context, was entitled to know who his client was and to whom his duty was owed. He was entitled to refuse to assume liability to any unknown lender, and was further entitled to refuse to assume liability to any known lender with whom he had not agreed. The court went on to say that he was entitled to increase the fee (or would have been) as a term of permitting the second lender to rely on the valuation, because it could be more expensive to be sued by two lenders rather than one:

> "if the second lender was not prepared to pay what is asked, it seems ... that the valuer would have been entitled to refuse to assume that liability to the bank, and the 1977 Act would not have required the contract to be rewritten."

It was pointed out that, in this case, the first claimant, when introduced, recognised the valuer's right to know who his client was. They had acted "properly", sought the valuer's permission and become clients. They received his report and the disclaimer; they never objected to the terms of the disclaimer; they never asked for permission to disclose it to their co-lenders; they were prepared to approbate the contract in the sense of acting and relying on the disclaimer, but they seem to have reprobated it by disclosing it to their co-lenders without having obtained the permission of the valuers first. If they had raised the question with the valuers, the second claimant could have been accepted as clients and risk could have been assumed by them: but only if the valuers were prepared to assume responsibility, and not otherwise. As the court concluded, it seemed that the first claimant was only entitled to put the valuation before the second claimant for reliance if they had sought permission from the borrowers, and the fact they did not would, on the face of it, seem to be a prima facie breach of contract on their part unless the clause was invalid under the Act.

9–029

In the light of all these circumstances, the Court of Appeal disagreed with the High Court and held that the disclaimer was a fair and reasonable one. It was apparently accepted that the clause could be unfair and yet reasonable, since the Court of Appeal said that this disclaimer was neither unfair nor was it unreasonable. It was also noted that public policy could be taken into account when assessing the reasonableness of a clause, but no such issue was relevant to the present case. It was further pointed out that the presence of the disclaimer was fatal to the second claimant's action, although this did not seem to point one way or the other. Accepting that it was first and foremost a matter for the trial judge to balance the conflicting interests, it was still the case that the conclusion reached here by the trial judge "was outside the margin of appreciation that is afforded to him, and in the circumstances ... wrong".

The *Omega* case was central to the decision in *Rehman v Jones Lang Lasalle Ltd*.[64] Referring to the observation in that case that it involved a professional valuer dealing with an expensive property, the court said that here too "was a professional valuer valuing an expensive property in a commercial context. Whether or not the Claimants were sophisticated in commercial property does not in my judgment alter the general proposition. Something most unusual would be required to upset that general proposition". The "general proposition" referred to is presumably that, in such circumstances, disclaiming liability will satisfy the reasonableness test.

The difference between the domestic transaction which was involved in the *Smith* case, and a major commercial transaction, was highlighted in *Bank of*

---

[64] [2013] EWHC 1339.

Scotland v Fuller Peiser.[65] Fuller Peiser had been instructed by the prospective purchaser of a hotel to prove a survey report and a valuation certificate. The report contained a disclaimer which stated that the report was "for loan security purposes and for the use of the client only"; and that Fuller Peiser accepted "no responsibility whatsoever to any party other than the client. Any such party relies on the report at their own risk". Distinguishing this case from *Smith* the court stressed that this case did not involve the purchase of houses of modest value, in relation to which the court in that case had been "careful to confine its judgment". It noted that the transaction in the present case "was plainly a commercial transaction, albeit of a modest value", and was treated as such by both parties. The court pointed out that the pursuers were a large commercial banking entity with ready access to legal advice and they were well able to appreciate the meaning and effect of the disclaimer in the defenders' report. It was accepted on their behalf that the pursuers could readily have obtained advice from another surveyor and that there were no constraints in terms of finance or urgency upon their so doing. It was also accepted that, as an alternative course, the pursuers could have asked the defenders to advise them separately as clients in a direct relationship for which a fee might well be payable. It was accepted also by the pursuers that they were of at least equal bargaining power with the defenders. The defenders had insurance, but the pursuers were no less able to bear such loss as may have been occasioned by this particular act of lending on their part. The court accepted that it was open to the pursuers to proceed on the basis of a "without responsibility" report but if that was what they chose to do, the court said, then it was hard "to see that recognition of their knowingly proceeding on that basis involves material unfairness to them". The test of reasonableness was satisfied.

Local authorities

9–030   By their nature, local authorities stand somewhere between consumers and businesses. The extended definition of "business" in s.14 of the 1977 Act, provides that "business" includes "the activities of any government department or local or public authority". Scott Baker J. in the *St Albans* case outlined the difference between them and "ordinary" businesses when he said that council officials are not:

> "in the ordinary sense of the word 'businessmen', although it is to be hoped that they act in a business-like way. Their contracts are governed by specific financial restraints, the need for public evaluation and, often, competitive tendering. They do not operate in the same commercial field as a business, and probably find it impractical to insure against commercial risks."[66]

That case concerned the supply of computer software which was defective.[67] A clause limited liability to £100,000 against a claim for over £1.3 million. Since

---

[65] 2002 S.L.T. 574.
[66] See *St Albans City and District Council v International Computers Ltd* [1996] 4 All E.R. 481.
[67] Without specifically deciding the matter, Scott Baker J. indicated that computer software was "goods" for the purposes of the Sale of Goods Act 1979 and the Supply of Goods and Services Act

this was a limitation clause, the judge first considered issues of insurance as required under s.11(4).[68] He stressed that the defendants were a substantial company with ample resources to meet any liability, and that they also had worldwide product liability cover for £50 million.

The judge also considered the relative bargaining strength of the parties, and it was here that he referred to the strength of the defendants' position in that they were one of the few companies meeting the claimants' requirements, all of whom dealt on similar terms, and the very tight timescale. He accepted that the claimants could have raised the question of the limitation clause earlier, but he did not feel confident that they would have achieved anything very different.

The Sch.2 guidelines also require a court to consider whether a customer received an inducement to agree to the particular term, or had the chance of entering a similar contract with someone else, but without the term in question. On this point, the judge found that the claimants received no such inducement, nor had any such chance as referred to in the guidelines. The judge also found, in making use of another of the guidelines, that the claimants knew of the exemption clause and made representations about it.

In reaching his decision that the defendants had failed to show that the limitation clause was reasonable, Scott Baker J. found the determining factors to be that: the parties were of unequal bargaining power; that the defendants were insured; and that the defendants had failed to justify a limitation figure of £100,000 which was small, in relation to both the potential risk and the actual loss. As he also pointed out, the fact that the 1988 General Conditions, which should have been used, had increased liability to £125,000 made it harder to argue that the limitation in the 1985 General Conditions was reasonable. The judge also drew attention to the practical consequences of any decision on the question of reasonableness.[69] It was, he said, better that the loss fell on an international computer company which was insured, and could pass the cost on to customers, than on a local authority where the loss would be borne by the local population. He added that it was not unreasonable "that he who stands to make the profit [International Computers Ltd] should carry the risk". This meant that a consideration of the practical consequences counted in favour of the claimants. A consideration of these various factors, he said, outweighed the fact that contracting parties should be free to make their own bargains; that the council went into this contract with its eyes open; that limitation clauses of this kind were common in the industry; and that the software used was a developing area. **9–031**

None of this is to suggest that local authorities are a privileged body so far as the issue of reasonableness is concerned, but the recognised restrictions on how they do business perhaps indicates a greater difficulty in showing a term to be reasonable than where the contract is between two fully-fledged businesses.

1982. On appeal, Sir Iain Glidewell was of the same view: [1996] 4 All E.R. 481 at 492–493. Digital content is covered specifically by the Consumer Rights Act 2014.

[68] See the discussion at para.9–007.

[69] The judge here was following the approach adopted by Lord Griffiths in *Smith v Eric S Bush; Harris v Wyre Forest DC* [1990] 1 A.C. 831 at 858. The issue of reasonableness was not discussed when the *St Albans* case went on appeal.

THE SOLE TRADER

9–032   It is also the case that, while contracts might be made between businesses, one of the businesses might be small indeed when compared to the size of the other contracting party. In *AEG (UK) Ltd v Logic Resource Ltd*,[70] it was indicated that a clause would fail the reasonableness test in the circumstances of that case, given that the sellers were a "large and well-known multi-national", while the buyers were a "one man show".[71]

FINANCE COMPANIES

9–033   An exclusion clause, stigmatised by the Court of Appeal as containing all the exclusions "known to mankind", was similarly found to be unreasonable in *Lease Management Services Ltd v Purnell Secretarial Services Ltd*.[72] An agreement was entered into with a finance company for the lease of a photocopying machine. This machine was stated by the manufacturers to have a certain capacity, and it was on the basis of that assurance that the lease contract was made with the finance company to whom the manufacturers sold the machine. The agreement signed with the finance company was so designed (a business practice strongly condemned by the Court of Appeal) to make it appear that the agreement was in fact made with the manufacturers.[73] This gave rise to an estoppel against the manufacturers who could therefore not deny that this agreement contained the assurance as to the quality of the machine being supplied.

The agreement contained a clause which offered to obtain for the lessee the benefits of any manufacturer's guarantee, but which proceeded to exclude all liability:

> "in respect of any conditions warranties or representations relating to the condition of the equipment or to its merchantability or suitability or fitness for the particular purpose for which it may be required whether such conditions warranties or representations are express or implied and whether arising under the agreement or under any prior agreement or in oral or written statements made by or on behalf of the lessor or its agents in the course of negotiations in which the lessee or its representatives may have been concerned prior to the agreement."

After reciting this clause, the Vice-Chancellor observed that:

> "We would like to think that the days of such blanket exclusion clauses, daunting to anyone and incomprehensible to an ordinary customer are passed. One would hope that finance companies and suppliers of expensive equipment no longer use small pre-print standard conditions as a means to avoid liabilities otherwise attaching to them for breach of pre-sale representations or breach of implied warranties."

The county court had upheld the clause, mainly because the finance company was involved in the contract only in a technical sense: it was not itself the

---

[70] [1996] C.L.C. 265.
[71] In fact, the issue was not formally decided since, by a majority, the Court of Appeal ruled that the relevant clause had not been incorporated into the contract.
[72] [1994] C.C.L.R. 127.
[73] Such a practice could well be an offence under the Business Protection from Misleading Marketing Regulations 2008 (SI 2008/1276).

manufacturer or producer of the goods. The Court of Appeal, however, did not see this as having any real bearing on the matter:

> "Self-evidently, it cannot be reasonable to exclude liability for breach of a warranty or condition which has been expressly given. Otherwise the customer will find himself snared: he is given an express warranty and he relies on that and binds himself to take the equipment."

He is later told that there is in "obscure small print", which he "did not read and could not sensibly be expected to read some exclusion clause requiring him to accept a machine which was incapable of doing what he had been assured it could do". Accordingly, and notwithstanding that the lessee in this case was experienced in the business, the Court of Appeal reversed the county court and held that the clause had not been shown to be reasonable.

This comes very close to saying that no clause can ever exclude liability for breach of an express term. The Court of Appeal said that there could be circumstances where such a clause would satisfy the test of reasonableness, but stated that it was not reasonable to suppose that a buyer would appreciate that such a term would override a statement made expressly by the seller. The buyer, it was said, would normally need to be told of the existence of the clause. Since it is hard to see such advice ever being given, it may be supposed that, as a practical matter, this decision assures the validity of the express terms of a contract.[74]   **9–034**

The Court of Appeal also made it clear that, when it came to an application of the reasonableness test, finance companies were not to be treated favourably just because they had no real contact with the goods. If it were otherwise, this would present a "trap" for the other party, his rights depending on what method of acquisition he preferred.

This statement of principle was noted with approval in *Danka Rentals Ltd v Xi Software Ltd*,[75] where the question arose as to the reasonableness of this clause:

> "The equipment and the supplier have been selected by you relying entirely on your own judgment. If you require any warranties or guarantees in respect of the equipment, its maintenance or suitability for any purpose, you must obtain them from the supplier. We exclude all express or implied warranties, conditions or guarantees from this agreement, and in no event will our liability under this agreement exceed the aggregate of the rentals paid by you at the time the liability arises.
>
> In no event will we be liable to you in contract, tort or otherwise including any liability for negligence
> (a)   for any loss of revenue, business, anticipated savings or profits, or any loss of use or value; or
> (b)   for any indirect or consequential loss howsoever arising.
> 'Anticipated savings' means any expense which you expect to avoid incurring or to incur in a lesser amount than would otherwise have been the case."

This was contained in a contract between a finance company and the lessee of a photocopier, the machine being not of merchantable quality.

Looking first to the statutory guidelines as to reasonableness, the court considered first the relative bargaining strength of these parties, taking account of   **9–035**

---

[74] See, however, *Nippon Yusen Kaisha Ltd v Scindia Steam Navigation Co Ltd* [2000] 1 All E.R. (Comm) 700.
[75] [1998] 17 Tr. L.R. 74.

alternative means by which the customer's requirements could have been met. The court regarded this as favouring the finance company, given that the lessee was an "experienced and intelligent" party who belonged to a trade body and who would have had legal advice available. As for the customer's knowledge of the existence or extent of the relevant term, the court accepted that the lessee had all the actual knowledge.

The finance company also argued that the courts tend to accept the argument that finance companies are acting reasonably when they exclude the implied terms as to quality and fitness where the lessee knows that the former has had no chance to examine the relevant equipment. After referring to the *Lease Management* case, the court rejected this approach. Noting the "awful" quality of the equipment in this case, the court asked if it would really be reasonable for the finance company to state that, while they were owners, and had leased out the equipment for a long, fixed term, they could still require the lessee to say:

> "however useless and defective that equipment will be from the outset, we can require you to look to the suppliers as the people who sold it to us for your remedy and we can require you to continue paying the rent meanwhile."

The court said that "would not be and is not reasonable ... nor would it be fair". The finance company had said that the proper and reasonable thing for parties such as the present lessee to do was to pursue his grievances against the actual supplier. There was evidence in the present case that the lessee had obtained judgment against the suppliers in third party proceedings. There was also evidence of a "reasonably widely drawn" guarantee furnished by the supplier. The court, however, indicated that it was not reasonable to expect a lessee to throw up his rights against a lessor in return for perhaps more dubious rights against a supplier who might prove awkward or who might go out of business. It was also always open to a lessor to preserve its own remedies against a supplier. The lessor would probably be in a good position to assess the reliability and solvency of the supplier, more than the lessee.

The court was also influenced by the background to the present agreement which, in large part, was influenced by the lessee's unhappy previous experiences with this finance company. The financial terms of the current agreement had been reached so as to provide the lessee with an incentive to settle disputes relating to the earlier agreement without recourse to law.

Finally, the court pointed to a further statutory guideline which requires it to consider where the term excludes or restricts any relevant liability if some condition is not complied with, "whether it was reasonable at the time of the contract to expect that compliance with that condition would be practicable". The court said that: "It would ... be perfectly reasonable to expect the [finance company] to comply with the conditions purported to be excluded". In its judgment, therefore, the court concluded that "whilst there are factors relating to the reasonableness test on either side of the line, the [finance company has] decisively failed to show that the exclusion clauses satisfied the requirement of reasonableness".

9–036 The difficulty faced by finance companies seeking to uphold exclusion or limitation clauses was also emphasised in *Sovereign Finance v Silver Crest*

Furniture.[76] Goods had been obtained from a supplier but the actual contract was made with a finance company. This contract contained the following clause:

"ACKNOWLEDGEMENT AND INDEMNITY
(A)   The hirer acknowledges that:
  1.   The goods are required for the purpose of a business carried on by him, were selected by him and acquired at his request by the company for the purpose of this agreement from the supplier;
  2.   In selecting the goods the hirer does not rely on the skill or judgment of the company but on his own or that of his supplier;
  3.   Save for the extent that any statutes may provide otherwise, the supplier is not the agent of the company;
  4.   Acceptance by the hirer of delivery of the goods is conclusive proof that the hirer is satisfied that they are in all respects in good working order and in conformity with the hirer's requirements;
  5.   The delivery of the goods by the company depends on the supplier of the goods fulfilling its obligation to supply and the company shall not be liable for any delay in the delivery of the goods howsoever caused or arising.
(B)   As the goods have been selected by the hirer and have not been inspected by the company, the company does not make or give any representation, warranty, stipulation or undertaking, express or implied, by statute, Common Law or otherwise, as to the age, state, quality or performance of the goods or their correspondence with description, merchantable quality or their fitness for any particular purpose."

The finance company's fundamental submission was that the nature of the transaction was such that it was reasonable for the buyers to bear the risk of any defect in the machine. They selected the machine. They had, at the time of entering into the agreement, opportunities to inspect the machine and had, in fact, done so on two occasions. Whether or not they did so thoroughly was their own business. It was never envisaged that the finance company would have any opportunity to inspect the machine and, in any event, it was the buyer, not the finance company, who possessed the expertise to make such an inspection. The quality of the goods did not form a dimension of the service envisaged by the parties that would be provided by the company, which was the mere provision of finance. Nor was it commercially viable to impose such an obligation on a finance company in such circumstances. It was said that the clear nature of the agreement was indicated by the fact that it was for the buyer to maintain the goods.

The High Court pointed to what it felt was a difference in emphasis between *R&B Customs Brokers Co Ltd v United Dominions Trust Ltd*[77] and the *Lease Management* case. In the former, albeit obiter, Dillon L.J. had found that a clause in a finance company's contract was reasonable. Longmore J. preferred to follow the latter case "where the reasonableness of the clause arose from direct decision rather than be guided by *obiter dicta* of a single Lord Justice".

Seeking to uphold the clause, the company said that the clause in the present case was narrower than that in the *Lease Management* case and approximated closely to that in *R&B Customs Brokers Co Ltd v United Dominions Trust Ltd*;

---

[76] (1997) 16 Tr. L.R 370.
[77] [1988] 1 All E.R. 847.

and that the former dealt with an express contemporaneous warranty which would be unreasonable to exclude and not with the statutory implied warranties with which this case was concerned.

The High Court rejected this argument. First, the clause purported to say that no express representations were made or warranties given. The company argued that if an express representation were made, or an express warranty given, whether by the finance company or supplier, the clause would not exclude liability for non-compliance with such representation or warranty. The court, however, took the view that, on its ordinary wording, the clause did seek to exclude such liability. The natural meaning of the clause was that there was to be no liability for any express representation or warranty. It amounted to a total exclusion of all liability:

> "That natural meaning is offensive to reason... Any clause with that meaning is, therefore, prima facie unenforceable. The fact that the clause, on its true construction, is too wide to be reasonable, means that the clause, as a whole, must be regarded as unenforceable even though the parties relying on the clause may wish to rely on an obligation which it might be reasonable to exclude if it were excluded on its own. The way in which the term is in fact operated or relied on is irrelevant."

The court also said that, while it was true that the *Lease Management* case did deal with an express or implied warranty made contemporaneously with the contract, and that the present case dealt with an exclusion of implied warranties, the language used in that case applied equally to implied warranties of the kind relevant in the present case. The clause in the *R&B Customs Brokers Co Ltd*[78] case was drawn more narrowly and was a "conscious attempt to accept some liability and to exclude merely the terms implied by statute". The clause in the present case was more wide-ranging and was unreasonable.

9–037   A contrary view was taken, but with clear regret, by Court of Appeal, in *BTE Auto Repairs Ltd v H&H Factors Ltd*.[79] The claimant had leased an item of machinery for a fixed period of three years.

The machinery was supplied to the defendants, a finance company, which obtained it in the usual way from the importers. The machine eventually proved defective but the claimant was faced with this clause in the leasing contract:

> "The lessee has satisfied himself as to the condition of the goods and acknowledges that no condition or warranty whatsoever has been or is given by the lessor as to their fitness for any purpose and all conditions or warranties express or implied and whether by statute or otherwise are expressly excluded and delivery of the goods to the lessee shall be conclusive evidence that the lessee has examined them and found them to be completely in accordance with the description overleaf, in good order and condition, fit for any purpose for which they may be required and in every way satisfactory. The lessee shall not be entitled to any remission of rental in respect of any period during which the goods or any of them are unserviceable and the lessor shall not be liable to provide the lessee with any replacement goods during any such period or at all. The lessor shall use all reasonable efforts to obtain for the lessee the benefit of the manufacturers guarantees and warranties (if any) given to the lessor."

---

[78] *Supra* fn.75.
[79] Unreported January 26, 1990.

In the county court, the judge had taken note of the statutory guidelines, saying that, in the context of the present case, these required him to have regard to the relative bargaining power of the parties; any alternative means by which the claimant's requirements could have been met; and whether he knew of the existence and extent of the disputed term.

In applying the guidelines, he stated that, because the defendants were "better endowed" than the claimant, this did not of itself indicate the relative strength of the parties. In this context, regard had to be had to the nature of the transaction and its essential features, and here he pointed out that the defendants, as a finance company, never had the machinery in their possession at any time. This militated much in their favour.[80]

The county court also drew attention to the fact that the defendants had agreed under the contract to make all reasonable efforts to pass on to the claimant the benefit of any manufacturer's guarantee. That guarantee was limited to a period of 12 months, and itself excluded any other express warranties and conditions, and any warranties or conditions implied by statute or otherwise. The court thought it reasonable that a finance house should decline to accept liability more extensive than any remedy they might have against their own suppliers and upheld the exclusion clause.

In the Court of Appeal, it was argued on behalf of the claimant that the consequence of giving force to the exclusion clause was serious, in that he would receive only a worthless piece of equipment and have rights against his suppliers and the manufacturers which were at best conjectural. The attention of the court was drawn here to the observations of Lord Griffiths that regard should be paid to the consequences of giving effect to an exclusion clause.[81] For the finance company, on the other hand, this was just one of a series of transactions, and they were also able to amend the terms of their contracts with their suppliers. Even so, the court found no reason to depart from the lower court's finding and upheld the clause.

9–038

A similar finding, but this time with no regret, was made in *Anglo Group Plc v Winther Browne & Co Ltd*.[82] WB, a distributor of goods for the DIY market, entered into a written agreement on BML's standard terms that BML would supply computer hardware and a standard software package to WB. WB alleged that BML made a number of representations to WB in order to induce it to enter into a standard form leasing agreement with Anglo in respect of the equipment. WB alleged that the equipment suffered from numerous defects, such that Anglo, by reason of the representations made by its agent BML, was in breach of a condition or warranty as to the fitness or quality of the equipment, which was to be implied into the leasing agreement under s.9 of the Supply of Goods and Services Act 1982. Anglo relied upon express terms of its leasing agreement, by which WB confirmed that BML was not the agent of Anglo, and that Anglo was not liable for any loss consequential upon the equipment not functioning properly. As against BML, WB claimed for loss and damage by way of loss of net

---

[80] The county court judge had relied here on the observations of Dillon L.J. in *R&B Customs Brokers Co Ltd v United Dominions Trust Ltd supra*.
[81] *Racal Communications Ltd v Pay Board* [1974] 3 All E.R. 263.
[82] 72 Con. L.R. 118.

profits and wasted expenditure. BML relied upon the terms of its agreement to the effect that it was WB's responsibility to select a computer system which was adequate for WB's purposes. Both Anglo and BML asserted that their standard terms satisfied the requirements of the 1977 Act. After referring to both the *Purnell* and *Sovereign* cases, the judge said that WB had a right of recourse against BML and that the inclusion of the clause did not place WB in the position where acquisition by hire from a finance company rather than by purchase from a supplier became a trap. He took account of the statutory guidelines and all the circumstances of the case, noting in particular that WB was not bound to obtain its finance from Anglo. It could have done so from other sources. The customer was aware of the terms and accepted them. Although the system purchased was standard, the process, to be successful, required considerable input and co-operation from the purchaser. The judge also took into account that Anglo had not been involved in the negotiations which led to the contract between WB and BML. The exclusion clauses were held to be reasonable.

The uncertainty felt by the courts in such matters is amply demonstrated by the decision of Buckley J. in *Scania Finance Ltd v Monteum Ltd* and *Gray & Adams*.[83] Scania brought an action for damages arising out of the alleged repudiatory breach by the first defendant of a hire-purchase agreement. By the agreement Monteum hired a cab and chassis unit manufactured by Scania which was fitted with a body unit manufactured by the second defendant. Both Scania and G&A knew the purpose for which the vehicle was required and that the body unit had to be watertight, apart from specific drain holes. After delivery to Monteum, G&A repaired two reported leaks in the bulkhead of the body unit and screwed down the floor. Six months after delivery, Monteum purported to reject the body unit, and hence the vehicle, as being of unsatisfactory quality. Scania claimed damages for breach of the agreement, and Monteum counterclaimed for damages for loss of use of the vehicle whilst it was under repair. An issue arose on the counterclaim concerning the reasonableness of an exclusion clause in the agreement excluding all conditions, warranties and stipulations save those implied by the Supply of Goods (Implied Terms) Act 1973.

The judge felt that it was better to adopt the course taken by Longmore J. in the *Silver Crest* case and hence to follow the ruling in the Lease Management case, and thus to find the clause unreasonable. He did so, however, while acknowledging that he could see "considerable force" and a "strong contrary argument" in regard to the argument that the clause should be upheld. He noted that, in a contract of this sort, where the goods are to a specification agreed between the ultimate purchaser and the manufacturer, and the finance company is simply there to facilitate the deal, there were good reasons for saying that clause should be upheld. He drew attention also to the fact that commercial parties should be free to draft their own clauses and to do so without judicial interference. There was also a manufacturer's warranty with which all three parties were happy.

---

[83] Unreported January 30, 2001 (High Court).

It is perhaps better always to approach such issues on a fact-by-fact basis, so that each case should be judged on its own facts. No case can ever be a binding precedent as to the reasonableness of a clause, whether in the context of a finance company or not.

WHERE THE CLAUSE HAS PREVIOUSLY BEEN RELIED ON

In *George Mitchell (Chesterhall) Ltd v Finney Lock Seeds Ltd*,[84] the party seeking to rely on a disputed clause had rarely, if ever, invoked it in the past. The evidence showed clearly that the clause was not relied on "to the letter", that neither party expected it to be applied literally, and that its existence "merely provides a basis for the negotiation of mutually acceptable settlements".[85] Lord Bridge said that the conduct of the parties in relation to the clause "indicated a clear recognition by [the parties] that reliance on the limitation of liability imposed by the relevant condition would not be fair or reasonable".[86]

9–039

In the *Overland Shoes Ltd v Schenkers Ltd*[87] case, however, Pill L.J. saw "little merit" in the argument that the disputed clause had not in practice been relied on. Such practice "was admirable and conducive to a good business relationship" but, in contrast to the *George Mitchell* case, where there was recognition that reliance on the clause was unreasonable, there was no such recognition in the instant case.

NOTICES NOT HAVING CONTRACTUAL EFFECT

In relation to notices not having contractual effect, where the test is whether it is "fair and reasonable" to permit reliance on the notice,[88] the Divisional Court in the *British Airports Authority* case considered the following clause in the Authority's contract:

9–040

> "Neither the Authority nor any servant or agent of the Authority shall be liable for loss of or damage to the aircraft, its parts or accessories or any property contained in the aircraft, occurring while the aircraft is in the airport or is in the course of landing or taking off at the airport, or being removed or dealt with elsewhere ... arising or resulting directly or indirectly from any act or omission or default, on the part of the Authority its servants or agents unless done with intent to cause damage or recklessly and with knowledge that damage would probably result."

The judge ruled that it was fair and reasonable to allow reliance on the clause. He gave no specific reasons, but he was clearly impressed by the effect the clause would have in enabling the Authority to limit its costs and in freeing it from any involvement in disputes and accidents, the facts of which would be almost entirely unknown to it.

---

[84] [1983] 1 All E.R. 108 (CA).
[85] [1983] 1 All E.R. 108 (CA) at 135, per Kerr L.J.
[86] [1983] 2 A.C. 803 at 817.
[87] [1998] 1 Lloyd's Rep. 498.
[88] Unfair Contract Terms Act 1977 s.11(3).

PRE-1978 AUTHORITIES

9–041   Under the Supply of Goods (Implied Terms) Act 1973, the test of reasonableness, now replaced by the provisions of the Unfair Contract Terms Act 1977, was that the relevant clause was unenforceable to the extent that "it would not be fair or reasonable to allow reliance" on it.[89] This differs from the 1977 Act, which asks instead whether the particular term was a fair and reasonable one to incorporate.

In *Green Ltd v Cade Bros Farms*,[90] the contract was for the sale of seed potatoes to a farmer. The contract imposed a time limit for the making of complaints, and also limited damages to the contract price. The judge ruled against the time limits since no one, at the time the contract was made, would have reckoned it a practical matter to have complained of the particular defect within the prescribed time, a finding which virtually applies the test now found in the 1977 Act. In relation to the limitation of liability, this was upheld because the contract was one negotiated by trade associations representing both sides to the contract and because the potatoes in this case were cheaper because they were uncertified.

In *George Mitchell (Chesterhall) Ltd v Finney Lock Seeds Ltd*,[91] a contract for the supply of cabbage seeds to a farmer limited liability to replacing defective seed or repaying the price. The value of the contract was £201.60, whereas the loss to the farmer was over £61,000. The Divisional Court[92] ruled against the clause, stressing also that the sellers could have obtained insurance cover without thereby causing any material increase in the cost of the seed.

In the Court of Appeal,[93] Lord Denning accepted this point, also noting that the buyers, unlike the sellers, had no way of discovering the defect in the seed; that the parties were not of equal bargaining power, the term having been inserted by the seedsmen generally with no negotiation with the farmer; that the error in the supply had been caused by "serious negligence"; and finally that it had never been the practice to rely on the strict letter of the exclusion clause. The House of Lords accepted all these points, but was particularly influenced by the fact that seedsmen had not generally sought to rely on the clause:

> "This evidence indicated a clear recognition by seedsmen in general, and the appellants in particular, that reliance on the limitation of liability imposed by the relevant condition would not be fair or reasonable."[94]

ACKNOWLEDGMENT OF EXAMINATION CLAUSES

9–042   The point has been made earlier[95] that a contract term by which a party agrees that he has examined the goods and found them in good condition, perhaps also indicating that the supplier was not advised of the purpose for which the goods

---

[89] [1983] 2 A.C. 803 at 817.
[90] [1978] 1 Lloyd's Rep. 602.
[91] [1983] 2 All E.R. 737.
[92] [1981] 1 Lloyd's Rep. 476 at 480, per Parker J.
[93] [1983] 1 All E.R. 108 at 115.
[94] [1983] 2 All E.R. 737 at 744, per Lord Bridge.
[95] See the discussion at para 2–050.

were wanted, will be effective, if at all, only if the facts give rise to an estoppel. This point has been further examined in the context of the reasonableness test.

In the *Photoprint* case,[96] one clause read:

> "the customer declares that he has examined the goods and that they are in every respect satisfactory and suitable for the purpose for which they are required and that he has relied on his own skill and judgment in choosing the goods."

The claimants argued that this was an attempt to avoid the implied term as to merchantable quality by seeking to establish facts rendering that term inapplicable; that it was not promissory in form; that it should be read as a statement only which may in appropriate cases tend to prove the truth of what it says; and that it sometimes raises an estoppel, but that where the facts acknowledged were not true, an estoppel could not normally arise. No estoppel was raised in the present case, so the reliance by the claimants on *Lowe v Lombank*[97] was held of no avail. The court also pointed out that the relevant clause in the earlier case covered patent not latent defects.

The deputy judge accepted the submission of the first defendants that the presence of the particular clause was one of the facts to be taken into account when determining whether the exclusion clause also contained in the contract was reasonable. Photoprint had put forward as an argument the fact that the quality of the machine could not be determined until it had been up and running for a couple of weeks. This, however, was not known to the defendants when the contract was made. All that they had was the acknowledgment clause referred to above. Without making any specific comment on the clause, the deputy judge appeared to treat it as one factor among many in his decision to uphold the exclusion clause.

A more specific finding that a non-reliance clause can be reasonable was made by the Court of Appeal in *Grimstead & Son Ltd v McGarrigan*.[98] The court had no doubt that:

> "In such a case it seems ... wholly fair and reasonable that the purchaser should seek his remedies ... within the four corners of the agreement and should not be permitted to rely on pre-contractual representations which are, deliberately, not reflected in contractual warranties."

In the *BTE Auto Repairs* case,[99] the exclusion clause in question began with an acknowledgment by the lessee that he had:

> "satisfied himself as to the condition of the goods and acknowledges that no condition or warranty whatsoever has been or is given by the lessor as to their fitness for any purpose and all conditions or warranties whether expressed or implied and whether by statute or otherwise are expressly excluded and delivery of the goods to the lessee shall be conclusive evidence that the lessee has examined them and found them to be completely in accordance with the description ... in good order and condition, fit for any purpose for which they may be required and in every way satisfactory."

---

[96] See para 9–010.
[97] [1960] 1 W.L.R. 196.
[98] [1998] EWCA Civ 1523.
[99] See para.9–037.

The county court judge pronounced himself "not impressed" by this clause: "the defects were not apparent at the time". Neither this observation, nor the clause itself, was commented on in the Court of Appeal. It seems clear enough that, whether or not an acknowledgment of examination clause raises an estoppel or is material in determining the reasonableness of an exclusion clause, it has no impact where the defect of which complaint is made is latent, certainly where it is not expressed to cover such defects.

9–043   That a non-reliance clause, or its equivalent, can give rise to an estoppel (even though misapplied in the instant case) was evidenced *by Olympic Airlines SA v Misrepresentati ACG Acquisition XX LLCon*.[100] The parties had entered into a five-year lease of a Boeing 737. Clause 7.9 provided as follows: "Delivery by lessee to lessor of the certificate of acceptance will be conclusive proof as between lessor and lessee that lessee has examined and investigated the aircraft, that the aircraft and the aircraft documents are satisfactory to lessee and that lessee has irrevocably and unconditionally accepted the aircraft for lease hereunder without any reservations whatsoever (except for any discrepancies which may be noted in the certificate of acceptance)".

The High Court held that statements made in the Certificate of Acceptance gave rise to an estoppel by representation, on which the other had reasonably relied to its detriment, in accepting redelivery from the previous lessee which precluded Olympic from arguing that the aircraft was not on delivery in the contractually required condition.

The Court of Appeal ruled that the lower court had come to the right conclusion but for the wrong reason. It had rejected the contention that the contractual terms rendered the Certificate of Acceptance conclusive proof that the aircraft complied in all respects with the condition required at delivery; if cl.7.9 of the lease did not provide that delivery of the Certificate of Acceptance was conclusive proof of compliance of the aircraft and of the aircraft documents with the contractual requirements, it was not possible to regard it as nonetheless giving rise to an estoppel by representation to the same effect. The Court of Appeal said that natural meaning of the relevant provisions was clear. There was no ambiguity: Olympic as lessee confirmed that the aircraft at delivery complied in all respects with the condition required under the contract. Clause 7.9 provided that delivery by the lessee to the lessor of a certificate in that form would be conclusive proof that the aircraft and the aircraft documents were satisfactory to the lessee. There was no difficulty in deciding what was meant by the aircraft being "satisfactory" to Olympic. The contract provided only one yardstick by which its satisfaction with the aircraft was to be measured, and that was compliance with the conditions required by the agreement. When Olympic as lessee confirmed that the condition of the aircraft at delivery complied in all respects with that required under the agreement, it was confirming that the aircraft was satisfactory to it in the only sense in which it was entitled, or expected, to express its satisfaction. The court said that other factors supported such a conclusion. For example, it was commonplace for parties in this market to contract on a basis which, at first sight, appeared to be intended to provide a

---

[100] [2013] EWCA Civ 369.

structure whereby a lessee elected whether or not to accept an aircraft on lease and with it the risk of non-compliance with the required delivery condition becoming apparent later. Further, the parties would know that neither could be absolutely certain of an aircraft's condition at the point at which the lessee was called on to accept delivery and the ongoing risk. In addition, the lease itself contained an extensive provision of facilities for inspection by Olympic of the aircraft and its associated documents before it was required to elect whether to accept delivery.

Although the issue of reasonableness was not raised, the stress on these last factors indicates strongly that the clause would have been upheld.

Misrepresentation

A contract term seeking to avoid or limit liability for any pre-contract misrepresentation, or to avoid or restrict any remedy otherwise arising by reason of such a misrepresentation is subject to the reasonableness test.[101] In *Howard Marine & Dredging Co Ltd v Ogden*,[102] the term provided that:

9–044

> "...charterer's acceptance of handing over the vessel shall be conclusive that [she is]...in all respects fit for the intended and contemplated use by charterers and in every other way satisfactory to them."

The Divisional Court found that it was not fair and reasonable to rely on this clause,[103] a view which the majority of the Court of Appeal were not prepared to disturb though no specific view was expressed. Lord Denning, however, pointing out that the parties were commercial concerns of equal bargaining strength, and that the term was not foisted by one party on another, but contained in a contract the drafts of which had been passed between the parties, and also noting that the dispute which had arisen was just what such a clause sought to avoid, ruled that it was fair and reasonable to rely on this clause.[104] It seems fair to assume that Lord Denning would also have found that this term was fair and reasonable to include in the contract.

A specific finding as to fair and reasonable inclusion was made in *Walker v Boyle*.[105] A clause in the then edition of the National Conditions of Sale provided that there was no right of rescission for errors, mis-statements or omissions in the preliminary answers, or in the sale plan or special conditions:

> "nor (save where the error, mis-statement or omission is in a written answer and relates to a matter materially affecting the description or value of the property) shall any damages be payable or compensation allowed by either party in respect thereof."

---

[101] Misrepresentation Act 1967 s.3, as substituted by the Unfair Contract Terms Act 1977 s.8. There is no equivalent Scottish provision.
[102] [1978] 2 All E.R. 1134.
[103] This being the test prevailing under the Misrepresentation Act 1967 before it was amended by the Unfair Contract Terms Act 1977.
[104] [1978] 2 All E.R. 1134 at 1143.
[105] [1982] 1 All E.R. 634.

Without specifying his reasons, the judge ruled that this clause had not been shown to be reasonable. He appears to have been influenced by the fact that the condition excluded compensation for any oral mis-statement, however grave, even to the extent of being fraudulent.

This case was distinguished in *Morgan and Morgan v Pooley and Pooley*.[106] A special condition in a sale of real property stated that the buyers acknowledged they did not rely upon any pre-contract representations made by the vendors, except those made in writing by the vendors' conveyancers. Finding the clause reasonable, the court said that the buyers, or at least their solicitors, knew of the clause and had every opportunity to challenge it if they had thought fit to do so. Had that been done, the court thought that the sellers might well have been advised to stand firm with the result that the buyers would not have pressed the point. The court accepted that it was difficult to say but it said that the buyers were obviously very keen on the property and the court believed, that, on balance, they would probably have accepted the non-reliance clause if it had been a sticking point. In those circumstances, the term was fair, though what would not be fair would be to allow a purchaser to keep silent at the stage when he is presented with a draft contract containing the relevant term in a fairly prominent form, with plenty of time in which to consider it, and then to permit him to assert later that he should not be bound by the term.

Walker v Boyle was distinguished as a decision which turned essentially on its facts. The court saw a significant difference between a term that is "very clearly set out in a set of special conditions that are communicated to the purchaser well before the contract is signed, and a provision that is tucked away in one clause in the National Conditions of Sale".

9–045 Much the same view, but with more play given to the circumstances of the contract parties, was reached in *Lloyd and Lloyd v Browning and Browning*.[107] L had retained a planning consultant and an architect before exchanging contracts to purchase farmland from B. Planning permission had been granted in respect of the farm land which L believed, relying on an alleged oral statement by B, included permission to extend a barn. When L's advisers inspected the planning file there was no planning permission filed. A planning consultant reported that there was nothing to indicate that there was permission for an extension, but that she did not consider that to be a problem. The contract for the sale contained a clause, which had been in common usage by a regional law society, stating that the buyer had entered into the agreement solely on the basis of an inspection that he admitted having undertaken, and that he had not been induced by any statement made by the seller, except for written responses by the seller's conveyancers to written pre-contractual enquiries made by the buyer's convey-ancers. Following completion, L became aware of the true planning position that there was no permission for an extension and brought a claim against B for misrepresentation. The judge held that, although L had been induced by a misrepresentation that there was planning permission for an extension, and that the land was worth approximately £55,000 less than it would have been had

---

[106] [2010] EWHC 2447.
[107] [2013] EWCA Civ 1637.

planning permission been granted, the exclusion clause had removed B's liability. The issue was whether the exclusion clause had fairly and reasonably been included within the contract.

The Court of Appeal agreed with the county court that the test of reasonableness had been passed. Davis L.J. singled out these matters:

(1) First, each side had, and as they each knew, legal advisers. That was, as the judge duly found, plainly material as to the reasonableness of including this particular condition into the contract. Moreover, it was the case, as was known to all concerned, that the claimants had in addition instructed architects and planning consultants. That was a relevant factor, too.

(2) Second, the contract was one for the sale of land. It is generally well known that such contracts do indeed, as the judge put it, have a status of "formality" about them. Contracts relating to the disposition of property are designed by law to require that all the agreed terms are set out in one contractual document signed by each party.

(3) This condition was not a "take it or leave it" condition of the kind sometimes imposed in small print on consumers, acting without legal advice, in consumer transactions. It was a special condition agreed by the parties' lawyers in circumstances where the parties had equal and corresponding negotiating positions. Moreover, such condition had the general imprimatur of the Eastbourne Law Society and was, it was to be inferred, in common use. That, too, was a further factor indicating reasonableness.

(4) And this was thought to be "a particular striking feature in the present case"; the condition, expressly by its terms, permitted the claimants to rely on written statements made by the defendants' solicitors in replying to pre-contract enquiries or otherwise in correspondence. Thus, if the claimants had wished to rely on what had been said to them orally the means for giving legal effect to that were readily available: that is, by an appropriate written pre-contract enquiry or solicitor's letter. Such a request would have revealed just what the defendant vendors were prepared formally to commit themselves to.

A fifth reason was added by Arden L.J. She noted that the pressure to exchange came from the appellants as purchasers and not from the respondent vendors.

In reaching its decision, the Court of Appeal endorsed the approach adopted *FoodCo UK LLP v Henry Boot Developments Ltd.*[108] There, in a non-reliance clause of a broadly similar kind to the one before it, the High Court had listed the particular features relevant to the assessment of the fairness and reasonableness of a condition such as that contained in a contract for the disposition of land. Those observations corresponded to the ones listed by Davis J. and were endorsed by him.

---

[108] [2010] EWHC 357.

A different finding on the National Conditions of Sale was made in *Cleaver v Schyde Investments* Ltd.[109]Cleaver had orally agreed to sell a garage property to Schyde with a view to residential development. A local doctor was interested in purchasing the property for development as a medical centre. Cleaver had replied to the commercial property standard enquiries from Schyde's solicitors to the effect that there was no planning application, letter or notice outstanding in relation to the property. Cleaver then received notice from the doctor that he had made a planning application for the erection of a health centre and four flats on the property. Cleaver informed their solicitor but the latter failed to correct the answers to the enquiries. Contracts were exchanged incorporating the *Standard Conditions of Sale* (4th edition). The doctor pursued his planning application notwithstanding that the property had been sold and that came to the attention of Schyde. The latter thought that the doctor's application, if successful, would create real difficulties in the way of any application for purely residential development. Schyde therefore gave notice to rescind. It was accepted that Cleaver's replies to the standard enquiries had contained innocent misrepresentations which would have entitled Schyde to rescind but for standard condition 7.1.3 which excluded error or omission except in the case of fraud or recklessness or where the property differed substantially in quantity, quality or tenure from what the purchaser had been led to expect. The judge held that standard condition 7.1.3 was not fair and reasonable.

9–046   This decision was upheld by the Court of Appeal. There was nothing self-evidently offensive, in terms of reasonableness and fairness, in a contractual term which restricted a purchaser's right to rescind in the event of the vendor's misrepresentation to cases of fraud or recklessness or where the property differed substantially in quantity, quality or tenure from what the purchaser had been led to expect, and to confine the purchaser to damages in all other cases. The argument in favour of upholding such a provision was particularly strong where, as in the instant case, the term had a long history, it was a well established feature of property transactions, it was endorsed by the Law Society, both sides were represented by solicitors and the parties had negotiated variations of other standard provisions. It would require some exceptional feature or combination of features to enable a court to conclude that standard condition 7.1.3 failed to satisfy the test of reasonableness. It was noted, however, that respect had to be given to the rulings of a lower court.[110] The Court of Appeal went on to say that the judge was entitled to find that the planning application had a significant negative impact on Schyde such that had it known of the application it would not have exchanged contracts for the purchase. At the date of the contract Cleaver knew of the planning application and that it would be material to the former's intentions. Cleaver had that knowledge and failed to disclose the fact that the application had been made at the very time that they were entering into a contract which would remove the right that Schyde would otherwise have to rescind for misrepresentation. Moreover, they were doing so notwithstanding their express promise in the standard enquiries to notify Schyde on becoming aware of anything which might cause any reply they had given to be incorrect and

---

[109] [2011] EWCA Civ 929.
[110] See para.9–049.

notwithstanding the fact that the replies to pre-contract enquiries were excluded by agreement from the entire agreement clause in special condition 12. The judge was entitled to regard that combination of circumstances as taking the case out of the general run and to hold that Clever failed to show that standard condition 7.1.3 was fair and reasonable in the instant case.

The difficulty of showing that a clause is reasonable was also demonstrated in *South Western General Property Co v Josef Marton*.[111] Land had been bought at auction in reliance upon a misrepresentation. The relevant clause stated:

> "The property is believed to be and shall be taken to be correctly described and any incorrect statement, error or omission found in the particulars or conditions of sale shall not annul the sale or entitle the purchaser to be discharged from his purchase."

The purchaser was also denied the right to take any point under town and country planning legislation, requiring him to "take the properties as they are under the said Acts, rules and regulations". A further clause, "quite obviously designed to avoid the effects" of the Misrepresentation Act 1967 provided:

> "(1) All statements contained in the foregoing particulars are made without responsibility on the part of the auctioneers or the vendor and are statements of opinion and are not to be taken as or implying a statement or representation of fact and any intending purchaser must satisfy himself by inspection or otherwise as to the correctness of each statement contained in the particulars.
>
> (2) The vendor does not give or make any representation or warranty in relation to the property nor has the auctioneer or any person in the employment of the auctioneer any authority to do so on his behalf."

The vendors argued that the circumstances of auction sales necessitated such clauses, while the purchaser said that the misrepresentation was derived from matters solely within the knowledge of the vendors.

The vendors further argued that the particulars did stress the need for purchasers to make their own enquiries, and that they were catering not just for private buyers, such as the present party, but also for other categories including speculators.

The judge, however, ruled that parties might well come to an auction, as did this particular buyer, when time no longer allowed for enquiries to be made. He stressed that he was to judge this particular contract and the particular circumstances of the case, also noting that the facts on which the misrepresentation was based were central to the purchase and peculiarly within the vendors' knowledge. He held that they had not shown that the exclusion was reasonable: if it were otherwise, the vendors could have avoided liability "for a failure to tell more than only a part of the facts which were among the most material to the whole contract of sale".

---

[111] (1982) 263 E.G. 1090; (1983) 2 Tr. L. 14 QBD.

9–047 This can be neatly contrasted with *McCullough v Lane Fox & Partners Ltd*,[112] which involved the purchase of property which had a smaller acreage than stated in the particulars. An exclusion clause was upheld, not least because the purchaser:

> "had ample opportunity to regulate his conduct having regard to the disclaimer. He could have obtained, had he so chosen, an independent check on the acreage. Indeed, he appears to have accepted in evidence that, even within the tight timetable which he was following, he did have the opportunity had he wished to avail himself of it."

Another clause upheld, albeit obiter, was the following:

> "Each of the parties agrees that it shall not commence any lawsuit or assert any claim, whether known or unknown, against the other party or any of its affiliates based on actions, discussions or agreements (except for the Application Letter Agreement signed by the parties in anticipation of this Agreement) which occurred prior to the signing of this Agreement."[113]

As the judge said: "The Agreements were sophisticated agreements that were entered into by substantial entities in respect of a major transaction. There was no inequality of bargaining power".[114]

THE VALUE OF PRECEDENT

9–048 Each case falls to be judged in relation to its individual facts. Accordingly, a ruling on the issue of reasonableness of a particular clause is no guarantee that the same finding would be made in relation to that clause in any future case since each case "has to be considered in the light of the particular circumstances of the parties in question at the time the contract was made".[115]

It is possible for an identical clause to be reasonable in one case, and yet unreasonable in another, precisely because the statutory test requires the issue of reasonableness to be determined on the basis of the individual circumstances. A particularly good example occurred in *Fillite (Runcorn) Ltd v APV Pasilac Ltd*.[116] Simultaneous contracts were made for the supply of a drier and a rate feeder. The separate orders arose out of one particular set of negotiations. The contracts were identical, and each contained this clause: "No claim for direct or consequential losses can be accepted." The High Court found that the clause in the drier contract was reasonable, while in the feeder contract, it was unreasonable. The Court of Appeal reversed the finding in relation to the drier, but upheld it in relation to the feeder. There was nothing in the Court of Appeal's ruling to indicate that it could never be right to rule that the same clause could not in

---

[112] [1995] E.G. 195 (C.S.). An appeal was dismissed: [1996] 1 EGLR 35. See also *Government of Zanzibar v British Aerospace (Lancaster House) Ltd* [2000] 1 W.L.R. 2333.
[113] *Six Continents Hotels Inc v Event Hotels GmbH* [2006] EWHC 2317 (QB).
[114] The judge approved of the approach taken in the *Grimstead* case; [1998] EWCA Civ 1523.
[115] *British Fermentation Products Ltd v Compair Reavell Ltd* [1999] EWHC 227 (TCC), per Bowsher J.; see also the discussion of the *Fillite* case immediately below.
[116] Unreported January 26, 1995 (CA).

principle be reasonable in one contract, but unreasonable in another. The findings were directed solely to issues of reasonableness and different criteria were applied to the disputed clauses.

UPHOLDING LOWER COURT RULINGS

In the *George Mitchell* case, Lord Bridge had said:

9–049

> "There will sometimes be room for a legitimate difference of judicial opinion [on the question of reasonableness] where it will be impossible to say that one view is demonstrably wrong and the other demonstrably right. It must follow ... that, when asked to review such a decision on appeal, the appellate court should treat the original decision with the utmost respect and refrain from interference with it unless satisfied that it proceeded upon some erroneous principle or was plainly and obviously wrong."[117]

Thorpe L.J. quoted these words with approval in *Overland Shoes Ltd v Schenkers Ltd*[118] and in the *St Albans* case, the Court of Appeal upheld the finding of the lower court on the issue of reasonableness, Nourse L.J. saying that he was "certainly not satisfied that [the judge below] proceeded upon some erroneous principle or was plainly and obviously wrong".[119]

Findings of the lower court, however, are not always sacrosanct. In *Fillite (Runcorn) Ltd v APV Pasilac Ltd*,[120] a contract for the supply of a drier (used when dealing with industrial waste) provided that: "No claim for direct or consequential losses can be accepted". The High Court had found that the parties were of equal bargaining power. Fillite had had ample time and money to buy the drier and had understood the contract terms. Neither party could have insured. The High Court had also stressed that the costs to Fillite of a failure of the equipment were likely to be very high in relation to the profits which APV would expect to make. It duly found the clause to be reasonable. The Court of Appeal, however, held otherwise. This exclusion clause had sought to invalidate express promises made in the contract:

> "If the judge had considered the reasonableness of the exclusion clause overriding the specific delivery schedule, it seems likely that he would have held it to be unreasonable."

APV argued that the presence of the exclusion clause did not render the delivery schedule wholly without effect, since the latter would still entitle Fillite to accept failure to comply with the time limits as a repudiation of the contract. The Court of Appeal said that that would have been a "scant consolation".

Similarly, the Court of Appeal reversed a decision to declare a term unreasonable in *Grimstead & Son Ltd v McGarrigan*.[121] The evidence showed that the draft accounts had been available and that the purchaser did indeed have

---

[117] [1983] 2 All E.R. 737 at 743.

[118] [1998] 1 Lloyd's Rep. 498. See too *Cleaver v Schyde Investments Ltd* [2011] EWCA Civ 929.

[119] [1996] 4 All E.R. 481 at 492. "There is, as it were, to be accorded a margin of appreciation to a trial judge's decision in this regard": *Lloyd and Lloyd v Browning and Browning* [2013] EWCA Civ 1637, per Davis L.J.

[120] Unreported January 26, 1995 (CA).

[121] [1998–99] Info. T.L.R. 384.

the chance to make a full investigation of the books and records. When the agreement was made, it was entered into with the benefit of advice from accountants and solicitors on both sides. It was also the case that the party making the allegedly false statements had been prepared to enter into the contract on the basis that the other side relied on its own investigations and judgment.[122]

9–050 Where the lower court had misinterpreted the clause in question, it becomes easier for the appellate court to reverse any decision on its reasonableness. In *Granville Oil & Chemicals Ltd v Davis Turner & Co Ltd*,[123] the relevant clause was as follows:

> "30(A) Any claim by the customer against the company in respect of any service provided for the customer or which the company has undertaken to provide should be made in writing and notified to the company within 14 days of the date upon which the customer became or should have become aware of any event or occurrence alleged to give rise to such claim and any claim not made and notified as aforesaid shall be deemed to be waived and absolutely barred except where the customer can show that it was impossible for him to comply with the time limit and that he has made the claim as soon as it was reasonably possible for him to do so.
>
> (B) Notwithstanding the provisions of subparagraph (A) above the company shall in any event be discharged of all liability whatsoever howsoever arising in respect of any amount provided to the customer or which the company has undertaken to provide unless suit be brought and written notice thereof given to the company within nine months from the date of the event or occurrence alleged to give rise to the cause of action against the company."

The High Court had held that this clause was apt to cover fraud and claims which had been fraudulently concealed. Such a clause, it had ruled, was unreasonable.

The Court of Appeal ruled that the judge had misinterpreted the clause, finding that it was instead designed to meet ordinary contractual claims, such as were made in the case itself, which a freight forwarder would expect to have to face in the ordinary course of business. In so finding, the Court of Appeal said that it was therefore less "inhibited" as to possibly reversing the lower court on the issue of reasonableness.

In determining if the particular clause was reasonable, the court noted that the parties were of equal bargaining power. The respondent, from its general business experience, ought also to have known of the particular term. The court concluded that the time limit was reasonable in the case of a claim for loss or damage to goods in transit. The loss or damage could be ascertained on delivery, and nine months was ample time for the customer to decide whether to start proceedings. It said that such a limit was "necessary to enable the freight forwarded to claim under the 12-month time limit which applies to many contracts of carriage".

9–051 The court pointed out, however, that that was a finding in relation to "the typical claim". As the case itself showed, however, the freight forwarder might also be faced with a claim for failure to insure. It held that the facts of the instant case "did not compel the conclusion that [the clause] is unreasonable". In the ordinary case, the customer would know whether he has cover relatively soon after his

---

[122] See also the observations of the court quoted at para.9–042.
[123] [2003] EWCA Civ 570.

goods are damaged. The loss for failure to insure will be related to the amount of the claim for damage. In those circumstances:

> "it is fair and reasonable to fix the same time limit for a claim based on failure to insure the goods as is fixed for the claim for damage to those goods."

The contrast to be made was between a practicable time limit to claim for damage and one to claim for failure to insure. Given the period of nine months allowed, it was "fair and reasonable that they should be the same". The court below, the court concluded, had been "plainly wrong".

An error in the interpretation of the clause also lay at the heart of *Regus (UK) Ltd v Epcot Solutions Ltd.*[124] The clause in question excluded all liability "in any circumstances" for certain kinds of losses, namely "loss of business, loss of profits, loss of anticipated savings, loss of or damage to data, third party claims or any consequential loss". The judge had wrongly said that this would leave the innocent party without remedy, and ruled it unreasonable. Such a reading of the clause was incorrect since it left untouched the right to claim for a diminution in value of the services promised. For the following reasons, the Court of Appeal held that the clause was reasonable:

(i) The judge himself had said that "in principle it was entirely reasonable for Regus to restrict damages for loss of profits and consequential losses from the categories of loss for which it will become liable when in breach of contract."

(ii) Epcot's Mr Randhawa was an "intelligent and experienced businessman".

(iii) He accepted in evidence that he was well aware of Regus's standard terms when he entered into the contract. Indeed, he had contracted before on identical terms.

(iv) He also accepted that he used a similar exclusion of liability for indirect or consequential losses in his own business.[125]

(v) Epcot sought to renegotiate terms of the contract frequently and energetically, albeit not the disputed clause: despite Mr Randhawa's evidence, which the judge did not accept, that he had told Regus that this clause was not acceptable.

(vi) There was no inequality in bargaining power.

(vii) The disputed clause advised Regus's customers to protect themselves by insurance for the losses with which it was concerned.

The judge had been unable to make any finding about the availability of insurance to either party, in the absence of any evidence on the subject before him, and had treated this as a neutral matter. The Court of Appeal, however, felt that the probability was that it would have been easier for each customer to insure himself against business losses, than for Regus to insure all of its "constantly changing phalanx" of customers in respect of their own interests.

---

[124] [2008] EWCA Civ 361.
[125] Reference was made here to *Watford Electronics Ltd v Sanderson CFL Ltd*, discussed at para.9–013 and following.

It can perhaps be noted here that in *Director General of Fair Trading v First National Bank Plc*,[126] a case heard under the Unfair Terms in Consumer Contracts Regulations, the Court of Appeal reversed the finding of the lower court on the issue of fairness, but that the decision of the Court of Appeal was itself reversed by the House of Lords.

Fair and reasonable

9–052   The Unfair Contract Terms Act 1977 requires a clause to be "fair and reasonable". In the *BTE Auto Repairs*[127] case, Sir John Megaw said that these words might be tautologous, but it was his view that they were not to be interpreted in the same way. He noted that in *George Mitchell (Chesterhall) Ltd v Finney Lock Seeds Ltd*, the House of Lords made specific reference to what is "fair and reasonable",[128] though it has to be said that nothing was said to indicate that this was to do other than repeat the wording of the Act. Neill L.J., though, agreed with Sir John Megaw that the reasonableness test did require "the element of fairness as well as the element of reasonableness". It is also the case that, in *Omega Trust Co Ltd v Wright Son & Pepper*,[129] the Court of Appeal made specific, separate, findings that a particular clause was both fair and reasonable.

It is just about possible, though in practice it is hardly likely to happen often, for a term to be unfair, but, in the circumstances of the case, reasonable. A small business might limit its liability to £100 if this is the most that it could afford, even though the item being supplied, because of its nature, could cause enormous damage if it malfunctioned. This might be unfair on the injured party but still reasonable as far as the business was concerned. In such a case, the business would be unable to rely on the clause since both limbs of the test must be satisfied.

Consequences of unreasonableness for the contract-severing the unfair term

9–053   Where a term is rendered ineffective by the 1977 Act, nothing is stated as to the effect this has on the rest of the contract.[130] However, common law principles would apply so that if the substance of the contract remains untouched by the elimination of the offending clause, the contract remains enforceable. The courts have, however, no jurisdiction to rewrite the contract.[131]

In the *Regus* case,[132] the relevant paragraph contained both a limitation clause and an exclusion clause. The paragraph itself read continuously and was not

---

[126] [2002] 1 All E.R. 97.
[127] Unreported January 26, 1990.
[128] [1983] 2 All E.R. 737 at 743.
[129] (1998) 75 P & C.R. 57.
[130] Compare this with the position under the Unfair Terms in Consumer Contracts Regulations, para.10–080.
[131] See the discussion in Cheshire, Fifoot and Furmston, *Law of Contract* (15th edn), pp.541 and following.
[132] See para.9–006.

broken down into subparagraphs. The judge had held that he had no power to sever the exclusion clause, which he had found to be unreasonable, but it was conceded before the Court of Appeal that the judge had been wrong to say he had no such power. Such a concession was regarded as "well made". The Court of Appeal pointed out that, even though the paragraph was not broken down, the provisions in that paragraph were independent, being in part a limitation of liability and in part an exclusion of liability, thus serving different purposes.

In so deciding, the court followed *Watford Electronics Ltd v Sanderson CFL Ltd*.[133] The Court of Appeal in that case said that the relevant contract term contained two sentences:

(i) "Neither the Company nor the Customer shall be liable to the other for any claims for indirect or consequential losses whether arising from negligence or otherwise".

(ii) "In no event shall the Company's liability under the Contract exceed the price paid by the Customer to the Company for the [Equipment/Software] connected with any claim". These sub-divisions were not in the contract term itself.[134]

The Court of Appeal disagreed with the lower court which had said that the whole term had to be read as one and was, therefore, not capable of being subject to any "blue pencil" exercise. According to Chadwick L.J.: "It is, to my mind, plain that the reason why the clauses each contain two sentences is that each sentence is intended to have its own separate and distinct purpose". He added that the need to recognise that each of the two sentences in the clause had a separate and distinct purpose—and to identify that purpose—was not to be dismissed as "a blue pencilling exercise".

It has also been said that the whole of a disputed clause must be reasonable and not just part of it the court cannot engage in any blue-pencil exercise.[135]

Action against unreasonable terms under other enactments

One possibility is that the Financial Conduct Authority, acting under its powers to licence consumer credit or consumer hire businesses, could withhold from, suspend or withdraw the licence of, a trader who used unfair or unreasonable terms in his contracts.[136]

9–054

Another is for action to be taken under the Enterprise Act 2002. The 1977 Act has been specified by the Enterprise Act 2002 (Part 8 Domestic Infringements) Order 2003.[137] The use of unreasonable terms would thus amount to a domestic infringement, entitling the Competition and Markets Authority, a weights and

---

[133] [2001] EWCA Civ 317.
[134] See para.9–013 and following.
[135] *Stewart Gill Ltd v Horatio Myer & Co Ltd* [1992] Q.B. 600, per Lord Donaldson M.R.
[136] Consumer Credit Act 1974 ss.31, 32 32A and 32B.
[137] SI 2003/1593.

measures authority or any public body designated by the Secretary of State to seek a court order against such conduct, or to seek an assurance that such conduct will cease.[138]

---

[138] Enterprise Act 2002 ss.217–219.

CHAPTER 10

UNFAIR TERMS IN CONSUMER CONTRACTS

INTRODUCTION

The Consumer Rights Act 2014 repealed the Unfair Terms in Consumer **10–001**
Contracts Regulations.[1] The effect of the Regulations was to create a regime quite
distinct and separate from the Unfair Contract Terms Act 1977 and hence
consumers could take action under either or both enactments, though the scope of
the Regulations was wider than that of the Act. In the main, the Act dealt with
exclusion clauses in both consumer and business contracts whereas the
Regulations applied solely to terms in contracts with consumers. The Act could
apply to negotiated contracts, whereas the Regulations applied only to consumer
contracts which had not been individually negotiated. The Act covered exclusion
clauses contained in notices, whereas the Regulations did not. Finally, unlike the
Act, the Regulations were not limited to exclusion or limitation clauses. The 2014
Act, however, has disapplied the 1977 Act from consumer contracts, the result
being that consumer contracts now fall solely under the 2014 Act.

SCOPE OF THE 2014 ACT

The Act applies to any term in a contract concluded between a trader[2] and a **10–002**
consumer. The Regulations did not apply to non-contractual notices but the 1977
Act does. The 2014 Act is, however, broader than the 1977 Act in that the latter
refers only to notices excluding or restricting liability for negligence whereas the
2014 Act contains no such limitation. Notices are also within the 2014 Act if,

---

[1] Unfair Terms in Consumer Contracts Regulations 1999 (SI 1999/2083) themselves repealing and
replacing the Unfair Terms in Consumer Contracts Regulations 1994 (SI 1994/3159). The Regulations
and now the 2014 Act implemented Council Directive 93/13/EEC of 5 April 1993 on unfair terms in
consumer contracts. The Directive is a minimum harmonisation Directive so a Member State is free to
offer its consumers a greater level of protection from unfair terms than that provided for in the
Directive: *Perenièová v SOS financ spol. s.r.o.* (C-213/10) [2012] EUECJ.
[2] That is to say "a person acting (personally or through an agent) for purposes relating to that person's
trade, business, craft or profession"; Consumer Rights Act s.2(2). "Business" includes "the activities
of any government department or local or public authority"; *ibid.* s.2(7). A council which has a
statutory duty to provide housing for the homeless has been held to be a supplier for the purposes of
the Regulations.The court had noted that the preambles to the Directive referred to activities of a
"public nature": *Khatun v Newham LBC* [2004] EWCA Civ 55.
  Note too that the Unfair Commercial Practices Directive 2005/29/EC applies to a public law body
charged with a task of public interest, such as the management of a statutory health insurance fund:
*BKK Mobil Oil Körperschaft des öffentlichen Rechts v Zentrale zur Bekämpfung unlauteren
Wettbewerbs eV* (C-59/12); European Court of Justice, 3 October 2013.

even though not expressed to apply to a consumer, it is reasonable to assume that the notice was intended to be read by a consumer.[3]

A "CONSUMER"

10–003   A consumer is an "individual acting for purposes that are wholly or mainly outside that individual's trade, business, craft or profession".[4] "Craft" has been added to the definition contained in the Regulations, though it cannot be doubted that a craft also fell within the Regulations as being a trade or profession.

This wording suggests that a person can only be a consumer if he has a trade, business or profession outside which he can act. The bizarre conclusion to which this literal reading would lead, that at the very least those with no occupation at all are outside the Act, cannot seriously be expected to be maintained. It is therefore much more likely that the definition will be read as "outside such business, if any, as he might have". This, at any rate, is commensurate with the approach adopted in relation to s.25(1) of the Sale of Goods Act 1979, where a sale by a buyer in possession is to have effect as if that person were a mercantile agent. If that person is not a mercantile agent, it seems impossible for him to fulfil the further requirement that he must be acting in the ordinary course of such agency. The Court of Appeal has attempted to resolve this problem by saying that the buyer in possession must be treated as a notional mercantile agent, with the court having to ask if the sale would have been in the ordinary course of business had he in fact been a mercantile agent.[5]

It would seem enough to satisfy the definition that just one of the purposes for entering into the contract was private, even if other reasons related to business. In *Evans v Cherry Tree Finance Ltd*,[6] E and his wife had carried on an antique restoration business from a property that they owned. The property was partially residential accommodation and partially business premises. The residential accommodation and business premises had separate addresses. E's wife initiated divorce proceedings and the partnership was dissolved. E applied to C for a loan so that he could buy his wife's interest in the property as part of the divorce settlement. The application form was entitled a "Secured credit agreement for a commercial loan". In completing the form, E gave his address as the residential accommodation and gave the business premises as the property to be offered as security under the loan. The contact telephone numbers given for the residential accommodation and the business premises were the same. E stated on the application form that the purpose of the loan was to repay an existing mortgage and to pay his ex-wife the balance due under his divorce settlement. E soon defaulted on the loan repayments and in due course the property was sold by C. C realised the amount due under the loan, which also included a sum in respect of an early redemption penalty. E brought proceedings against C claiming that he

---

[3] Consumer Rights Act s.61(6).
[4] Consumer Rights Act s.2(3): the burden is on the trader to show that the individual was not so acting; *ibid* s.2(4).
[5] *Newtons of Wembley Ltd v Williams* [1965] 1 Q.B. 560; see particularly *ibid.* at 578, per Pearson L.J.; *R&B Customs Brokers Co Ltd v United Dominions Trust Ltd* [1988] 1 All E.R. 847.
[6] [2008] EWCA Civ 331.

was not bound by the terms imposing the penalty because they were unfair. Upholding the High Court, the Court of Appeal ruled that that the loan was for a purpose outside E's business or trade. Looked at objectively the loan was to enable E to continue his livelihood, but that was not the only purpose of the loan. The stated purposes on the application form were equivocal. In particular the statement that one purpose of the loan was to pay off a mortgage. Moreover, C could have deduced from the information supplied to it that E had been both living and working at the property.

The strength of this case is somewhat weakened by the concession made by the lender that it was enough if just one of the purposes of the loan was not business-related. Sir Anthony Clarke M.R. made the point that, given the concession, it had not been necessary to consider the true meaning of "consumer", though he added that he was not suggesting that the concession was "not correctly made".

More specific guidance was given in *Heifer International Inc v Christiansen*,[7] which was not cited in the previous case. Judge Toulmin said that "purpose connotes intention. If a party acts in a way which furthers its intention, i.e. to further its trade, business or profession, its actions are excluded from the Regulations. If an action is for a different purpose but which has an incidental result which furthers its trade, business or profession it does not result in the contract being excluded from the protection of the Regulations". This of course applies equally to the 2014 Act.

In that case, the applicants (D1 to D5) applied to stay the proceedings pursuant to the Arbitration Act 1996. D1 was a Danish architect and D2 was his firm, a Danish legal entity. The respondent (H) was a British Virgin Islands company owned by the family of a wealthy Russian (T) who lived in England. T had decided that D1 would be engaged to refurbish a house in Surrey owned by H. D3, D4 and D5 were Danish sub-contractors who had carried out work on the property. H had given D1 a power of attorney to enter into contracts with craftsmen and to authorise payments to them. The court held that, in making the contract, H acted for purposes outside its trade, business or profession and therefore as a consumer.[8]

10–004

In *Office of Fair Trading v Foxtons Ltd*,[9] Mann J. considered the nature of a consumer. He said that "it is accepted that some of the people with whom Foxtons deal are consumers though many are not, being 'professional or 'commercial landlords' ". Finding that the company did deal with consumers, the court accepted evidence put forward by the OFT as follows:

"there are numerous individuals who find themselves in a position of requiring the services of an individual letting agent who cannot be classified as doing so for the purposes of a trade, business or profession within the meaning of the UTCCRs ... They include individuals who decide to let out their only property whilst travelling temporarily abroad, as a result of relocation by their employer or for other reasons connected to 'lifestyle' choice, individuals

---

[7] [2007] EWHC 3015.
[8] See this case further considered at para.10–061.
[9] [2009] EWHC 1681.

who let out part of their property in order to fund their mortgage on the remainder, and individuals for whom their property investment represents part of their pension plan or other long term saving."

This approach was followed in *Chesterton Global Ltd v Finney*.[10] The claimant had argued that the defendant was not acting as a consumer. It was accepted that the defendant had acted in his personal capacity and that the contract had no connection with the defendant's business which was a public affairs business for lobbying Parliament and had no dealings or connection with the property. The defendant gave evidence that he and his co-owner had purchased the property as a "buy to let". They were hoping for capital growth and that the rental income would pay the interest on the mortgage. The margins were tight. The District Judge, after referring to Mann J.'s observations, said that a consumer is someone who is regarded as a "weak party" who needs special protection. He said that the Regulations defined a "consumer" as "any natural person who, in contracts covered by the Regulations, is acting for purposes which are outside his trade business or profession". The conclusion was that Mr Finney was neither a professional landlord—his profession being entirely different—nor a commercial landlord—"that term implies a significant business as landlord and is not consistent with Mr Finney's position where he owned a single property as part of his pension plan or long term savings".[11]

The whole issue was usefully put in its European context (for, as noted, the 1999 Regulations and in turn the 2014 Act implement EU law) in *Turner & Co (GB) Ltd v Fatah Abi*.[12]

The defendants ran a printing business with two other shareholder directors. They engaged the claimants to sell the business and signed a blank agreement on Turner's standard terms. The agreement entitled Turner to commission where a transaction had taken place during the currency of their appointment. Turner advertised the sale and the defendants later terminated the agreement and around the same time the two shareholders resigned as directors of the business and transferred the majority of their shares to the defendants. Notice of the transfer was not registered until some months after it had taken place. Turner requested details of the transfer when he became aware of it, but the defendants failed to provide an adequate response. It was argued inter alia that the terms as to commission were unfair under the Regulations.

---

[10] Unreported April 30, 2010 (Lambeth CC). See too *Barclays Bank Plc v Alfons Kufner* [2008] EWHC 2319 (individual guarantor of business loan to company not provided by person acting as consumer).

[11] See *France v Di Pinto* (C-361/89) [1991] ECR 1-1189 (distance selling); *Benincasa v Dentalkit* (C-269/95) [1997] ECR 1-3767; *Gruber v Bay Wa AG* (C-464/01) [2005] ECR 1-439 (both concerning the Brussels Convention on jurisdiction and the enforcement of judgments in civil and commercial matters It has been said that there is no "substantial" difference between the meaning of "consumer" in the 1999 Regulations and the Brussels Convention on jurisdiction and the enforcement of judgments in civil and commercial matters: *Standard Bank London Ltd v Apostolakis* [2001] Lloyd's Rep Bank 240; *Maple Leaf Macro Volatility Master Fund v Jacques Rouvroy* [2009] EWHC 257.

[12] [2010] EWHC 2078.

The court looked to decisions of the European Court of Justice which had looked **10–005** at the definition of "consumer", albeit not in the context of Unfair Terms Directive.[13] The court drew particular attention to this observation in the *Benincasa* case:

> "A person will not be acting as a consumer unless they (sic) are contracting primarily for their family or personal needs. On that basis, it may be said that only contracts concluded for the purpose of satisfying an individual's own needs in terms of private consumption, come under the provisions of community law designed to protect the consumer as the party deemed to be the weaker party economically".

The court concluded that it was clear that "consumer" was to be given an interpretation not grounded in any national law, but which was of general application across the community. It said that guidance from the European Court of Justice on the definition of "consumer" was not to be taken as introducing a new and different test for what was a consumer, or to replace with its own words the definition of consumer in the Directive. Applying the Directive and Regulations, and taking into account the spirit of the ECJ guidance, the court thought it clear that the defendant had made the agreement for the purposes of his business. It was not made for his family or personal use.

The court held that the following principles emerged from the cases:

1. The expression "consumer" for the purposes of Council Directive 93/13 should be given an autonomous, community-wide interpretation, rather than one anchored to the particular jurisprudence of any individual Member State.
2. At least where the language adopted in community instruments is substantially the same and they have as their objective, at least in part, the protection of consumers, a similar approach to the construction and application of the expression should be adopted unless the context and purpose of the relevant instrument requires a different approach.
3. It is a question of fact for the court seised of the dispute to decide the purpose or purposes for which a person was acting when entering into a contract of a kind which might be covered by the Directive; and it is similarly a question of fact as to whether he was so acting for purposes outside his trade, business of profession.
4. The court must resolve these factual issues on the basis of all of the objective evidence placed before it by the parties; but that evidence is not confined to facts and matters which were or ought reasonably to have been known to both parties.
5. Though the words of the Directive must ultimately prevail, a party will normally be regarded as acting for purposes outside his trade, business or profession if, and only if, the purpose is to satisfy the individual's own needs in terms of private consumption.
6. Furthermore, where the individual in question is acting for more than one purpose, it is immaterial which is the predominant or primary purpose; and

---

[13] See the cases cited *supra* fn.11.

he will be entitled to the protection of the Directive if and only if the business purposes are negligible or insignificant.

7.   However, even where the objective purpose or purposes for which the individual was acting were, in fact, wholly outside his trade, business or profession, he may be disentitled from relying upon the protection afforded to him by the Directive if, by his own words or conduct, he has given the other party the impression that he was acting for business purposes so that the other party was and could reasonably have been unaware of the private purpose or purposes.

This decision was cited with approval in *Alfred Overy v Paypal (Europe) Ltd*.[14] The claimant, who was a photographer, had intended to sell his house. In order to obtain more profit than he would have from a conventional sale, he had devised a competition for which contestants paid to enter and in which the house was the prize. He entered into an agreement with Paypal for the provision of electronic payment services. After the competition was launched, a significant number of entry fees were electronically processed through the latter's facilities in accordance with the agreement. However, Paypal subsequently suspended and then terminated the service. Overy commenced proceedings for breach of contract. The court concluded that any loss suffered by Overy as a result of the suspension of those services was not caused by any breach of contract on Paypal's part but its determination in relation to those issues was expressly stated to be subject to any question as to the impact of the 1999 Regulations.

The court concluded that a contract would be treated as having been concluded by a person for a purpose which could be regarded as being outside his trade or profession only if any business purpose was insignificant or negligible and the contract satisfied an individual's own needs in terms of private consumption. If the only reason for which Overy had opened the account with Paypal had been to operate the competition, that would have been a purpose outside any trade or profession with which he was involved. Since, however, he had also intended to facilitate the receipt of goods and payments for his photography business via his account with Paypal, he could not be regarded as a consumer. In any event, by the nature of the application which he made to Paypal online and the information which he provided in so doing, Overy had clearly conducted himself in such a way as to lead to the obvious conclusion that he was acting in his trade or professional capacity.

The consumer as a legal person

10–006   In the special circumstances provided for in the Arbitration Act 1996, the 2014 Act can apply to legal as well as natural persons. Sections 89 and 90 of the Act extend the provisions of the Act to cases where the consumer is a legal person where the relevant term constitutes an arbitration agreement. Section 89(1)

---

[14] [2012] EWHC 2659.

defines such an agreement as one where there is an agreement "to submit to arbitration present or future disputes (whether or not contractual)".[15]

Mandatory provisions, etc.

The 2014 Act does not apply to terms which reflect a mandatory statutory or regulatory provision[16]; nor to the provisions or principles of international conventions to which the United Kingdom or the European Union is party.[17]   **10–007**

These provisions above would, for example, cover a term in a package holiday contract laying down the conditions under which a surcharge is to be applied providing it follows the provisions of the Package Travel, Package Holidays and Package Tours Regulations 1992.[18]

The Act also recognises, in particular, the exclusions permitted in international conventions relating to transport.[19] The inclusion of the phrase "or principles" recognises that conditions of contract may:

(1)   apply international convention provisions with amendments (e.g. increase of limits) to domestic carriage;
(2)   apply such provisions but with amendments (e.g. increase of limits) in the field of international carriage offered voluntarily by the carrier or under compulsion nationally; or
(3)   reflect private law conditions of carriage that are based on the principles but not the exact provisions of a convention.

Not all national legislation, however, will fall outside the test of fairness imposed by the Act. In *RWE Vertrieb AG v Verbraucherzentrale Nordrhein-Westfalen e.V.*,[20] a local consumer association challenged a standard contractual term by which RWE, a German undertaking supplying natural gas, reserved the right unilaterally to amend the price charged to its customers if they were on a special tariff. Instead of opting for the standard tariff which German gas suppliers are obliged to offer consumers, those customers entered into contracts on the basis of freedom of contract.

RWE considered that the disputed term, which formed part of the general terms and conditions applicable to the customers in question, could not be reviewed for unfairness. The term merely referred to the German legislation applicable to standard tariff contracts. That legislation allowed the supplier to vary gas prices unilaterally without stating the grounds, conditions or extent of such a variation, while ensuring, however, that customers would be notified of the variation and would be free, if appropriate, to terminate the contract.

---

[15] See the 1996 Act further discussed at para.2–049.
[16] Consumer Rights Act 2014 s.73(1)(a). This includes "rules which, according to law, apply between the parties on the basis that no other arrangements have been established"; *ibid.* s.73(2).
[17] Consumer Rights Act 2014 s.73(1)(b).
[18] SI 1992/3288.
[19] See art.1(2) of the Directive. See also the comparable provisions contained in s.29(1) of the Unfair Contract Terms Act 1977.
[20] (C-92/11) Unreported April 14, 2013.

The European Court of Justice ruled that such terms must be subject to review for unfairnessif the statutory provisions they reproduce are applicable only to another category of contracts. It said that the exclusion of review for unfairness of contractual terms that reflected the provisions of national legislation governing a certain category of contracts was justified by the fact that it could legitimately be assumed that the national legislature struck a balance between all the rights and obligations of the parties to those contracts. That reasoning did not apply, however, to terms in a different contract. The ECJ said that to exclude a term in such a contract from review for unfairness merely because it reproduced legislation that applied only to another category of contract would call into question the protection of consumers aimed at by EU law.

Auction sales

10–008   The 1977 Act excluded certain sales by auction or competitive tender. There had been no such exclusion in the 1999 Regulations, but s.2(5) of the 2014 Act states that a person is not a consumer in relation to a sales contract if (a) the goods are second hand goods sold at public auction; and (b) individuals have the opportunity of attending the sale in person. Purely internet auctions will therefore still be consumer sales as will be, the no doubt rare auctions, where services or digital content are for sale. Section 2(6) partially qualifies this exclusion of auction sales from the Act in relation to any statement as to the characteristics of the goods, and in relation to delivery and risk.

Excluded contracts

10–009   Section 61(2) of the 2014 Act excludes from the Act contracts of employment or apprenticeship. Similarly, s.61(5) excludes notice which relates to the rights, obligations or liabilities as between employer and employee. There had been no such exclusions in the Regulations (though there had been in the 1994 Regulations repealed and replaced by the 1999 Regulations). It is difficult to see that such contracts could ever be regarded as contracts with "consumers" and it may be that the exclusion was inserted into the Act to avoid the confusion which had arisen in this context under the Unfair Contract Terms Act.[21]

The OFT had regarded vocational training contracts as consumer contracts within the Regulations, despite the fact that they are designed to enable persons to become suppliers rather than consumers, since they are sold to persons who are consumers at the time of the contract.[22] The same view would surely hold under the 2014 Act.

---

[21] See para.8–017.
[22] Unfair Contract Terms Bulletin, Issue 8, December 1999.

Choice of law

Section 77 of the Act says that where the contract has a "close connection" with **10–010** the United Kingdom, the provisions of the Act relating to unfair terms still apply notwithstanding a term of the contract which would apply the law of a non-EEA state.[23]

Terms automatically void

Negligence liability

The 2014 Act disapplies the provisions of the Unfair Contract Terms Act as to the **10–011** exclusion of negligence in relation to consumer contracts or notices directed at consumers.[24] There are, however, corresponding provisions in the 2014 Act. Sections 68(1) provides that no term in a consumer contract or notice excludes or restricts liability for negligence resulting in death or personal injury.[25] Sub-section (2) further provides that the consumer's knowledge of the provision is not to be construed as acceptance of any risk. Section 2(2) of the 1977 Act further provided that where negligence resulted in a category of injury other than death or personal injury, any exclusion of limitation clause would be subject to the reasonableness test. No such provision is contained in the 2014 Act, but any such term will of course be subject to the fairness test.

Section 68(4) provides that negligence means the breach of:

(a) any obligation to take reasonable care or exercise reasonable skill in the performance of a contract where the obligation arises from an express or implied term of the contract;
(b) a common law duty to take reasonable care or exercise reasonable skill;
(c) the common law duty of care imposed by the Occupiers. Liability Act 1957 or the Occupiers Liability Act (Northern Ireland) 1957; or
(d) the duty of reasonable care imposed by s.2(1) of the Occupiers Liability (Scotland) Act 1960.

Subsection (5) provides that it is immaterial for the purposes of subsection (4) whether a breach of duty or obligation was inadvertent or intentional, or whether liability for it arises directly or vicariously.

Section 66 excludes from the operation of the foregoing provisions:

(a) any contract so far as it is a contract of insurance, including a contract to pay an annuity on human life; or
(b) any contract so far as it relates to the creation or transfer of an interest in land.

---

[23] For "close connection", see see para.10–088. See too *Martrade Shipping & Transport GMBH v United Enterprises Corp.* [2014] EWHC 1884.

[24] See s.2 of the 1977 Act.

[25] "Personal injury" extends to "any disease and any impairment of physical or mental condition"; Consumer Rights Act 2014 s.65(3).

In addition, s.65 does not affect the validity of any discharge or indemnity given by a person in consideration of the receipt by that person of compensation in settlement of any claim the person has.

Section 65 also does not apply to the liability of an occupier of premises to a person who obtains access to the premises for recreational purposes if (a) the person suffers loss or damage because of the dangerous state of the premises, and (b) allowing the person access for those purposes is not within the purposes of the occupier's trade, business, craft or profession.[26]

The implied terms

10–012 The Consumer Rights Act implies into contracts a number of terms. Section 31 provides that liability cannot be excluded or restricted in relation to the implied terms as to: satisfactory quality; fitness for purpose; description; pre-contract information to be included in a contract; goods to match sample; goods to match model seen or examined; installation as part of conformity of goods with contract; goods not conforming to contract if digital content does not conform; trader to have right to supply; delivery of goods; passing of risk.

The use of terms automatically void may give rise to a criminal offence.[27]

Other non-excludable terms

10–013 Section 47 of the 2014 Act provides that there can be no exclusion of the following terms in relation to digital content: to be of satisfactory quality; fit for purpose; description; right to supply; remedy for damage to device or other digital content. Section 57, which relates to the provision of services provides that there can be no exclusion or restriction of the duty to provide a service with reasonable care and skill. Information about the trader or service is to be binding and this cannot be excluded or restricted. Section 57 also provides that a term is not binding in relation to these matters (and also in relation to the duty as to charging a reasonable price and doing the job within a reasonable time) if the term would prevent the consumer from recovering the price paid or the value of any other consideration. The section adds that if the term did not have this effect, the provisions as to unfair terms may apply. It should be added that, as noted above, the use of terms automatically invalid under ss.47 and 57 may constitute a criminal offence.

---

[26] These exclusions reflect in part the provisions of s.1(3) and Sch.1 of the 1977 Act.
[27] i.e. under the Consumer Protection from Unfair Trading Regulations 2008 (SI 2008/1278). See para.5–004.

Contracts relating to land

In *Khatun v London Borough of Newham*,[28] the claimants were persons provided   **10–014**
with accommodation under the provisions of the Housing Act 1996. The question
arose whether the Regulations extended to contracts relating to land, including
contracts for the grant of a lease.

In reaching its decision, the Court of Appeal paid particular attention to the
terms of the Directive. It pointed out that it had been adopted under art.100(a)
(now art.114 of the Treaty on the Functioning of the European Union) of the EU
Treaty which required the European Commission, in drafting legislation, to "take
as a base a high level of protection". The court felt that any exclusion of land
transactions from the Directive, and hence the Regulations, would "cut across"
such a provision.

There was also the fact that the language of the various documents linked to
the Directive (such as the Commission's explanatory papers, and other country's
texts) pointed strongly to the inclusion in the Directive of contracts relating to
land. The French term "biens" (and similar words in the Italian, Portuguese and
Spanish texts) comprehended immovables as well as movables, and thus
embraced land.

The Directive did, though, refer only to goods and services, and it had been
argued that these should be interpreted as an English lawyer would interpret
them. The Court of Appeal found no justification for this, not least because
European legislation was to be read as "a single corpus of law binding across
member states". The court also said that such an argument lead to absurdity since
a licence of land, which is a service, would be within the Directive but a lease or
a tenancy would not. Similarly, the sale of a fixture would be outside the
Directive but the sale of the same item when not fixed to the land would be
within it. The court said that any such distinction, in the context of "a
Europe-wide measure would be untenable". This reasoning applies no less
forcefully to the position under the 2014 Act.

Implied terms

In *Baybut v Eccle Riggs Country Park Ltd*,[29] it was said that the fairness test   **10–015**
could not be applied to terms which were implied by law. Pelling J. said it was
difficult to see how a term which was implied in order to make a contract work
and make good a gap in the contract could ever be shown to be unfair. He added
that terms were implied at common law in order to give effect to "the obvious
common but unspoken intention of both parties. Again, it was difficult to see how
such a term could ever be unfair". He further noted that none of the indicative list
of unfair terms could be regarded as implied terms.[30]

---

[28] [2004] EWCA Civ 55. See also Sta*rmark Enterprises Ltd v CPL Distribution Ltd* [2002] 4 All E.R.
264; *Financial Services Authority v Asset LI Inc* [2013] EWHC 178.
[29] *The Times*, November 13, 2006.
[30] For the Indicative List, see para.10–025.

Broadly the same line was taken in *Direct Line Insurance Plc v Khan*.[31] That case dealt with a rule of law known as the rule in *Britton v Royal Insurance Co*[32] under which a person making a fraudulent insurance claim is not allowed to recover anything at all. Arden L.J. had this to say:

> "As I read these Regulations they do not apply to a situation where a contract is affected by a rule of law, even though the contract is made with a consumer and is otherwise within the purview of these Regulations. Such a term could not be described as one which has been 'drafted in advance'. Moreover, I would find it a startling proposition if any rule of law could be reviewed under these Regulations. It seems to me to be well outside the purpose and spirit of the Regulations and might produce some surprising results."[33]

Oral agreements

10–016 There is no specific reference in the Act to oral agreements, but the wording of the various provisions is apt to cover such agreements. In any event, recital 11 to the Directive states categorically that "the consumer must receive equal treatment under contracts concluded by word of mouth and written contracts . . .".

TRANSACTIONS OUTSIDE THE ACT

10–017 Since the Act applies to transactions between traders and consumers, transactions between private individuals are excluded from its scope. An issue of a financial security would also be outside the Act since such security is no more than evidence of indebtedness and it will be the provision of the money covered by the security which will constitute the service and which alone would fall within the Act. Similarly, contracts for the issue of commodity futures and options are contracts for the sale of goods and hence within the Act in so far as they are contained within consumer transactions.

Guarantees

10–018 In *Bank of Scotland v Singh*,[34] the claimant bank sought the sum due under a guarantee given by the defendant in respect of the indebtedness of his company. The company of which he was the sole director and sole shareholder provided small businesses with the services of a personal assistant online. The bank had granted the company a facility of £900,000 personally guaranteed by the defendant. There had been discussions between the parties about a partnership arrangement under which the company's services would be marketed to the claimant's customers. The claimant sought repayment from the company and

---

[31] [2002] Lloyd's Rep I.R. 364.
[32] (1866) 4 F.&F. 905.
[33] These words were quoted with approval by Seymour J. in *Direct Line Insurance Plc v Fox* [2009] EWHC 386 (QB).
[34] Unreported June 17, 2005. Followed in *Manches LLP v Freer* [2006] EWHC 991 and *Williamson v Governor of the Bank of Scotland* [2006] EWHC 1289.

called on the guarantee. The company went into administration. The defendant submitted that the terms of the guarantee were unfair because they excluded set off or counterclaim.

In ruling that the Regulations did not apply to such guarantees, Kershaw J. said this:

> "In a contract between a bank and a company director the benefit of the contract flows one way: from guarantor to lender. The bank supplies a service, and does so for purposes relating to its business, but it does so under a contract with the borrower, who becomes the debtor. The guarantor will be normally be happy that the service is supplied to the company and will often, in his capacity as a director of the company, have engineered the loan, but he does not himself have a trade, business or profession as a guarantor (or, more broadly, as a provider of assorted financial services)."

The judge regarded any other decision as contrary to the wording of the Regulations. What he called the "immediate target" of the Regulations were unfair terms which caused a "significant imbalance in the parties' rights and obligations *arising under the contract* ... That wording is apt for a conventional contract for the supply of goods or services. It is not apt for a guarantee, in which ... all the contractual benefit flows one way and all the contractual burden flows the other way leaving no scope for a balance or imbalance."

This decision was dissented from in *Barclays Bank Plc v Alfons Kufner*.[35] The court referred to the ruling in *Bayerische Hypothetken v Dietzinger*,[36] where the court had to consider identical provisions in Council Directive 85/557/EEC to protect the consumer in respect of contracts negotiated away from business premises.[37] In giving judgment, the court in that case said this:

> "In determining whether a contract of guarantee securing performance of a credit agreement by the principal debtor can fall within the scope of Directive 85/577, it should be noted that ... the scope of the Directive is not limited according to the nature of the goods or services to be supplied under a contract; the only requirement is that the goods or services must be intended for private consumption. The grant of a credit facility is indeed the provision of a service, the contract of guarantee being merely ancillary to the principal contract, of which in practice it is usually a precondition. Furthermore, nothing in the wording of the Directive requires that the person concluding the contract under which goods or services are to be supplied be the person to whom they are supplied. Directive 85/577 is designed to protect consumers by enabling them to withdraw from a contract concluded on the initiative of the trader rather than of the customer, where the customer may have been unable to see all the implications of his act. Consequently a contract benefiting a third party cannot be excluded from the scope of the Directive on the sole ground that the goods or services purchased were intended for the use of the third party standing outside the contractual relationship in question."

Field J. held that this was the correct approach to the 1999 Regulations, saying that: "the Regulations apply to a bank guarantee, at least where the guarantor and the principal debtor each entered into their respective contracts as natural persons and were not acting in the course of their trade or profession."

---

[35] [2008] EWHC 2319 (Comm).
[36] (C-45/96) [1998] 1 W.L.R. 1035.
[37] Now contained in the Consumer Contracts (Information, Cancellation and Additional Charges) Regulations 2013 (SI 2013/3134).

It was this approach which was followed in *United Trust Bank Ltd v Dohil*.[38] The claimant had entered into a loan agreement with a company to finance the purchase of a property. The agreement provided that the security for the loan was to include a guarantee from the defendant, who was a director of the company, and that the total amount recoverable should not exceed £250,000. The Deputy Judge followed Field J. and ruled that the Regulations have no application to the guarantee in the present case, since the principal debtor, the company, was neither a natural person nor contracting as a consumer when it entered into the loan, and if the Regulations are to apply, it is necessary that both the guarantee and the loan to which it is ancillary should have been executed by a "consumer". Such an approach of course, applies with equal validity to the 2014 Act.

INDIVIDUAL NEGOTIATION

10–019 The requirement that the fairness test applied only if the particular term had not been individually negotiated, contained in the 1999 Regulations, is not repeated in the Act. Accordingly, a term which has been so negotiated can be subject to the fairness test, though may not often fail that test. Everything will, of course, depend on all the facts of the particular case.

RULES FOR ASSESSING FAIRNESS

10–020 Section 62(4) of the Act says that a contract term is unfair "if, contrary to the requirement of good faith, it causes a significant imbalance in the parties. rights and obligations under the contract to the detriment of the consumer".[39] Sub-section (6) applies the same test to notices. While it appears that the issues as to good faith and a significant imbalance appear as separate ingredients, it has been said that the two requirements do "overlap substantially" because a term: "which gives a significant advantage to the seller or supplier without a countervailing benefit to the consumer (such as a price reduction) might fail to satisfy this part of the test of an unfair term."[40]

That these requirements do have a separate role. however, was made clear in the *First National* case when it reached the House of Lords. Lord Steyn referred to the element of consumer detriment, good faith and significant imbalance as being "three independent requirements [though] the element of detriment to the consumer may not add much".[41]

Like the Regulations, s.62(5) provides that fairness is to be judged taking into account the nature of the subject matter of the contract, and by reference to all the circumstances existing when the term was agreed and to all of the other terms of

---

[38] [2011] EWHC 3302.

[39] The Regulations referred to rights and obligations "arising" under the contract, but otherwise the Act makes no changes.

[40] *Director General of Fair Trading v First National Bank Plc* [2000] 2 All E.R. 759 at 768, per Peter Gibson L.J; [2002] 1 All E.R. 97 at 113, per Lord Steyn.

[41] *Director General of Fair Trading v First National Bank Plc* [2000] 2 All E.R. 759 at 768, per Peter Gibson L.J; [2002] 1 All E.R. 97 at 113, per Lord Steyn. See too *UK Housing Alliance (North West) Ltd v Francis* [2010] EWCA Civ 117.

the contract or of any other contract on which it depends. Section 62(7) applies this test too to notices. It was said in *Pereničová v SOC financ spol sro*[42] that the requirement to have regard to all the existing circumstances "gives a particularly wide definition of the criteria for making such as assessment". Noting this, the court in *Financial Services Authority v Asset LI Inc*[43] rejected an argument that a telemarketing sales pitch could not be taken into account when determining issues of fairness, even if the telemarketers had no authority to say what they did.

It would appear from such provisions that a term which might of itself be unfair can lose that attribute if it is counterbalanced by other terms in the contract. For instance, a contract for the sale of expensive equipment might require a 100 per cent payment in advance. If this were to be regarded as unfair,[44] it might be counterbalanced by another term stipulating that interest at an appropriate rate is to be paid on such monies. Again, a contract term limiting compensation to a specific sum might of itself be unfair, but could be counterbalanced by another term which gave a right to compensation in different circumstances beyond that which would otherwise be required.

Although neither the Act nor the Directive make it clear, it would appear that the other terms to which reference may be made when considering the fairness of a particular term must be terms which have a specific relevance to the disputed term. Thus, a term demanding an advance payment may be unfair, and this would be unaffected by another term which accepted a degree of liability greater than was otherwise imposed by law.

Secondary contracts

Section 72 of the 2014 Act provides that the fairness test applies to a term of a **10–021** contract, the so-called "secondary contract", where a term reduces the rights or remedies or increases the obligations of a person under another contract, the "main contract". Sub-section (2) says that the fairness test will still apply to the secondary contract, even if the parties are not the same as in the main contract, and whether or not the secondary contract is a consumer contract. Sub-section (4) lays down, however, that the above provisions do not apply if the secondary contract is a settlement of a claim arising under the main contract. There was no such provision in the Regulations, though the provisions of the 2014 Act in some way reflect the more limited provisions in the Unfair Contract Terms Act which would of course have had relevance for consumer transactions.[45]

Thus, a maintenance agreement might specify very restricted call-out times, but the contract for the goods to which that agreement relates might provide for replacement equipment to be available on a 24-hour basis, and hence remove any element of unfairness from that restrictive term. If, in the circumstances just

---

[42] [2012] EUEJC-453/1

[43] [2013] EWHC 178.

[44] The Office of Fair Trading did take action under the 1994 Regulations against home improvement companies which demanded full or almost full payment in advance; *Consumer Law Today*, March 1999. See too Guidance on Unfair Terms in Home Improvement Contracts (OFT: edition 03/05; 2005).

[45] See para.7-001.

described, the maintenance agreement were with a husband as consumer, but the related contract were referable to the same goods, but with the wife as the other party, the Act would apply the fairness test to the contract with the wife. Similarly, the supplier of the maintenance might well be different from the supplier of the relevant goods, but this too would not prevent the applicability of the fairness test.

GOOD FAITH

10–022 The 1994 Regulations listed a number of matters which were to be taken into account when determining the issue of good faith. The 1999 Regulations, however, contained no such list and nor does the 2014 Act. This is presumably because, as experience under the Unfair Contract Terms Act 1977 has shown, such a list is generally regarded by the courts as containing no more than those matters which a court would generally refer to anyway.[46]

There is at the same time some guidance as to the meaning of "good faith" in the observations of Bingham L.J. in *Interfoto Picture Library Ltd v Stiletto Visual Programmes Ltd*,[47] when he said that "good faith" does not: "simply mean that [the parties] should not deceive each other ... its effect is perhaps more aptly conveyed by such metaphorical colloquialisms as 'playing fair', 'coming clean' or 'putting one's cards upwards on the table'. It is in essence a principle of fair and open dealing."[48]

Lord Bingham later elaborated on this approach when he said that the requirement of good faith, being one of "fair and open dealing" requires that the terms should be expressed: "fully, clearly and legibly, containing no concealed pitfalls or traps. Appropriate prominence should be given to terms which might operate disadvantageously to the consumer. Fair dealing requires that a supplier should not, whether deliberately or unconsciously, take advantage of the consumer's necessity, indigence, lack of experience, unfamiliarity with the subject matter of the contract, weak bargaining position or any other factor listed in or analogous to those listed in Sch.2 of the Regulations. Good faith in this context is not an artificial or technical concept ... It looks to good standards of commercial morality and practice."[49]

Lord Millett was even more expansive. Referring to what was "fair", he said that:

---

[46] See para.9–002.
[47] [1988] 1 All E.R. 348.
[48] [1988] 1 All E.R. 348 at 352. These words were quoted, with approval, by the Court of Appeal in *Director General of Fair Trading v First National Bank Plc* [2000] 2 All E.R. 759 at 768, per Peter Gibson L.J. and [2002] 1 All E.R 97 at 113 per Lord Steyn. See also *Office of Fair Trading v Foxtons Ltd* [2009] EWHC 1681 (Ch); and *Turner & Co (GB) Ltd v Fatah Abi* [2010] EWHC 2078 (QB).
[49] *Director General of Fair Trading v First National Bank Plc* [2002] 1 All E.R. 97 at 108. This was quoted with approval in *West and West v Ian Finlay Associates* [2013] EWHC 868; *Deutsche Bank (Suisse) SA v Khan* [2013] EWHC 482. As pointed out above the Schedule was dropped from the 1999 Regulations. For a consideration of the need for good faith and fair dealing in contracts generally, see *Yam Seng Pte Ltd v International Trade Corp Ltd* [2013] EWHC 111.

"There can be no one single test of this. It is obviously useful to assess the impact of an impugned term on the parties' rights and obligations by comparing the effect of the contract with the term and the effect it would have without it. But the inquiry cannot stop there. It may also be necessary to consider the effect of the inclusion of the term on the substance or core of the transaction; whether if it were drawn to his attention the consumer would be likely to be surprised by it; whether the term is a standard term, not merely in similar non-negotiable contracts, but in commercial contracts freely negotiated between parties acting on level terms and at arms' length; and whether, in such cases, the party adversely affected by the inclusion of the term or his lawyer might reasonably be expected to object to its inclusion and press for its deletion. The list is not necessarily exhaustive; other approaches may sometimes be more appropriate."[50]

Help in interpreting the requirement of good faith is also provided by the preamble to the Directive: **10–023**

"Whereas the assessment, according to the general criteria chosen, of the unfair character of terms, in particular in sale or supply activities of a public nature providing collective services which take account of solidarity among users, must be supplemented by a means of making an overall evaluation of the different interests involved; whereas this constitutes the requirement of good faith; whereas, in making an assessment of good faith, particular regard shall be had to the strength of the bargaining positions of the parties, whether the consumer had an inducement to agree to the term and whether the goods or services were sold or supplied to the special order of the consumer; whereas the requirement of good faith may be satisfied by the seller or supplier where he deals fairly and equitably with the other party whose legitimate interests he has to take into account."

In *Office of Fair Trading v Abbey National Plc*,[51] Andrew Smith J., referring to the reference to "bargaining position", said that it was not obviously part of the "procedure" or the "process" whereby the contract was made". This was a reference to the observations of Lord Steyn in the *First National* case that any argument that the requirement of good faith was predominantly concerned with procedural defects in negotiating procedures "cannot be sustained".[52]

Substantial or procedural unfairness

In *Director General of Fair Trading v First National Bank Plc*,[53] Evans-Lombe J.   **10–024**
noted that unfairness under the Regulations could amount to "substantive unfairness", which is the imposition of an onerous term out of proportion to a reasonable assessment of the obligations of the parties; and "procedural unfairness", where a consumer becomes unwittingly subject to an onerous term which need not of itself be substantively unfair, but which materially affects the balance of advantage of the consumer in entering into the contract. The judge thought that, given such an interpretation, the words "causes a significant imbalance in the parties' rights" add little to the words "good faith". He concluded that, in practice, a court considering whether a term was unfair would look at all the circumstances of the case and its judgment "will be based on an amalgam of perceived substantive and procedural unfairness".

---

[50] *Director General of Fair Trading v First National Bank Plc* [2002] 1 All E.R. 97 at 118.
[51] [2008] EWHC 875 (Comm).
[52] *Director General of Fair Trading v First National Bank Plc* [2002] 1 All E.R. 97 at 113.
[53] [2000] 1 All E.R. 240 at 251.

A "significant imbalance"

10–025   The need for the imbalance to be "significant" has echoes of s.3(2)(b) of the 1977 Act when it refers to a performance "substantially" different from that which was reasonably expected, with similar difficulties of interpretation. The 2014 Act does not catch those terms whose unfairness is minimal or moderate, but there can be no concrete rule for determining just when a term has crossed the line from insignificant to significant. In the *First National* case, Lord Steyn accepted that the test of a significant imbalance "obviously directs attention to the substantive unfairness of the contract".[54] Lord Bingham regarded the requirement as to significant imbalance as met if the particular term is:

> "so weighted in favour of the supplier as to tilt the parties' rights and obligations under the contract significantly in his favour. That may be by the granting of a beneficial option or discretion or power, or by the imposing on the consumer of a disadvantageous burden or risk or duty."[55]

What is clear is that significance has to be judged in the context of the whole of the obligation undertaken by the parties. If such a survey shows a contract which overall parcels out the duties and obligations in a way not leaning too heavily in favour of the seller or supplier, then the term under review would not have caused a "significant" imbalance.

The Act also makes it clear that it must be the disputed term itself which causes the imbalance. This raises the possibility that a contract may well contain a number of terms inimical to the interests of the consumer, but not any individual one causing the significant imbalance. This would mean in turn that none of the terms could be arraigned as unfair. This could well turn out to be a fatal flaw in the Act which, in this respect, accurately implement the Directive. There is a clear possibility that a contract could overall be tilted hugely in favour of the seller or supplier but, because no one term causes the necessary significant imbalance, no one term therefore can be judged unfair.

The Act further requires that the significant imbalance must be to the "detriment" of the consumer. It is clearly assumed that there can be such an imbalance, yet no detriment to the consumer. It would appear, though, that the detriment need only exist; it need not of itself be of any particular degree. A term requiring a non-refundable deposit would be to the detriment of the consumer, even if the amount required was no more than a token.

Unfair terms

10–026   Section 63(6), repeating the 1999 Regulations, provides that a term is always unfair if its effect is such that the consumer bears the burden of proof of showing compliance by a distance supplier or intermediary with requirements derived from relevant EU law.[56]

---

[54] [2002] 1 All E.R. 97 at 113.
[55] [2002] 1 All E.R. 97 at 107.
[56] The Act refers here to EU Directive 2002 2002/65/EC ("The Distance Marketing Directive") implemented by the Financial Services (Distance Marketing) Regulations 2004 (SI 2004/2095).

Schedule 2 Pt 1 to the Act contains an indicative, non-exhaustive, list of terms which may be regarded as unfair, and hence as automatically causing a significant imbalance to the detriment of the consumer.

It must be appreciated, however, that Sch.2 does no more than list types of term which may be unfair. They are not automatically unfair[57] and it will still be for the consumer to demonstrate on the above principles that the particular term is unfair though no doubt the burden is eased by the presence of the particular term in the list. This raises the question of whether the Schedule has any real value, though it may help those drafting contracts and those wishing to challenge a contract term.

The role of the indicative list has been made clear by the European Court of Justice:

> "It is not disputed that a term appearing in the list need not necessarily be considered unfair and, conversely, a term that does not appear in the list may none the less be regarded as unfair ... In so far as it does not limit the discretion of the national authorities to determine the unfairness of a term, the list contained in the annex to the Directive does not seek to give consumers rights going beyond those that result from Articles 3 to 7 of the Directive ... Inasmuch as the list contained in the annex to the Directive is of indicative and illustrative value, it constitutes a source of information both for the national authorities responsible for applying the implementing measures and for individuals affected by those measures."[58]

Again:

> "If the content of the annex does not suffice in itself to establish automatically the unfair nature of a contested term, it is nevertheless an essential element on which the competent court may base its assessment as to the unfair nature of that term."[59]

Some of the terms listed in Sch.2 are provisions which are already subject to the 2014 Act. Thus, term 1, which deals with excluding liability for death or personal injury is automatically void under the Act.[60]

Additions to the list

Three additions are made to the original list, these accepting a report by the Law Commissions. The three additional terms: **10–027**

- A term which has the object or effect of requiring that, where the consumer decides not to conclude or perform the contract, the consumer must pay the trader a disproportionately high sum in compensation or for services which have not been supplied.

---

[57] As noted by Lord Walker the grey list was originally proposed as a blacklist of terms which would be conclusively presumed to be unfair: *Office of Fair Trading v Abbey National Plc* [2009] UKSC 6.
[58] *Commission v Sweden* (C–478/99) (2002) ECR I-4147.
[59] *Nemzeti Fogyasztovedelmi Hatosag v Invitel Tavkozlesi Zrt* (C-472/10) [2012] 3 C.M.L.R. 1; [2012] C.E.C. 1375 ECJ.
[60] See the report "Unfair Terms in Consumer Contracts" March 19, 2013.

- A term which has the object or effect of permitting the trader to determine the characteristics of the subject matter of the contract after the consumer has become bound by it.[61]
- A term which has the object or effect of enabling the trader to alter unilaterally without a valid reason any characteristics of the goods, digital content or services to be provided.

Part 2 to Sch.2 contains some exceptions to the list. these relate to certain paragraphs in Pt 1 dealing with: financial services contracts; contracts which last indefinitely; contracts for sale of securities, foreign currency, etc.; and price index clauses.

It also follows from the status of the list as purely indicative that the exclusion of a term from the list does not create a presumption that it is fair. This is particularly important when assessing the position with regard to clauses referred to in the list, but which are then excluded from the list in certain defined circumstances, as noted above. For instance, the list refers to a term which has the object or effect of enabling the trader to terminate a contract of indeterminate duration without reasonable notice except where there are serious grounds for doing so. This goes on to say that this provision is subject to further terms in the list dealing with financial services contracts and contracts for sale of securities, foreign currency, etc.

EXCLUSION OF CORE PROVISIONS

10–028   A term of a consumer contract subject to the requirements of transparency and prominence,[62] may not be assessed for fairness to the extent that.

(a)   it specifies the main subject matter of the contract;
(b)   the assessment is of the appropriateness of the price payable under the contract by comparison with the goods, digital content or services provided under it.[63] Regulation 6(2) of the 1999 Regulations referred "(a) to the definition of the main subject matter of the contract; or
(c)   to the adequacy of the price or remuneration, as against the goods or services supplied in exchange". The change in wording is more a question of greater clarity than of any substantive change.

It should be noted that the exclusion of the "appropriateness of the price" does not relate to all terms relating to the price agreed, since the Indicative List indicates that price variation clauses can be assessed for fairness.[64]

Recital 19 to the Directive declares that "assessment shall not be made of terms which describe the main subject matter of the contract nor the quality/price ratio of the goods or services supplied...". One example of a core provision covers the terms in an insurance contract which define and circumscribe the

---

[61]   This is stated to be subject to those provisions of the list dealing with contracts lasting indefinitely.
[62]   See para.10–038 below.
[63]   Consumer Rights Act 2014 s.64(1)–(4).
[64]   See para.10–038.

insured risk and the insurer's liability. Originally, this was to feature as a specific exclusion from the Regulations, but was considered as adequately covered as an example of a core provision. Certainly, Recital 19 deals with these matters as an example of a core provision. There was the further consideration that, if insurance contracts were subject to a specific exclusion, the rule as to plain and intelligible language would not apply to such contracts. It is clear from this that an excessive price or charge for goods or services cannot itself be deemed unfair for the purposes of the Act.

It is important to note that s.64(6) of the 2014 Act states that the core provision exemption does not apply to terms listed in the Indicative List.

Invaluable guidance as to what is meant by this exclusion is given in *Kasler Arpad, Kaslerne Rabai Hajnalka v OTP Jelzalogbank Zrt.*[65] The borrowers had made a contract for a mortgage in foreign currency with a Hungarian bank. The bank granted them a loan in forints, the equivalent value of which was fixed in Swiss francs. The borrowers were formally notified that the related interest, default interest and administration fees were also to be determined in Swiss francs. The contract also stipulated that the amount of the loan in Swiss francs was to be determined at the buying rate applied by the bank at the date when the loan was advanced. Under the contract, however, the amount in forints for the monthly payments was determined on the day before the due date on the basis of the rate of exchange applied by the bank for the sale of Swiss francs.

The borrowers challenged this latter term, claiming it to be unfair because it provided for repayment to be based on a rate of exchange different to that which applied to the loan. The question referred to the European Court of Justice was whether a term determining the rates of exchange applicable to a loan contract denominated in a foreign currency related to the main subject matter of the contract or to the value for money of the services supplied under it.   **10–029**

The ECJ made a number of points. To begin with, the prohibition on determining the unfairness of terms relating to the main subject-matter of the contract must be interpreted strictly and may be applied only to terms laying down the essential obligations of the contract. Next, the examination of the unfairness of the term at issue could not be avoided on the ground that that term related to adequacy of the price and the remuneration on one hand as against the services or goods supplied on the other. That term in fact merely determined the conversion rate between Hungarian florints and Swiss francs for the purpose of calculating the repayments, without the lender providing any foreign exchange service. In the absence of such a service, the financial costs resulting from the difference between the buying and selling rates of exchange, which must be borne by the borrower, could not be regarded as remuneration due as consideration for a service. The ECJ made the point that a term defining the main subject matter of the contract was exempt from an assessment of its unfairness only if it were in plain, intelligible language. In that connection, the Court made the point that that requirement was not limited to clarity and intelligibility from a purely structural and grammatical point of view. What the loan contract had to do was set out in a transparent fashion the reason for and the particularities of the

---

[65] (C-26/13) Unreported April 30, 2014.

mechanism for converting the foreign currency. It was for the national court to determine whether the average consumer, who was reasonably well informed and reasonably observant and circumspect, on the basis of the promotional material and information provided by the lender in the course of negotiating the loan contract, would not only be aware of the existence of the difference between the selling rate of exchange and the buying rate of exchange of a foreign currency, but also be able to assess the consequences arising from the application of the selling rate of exchange for the calculation of the repayments and for the total cost of the sum borrowed.

The separateness of the exemptions

10–030 It has been said in the context of the 1999 Regulations, and this is valid also for the 2014 Act, that these provisions are to be read disjunctively. Regulations 6(2)(a) and 6(2)(b), and now s.64(1) of the Act, provide for two separate exemptions from assessment of fairness, and the reference to "the main subject matter" does not on its face limit the effect of the provision relating to the appropriateness of the price. The two provisions are linked by the conjunction "or", and within the provision relating to price, the phrase "the goods and services supplied" (to which is now be added "digital content") is not qualified. This reflects the Directive in that art.4(2) provides that: "[a]ssessment of the unfair nature of the terms shall relate neither to the definition of the main subject matter of the contract nor to the adequacy of the price or remuneration, on the one hand, as against services or supplied in exchange, on the other . . .".

This was somewhat qualified in the Supreme Court where it was said that:

> "the two paragraphs must be given their natural meaning, and read in that way they set out tests which are separate but not unconnected. They reflect (but in slightly different ways) the two sides (or quid pro quo) of any consumer contract, that is (a) what it is that the trader is to sell or supply and (b) what it is that the consumer is to pay for what he gets."[66]

Relevant case law

10–031 In *Director General of Fair Trading v First National Bank Plc*,[67] a loan agreement contained the following clause:

> "The rate of interest will be charged on a day to day basis on the outstanding balance and will be debited to the customer's account monthly in arrears. Payments made by the customer may be credited first to capital or interest outstanding under this agreement at the discretion of First National Bank."

It was accepted by the Director General that this was a core provision, being the provision fixing the contractual rate of interest and accordingly dealing with "the adequacy of the . . . remuneration as against the . . . services . . . supplied".

The agreement also contained this clause:

---

[66] *Office of Fair Trading v Abbey National Plc* [2009] UKSC 6, per Lord Walker.
[67] [2002] 1 All E.R. 97.

"Time is of the essence of making all repayments to First National Bank (the Bank) as they fall due. If any repayment instalment is unpaid for more than seven days after it became due, FNB may serve a notice on the customer requiring payment before a specified date not less than seven days later. If the repayment instalment is not paid in full by that date, FNB will be entitled to demand payment of the balance on the customer's account and interest then outstanding together with all reasonable and legal costs charges and expenses claimed or incurred by FNB in trying to obtain repayment of the unpaid instalment or of such balance and interest. Interest on the amount which becomes payable shall be charged in accordance with condition 3, at the rate stated in paragraph D overleaf (subject to variation) until payment after as well as before any judgment (such obligation to be independent of and not to merge with any judgment)."

It was argued that this, too, was a core provision. It was contended, and accepted by the court, that "adequacy" must be read as meaning the equivalent of "the extent of remuneration".[68] In the House of Lords, however, it was felt that such an interpretation could "risk watering down what the Directive may have intended". Lord Rodgers went on to say that the language used in the French and German texts of the Directive suggested that what was in issue was the "appropriateness" of the price or remuneration as compared with the services or goods: "in other words whether there is an equivalence between the services or goods and the consideration for them ... It may therefore be that 'adequacy' ... should be interpreted in that spirit".[69]

The Bank contended that the interest provision was a "core" term of the loan agreement, within reg.3(2) of the Regulations, in that it concerned the adequacy of the price or remuneration, as against "the ... services ... supplied". This was rejected by the court. This particular term was not one which defined the main subject matter of the contract and could not realistically be said to concern the adequacy of the remuneration, "relating as it does only to a case where the borrower is in default and then merely providing for the continuation of the contractual rate after judgment". The court accepted the view that, if this term were to be regarded as a core term, then "almost any provision containing any part of the bargain" would be capable of being construed as a core term.[70]

In *Bairstow Eves London Central Ltd v Smith*[71] an estate agency contract **10–032** contained a term providing for 1.5 per cent commission if paid within 10 days of completion, failing which commission was charged at 3 per cent. A further term provided that if commission were not payable in full after 10 days, then interest would be payable at 3 per cent above NatWest base rate. The court said that the question whether the Regulations applied turned on the question:

1. Did the agreement provide for a 3 per cent rate with the sellers having the option, but no obligation, to pay 1.5 per cent; or

---

[68] [2000] 1 All E.R. 240 at 248.

[69] [2002] 1 All E.R. 97 at 120.

[70] [2000] 2 All E.R. 759 at 768, per Peter Gibson L.J. The Court of Appeal was upholding the decision of the High Court on this point. See also words to like effect in the House of Lords [2002] 1 All E.R. 97 at 105 and 112 per Lords Bingham and Steyn respectively, the latter stressing that the notion of a core provision had to be construed restrictively.

[71] [2004] EWHC 263 (QB). See also *Maple Leaf Macro Volatility Master Fund v Jacques Rouvroy* [2009] EWHC 257 (Comm) where it was held that a clause providing for a 25 per cent return on an investment did relate to the adequacy of the "price or remuneration".

2.   did the agreement place the sellers under an obligation to pay a price of 1.5 per cent with a default provision, exercisable at the option of the agency, to insist on a payment of 3 per cent?

If it were the former, then the term would be a core provision; if the latter, then it would fall to be judged on its fairness.

The court held that it was clear on the evidence that the parties contemplated that the second alternative was the case, and that was for the following reasons:

- The branch manager had recognised that, in the then state of the market, it would not have obtained business had 3 per cent been the commission rate.
- It was not disputed that the negotiations had focused exclusively on the 1.5 per cent.
- The parties had proceeded on the basis that the commission would be paid within 10 days. They had no reason to suppose otherwise. The completion monies would of necessity be available from day one of the period. Furthermore, the fact that the 3 per cent was stated to be payable only at the agency's option militated against the 3 per cent being the contract price. In addition, the provision as to interest being payable assumed an obligation to pay the 1.5 per cent commission in full within the 10-day period.

The existence of the interest provision was not appropriate to the idea that payment of the 1.5 per cent commission was only an option on the part of the sellers. The provision charging 3 per cent was not therefore a core provision and the question of its fairness had therefore to be considered.

In *Bond v British Telecommunications Plc*[72] the action involved a charge of £4.50 made on the claimant for not paying her bills by direct debit. The court had no doubt that this was a core provision:

> "This was a charge for operating the total telecommunications service that she received from BT. It is quite clear what it is for. In my judgment, it is a charge for services rendered."

10–033   Perhaps the most detailed consideration of what constitutes a core provision came in the *Abbey Life* case.[73] The charges imposed by the banks, and which were at the heart of the case, comprised unpaid item charges, paid item charges, overdraft excess charges and guaranteed paid item charges (the relevant charges). The banks contended that any such investigation would be circumscribed by the provisions of reg.6(2) as being core provisions. Reversing the Court of Appeal, which had upheld the High Court, the Supreme Court ruled that these terms were core terms and their fairness could, therefore, not be assessed.

The High Court had rejected the banks' argument because the relevant charges were not the "price or remuneration" for "services supplied in exchange". They were not charged "in exchange" for anything. While most of the charges were triggered by the provision of an individual service they were not imposed by way of payment for those services. They were charges levied because the services in question were supplied by the banks "in particular circumstances".

---

[72] Unreported March 28, 2008 (Walsall CC).
[73] [2009] UKSC 6. See too *Foster-Burnell v Lloyds Bank*; Taunton County Court; June 21, 2014.

The Court of Appeal upheld the High Court but by a different route. In relation to unpaid item charges the court held that giving consideration to a request to honour a cheque on an overdrawn account was a service, even if the request was turned down. Thus each of the events that triggered a liability to pay relevant charges involved the provision of a service. It was not, however, realistic to consider that each relevant charge was payment for the individual service that occasioned its imposition. Rather, the substance of the contract had to be analysed as a package. The court then went on to divide the package into the "core or essential bargain" and provisions that were "incidental or ancillary", holding that reg.6(2) only applied to the former. The core or essential bargain was comprised of those matters to which the typical consumer would have regard when deciding whether to enter into the agreement with the banks. The latter would be those to which he would not attach importance when concluding the contract.

The court decided that charges which were contingent upon the customer overdrawing on his current account would not have been considered of significance by the typical customer at the time of establishing the account. The charges would only be imposed in contingent circumstances and were akin to default charges triggered by a breach of contract, although they were not in fact triggered by a breach of contract because of the manner in which the contractual relationship had been expressly framed. The customer would not consider the contingent liability to pay the relevant charges in the event of overdrawing on his account an essential part of the Bank's agreement to provide these services without charge provided that he remained in credit. It followed that the liability to pay the relevant charges was not part of the core or essential bargain and did not fall within the ambit of reg.6(2). The court accepted that the contract between bank and customer had to be treated as a package. It did not exclude from the package services that were supplied at a time when the current account was overdrawn. The court accepted that the relevant terms were terms that provided for payment of price or remuneration. It held, however, that they were not "core" payment terms but "ancillary or incidental price, remuneration or payment terms" which did not constitute price or remuneration that fell within reg.6(2).

For his part, Lord Phillips could see:

> "no justification for excluding from the application of Regulation 6(2) price or remuneration on the ground that it is an 'ancillary or incidental price or remuneration'. If it is possible to identify such price or remuneration as being paid in exchange for services, even if the services are fringe or optional extras, Regulation 6(2) will preclude an attack on the price or remuneration in question if it is based on the contention that it was excessive by comparison with the services for which it was exchanged. If, on analysis, the charges are not given in exchange for individual services but are part of a package of different ways of charging for a package of varied services, this does not mean that they are not price or remuneration for the purpose of Regulation 6(2)."

The Court of Appeal had accepted that the object of reg.6(2) was to exclude from assessment for fairness that part of the bargain that will be the focus of a customer's attention when entering into a contract, that is to say the goods or services that he wishes to acquire and the price he will have to pay for doing so. Market forces could and should be relied upon to control the fairness of this part   **10–034** of the bargain. Contingencies that the customer does not expect to involve him will not be of concern to him. He will not focus on these when entering into the bargain. The relevant charges, it was said, fell into this category. Free-if-in-credit current accounts are opened by customers who expect to be in credit. Customers who go into debit without making a prior agreement for an overdraft normally do so because of an unforeseen contingency.

Customers do not have regard to the consequences of such a contingency when opening a current account. Accordingly, so the Court of Appeal held, the relevant charges that were then levied did not fall within reg.6(2). It was Lord Phillip's view that this reasoning was "relevant not to the question of whether the relevant charges form part of the price or remuneration for the package of services provided but to whether the method of pricing is fair".

Lord Phillips also took issue with the reasoning deployed in the High Court. Andrew Smith J. had said that it was not a natural use of language to say that the relevant charges were levied or paid in exchange for those services supplied when an account was in credit. It was Lord Phillips' view that there were not many customers who ran a current account that was permanently overdrawn in circumstances where they had not specifically agreed an overdraft facility. He thought that most customers who incurred relevant charges ran current accounts that are in credit most of the time: "I do not think that it is an unnatural use of language to say that the relevant charges that they pay are paid as *part* of the price or remuneration provided in exchange for the package of services that they receive".[74]

It had been argued in the Court of Appeal that, if the relevant charges were not, as the High Court had held, to be regarded as the price of remuneration paid in such an exchange, then they should be regarded as default charges. The Court of Appeal accepted that the charges were akin to default charges since they were only payable in what were called "aberrant circumstances". The Supreme Court, however, felt it clear that the relevant charges were not concealed default charges designed to discourage customers from overdrawing on their accounts without prior arrangement. Whatever may have been the position in the past, the banks now relied on the relevant charges as an important part of the revenue that they generated from the current account services. If they did not receive the relevant charges they would not be able profitably to provide current account services to their customers in credit without making a charge to augment the value of the use of their funds. The conclusion had to be that the relevant charges were, as the banks had argued, charges that they require their customers to agree to pay as part of the price or remuneration for the package of services that they agree to supply in exchange

In the light of the Supreme Court ruling, doubt must be cast on the decision of Mann J. in *Office of Fair Trading v Foxtons Ltd*.[75] The judge, ruling that the commission charges were not core provisions, said it was necessary to consider how the matter would be perceived by the typical consumer and the supplier. This meant that, if the renewal commission were to be treated as part of the core bargain, the typical consumer would have to consider it so as well as the supplier.

---

[74] The emphasis is that of Lord Phillips.
[75] [2009] EWHC 1681 (Ch).

On the facts, the obligation to pay renewal commission had not been part of the core bargain between the parties, "since a typical consumer would have approached Foxtons for help in finding a tenant for an initial term of engagement and the prospect of a renewal would have been a subsidiary matter receiving little focus at that time. Furthermore, the provision for renewal commission was hidden away in the document and played no part in the activities under focus, namely those of finding a tenant. A re-wording of the clause to expressly make the renewals commission part of the overall contract price or core bargain did not alter the real position". The judge expressly followed the decision of the Court of Appeal in the *Abbey Life* case. The Supreme Court noted only that this had been so without further comment, but it is fair to assume that the ruling by Mann J. is incompatible with that of the Supreme Court.

In *Financial Services Authority v Asset L.I. Inc*,[76] the services clause ran thus: **10–035**

> "For the avoidance of doubt, the Seller is not obliged to and will not apply for planning permission in relation to the Property or in relation to the land as a whole of which the Property forms part, nor will the Seller provide any other services to the Buyer following the purchase of the Property by the Buyer to the extent that the provision of such services would constitute the carrying on by the Seller of regulated activities for the purposes of the FSMA unless the Seller is authorised under that Act and permitted by the [FSA] to carry on the relevant regulated activities. Notwithstanding the foregoing, the Seller reserves the right to (but is not obliged to) apply for planning permission in relation to any land owned by the Seller which forms part of the land of which the Property forms part."[77]

Andrew Smith J. began by saying that he did not necessarily accept that the contracts were for the sale and purchase of land, and that was their main subject matter. He went on to say that, even if it were correct that the services clause "defines the scope of the service which [Asset Land] is to provide", he did not see how it could be said to relate to the *main* subject matter of the contracts:

> "Moreover, the written contracts expressly stated that the price was paid for the property: 'The Seller shall sell and the Buyer shall buy the property ... for the price ...'. The services clause did not relate to the adequacy of the price as against what was supplied in exchange".

The nature of the assessment excluded

Although it was not required to do so, the Supreme Court in *Abbey Life* also **10–036** considered this issue: whether, if reg.6(2) did apply to a term, was any assessment of its fairness excluded, or did it exclude only an assessment relating to the adequacy of the price.

The court ruled that the latter was the correct interpretation. It pointed to arts 4(1) and (2) of the Directive:

> "(1) ... the unfairness of a contractual term shall be assessed, taking into account the nature of the goods or services for which the contract was concluded and by referring, at the time of conclusion of the contract, to all the circumstances attending the conclusion of the contract and to all the other terms of the contract or of another contract on which it is dependent. (2)

---

[76] [2013] EWHC 178. For the facts of this case, see para.10–068.
[77] FSMA is a reference to the Financial Services and Markets Act 2012 and the reference to FSA is to the Financial Services Authority, now the Financial Conduct Authority.

> Assessment of the unfair nature of the terms shall relate neither to the definition of the main subject matter of the contract nor to the adequacy of the price and remuneration, on the one hand, as against the services or goods supplied in exchange, on the other, in so far as these terms are in plain intelligible language."

As the court said:

> "Article 4(1) is directed to how the unfairness of a contractual term is to be assessed. Article 4(2) specifically states that the 'assessment' shall not relate to the exempted matters. It is not to relate to one aspect of the price or remuneration, its adequacy as against the goods or services supplied in exchange (just as an assessment relating to the definition of the main subject matter, and not an assessment relating to any term that defines the main subject matter, is excluded from assessment for fairness)."

The court also singled out the wording of reg.6(2), where the subject of "shall not relate" was "assessment". This approach is not negated by the fact that s.64(1)(b) of the 2014 Act in different wording precludes an assessment for fairness where such "assessment is of the appropriateness of the price payable . . .".

It was also noted that art.4(2) was introduced into the Directive by the Council of Ministers, who explained in their reasons for the common position that they adopted that the wording was intended to "clarify the procedures for assessing the unfairness of terms and to specify their scope while excluding anything resulting directly from the contractual freedom of the parties (*e.g.* quality/price relationship)".

10–037   It had been argued that the construction ultimately adopted by the court could not be correct, since "Once a payment obligation is categorised as a price . . . there is no difference between investigating whether the price is fairly charged at all and investigating the fairness of its amount". The court accepted that, while there might not be "a clear line between an investigation into a pricing structure and an investigation into the adequacy of the price", that did not mean that the Regulations did not require a judgment to be made as to where the line fell. The court said that the assessment required by reg.5(1) was into the overall balance of the parties' rights and obligations under the contract: "While this might entail some consideration of the level of the price paid by consumers as against what they receive in exchange, the assessment under Regulation 5(1) is a broader one"; it involved looking at the contract as a whole. There was support for this in Recital 19[78] to the Directive which makes clear that a distinction is to be drawn "between (permissibly) taking into account the price/quality ratio when assessing fairness and (impermissibly) assessing the price/quality ratio itself".

This view was adopted in *Office of Fair Trading v Ashbourne Managements Services*.[79] A clause in a gym membership contract provided that a member was liable to pay the monthly membership subscription for the minimum membership period and may be obliged to do so even if the member would prefer to cancel the agreement. Kitchin J. held such a clause to be a core provision since "it defines the period during which the member is entitled to use the facilities of the gym club and, in return, must pay a particular monthly subscription". The clause thus

---

[78] See para.10–027.
[79] [2011] EWHC 1237.

related to the main definition of the main subject matter of the contract within reg.6(2)(a). Following the Supreme Court, the judge further ruled that this did not mean that the clause still could not be subject to the fairness test. It could still be so subject in that the fairness test would relate to the obligation upon members to pay monthly subscriptions for the minimum period when they have overestimated the use they will make of their memberships and failed to appreciate that unforeseen circumstances may make their continued use of a gym impractical or their memberships unaffordable: "Put another way, it relates to the consequences to members of early termination in light of the minimum membership period". He ruled the clause unfair.

USING CORE PROVISIONS TO JUDGE OTHER TERMS

Regardless of whether the core provisions can themselves be assessed for fairness, they can always be taken into account when determining if some other term of the contract falls to be so assessed. This is clear from the provisions of s.62(5)(b) of the 2014 Act which states that regard can be paid when determining fairness "to all the other terms of the contract". If, for example, a consumer is required to pay a specific sum in the event of cancellation, the price of the goods or services may well be relevant in determining if this particular clause is fair. **10–038**

Transparency and prominence

Regulation 6(2) of the Regulations stipulated that the exclusion of "core provisions" would apply only if the relevant term was in "plain, intelligible language". The Act adopts a different approach by saying that the exclusion applies only if the relevant term is "transparent and prominent."[80] Section 64(3) and (4) expand this by stating, respectively, that a term is transparent "if it is expressed in plain and intelligible language and (in the case of a written term) is legible". A term is regarded as prominent if it is brought to the consumer's attention in such a way that an average consumer would be aware of the term.[81] **10–039**

To a high degree, this new wording represented the view taken of the meaning of "plain and intelligible" taken by the then Office of Fair Trading (now the Competition and Markets Authority). It was its view[82] that, to avoid the Regulations, core terms must be brought to the attention of the consumer. It also said[83] that it would be difficult to claim that a term was a core term unless central to how consumers perceived the bargain. A supplier would "surely find it hard" to sustain the argument that a contract's main subject matter was defined by a term which a consumer had no real chance to see and read prior to signature: in other words, where a term has not been drawn properly to the consumer's attention: "We regularly see terms which are claimed to be 'core terms' but which are given no prominence and are indeed rather coyly tucked away in the small print". While

---

[80] Section 64(2).
[81] Unfair Contract Terms Bulletin, Issue 1, May 1996.
[82] Unfair Contract Terms Bulletin, Issue 2, September 1996.
[83] Unfair Contract Terms Bulletin, Issue 2, September 1996.

this approach was perhaps not immediately obvious from the use of the simple words "plain" and "intelligible" it was consonant with the intent of the Regulations and has now been endorsed by the 2014 Act.

It will follow from the above that "consideration" may have to be dropped in favour of "price" or "charge". Latinisms may also have to be removed. The long paragraph may also have to be removed, with greater attention being placed on short sentences, with key words perhaps being highlighted. In one contract, an expiry date was not adequately drawn to the consumer's attention. Such a term would have been a core term, and hence outside the Regulations, but for the fact that, since it was not sufficiently drawn to the consumer's attention, it failed the requirement that it be plain and intelligible.[84] The OFT has also said what is required:

> "is that terms are intelligible to ordinary members of the public, not just lawyers. They need to have a proper understanding of them for sensible and practical purposes. It is not sufficient for terms to be clear and precise for legal purposes, except in contracts normally entered only on legal advice."[85]

10–040   In the view of the OFT, the purpose of the exemption given to the two kinds of "core" term is to allow freedom of contract to prevail in relation to terms that are genuinely central to the bargain between consumer and supplier. As such, the "core terms exemption" is seen as conditional upon such terms being expressed and presented in such a way as to ensure that they are, or at least are capable of being, at the forefront of the consumer's mind in deciding whether to enter the contract. The concern of the Regulations is with the "object or effect" of terms, not their form. A term that has the mechanism of a price term, or which purports to define what the consumer is buying, will not be treated as exempt if it is clearly calculated to produce the same effect as an unfair exclusion clause, penalty, variation clause or other objectionable term. This particularly applies to the termination charges that have the effect of unfair cancellation penalties.[86]

That the Financial Services Authority (now the Financial Conduct Authority) took this broader view is evidenced by the undertaking accepted in the case where it:

> "considered that Clause 11.6 was not drafted in plain, intelligible language in line with Regulation 7.[87] This is because Clause 11.6 refers to paragraph 2 of the terms and conditions. Paragraph 2 only discusses cancellation by the consumer within a 14-day cooling-off period. As such, we considered that it was not clear what would happen to a consumer's investment in the event that the consumer terminated the contract outside of the 14-day cooling-off period and what refund, if any, a consumer would receive back on such an early redemption outside of the 14-day cooling-off period."

---

[84] See the Unfair Contract Terms Bulletin, Issue 6, April 1999. The OFT said also that, if a core term were hidden away in the small print as if it were unimportant, when potentially burdensome, it would be considered potentially unfair: Unfair Terms in Consumer Contracts Regulations 1999 reg.6(2). The OFT has required the removal of "indemnify" and "joint and several liability" as being unacceptable "jargon": See the Unfair Contract Terms Bulletin, Issue 20, November 2002.

[85] See Unfair Contract Terms Guidance, September 2008.

[86] See Unfair Contract Terms Guidance, September 2008.

[87] Reg.7 of the Unfair Terms in Consumer Contracts Regulations requires written agreements to be in plain, intelligible language. See now s.68 of the Consumer Rights Act 2014 and para.10–077.

It considered that the revised cl.11.6 was "more likely to be plain and intelligible under the Regulations as it is clearer what the cancellation process is: (i) for cancellations within the 14-day cooling-off period; and (ii) for cancellations outside the 14-day cooling-off period. It also gives clearer information about how the early redemption fee is calculated, which is payable for cancellations outside the 14-day cooling-off period".[88]

There are, however, limitations to the test of prominence and transparency. A clause may lack any real meaning, or even give rise to uncertainty, but this does not necessarily mean that it fails the test. To state, for example, that the given price may vary to take account of any changes in "Government charges" may lack precision, but is still a phrase which is prominent and transparent. On the other hand, Lord Wright in *Scammel and Nephew Ltd v HC/JG Ouston*,[89] regarded these words: "This order is given on the understanding that the balance of the purchase price can be had on hire-purchase terms over a period of two years" as suffering from "actual vagueness and unintelligibility".[90] The main reason for the decision, that no binding contract existed, was that there was no certainty at all as to what "hire-purchase terms" meant and that the parties had never got beyond the point of negotiation.[91] For all it lacked a clear content, it is still the case that the disputed clause was plain and intelligible. Lord Wright also said that "difficulty is not synonymous with ambiguity",[92] but, in the context of the Act, difficulty may equate with lack of intelligibility.

INTELLIGIBILITY CONSIDERED

In *Bankers Insurance Co Ltd v South*,[93] an insurance contract contained these words:

10–041

> "Personal Liability: For each Person-Insured we will pay for the following Events Insured. Up to . . .,000,000 including costs agreed between us in writing for which you are legally liable to pay, if they relate to an event caused by you which results in A. Injury . . . of any person . . . For each Person-Insured we will not pay for . . . compensation or other costs arising from accidents involving your ownership or possession of any . . . mechanically propelled vehicles and any trailers attached thereto, aircraft, motorised waterborne craft or sailing vessels or wind-surfing."

This was held to be in plain and intelligible language.
In the *Abbey* case,[94] Abbey used the following:

> "3.3 Instant Overdrafts
> 3.3.1 Without contacting us at all, you may also request an overdraft by trying to make a payment from your current account, where that payment would:

---

[88] Notice of Undertaking Investec Bank plc; Financial Services Authority (now FCA); February 26, 2013.
[89] [1941] A.C. 251.
[90] [1941] A.C. 251 at 268–269.
[91] [1941] A.C. 251 at 268–269.
[92] [1941] A.C. 251 at 268–269.
[93] [2003] EWHC 380.
[94] [2009] UKSC 6.

> (i)   cause your current account to go overdrawn without an Advance Overdraft in place; or
>
> (ii)   cause your current account to go over any Advance Overdraft limit we have previously agreed with you.
>
> In either case this is referred to as an Instant Overdraft request.
>
> 3.3.2   You will be treated as making an Instant Overdraft request to us automatically if you do not have enough money in your current account, or enough unused Advance Overdraft with us and you do any of the following:
>
> (i)   you try to purchase goods or services using your debit card or by cheque;
>
> (ii)   you try to withdraw money from your current account;
>
> (iii)   you try to make a payment from your current account against a cheque which is later returned unpaid or against any other deposit in your current account which has not been processed; or
>
> (iv)   an automated payment you have set up, such as a Direct Debit or a standing order, is requested to be paid.
>
> 3.3.3   An Instant Overdraft Request Fee will be payable by you each time that you use the Instant Overdraft service. The Instant Overdraft Request Fee is payable regardless of whether we agree to give you the Instant Overdraft requested.
>
> Important: Payment of the Instant Overdraft Request Fee may result in you becoming overdrawn (or, if you already have an overdraft, further overdrawn) even if we do not agree to give you the Instant Overdraft.
>
> 3.3.4   We may give you an Instant Overdraft or we may refuse to do so. If we agree, we will give you an Instant Overdraft to cover the amount of the withdrawal or the payment involved. An Instant Overdraft Monthly Fee will by (sic) payable by you monthly for every calendar month in which you have used our Instant Overdraft service (including where you continue to use an existing Instant Overdraft facility). Interest will also be payable by you at the Instant Overdraft Interest Rate on any money you borrow by way of an Instant Overdraft. If we refuse your Instant Overdraft request but your account is in credit or, if you have an Advance Overdraft and your account still has some unused Advance Overdraft on it, then you will not have to pay the Instant Overdraft Monthly Fee."

This was not in plain, intelligible language.

In the same case, the court considered that the following HSBC terms were plain and intelligible:

> "If an electronic payment is fraudulently or mistakenly paid into your account, the amount of the payment may subsequently be deducted. This may happen even if you have used the funds to make a payment, transferred or withdrawn all or part of them. If the deduction of the electronic payment from your account would either make your account go overdrawn or go over an existing overdraft limit, we will treat this as an informal request for an overdraft please see clause 7.3 for further details."

10–042   Clause 4 is headed "Payments from your account", and in clause 4.1 HSBC says that:

> "We will make payments from your account if:
> - you authorise them in any of the ways set out in these Terms, but we may decline to make a payment if the amount exceeds any limit we set for monitoring or fraud prevention purposes; and
> - there are cleared funds in your account or they are covered by an overdraft that we have agreed following a formal or informal request from you, made in one of the ways described in clause 7.3. We may consider any other payments we have made or agreed to make from your account, or which have already been authorised, such as card transactions. This will be regardless of whether or not these transactions have already been deducted from your account."

Clause 4.2 provides:

"If we receive:
- any cheque drawn by you (including any cheque guaranteed by an appropriate card . . . that we may be bound to honour); or
- any debit card transaction on your account; or
- any other payment or withdrawal instruction or request made by you (or by anyone with your authority) to us in any way;
- that would, if honoured by us, either make your account go overdrawn or go over an existing overdraft limit, we will treat this as an informal request from you for an overdraft please see clause 7.3 for further details."

Clause 7 is about "Borrowing from us". Clause 7.1 states that the customer must be at least 18 years of age to borrow from HSBC. Below clauses 7.3, 7.4 and 7.5 are set out.

"7.3   You can request an overdraft, or an increase to an existing overdraft, on your Bank Account . . . from us. You can do this in one of two ways, either:
- by way of a formal request, that is, you ask us for and we agree to provide you with, an overdraft or an increase to an existing overdraft limit before you authorise any payments or withdrawals from your account that, if made by us, would cause your account to go overdrawn or over an existing overdraft limit; or
- by way of an informal request, that is, where you authorise a payment or withdrawal to be made from your account which, if made by us, would cause your account to go overdrawn or over an existing overdraft limit without having agreed with us in advance an overdraft or an increase in an existing overdraft limit on your account to cover such payment.

7.4   If we receive a formal request for an overdraft or an increase to an existing overdraft limit from you, we will consider your request and, if we agree to it, we will give you a letter setting out the terms of the overdraft. An Arrangement Fee may be charged if we agree to your formal request. We may agree to provide you with another overdraft at the end of the term of your facility and, if we do so, an Arrangement Fee may be payable.
Please refer to clause 6 for more details of our charges.

7.5   If we receive an informal request for an overdraft or an increase to an existing overdraft limit from you, we will consider your request and if we agree to it, we will provide you with an overdraft or an increase to your existing overdraft to cover the item concerned for 31 days. An Arrangement Fee may be charged if we agree to your informal request.
You will not be charged further Arrangement Fee(s) provided your account does not go any further overdrawn. However, if your account goes into credit, or the overdrawn balance on your account decreases, and you then make another informal request for an overdraft and we agree to such a request, we may charge you a further Arrangement Fee.
If we do not agree to an informal request from you for an overdraft or an increase to an existing overdraft limit, then we will not make any payment authorised by you that would cause your account to go overdrawn or over any agreed overdraft limit. We may charge for considering and returning these informal payment requests.
Please refer to clause 6 for more details about our charges.
If you do require an overdraft or an increase to an existing overdraft, it would be in your interests to contact us to discuss your borrowing requirements as it would probably be cheaper for you to have a formal overdraft than several informal overdrafts."

As is apparent from the last two sentences, not all of cl.7.5 is of contractual effect, and it includes statements that are advisory or exhortatory in character.

"228.   Clause 6 explains that the Bank's charges are in the price list. The leaflet of 'Price List and Interest Rates' sets out under the heading 'Overdraft Service' an explanation (in terms essentially similar to condition 7.3) that the customer can make a formal or an informal request. It then states under the heading 'Arrangement Fees' that a first overdraft in 6 months is free and the fee for subsequent overdrafts is £25. As for Return Fees, it is said: 'We may not be able to grant every request you make for an overdraft. Where we decline an informal overdraft request we will not charge an Arrangement Fee but a Return Fee will be payable for considering and returning payment requests e.g., cheque, standing order, direct debit etc.'. The amount of the Return Fees is set out: 'Up to £10, no charge. Up to £25, £10 per item. Above £25, £25 per item.'"

10–043   The leaflet also sets out HSBC's "Fair Fees Policy" in the following terms:

"We always aim to be fair in the way we charge for our Overdraft services, therefore:
- we will not charge an Arrangement Fee provided, within the last 6 months, either:
    - we have not agreed to a request from you for an overdraft, or
    - before 1 November 2006, you have not exceeded your overdraft limit or gone overdrawn without a limit
- we will not charge an Arrangement Fee for an overdraft request of £10 or less
- we will not charge Arrangement Fees for informal overdrafts if covering funds are paid in before the end of the day
- we will give advance notice before Arrangement Fees are debited from your account
- if debited Arrangement Fees (or interest) cause your account to go overdrawn or further overdrawn we will not make a further charge
- Arrangement Fees charged will never be higher than the overdraft requested (e.g. a £15 overdraft will not cost you say, £50)
- we will not charge more than one Arrangement Fee a day".

In the *Foxtons* case,[95] these clauses fell for consideration:

"2.14.3 Renewal commission will become due in respect of renewals, extensions and hold-overs or new agreements where the original tenant remains in occupation. It will also become due where the incoming tenant is a person, company or other entity associated or connected with the original tenant, either personally, or by involvement or connection with any company or other entity with whom the original tenant is or was involved or connected. Where there is more than one tenant, renewal commission will be payable in full where any or all of them remain in occupation. Commission is due whether or not the renewal is negotiated by Foxtons.

2.14.4 Renewal commission is charged in advance, either as a percentage of the rental value of the new agreed term or where the tenant extends and/or holds over indefinitely, commission will be payable for the same period as the initial agreement subject to clause 1.5 above. The scale of commission fees charged is as set out on page 1."

Mann J. regarded the first clause as not plain and intelligible: "I do not think that the typical consumer looking at this clause would understand how far the obligation was said to go, and that is enough to render [this provision] as being one not in plain and intelligible language". He ruled, however, that cl.2.14.4 was plain and intelligible. This was despite the fact that reference in that clause to "page 1" should have been to "page 2". As Mann J. said:

"The consumer protection purposes of Regulation 6(2) (and Regulation 7, which also has a requirement for plain and intelligible language) does not require an absolute and pedantic rigour. That error seems to me to be one which will be obvious to the consumer, which does not, by itself, lead to a failure to fulfil the plain intelligible language requirement."

---

[95] [2009] EWHC 1681 (Ch).

In the *Ashbourne* case,[96] this was the disputed clause: **10–044**

"The Minimum Membership Period
    You have chosen the 'Minimum Membership Period' referred to overleaf.
    YOU MUST PAY THE MONTHLY MEMBERSHIP SUBSCRIPTION FOR THE
    MINIMUM MEMBERSHIP PERIOD UNLESS YOUR MEMBERSHIP IS TERMINATED
    WITHOUT LIABILITY, SUSPENDED OR TRANSFERRED AS SET OUT BELOW
    Your right to terminate this agreement without liability.
    Your right to terminate this agreement without liability is set out in clause 5. In particular,
you may terminate this agreement at any time if the facilities or the services we provide fall
well below the standard that you reasonably expect us to provide.
    Your right to suspend this agreement.
    We will suspend your membership during the minimum membership period if and when
you provide written confirmation that (a) you, your spouse or your partner has begun to claim
income support or (b) you provide a letter from your GP to prove that you (i) have been
advised not to use the gym for a medical reason (ii) are pregnant or (iii) gave birth in the last
3 months. We will review your circumstances every 2 months. If your circumstances have not
changed, we will suspend your membership for a further 2 months, unless you tell us that you
would prefer to cancel your membership which you may do without any further obligation on
your part. Whilst your membership is suspended, you will be relieved of your obligation to
pay your monthly membership subscription and we will be relieved of our obligation to allow
you to use the facilities at the club. Suspension will not affect the date when the minimum
membership period ends.
    Your right to cancel this agreement.
    We will cancel your membership during the minimum membership period without any
further obligation on your part if: (a) you provide a letter from your GP to prove that you have
been advised not to use the gym for the foreseeable future for a medical reason; (b) you
provide written confirmation (e.g. a letter from your employer) to prove that the location of
your main place of work has changed; or (c) you provide written confirmation (e.g. a utility
bill) to prove that you have moved more than 15 miles from your old address.
    Your right to transfer this agreement.
    We will transfer your membership to another person (Provided they do not have an existing
relationship with the gym) during the minimum membership period if (a) he or she agrees to
become a member for the remainder of the minimum membership period; (b) he or she agrees
to pay an induction fee of £35 and; (c) he or she is introduced to us by you."

The starting point for Kitchin J. was that the question whether a particular
term is expressed in plain intelligible language "must be considered from the
perspective of an average consumer. Here such a consumer is a member of the
public interested in using a gym club which is not a high end facility and who
may be attracted by the relatively low monthly subscriptions".

He noted that there was a difference in the terminology used on the front of
many of the agreements and that used in the body of the terms and conditions on
the reverse. On the front of the earlier agreements, under the space left for the
consumer's signature, appeared the words "I have read the terms and conditions
overleaf and understand that I am signing for a minimum of...". In later
agreements this wording had been modified to read "I have been advised that I
should read the terms and conditions overleaf and that I am signing for a
minimum term of... Months". He further noted that, in the case of one of the
agreements (agreement 13), the wording read: "MEMBERSHIP DETAILS &
LENGTH OF MINIMUM MEMBERSHIP PERIOD" and then, a little further

---

[96] [2011] EWHC 1237.

down the page: "YOU MUST PAY THE MONTHLY MEMBERSHIP SUB-SCRIPTION FOR THE NEXT... MONTHS ('THE MINIMUM MEMBER-SHIP PERIOD') UNLESS YOUR MEMBERSHIP IS TERMINATED WITHOUT LIABILITY, SUSPENDED OR TRANSFERRED AS SET OUT OVERLEAF".

10–045   On the reverse of the earlier agreements, cl.2 provided that the consumer will remain a member for "the minimum period of... year..." and, in the case of the later agreements, for a "membership period" or "minimum membership period".

Kitchin J. pointed to the desirability of there being a consistency in the terminology used in any agreement and, in this case, on the front of each of the agreements and in the terms and conditions on the reverse. In the case of many of the agreements, that consistency was lacking. Even so, he felt that the language used was plain and intelligible: "the average consumer reading each of the agreements reasonably carefully would have been left in no doubt that he was signing up for a minimum period". In the case of agreement 13, he felt that "the language is wholly consistent because the minimum membership period is defined". He added that, while in some of the earlier agreements it was not stated in terms that the member had no right to end the agreement during the minimum period, he felt this "self evident to the average consumer from the clearly expressed obligation to remain a member for the minimum period".

He accepted that there was no statement in cl.2 of the overall liability which is being incurred, but he said that that did not prevent the clause being clear or intelligible. Kitchin J. also agreed that there was no statement in cl.2 that the consequence of termination before the end of the minimum term may be an immediate liability for payments that would otherwise have been payable over the balance of the minimum term or for damages for loss of the bargain: "But this, it seems to me, is more a criticism of the fairness of the clause than its clarity or intelligibility". It may be felt that the approach in this case is a move away from the much broader view of "plain and intelligible" preferred by the Office of Fair Trading.

In the *Financial Services Authority* case, the services clause was held not to be plain and intelligible.[97] This was also the view of the court in relation to the representations clause which read thus:

> "The Buyer confirms that there are and have been no representations made by or on behalf of the Seller on the faith of which the Buyer is entering into this Agreement except and to the extent to which such representations are herein expressly set out or form part of written replies by the Solicitors for the Seller to the written Enquiries before Contract raised by the solicitors for the Buyer or the Seller's replies to Property Information Forms."

---

[97] See para.10–034.

Regulatory action

The Office of Fair Trading/Competition and Markets Authority

The OFT (now absorbed into the Competition and Markets Authority) took action as follows[98]:

10–046

Summary of changes to terms and conditions, associated documents and sales process

Bannatyne Fitness Limited

10–047

Extended provision for cancellation during the minimum term in the following circumstances:

- illness or injury which would preclude the consumer from using the gym for two months or more, and
- loss of employment (redundancy or otherwise).

Bannatyne's contract also provides for consumer cancellation during the minimum term when the company makes material changes or variations to the membership.

The notice period to cancel a contract with a 12-month minimum term has been reduced from three months to one-month before and after the expiry of the minimum term.

Bannatyne's has:

- clarified that it does not roll over minimum term contracts;
- improved its contract terms to clarify that the contract continues on a month-by-month basis after the expiry of the minimum term;
- committed to explaining this in the sales process.

Bannatyne's has committed to review its standard debt collection letters and not to use ones that the OFT considers misleading.

The OFT said that, in assessing fairness, it took note:

> "of how a term could be used. A term is open to challenge if it is drafted so widely that it could cause consumer detriment. It may be considered unfair if it could have an unfair effect, even if it is not at present being used unfairly in practice and there is no current intention to use it unfairly. In such cases fairness can generally be achieved by redrafting the term more precisely, so that it reflects the practice and current intentions of the supplier."[99]

---

[98] For the full undertakings (dated March 8, 2013) which involved other gym clubs, see *http://webarchive.nationalarchives.gov.uk/20140402142426/http://www.oft.gov.uk/shared_oft/ consumer-enforcement/gyms-table.pdf*.

[99] See *https://www.gov.uk/government/uploads/system/uploads/attachment_data/file/284426/ oft311.pdf*. See now Unfair contract terms: CMA guidance – OFT311; *https://www.gov.uk/ government/publications/unfair-contract-terms-guidance-2*.

The Financial Conduct Authority

10–048   The FCA took action as follows[100]:

BISL Ltd is a car and motorbike insurer that arranges and manages policies under several names that it owns and also for about a dozen other firms.

Why the terms were changed

10–049   BISL has agreed to change the cancellation terms in its policies. This is because we believe the original terms were confusing and unfair.

Our assessment is that the original terms did not explain clearly to customers who cancelled their policies early how BISL would calculate any refund of premium due to them. The contract terms allowed BISL to cancel a policy and either refund or keep the premium, depending on the circumstances, which needed to be explained more fully.

The contract changes

10–050   The new terms make it clear that:

- a customer cancelling a policy before the end of 12 months will be refunded on the basis of the number of days of cover remaining, provided no claim has been made;
- the company will charge a fixed cancellation fee, which will be set out in an 'Additional Important Information' document; and
- under certain circumstances BISL can cancel a policy—the new terms now include examples of these, including when the company can keep the premium.

The FCA has also published the following:

Unfair terms

10–051   Terms that:

- charge the consumer a large sum of money if they don't fulfil their obligations under the contract or cancel the contract (e.g. a consumer does not pay an insurance premium or mortgage repayment on time);
- tie a consumer into the contract, while letting the firm decide whether or not to provide the service;
- require the consumer to fulfil all their contractual obligations, while letting the firm avoid its own;
- automatically renew a fixed-length contract where the deadline for the customer opting not to extend is unreasonably short (e.g. these could apply to some renewable insurance contracts).

---

[100] Dated February 11, 2013. See *http://www.fca.org.uk/static/fca/documents/undertakings/fsa-undertaking-bisl.pdf.*

Other unfair terms:

- limit a firm's obligation to honour its agents' commitments to the consumer (e.g. whole agreement clauses);
- allow the firm to transfer its consumer obligations to a third party without the consumer's consent;
- mislead the consumer about the contract or their legal rights;
- exclude or limit the consumer's legal rights or remedies when the firm has failed to meet its obligations under the contract.[101]

Ofcom

Ofcom has published the following.[102]　　　　　　　　　　　　　　　　**10–052**
　　　Complainant: Ofcom own-initiative
　　　Investigation against: Communications providers offering fixed line telephony, mobile, broadband or Pay TV services to consumers
　　　Case opened: April 1, 2009
　　　Issue: Compliance with the Unfair Terms in Consumer Contracts Regulations 1999 in relation to Additional Charges, following Ofcom's publication of Guidance on what we consider to be the law in relation to such charges.
　　　Relevant instrument: Unfair Terms in Consumer Contracts Regulations 1999.

Update note—28 March 2013

Over the last six months under the Additional Charges Enforcement Programme　**10–053** (the Programme) we have continued our efforts in relation to ensuring consumer contract terms relating to Early Termination Charges (ETCs) in the communications sector are fair. Whilst complaints in the fixed voice and fixed plus broadband sector have fallen significantly since the Programme opened in September 2009, fairness of consumer contract terms in relation to Additional Charges is still an important area of Consumer Protection for Ofcom. We have therefore decided to extend the Programme for a further twelve months. In that time, we will continue to engage with relevant providers in the fixed voice and broadband sector where appropriate. In parallel, we will also be monitoring consumer complaints in relation to ETCs in all communications sectors and, along with consideration of other issues and developments in those sectors, this will help us to identify what our priorities should be under the Programme.

Words and pictures

Oral contracts and notices are within the Act and the above requirement as to　**10–054** plain and intelligible language is not expressed to be limited to written contracts or notices. This is made particularly plain by the provision that a notice, includes

---

[101] *http://www.fca.org.uk/firms/being-regulated/unfair-contracts/examples-unfair-terms.*
[102] *http://stakeholders.ofcom.org.uk/enforcement/competition-bulletins/open-cases/all-open-cases/ cw_01019.*

an announcement, whether or not in writing,[103] The problem will, of course, be one of proving that the particular verbal provision was expressed in the way the consumer maintains.

The Directive, and hence the Act, have overlooked the fact that goods may be defined or described pictorially as well as by a written statement. Unfairness cannot, therefore, extend to a representation of the goods to be supplied which, for example, creates uncertainty as to dimensions. It would be quite impossible to describe such a drawing as being "language" in any sense of the word.[104]

The relevant language

10–055 It is also to be noted that there is no requirement for the plain, intelligible language actually to be in English. This is to be contrasted with the express provisions of s.30(4) of the Act[105] which provide for a guarantee to be in plain, intelligible language and, where the product circulates in the United Kingdom, for that language to be English.[106] It may be that, in the context of the Act, the language will be taken to be English, yet this is by no means certain given the number of those in the country whose first language is not English.

Conformity with description

10–056 The impact of the exclusion of terms defining the main subject matter of the contract may well, however, be less severe than imagined. As is made clear by recital 19, the "definition" of the main subject matter is to be treated as coterminous with its description. That goods must conform to their description is set down in s.11 of the Act. It has been noted above that such requirement cannot be excluded or restricted by any provision.[107]

PRECEDENT ON UNFAIRNESS

10–057 It is accepted that the burden of proof lies on the party seeking to strike down the particular clause.[108] It would also appear to be the case that matters of fairness cannot be disposed of summarily since the court is required to take account of the nature of the goods or services for which the contract was concluded and to consider, as at the time of conclusion of the contract, all the circumstances

---

[103] Consumer Rights Act 2014 s.61(8).
[104] An offence could well arise, though, under the Consumer Protection from Unfair Trading Regulations 2008 (SI 2008/1277).
[105] Re-enacting in this context theprovisions of the Sale and Supply of Goods to Consumers Regulations 2002 (SI 2002/3045) which were repealed by the Act.
[106] The Regulations, and hence now the Act, are based on Directive 99/44/EC on sale of consumer goods and associated guarantees.
[107] See para.10–012.
[108] See, e.g. *Director General of Fair Trading v First National Bank Plc* [2000] 1 All E.R. 240 at 254, per Lombe-Evans J.

attending the conclusion of the contract and to all the other terms of the contract or of another contact on which it is dependent.[109]

Much the same message, that each case must depend on its own individual circumstances, emerges from *Tew v BoS (Shared Appreciation Mortgages (No.1)) Plc*.[110] The claimant borrowers sought to challenge the fairness of the terms of the mortgages under the Unfair Terms in Consumer Contracts Regulations. They had sought to obtain a group litigation order on the footing that it would be right for the court to determine, if it thought fit, that the criticised terms could be seen to be unfair by looking at the terms, their potential and actual effect, but excluding any consideration of the personal circumstances and qualifications of the borrowers or the actual circumstances of any of the loans. The claimants argued that their approach of excluding individuals' circumstances under the group litigation order would be an efficient and cheaper determination of their cases, and would allow them access to justice, which as individuals of often modest means they would otherwise be denied.

Mann J. said that fairness questions could best be tackled by taking lead cases. It was appropriate to do that within a group litigation order, which had some advantages in automatically binding all participants in relation to the genuinely common issues, and provided a useful umbrella for controlling other claims by means of stays. He said that:

> "even if it might be appropriate to try to get a determination of fairness, whether prima facie or not, without putting that question in a real factual transactional context, I have to consider the degree of likelihood of that turning out to be possible. It would be a positive disadvantage to this litigation to go through the exercise, make some findings of fact but to decide that the question of fairness cannot, after all, be decided at that stage. There would then have to be a significant hiatus while individual cases were prepared."

He also said that:

> "Fairness questions can best be tackled by taking lead cases... Sample cases can be taken which represent various parts of the spectrum. Technically speaking, the actual findings of unfairness in those cases will not bind other litigants."

Own initiative

Section 71(2) of the 2014 Act provides that national courts are not limited to a mere power to rule on the possible unfairness of a contractual term; they are also obliged to examine that issue of its own motion, where it has available to it the legal and factual elements necessary for that task, including when it is assessing whether it has territorial jurisdiction.   **10–058**

Such a provision was not contained in the 1999 Regulations, and, in so enacting, the 2014 Act was implementing the ruling in *Pannon GSM Zrt v Erzsébet Sustikné Győrfi*.[111] In December 2004, Erzsébet Sustikné Győrfi entered

---

[109] *Harrison v Shepherd Homes Ltd* [2010] EWHC 1398 (TCC).
[110] [2010] EWHC 203 (Ch).
[111] (C-243/08) [2009] E.C.R. I-4713. See also the ECJ rulings in *VB Pénzügyi Lízing* (C-137/08) [2010] E.C.R. 10847; *Erika Jőrös v Aegon Magyarország Hitel Zrt* (C-397/11) Unreported May 30, 2013.

into a subscription contract with Pannon for the provision of mobile telephone services. By signing the contract, Mrs Sustikné Győrfi also accepted the undertaking's general terms and conditions which stipulated that the Budaőrsi Városi Bíróság (Budaőrs District Court), the court for the place where Pannon had its principal place of business, had jurisdiction for any dispute arising from the subscription contract or in relation to it. Taking the view that Mrs Sustikné Győrfi had not complied with her contractual obligations, Pannon brought proceedings before the Budaőrsi Városi Bíróság which said that Mrs Sustikné Győrfi, who was in receipt of an invalidity allowance, had her place of permanent residence in Dombegyház, that is to say, 275 km from Budaőrs, with limited means of transport between those two places. The Hungarian court also noted that under the applicable rules of the Hungarian Code of Civil Procedure, in the absence of a term conferring jurisdiction in the subscription contract, the court with territorial jurisdiction would be that for the place where the subscriber resides.

In those circumstances, the Budaőrsi Városi Bíróság, having doubts as to the possible unfairness of the term conferring jurisdiction in the subscription contract, referred questions on the interpretation of the Directive to the ECJ, seeking a determination, inter alia, to whether it must, of its own motion, ascertain whether that term was unfair, in the context of verifying its own territorial jurisdiction. The Court ruled that the Directive on Unfair Terms in Consumer Contracts[112] provides that unfair terms used in a contract concluded with a consumer by a seller or supplier are not binding on consumers.

The Court ruled that the protection which the Directive conferred on consumers extended to cases in which a consumer who has concluded with a seller or supplier a contract containing an unfair term fails to raise the unfairness of the term, whether because he is unaware of his rights or because he is deterred from enforcing them on account of the costs which judicial proceedings would involve. The Court went on to say that:

> "Consequently, the role thus attributed to the national court by Community law in this area is not limited to a mere power to rule on the possible unfairness of a contractual term, but also consists of the obligation to examine that issue of its own motion, where it has available to it the legal and factual elements necessary for that task, including when it is assessing whether it has territorial jurisdiction."

The Court further ruled that, where the national court does consider such a clause to be unfair, it must not apply it, unless the consumer, after having been informed of it by the court, does not intend to assert its unfairness and non-binding status. Though this part of the ruling is not repeated in the Act, presumably a UK court would adopt this approach.

---

[112] Council Directive 93/13/EEC 1993 OJ L95/29 on unfair terms in consumer contracts.

Clauses held fair

(1) In *Broadwater Manor School v Davis*,[113] BMS brought an action for payment **10–059** of unpaid school fees under a standard term contract which included a provision that parents must give a term's written notice when cancelling acceptance of a place, failing which a term's fees were payable. A "term" was expressed to mean each of the three terms in a school year. The parent gave notice of cancellation by a letter received on June 8 concerning a place booked for September. The summer term began on April 21 and ended July 2, with the Autumn term due to start on September 2. BMS claimed that the notice was six to seven weeks too late. The court held that the term was not unfair. The economic rationale behind the notice period in a contract for education was not of itself unreasonable or unfair. Such a clause was common. Schools had to prepare in advance for their pupils, and they had to be able to contract to protect their legitimate interests in serving their -changing body of pupils in the best way possible and to fill the required number of places in good time to plan adequately and meet their costs.

(2) In *Gosling v Burrard-Lucas*,[114] G brought an action against B for recovery of a debt under a form of undertaking. The school required parents of prospective pupils to sign a standard form of undertaking when accepting the offer of a place. Parents undertook to pay a term's fees in the event that the child did not later take up the place. The court held that this clause was a long way from being unfair. The school was entirely dependent on fee income and the particular clause was designed to ensure financial planning could be done with some degree of certainty. There was no inequality of bargaining power: if anything, the fierce competition for pupils in the area meant that the parent was in the better position. There was no inducement for the parent to sign the undertaking, and prospective parents were told to postpone signing until they were certain that they could commit themselves. The school had at all times dealt fairly and equitably with the parent and the undertaking contained no attempt to limit the school's liability in the event of breach.

(3) In *Director General of Fair Trading v First National Bank Plc*,[115] the Director General of Fair Trading sought an injunction against the continued use of this clause:

> "Time is of the essence of making all repayments to First National Bank (the Bank) as they fall due. If any repayment instalment is unpaid for more than seven days after it became due, FNB may serve a notice on the customer requiring payment before a specified date not less than seven days later. If the repayment instalment is not paid in full by that date, FNB will be entitled to demand payment of the balance on the customer's account and interest then outstanding together with all reasonable and legal costs charges and expenses claimed or incurred by FNB in trying to obtain repayment of the unpaid instalment or of such balance and interest. Interest on the amount which becomes payable shall be charged in accordance with condition 3, at the rate stated in paragraph D overleaf (subject to variation) until payment after as well as before any judgment (such obligation to be independent of and not to merge with any judgment)."

---

[113] Unreported January 8, 1999 (Worthing CC).
[114] Unreported November 4, 1998 (Tunbridge Wells CC).
[115] [2000] 1 All E.R. 240; [2000] 2 All E.R. 759 CA; [2002] 1 All E.R. 97 HL.

The Director General's complaint was as to the operation of the clause once a court had extended time for repayment of the amount lent by making an instalment order. It was common ground that the effect of the clause was to make interest payable, at the contractual rate on the amount of principal advanced, together with the accrued unpaid interest existing at the date of judgment, during the period after judgment until discharge by payment.

The Director General maintained that the provisions of the disputed clause were unlikely to be noticed by the average consumer. The latter, who would have consented to judgment for the balance due payable by instalments, would be surprised, the argument ran, to find that, when he had discharged all the instalments due under the judgment, there still remained a substantial bill for interest, not least because, during the extended period for repayment, interest at the contract rate remained chargeable. The harsh effects of this clause could be considerably mitigated were the court to reduce the rate of interest, even to nil, under the terms of the Consumer Credit Act 1974. In practice, this appeared to happen rarely. In most cases, the borrower would consent to an instalment order which would be accepted by the lender, the court automatically making an order without any consideration of the terms of the agreement. A borrower would generally be unaware of the provisions of the disputed term, notwithstanding the practice of the bank in this case to draw attention to the clause in its claim forms and the presence in the "notes for defendants on replying to a claim form" of a sentence indicating that a claimant might be entitled to relief against further interest. While the only method of enforcing payment of interest after judgment was by county court action, where the provisions of the 1974 Act as to amending the agreement would apply, this again in practice did not happen. The borrower usually paid or the lender waived the further interest in whole or in part. The Director General submitted in the present case that the disputed clause operated in such a way in practice as to cause uncertainty and confusion among judgment debtors.[116]

10–060 The House of Lords upheld the clause, thus reversing the Court of Appeal and reinstating the judgment of the High Court. Lord Bingham pointed to the nature of the contract as making funds available to the consumer, to be repaid over time with interest. The borrower's obligations in this regard were clearly set out in the contract: "There is nothing unbalanced or detrimental to the consumer in that obligation; the absence of such a term would unbalance the contract to the detriment of the lender".[117] The question thus arose as to whether the provisions of the 1991 Order made the term unfair.[118] Lord Bingham was influenced by the fact that the Consumer Credit Act 1974, while laying down a number of terms with which agreements were to comply, did not prohibit terms which provided for post-judgment interest, even though claims to enforce agreements were to be

---

[116] Under the Consumer Credit Act 1974, as amended by the Consumer Credit Act 2006, the creditor or owner must now provide the customer with written notice of his intention to recover post-judgment interest.

[117] [2002] 1 All E.R. 97 at 108–109.

[118] This being a reference to the County Courts (Interest on Judgment Debts) Order 1991 (SI 1991/1184).

brought in the county courts which could not award statutory interest.[119] He also regarded it as "pertinent" that judgments based on consumer credit agreements appeared to have been excluded from the scope of the county court's power in response to observations made in *Forward Trust Ltd v Whymark*,[120] but that was a case based on a flat rate agreement, in which the judgment in default would include a sum for future interest not yet accrued, in contrast to a simple rate agreement of the kind in the instant contract:

"the logic underpinning exclusion of statutory interest in the one case would not apply, at any rate with the same force, in the other. It is understandable that when a court is exercising a statutory power to order payment by instalments it should not also be empowered to order payment of statutory interest if the instalments are duly paid, but the term is directed to the recovery of contractual and not statutory interest. I do not think that the term can be stigmatised as unfair on the ground that it violates or undermines a statutory regime enacted for the protection of consumers."[121]

Lord Bingham also pointed to the provisions of the 1974 Act which provided for a borrower's obligations to be re-drawn.[122] Problems had arisen in practice because borrowers were unaware of the provisions of the Act and because the default notices given to borrowers, and the county court forms, did not draw their attention to the rights under the Act.[123] He concluded that these procedural difficulties did not mean that the term itself was unfair. He pointed out that the Regulations were directed to the unfairness of a term, not the use which a supplier may make of a term which is in itself fair.[124] Lord Steyn also pointed out that the difficulty in the way of arguing that the term was unfair was that the disadvantage to the consumer arose, not from the term itself, but because of the 1991 Order. The term could not be said to be unfair "where the legislature has neither expressly nor by necessary implication barred a stipulation that interest may continue to accrue after judgment until payment in full".[125] According to Lord Millett:

"no lawyer advising a commercial borrower would dream of objecting to the inclusion of such a term, which merely reinforces and carries into effect what the parties themselves would regard as the essence of the transaction... this unfairness does not arise from any inherent unfairness of the term. It is due to the limited nature of the judgment and the fact that it does not cover the whole of the borrower's indebtedness to the lender."[126]

(4) In *Bankers Insurance Co Ltd v South*,[127] the judge considered that the following clause would have been fair but he was not required to make any finding because the relevant terms was a core provision expressed in plain, intelligible language:

---

[119] See in this context the provisions of the Act referred to at fn.118.
[120] [1989] 3 All E.R. 915 at 921, per Lord Donaldson M.R.
[121] [2002] 1 All E.R. 97 at 109.
[122] See *Southern & District Finance Plc v Barnes* [1995] C.C.L.R. 62.
[123] See now the provisions referred to at fn.118.
[124] [2002] 1 All E.R. 97 at 110.
[125] [2002] 1 All E.R. 97 at 114.
[126] [2002] 1 All E.R. 97 at 118–119. See also Lord Rodger at 121.
[127] [2003] EWHC 380 (QB).

"Personal Liability. For each Person-Insured we will pay for the following Events Insured. Up to ... including costs agreed between us in writing for which you are legally liable to pay, if they relate to an event caused by you which results in (A) injury ... of any person ... For each person-Insured we will not pay for ... Compensation or other costs arising from accidents involving your ownership or possession of any ... Mechanically propelled vehicles and any trailers attached thereto, aircraft, motorised waterborne craft or sailing vessels or windsurfing."

(5) In *Bank of Scotland v Singh*,[128] the court gave consideration to whether a contract of guarantee provided by a director to secure the company's debt was unfair. In deciding that the term was not unfair, the judge noted that, although it was unlimited, the defendant had complete control of the debtor company and could prevent the overdraft from exceeding the permitted £900,000. It was also the case that the overdraft agreement allowed the company to go beyond that limit. In a letter headed "Working Capital", the claimants had stated that the loan was not to be used to fund trading losses. The letter, on the basis of which the credit had been extended, required the debtor company to use its "best endeavours" to ensure that trading losses were met by the guarantor. Given that the relevant management team of the company was in fact the guarantor, who thus had to use his best endeavours to ensure that trading losses were met by himself as an individual, the relevant terms of the guarantee could not be said to generate any significant imbalance.

10–061 As for the contractual provision ruling out a set-off, reference was made to the indicative list of unfair terms contained in the Regulations, which regards as presumptively unfair a clause which limits or excludes a consumer's rights against the supplier in the event of total or partial non-performance by the supplier of any of its contractual obligations, "including the option of offsetting a debt" owed to the supplier against any claim which the consumer might have against him.[129] The problem with applying this provision, the court said, was that, if the bank could be assumed to be the supplier (which in fact was the defendant as provider of the guarantee) the bank still had no obligations under the term of the guarantee, there was nothing it could fail to perform under the guarantee. The court noted as the "most important factor" the fact that the defendant had had legal advice. He had received advice from his solicitor and signed the guarantee at his solicitor's office. The court thus held that it was not unfair for a lender to protect itself against the risk of set-off by a guarantor of a claim which, if viable, might be primarily a claim by the principal borrower and only a "reflective loss" claim in the hands of a guarantor who no longer controlled the principal debtor.

(6) In *Bond v British Telecommunications Plc*,[130] the applicant applied for summary judgment (in respect of a claim brought against it by the respondent). The respondent's claim was brought in respect of a £4.50 charge levied upon her by BT because she had elected not to pay her telephone bills by direct debit. She alleged that the company was profiteering and that the charge was likely to lead to a secret profit. The court said that, while that could well be a factor in

---

[128] Unreported June 17, 2005. This case was dissented from in *Barclays Bank Plc v Alfons Kufner* [2008] EWHC 2319 (Comm) but not on a point relevant here.
[129] Unfair Terms in Consumer Contracts Regulations 1999 (SI 1999/2083) Sch.2 para.1(b). See now Sch.2 Pt 1 para.2 of the Consumer Rights Act 2014.
[130] Unreported March 28, 2008 (Walsall CC).

unfairness, there was no legal requirement for a company to justify such a charge in strict cost terms. Even if it did make a secret profit, that would not make the charge unlawful. To be unfair, a term had to be contrary to the requirement of good faith, had to cause a significant imbalance in the parties' rights and obligations arising under the contract and had to be detrimental to the customer. In the instant case, the court said that there was no bad faith: BT had notified the respondent of the charge and she could have chosen to terminate her agreement without penalty. There was no significant imbalance in the parties' rights and, given that the respondent had had notice of the charge and could have terminated the contract without penalty, she had suffered no detriment.

(7) In *Heifer International Inc v Helge Christiansen*,[131] the applicants applied to stay the proceedings pursuant to the Arbitration Act 1996. One of the applicants was a Danish architect and another was his firm, a Danish legal entity. The respondent was a British Virgin Islands company owned by the family of a Russian who lived in England. The latter had decided that the architect would be engaged to refurbish a house in Surrey owned by the respondent. The remaining applicants were Danish sub-contractors who had carried out work on the property. The respondent had given the architect a power of attorney to enter into contracts with craftsmen and to authorise payments to them. On the basis that the work remained incomplete, the respondent claimed an account of moneys paid to the architects and the contractors and claimed damages for defects in the works and the design of the works. The architect claimed that he did not enter into any agreements personally. The other applicants claimed that they had carried out work pursuant to binding contracts which contained an arbitration clause referring disputes to Danish arbitration. The respondent contended, inter alia, that the arbitration provisions relied on by the applicants were unfair terms and were not binding.

It was held that, with respect to the agreement with the Danish firm, it was the respondent's Danish lawyers who prepared the agreement. The respondent was not prevented by the architect from being properly and effectively advised by its English lawyers. The respondent had granted the architect a power of attorney to enter into agreements with skilled Danish workmen for them to work on the project. The arbitration clause was not unfair either in respect of the Danish firm or the workmen. The Russian had chosen to have his house renovated by Danish workmen and a Danish architect. It was not inherently unfair that if something went wrong the dispute should be determined in the domicile of the Danish entities.

(8) In *UK Housing Alliance (North West) Ltd v Francis*,[132] the appellant appealed against a decision that the respondent was not required to pay him the sum of £37,500. The appellant had sold his house for £125,000 to the respondent, whose business it was to buy residential properties and then lease them back to their former owners. The sum of £87,500 was payable on completion, while the balance of £37,500 (the final payment) was due on the expiry of 10 years and the giving up of possession by the appellant. If the appellant terminated his tenancy at any time during the first six years, the final payment would not become

---

[131] [2007] EWHC 3015 (TCC).
[132] [2010] EWCA Civ 117.

payable. If he terminated it thereafter, he would receive a percentage of the final payment on a sliding scale depending on the date of termination. If, however, the respondent terminated the tenancy pursuant to any right to do so under the tenancy agreement, the sale contract provided that the appellant would cease to have any right to receive the final payment. The respondent terminated the tenancy for non-payment of rent.

10–062   The court held that for the purposes of the Regulations, it was necessary to consider whether the impugned provision caused or created a significant imbalance in the parties' rights and obligations to the appellant's detriment in a manner or to an extent which was contrary to the requirements of good faith. Having regard to the contract as a whole, the Court of Appeal stated that it could not be said that the retention of the final payment, on the grant of a court order for possession, created a significant imbalance. It was possible to conceive of circumstances where it might, especially if the original contract price was below the market price and the rental market (or perhaps the sale market) was buoyant at the time of the possession. The matter had, however, to be judged at the time when the contract was made and it would be equally possible to envisage a stagnant market in which the landlord would find it difficult to relet the property or even to resell it. In those circumstances, the retention of what was less than a third of the price did not cause any imbalance, let alone a significant one. Furthermore, the agreement that the respondent could retain the final payment was not contrary to the concept of good faith. It could not be suggested that the term was not fully, clearly and legibly expressed or was not given appropriate prominence. No doubt the appellant had been short of money when he made the contract for the sale and leaseback of the property, but it could not be said that he had been "taken advantage of" unfairly. The very nature of the transaction necessitated that he instructed a solicitor, which he did. He also had the protection of the court if and when a possession order was sought by the respondent. In the circumstances, there had been no failure to conform with "good standards of commercial morality and practice".

(9) In *Du Plessis v Fontgary Leisure Parks Ltd*,[133] the claimant had purchased a caravan which stood on a pitch on the defendant's site and she entered into a licence agreement with the defendant. The agreement provided that it complied with the Code of Practice for Selling and Siting Holiday Caravans, as issued by the British Holiday and Home Parks Association and the National Caravan Council. Under cl.7 the agreement stated that the defendant was entitled to review the pitch fee and that, provided at least 51 per cent of the caravan owners affected by an increase in the fee objected, it could proceed to arbitration. Under cl.7(d) the fee would be reviewed having regard to certain factors, including charges paid to third parties, changes in staff wages, changes in the length of the season and, finally, "any other relevant factor". The agreement also provided that the defendant could terminate it if the claimant was in serious breach of contract.

All caravan owners had been charged the same pitch fee although some had pitches in more desirable locations. Approximately one year after the claimant signed the agreement, on professional advice, the defendant informed all caravan

---

[133] [2012] EWCA Civ 409.

owners that it would be grading the pitches and charging different amounts accordingly but that if owners wished to move to a lower grade, and therefore a cheaper pitch, it would move their caravans at its own expense. Following the grading, the claimant was required to pay a higher fee. However, she refused to do so and the defendant served a notice terminating the agreement. The claimant suffered a substantial loss and attributed it to breaches of contract by the defendant.

Upholding the clause, the court ruled that it was part of a carefully balanced review procedure and in reviewing the fee the defendant could only take into account factors which were relevant to that exercise. Further, any individual caravan owner could challenge the legality of an increase in court. Nor did the clause fall within the relevant provisions of Sch.2 of the Regulations which listed terms which might be regarded as unfair. The claimant had referred to paras 1(i), (j), (k) or (l),. The court had said that, as to para.1(i) the claimant had a proper opportunity to become acquainted with the terms of the licence agreement before she entered into it. As to para.1(j) of Sch.2, cl.7 did not enable the defendant to alter the terms of the licence agreement unilaterally without a valid reason which was specified in the contract. As to para.1(k) of Sch.2, the defendant did not alter the characteristics of the service which it provided. As to para.1(l) of Sch.2, the licence agreement gave the claimant the right to terminate if she found the pitch fee to be unacceptable.

The court went on to say that the introduction of grading was also carried out in a fair manner. It duly ruled that, when tested against the criteria in the Regulations, cl.7 was a fair term. It further noted that there was good sense in permitting arbitration only if it was required by a substantial body of caravan owners. It would not be practicable to administer the leisure park if pitch fees were negotiated or determined on an individual basis. It would not make sense for the pitch fees for different caravans to be the subject of a series of arbitrations. Further, the caravan owners had the right to challenge in court any fee increases which went beyond the constraints of cl.7. This meant that the arbitration provisions of the agreement were fair within the meaning of the Regulations.

(10) In *Parker and Parker v National Farmers Union Mutual Insurance Society Ltd*,[134] it was held that a general condition in a property and contents insurance policy which required the policyholder to provide all the written details and documents asked for by the insurer if anything happened which might result in a claim was not unfair. The insurer's rejection of a claim on the grounds of breach of that condition was not in the circumstances unreasonable under the Insurance Conduct of Business Sourcebook.[135]

(11) In *IG Index Plc v James Colley*,[136] a spread-betting contract contained this term:　　　　　　　　　　　　　　　　　　　　　　　　　　　　**10–063**

> "(1) We reserve the right to void without your consent from the outset or to amend the terms of any Bet containing or based upon a manifest error. If, in our discretion, we choose to amend the terms of any such Manifestly Erroneous Transaction, the amended level will be such level

---

[134] [2012] EWHC 2156.

[135] This being a reference to the Financial Conduct Authority Handbook: *http://www.fshandbook.info/ FS/html/FCA/COBS*.

[136] [2013] EWHC 478.

as we reasonably believe would have been fair at the time the Transaction was entered into. A "Manifest Error" is any error that we believe to be obvious or palpable. In deciding whether an error is a Manifest Error we may take into account any relevant information including without limitation the state of the Underlying Market at the time of the error. Or any mistake in a lack of clarity of, any information source or pronouncement upon which we base our quoted prices. In making such a decision we will act in our sole discretion, reasonably and in good faith. Any financial commitment that you have entered into or refrained from entering into in reliance on a Bet with us will not be taken into account in deciding whether or not there has been a Manifest Error. (2) In the absence of wilful default or fraud we shall not be liable to you for any loss, cost, claim demand, or expense following a Manifest Error. In the event that a manifest error is made by any information source, commentator or official upon whom we reasonably rely we shall not, in the absence of wilful default or fraud, be liable to you for any loss, cost, claim, demand or expense. Following a Manifest Error we may decide to void the Bet, or, at your request, we may agree to amend the terms of the bet to what we believe would have been fair and reasonable at the time it was entered."

The court considered this fair because it served a legitimate commercial function and contained important limitations.

(12) In *Deutsche Bank (Suisse) SA v Khan*,[137] a number of clauses were in dispute:

(1)   Clause 9(c)(ii) which purported to prohibit a set-off.

This was held fair. It fulfilled a legitimate commercial function and contained important limitations.

(2)   Clause 9(d) which provided for an allegedly penal rate of interest on default. It provided for a rate of 3 per cent above the bank's costs of funding the relevant amount.

(3)   Clause 12 which referred to the conditions precedent at Appendix 3. In more detail, this clause stated:

"The obligation of the Bank to make the Facility available hereunder is subject to the condition that prior to the date on which any Tranche of the Facility is to be drawn the Bank shall have received in form and substance satisfactory to it the documents listed in Appendix 3".

The document relevant in this case was listed under para.2 of Appendix 3:

"A report on or valuation of each Property addressed to the Bank and signed by a chartered surveyor acceptable to the Bank and expressed to be for mortgage purposes".

(4)   Clause 15 which dealt with valuations of the Properties and maintaining a certain loan to value ratio fixed at 75 per cent.

In these further cases, the court also held that the terms were fair. They were commonplace. The defendants had legal advice and other sources of finance. For good measure, the court also held that the terms were reasonable under the Unfair Contract Terms Act, though that Act did not apply because of a choice of law clause.

---

[137] [2013] EWHC 482.

(13) In *West and West v Ian Finlay & Associates*,[138] a clause in an architect's contract ran: W and F had entered into an agreement in respect of renovation and improvement works to W's house. The contract included a net contribution clause (NCC) limiting F's liability. The NCC stated that F's "liability for loss or damage" was to be limited to the amount that it was reasonable for it to pay having regard to "the contractual responsibilities of other consultants, contractors and specialists appointed by [W]". F appointed a main contractor (X) and W engaged specialist contractors at various stages. The work took 11 months and W moved back into the property when it was completed. However, extensive damp was discovered which required considerable remedial works. X were subsequently wound up. W brought a claim against F for damages.

The judge held that F had breached its professional duties. He found that the losses were caused to some extent by X's breach of contract, but held that the NCC did not limit F's liability to W where the other party liable was the main contractor. F submitted that the judge should have found that the NCC limited its liability when any other contractor, including X, was responsible. W argued that, even if the judge were wrong, the NCC could not operate to exclude the principle of joint and several liability and, alternatively, that it was contrary to the requirements of good faith under the Unfair Terms in Consumer Contracts Regulations 1999. The Court of Appeal held that the judge had erred in his construction of the NCC. He had held that the parties' knowledge that W would instruct a number of specialist contractors directly meant that they should be taken to have intended the words referring to the persons to be "appointed by [W]" to refer only to those persons appointed directly by W, and not to the main contractor appointed through F's agency. In the instant case, the normal meaning of the words was clear. There was no limitation on the words "other consultants, contractors and specialists appointed by [W]", and they had to be taken to mean any such persons, including any main contractor ultimately appointed, excepting F. The NCC was not therefore ambiguous. It had a clear meaning and the relevant factual matrix did not lead to the conclusion that the parties should be taken to have used the wrong language to express their agreement.

It was further held that the NCC did grant F a beneficial limitation of liability and imposed a corresponding disadvantage on W. It also imposed a disadvantageous risk on W, namely the risk of the insolvency of the contractors. It also forced W to bring proceedings against any defaulting contractor who might be jointly and severally liable with F, and to await the outcome of any contribution proceedings before obtaining full satisfaction. Contrary to F's submissions, it was the NCC which created the imbalance in the parties' rights under the contract, to W's detriment, as it reduced F's liability in the event of it being jointly and severally liable with a contractor. F's failure to draw W's attention to the NCC and its effect, and the particular formulation of the clause, were factors that weighed in the balance against a finding that its inclusion satisfied the requirements of good faith. However, the openness of the presentation of the clause, F's fair dealing in relation to it and the reasonable equality of bargaining power weighed in favour of a finding that its inclusion satisfied the requirement of good faith. Weighing those factors, the imbalance caused by the NCC was not

---

[138] [2013] EWHC 868 (TCC); [2014] EWCA Civ 316.

significant and the NCC was not properly to be regarded as so weighted as to tilt the parties' rights and obligations under the contract significantly in F's favour, or as contrary to the requirement of good faith.[139]

Clauses held unfair

10–064 (1) In the Leeds County Court, the Regulations relieved former clients of an estate agency from liability to pay an excessive cancellation fee if the property was taken off the market. In the case of one version of the agents' standard form contract, it is understood that the cancellation fee would have exceeded the contractual commission payable had the property been sold.[140]

(2) In *Murphy v Kindlance*,[141] a consumer ceased his payments on a home improvement loan when the lender advanced him only £41,000. The lender demanded a redemption penalty of £73,000 and threatened to repossess the premises. The court said that the Rule of 78 used by the lenders to calculate the redemption sum was unfair. This rule adds up the total number of months in the year, based on 12 + 11 + 10 and so on, giving a total of 78. The number of months remaining in the agreement is worked out in like manner, and the remaining months over 78 gives the redemption penalty. Kindlance agreed to a settlement figure of £56,000.

(3) In *Falco Finance Ltd v Gough*,[142] a loan agreement stated that:

> "Providing instalments are made on their due date, you may deduct a discount of £125. We will thus accept the reduced instalment of £324.75 in lieu of the contractual instalment of £449.75."

The judge said that this was very harsh and meant that even if one payment, or a tiny part of one payment, was late, then for the next 25 years the borrower had to pay the higher rate. He added that a dual rate was lawful where it bore a relationship to the actual extra costs to the lender:

> "Where however the lower and higher rates bear no resemblance to the costs incurred on account of a borrower breaching his or her obligations, then it seems to me that on the face of it the added payment is either a penalty or a profit."

It was found that, if the borrower paid under the higher rate, which was 13.99 per cent, he would pay £104,925 in interest over the period of the loan. If the mortgage were calculated on the normal lenders' basis, then the total interest would have been just over £79,000. The difference resulted from a flat rate calculation basis for interest and a reducing basis. When the effective rate of interest was worked out on both bases, at the start the rates would be the same, but, by month 150, the rate would be 17.86 per cent and by month 250, when the

---

[139] It was also held that the clause was reasonable under the Unfair Contract Terms Act. The High Court had also fund the term fair under the 1999 Regulations.
[140] Consumer Law Today, November 1996.
[141] Consumer Law Today, November 1996.
[142] (1999) 17 Tr. L.R. 526; [1999] C.C.L.R. 16 CC (Macclesfield).

capital balance would have been about £5,100, the rate would have been 52.88 per cent and by the last month 2,697 per cent. The judge said:

> "The defendant throughout this mortgage, if it ran for 25 years, would be paying interest on vast sums of money which have already been paid. It seems to me as a precept of commonsense, looked at through the eyes of the ordinary layman, that it is almost the same as paying interest on money that was never borrowed at all."

The judge also referred to the principle that there should be "no clog on the equity **10–065** of redemption", meaning that everyone should be entitled to repay and clear a mortgage debt without unreasonable obstruction. A significant imbalance in the parties' respective positions was created contrary to the requirement of good faith, and a £5,200 redemption payment would have been a wholly unfair sum for the lender to have gained. The judge also pointed to the indicative list of unfair terms, and to the reference to "terms which have the object or effect of requiring any consumer who fails to fulfil his obligation to pay a disproportionately high sum in compensation".[143] It was held that the dual rate of interest was an unfair contract term.

(4) In *Bankers Insurance Co Ltd v South*,[144] the terms of an insurance policy required the "reporting in writing to us as soon as is reasonably possible, full details of any incidents which may result in a claim under the policy"; and also "forwarding to us immediately upon receipt, every writ, summons, legal process or other communication in connection with the claim". The judge noted that non-compliance by the insured could: "hopelessly prejudice the insurer's right of subrogation and chance of recovery from another party. Further, it is not asking a great deal of an insured to pass on information which he has or receives, to the insurer, at least within a reasonable time".

Such considerations alone would mean that there was no significant imbalance contrary to the interests of the consumer. Having said that, though, the judge then said that these clauses could deprive the consumer of the benefit he had bargained for, or provide the insurer with a bonus just because of a procedural shortcoming on the part of the consumer which did not prejudice the insurer. A breach by the consumer might not prejudice the insurer, even if notification by the consumer were very late. The judge thought that such circumstances could be contemplated, were not fanciful, and hence that the terms were unfair.

(5) In *Bairstow Eves London Central Ltd v Smith*,[145] an estate agency contract contained a term requiring commission of 1.5 per cent to be paid within 10 days of completion, failing which commission of 3 per cent would become payable, plus interest. The county court judge had ruled the provision as to the payment of 3 per cent commission was unfair:

> "The clause is a trap for consumers. It can operate where there is simply a misunderstanding between them and their solicitors, perhaps not even their fault, as indeed it was not their fault here. It can operate where, as here, the option was exercised effectively when just £387 [out of a commission of £2,925.75] was outstanding ... this is not a good standard of commercial

---

[143] Unfair Terms in Consumer Contracts Regulations 1999 (SI 1999/2083) Sch.2 para.1(e), now Sch.2 Pt 1 para.5 of the Consumer Rights Act 2014.
[144] [2003] EWHC 380 (QB).
[145] [2004] EWHC 263 (QB).

morality or practice ... it falls comfortably within the Regulations, and it follows that the provisions of the marketing agreement which require a 3% commission to be paid are not binding on the consumer."

The matter went on appeal, but there was no appeal against these particular findings.

10–066 (6) In *Office of Fair Trading v MB Designs (Scotland) Ltd*,[146] the contract related to the supply and fitting on behalf of consumers of windows, doors and conservatories. The relevant clause provided as follows:

> "The Customer should ensure that any representation or promise made before or at the time of signature to the contract not included in the printed form of the contract is added in writing to the face of the contract and signed by the Customer and the Company or its agent. In this way there will be no doubt as to the terms of the representation or promise. Any such statement not in written form must be agreed by the surveyor in writing."

The term was obscurely located; contained in the middle of detailed contractual provisions in small print which extended over one or two pages, and there was nothing to mark it out as a particularly important term. The court said that this was:

> "significant, because a term of this nature is of a different order from ordinary contractual terms. It is not a substantive term, but is designed to regulate the manner in which the contract is concluded. In particular, it regulates how alterations may be made to the substantive terms to meet the requirements of a particular contract. As such, it should in my opinion be placed in a prominent position, so that the customer who signs the contract is aware of what he must do to effect any necessary alterations to the printed form."

It was argued that this clause was unfair in that it had the potential for abuse. Such abuse was said to arise where pre-contractual representations were made by a representative of the first respondent to induce a prospective customer to enter into a contract. Pre-contractual representations of that nature might be inconsistent with or not reflected in the written contract terms. It was likely that unsophisticated consumers might reasonably rely on such representations or other verbal assurances in deciding whether to enter into the contract in question. Such consumers did not always or necessarily consider whether any written terms might apply, and might not be aware of the existence or effect of a term such as this particular one. It was in particular argued that such consumers might not be aware that such a term might displace all of the pre-contract representations made by representatives of the respondent; such consumers do not generally examine the written terms closely. It was further submitted that, even if such customers of the respondent were aware that there might be written contractual terms, or had such terms presented to them, good faith demands that the customers should be able to rely on representations or assurances made by sales personnel as inconsistent with any written contractual terms, and that such customers should not be obliged to draft additional contract wording to record any representations that may be made. The clause was ruled to be unfair.

---

[146] [2005] CSOH 85.

(7) *In Scheps v Fine Art Logistic Ltd*,[147] the claimant sought damages from the defendant in respect of the loss of a sculpture. The claimant had purchased the sculpture while it was being stored by an auction house. He had engaged the defendant to collect the sculpture and store it before it was taken to the artist's studio for some restoration work. When required, the sculpture could not be found in any of the defendant's storage units. The latter's view was that it had by accident been destroyed. He maintained that the agreement between the parties incorporated his standard terms and conditions which limited liability for the loss of the sculpture to £350 per cubic metre of its volume. He submitted that it was usual in the transport and storage trade for services to be provided on standard terms and conditions that limited liability and that the claimant must have been aware of that as a result of his considerable experience of arranging for the transport of works of art. The court said that it would be fair and reasonable under the Regulations for a company engaged in the business of fine art storage and transport to limit its liability to a fixed sum per weight or volume if the limit was clearly brought to the attention of the customer, but in the instant case the defendant had taken no steps to bring the limit to the claimant's attention and it would not have been fair and reasonable for the defendant to rely on the limit.

(8) In *Governors of the Peabody Trust Ltd v Reeve*,[148] the claimant social landlord claimed that it was entitled to exercise unilateral variations to its tenancy agreements in accordance with the procedure under the Housing Act 1985 s.103. Clause 5 of the tenancy agreements contained two subclauses; the first prevented the claimant from altering the terms of the tenancy, save in regards of rent, unless both the tenant and claimant agreed in writing; the second provided a mechanism whereby the claimant could change the provisions of its tenancies by serving a notice of variation under s.103. The court was asked to determine whether, on its true construction, cl.5 gave the claimant the ability to effect unilateral variations in the terms of its tenancy agreement using the s.103 procedure, and if he did have such a right, whether the clause was not binding by virtue of the Regulations. The claimant argued that cl.5 had to be interpreted to take into account the fact that with such a large number of properties and tenants under its control it needed to have a unilateral method of varying tenancy agreements, otherwise its housing stock would become impossible to manage; and that the ability to unilaterally vary the terms of the tenancy agreement was fair.

It was held that, although it was true that a unilateral variation would be useful to the landlord, and would avoid a risk of its housing stock becoming unmanageable, it was nevertheless a risk that the legislature had chosen to allow registered social landlords to run on the basis that they would be able to manage without such powers. As there was doubt as to the meaning of cl.5 as a whole, and, in the light of the contradictory nature of the subclauses, as to the meaning of the subclauses, the court was obliged by reg.7(2) of the Regulations to adopt the interpretation most favourable to the tenant.[149] Accordingly, there could be no variation of the tenancy agreement without the agreement, in writing, of both parties. The court went on to say that, if that were wrong, it was necessary to

10–067

---

[147] [2007] EWHC 541 (QB).
[148] [2008] 23 E.G. 116 (C.S.).
[149] Now s.69 Consumer Rights Act 2014. See further para.10–077.

consider the fairness of a unilateral variation clause. The landlord had incorporated two entirely contradictory clauses into the tenancy agreement and had then attempted to rely on one of them to enforce a power of unilateral variation; such actions, the court said, were contrary to any concept of fair and open dealing. The tenancy agreements already made ample provision for future events; there was no reason to suggest that the landlord would be left in an impossible position without a sweeping variation clause. To satisfy the requirements of the Regulations, any such unilateral variation clause would need at a minimum to take full and proper account of the commonsense guidelines set out by the Office of Fair Trading for tenancy agreements.[150]

(9) In *Chesterton Global Ltd v Finney*,[151] the claimant, a provider of property management services, sought payment of renewal commission under the terms of a contract it had made with the defendant landlord. The latter counterclaimed for payment of renewal commission that it had previously paid the claimant. He stated that he had bought the property to lease it, with the hope that he would profit on the capital and that the rent would pay the mortgage interest. Under the contract, the claimant was to find a tenant. The contract stated that 10 per cent of the total rent payable was due "at the commencement of each tenancy and/or renewal". A provision concerning renewed tenancies stated that commission was payable at 10 per cent of the total rent. The claimant found a tenant and charged 10 per cent of the rent payable for the initial term of the tenancy. The defendant agreed that the claimant had been entitled to do so. The tenant, by signing a renewal contract, later exercised an option to renew the tenancy and pay increased rent. The claimant invoiced the defendant for renewal commission of 10 per cent of the increased rent. The latter stated that he had queried that invoice but stated that the claimant had informed him that the fee was provided for in the contract and there was nothing that the defendant could do about it. Accordingly, he had paid that commission. The tenancy was later renewed again and the claimant invoiced for the commission but the defendant refused to pay it.

The District Judge said that the renewal commission terms were not drawn to the defendant's attention but they were not hidden from him; they were contained in a section which it was reasonable to assume he would read. That said there was a significant imbalance in the rights and obligations of the parties arising under the contract, to the defendant's detriment.[152] The District Judge said that the provision relating to the commencement of the tenancy was not sufficient to alert the defendant to the renewal commission. The provision relating to renewed tenancies of the property gave no definition of the term "renewed tenancy" and did not explain the circumstances in which a tenancy would be a renewed tenancy. The District Judge went on to say that a consumer who was employing an agent to find a tenant for 12 months was not likely to expect that he was signing up for potentially indefinite renewal commission. That was a sufficiently onerous provision that was not but should have been drawn to the defendant's attention or at the very least written in such clear language that a consumer

---

[150] This being a reference to the OFT Guidance on unfair terms in tenancy agreements; September 2005.
[151] Unreported April 30, 2010 (Lambeth CC).
[152] See this case further discussed at para.10–004.

reading it would be in no doubt what the provision meant. The claimant "had very little to do on renewal and yet each year would receive a higher payment because of the rent increase provisions". The renewal commission provisions were therefore unfair and the claimant was entitled to judgment on his counterclaim for the renewal commission previously paid.

(10) In *Mayhook v NCP*,[153] the terms on which cars were parked included this provision:

> "You acknowledge that you enter into this contract with us on the basis of these Terms and Conditions not only on behalf of yourself but also on behalf of any passengers in the vehicle and the legal owner of the vehicle. This means that we may enforce these Terms and Conditions against you or any passenger or the legal owner of the vehicle".

The recorder had no doubt but that this was unfair. There were likely to be very few occasions when someone other than the registered owner was the driver, but on those rare occasions, it would be a significant imbalance to say that the registered owner was deemed to have given authority to the driver to incur charges on his behalf. It was not necessary to the operation of the relationship and it was an unfair term. If the clause were upheld, he said, it would mean that car hire companies would be liable for charges incurred by those hiring the car, or parents being liable for charges incurred by sons or daughters. He also noted that DVLA had condemned the clause and that the current defendants had removed it from their terms and conditions.

(11) In *Financial Services Authority v Asset L.I Inc*[154]   **10–068**
     The fourth defendant was a director of P and the fifth defendant was a director of U. U and P had acquired land and sub-divided it into small plots. Salesmen invited consumers to purchase plots and verbally represented to them that U and P would seek to obtain planning permission in respect of the site as a whole, or otherwise seek to have the sites "re-zoned" for residential building purposes before facilitating the onward sale of the site to developers, for substantial profit. None of the defendants were authorised to undertake regulated activities under the 2000 Act. Certain contractual clauses stipulated that the buyer was not entering into the agreement on the faith of any representations from the seller and that the seller was not obliged to apply for planning permission. Investors were also asked to sign contract forms containing disclaimers set out in small print, to similar effect. The contract contained these clauses:

> "The Buyer confirms that there are and have been no representations made by or on behalf of the Seller on the faith of which the Buyer is entering into this Agreement except and to the extent to which such representations are herein expressly set out or form part of written replies by the Solicitors for the Seller to the written Enquiries before Contract raised by the solicitors for the Buyer or the Seller's replies to Property Information Forms."

The other clause (the "services clause") read:

---

[153] Unreported November 29, 2012 (Cambridge CC).
[154] [2013] EWHC 178.

"For the avoidance of doubt, the Seller is not obliged to and will not apply for planning permission in relation to the Property or in relation to the land as a whole of which the Property forms part, nor will the Seller provide any other services to the Buyer following the purchase of the Property by the Buyer to the extent that the provision of such services would constitute the carrying on by the Seller of regulated activities for the purposes of the [FSMA] unless the Seller is authorised under that Act and permitted by the [FSA] to carry on the relevant regulated activities. Notwithstanding the foregoing, the Seller reserves the right to (but is not obliged to) apply for planning permission in relation to any land owned by the Seller which forms part of the land of which the Property forms part."

In ruling the clauses unfair, the court took note that the indicative list of unfair terms referred to "Terms which have the object or effect of:... Limiting the seller's or supplier's obligation to respect commitments undertaken by his agents or making his commitments subject to compliance with a particular formality".[155] It then observed that the circumstances of the sales were that the plots were marketed as investments, often investments for no more than two years or so, and the statements supposedly of no effect because of the representations clause and the services clause were exactly what led the purchasers to decide to invest in the plots and they were made to induce them to do so. The nature of the plots was that their investment value was as a small part of sites that it was hoped would be made available for development and as such attract a developer. The statements and the sales were generally made to persons who were not financially experienced or sophisticated, who, as Asset Land's representatives knew, had no financial, legal or other relevant advice, and who were discouraged from seeking legal advice. The court noted in particular that Asset Land had deliberately conducted its business on the basis that the investors should not see the written contract and learn of the representations clause and the services clause until they had paid Asset Land the whole price; and then Asset Land did not transfer the plot, the consideration for what it had been paid, unless and until the investors signed the contracts. It was also the case that the "footers" on Asset Land's letters to some extent foreshadowed the substance of the services clause, but they were in small print and "readily overlooked". In consequence, the court concluded that each of these clauses caused "a significant imbalance in the parties' rights and obligations under the contract" and that it operated to the investor's detriment. Each operated only in Asset Land's favour and against the investor: neither clause purported to prevent Asset Land from relying on pre-contractual representations or exchanges. Its effect was to tilt the balance of the contract against the investor because it detracted from the investment potential of the purchase. It was also the court's view that each term was contrary to the requirement of good faith, which "requires that a supplier should not, whether deliberately or unconsciously, take advantage of the consumer's ... lack of experience, unfamiliarity with the subject matter of the contract, weak bargaining position..."[156] by introducing the representations clause and the services clause after investors had paid, Asset Land did just that. The court also decided that the representations clause failed the reasonableness test set out in the Misrepresentation Act.[157]

---

[155] See now Consumer Rights Act 2014 Sch.2 Pt 1 para.17.
[156] Here the court was quoting Lord Bingham in *Director General of Fair Trading v First National Bank Plc* [2001] UKHL 52.
[157] See para.9–044.

Contracts with building contractors

In a number of cases, the courts have had to deal with the special issues arising **10–069**
where a consumer employs a building contractor on the basis of written standard
terms but where the consumer has accepted those terms following professional
advice.

In *Lowell Products v Legg and Carver*,[158] the defendant consumers
approached the claimant to carry out extensive refurbishment works to their
home. The defendants' agent provided the claimant with a work specification and
accompanying drawings. The contract contained the following provision:

> "If any dispute or difference arises under this agreement either party may refer it to
> adjudication in accordance with the procedures set out in supplemental condition D. If under
> clause D2 the parties have not nominated a person as the adjudicator the nominator of the
> adjudicator shall be . . .".

This provision was challenged as unfair.

Schedule 2 to the Regulations (and now the Act) contained an indicative and
non-exhaustive list of terms which may be regarded as unfair. One such is any
clause:

> "Excluding or hindering the consumer's right to take legal action or exercise any other legal
> remedy, particularly by requiring the consumer to take disputes exclusively to arbitration not
> covered by legal provisions, unduly restricting the evidence available to him or imposing on
> him a burden of proof which, according to the applicable law, should lie with another party to
> the contract."

The court regarded this as not assisting the defendants because the disputed
contract term did not hinder or exclude the right to take legal action or exercise
any other remedy. Quite the opposite, in that an adjudication only bound the
parties until the dispute was resolved by legal action, arbitration or agreement.
The defendants were not required to take disputes exclusively to arbitration.
Furthermore, the term did not restrict the evidence available to them or alter the
burden of proof. In any event, the Regulations did no more than say that such a
term "may" be unfair, not "must".

The court thus had to consider more generally whether the disputed term was **10–070**
unfair. For this to be so, the court stressed that the clause must cause a significant
imbalance, as opposed to a relatively minor imbalance, and that such imbalance
must be contrary to the requirement of good faith. The court felt that neither
requirement was satisfied. The adjudication provision applied to both parties
equally. The adjudication in this case had resulted in a payment by the consumers,
but that was only because the dispute concerned the non-payment of sums due

---

[158] Unreported July 7, 2005 (TCC). See too these words of Master Ellison in *Swift Advance Plc v
Heaney* [2013] NIMaster 18: "I do not think a court should be asked to make an order for possession
of a person's property, let alone his home, in favour of a plaintiff lender not for the purpose of
realising or protecting its security but apparently to hold a threat of eviction over him so as to coerce
him into payment or punish him for his default. Suffice to say that if there were a mortgage condition
in terms permitting a lender to take possession (in the event that equity is non-existent) for such
purposes I believe it would be void, whether as being unconscionably close to a penalty *in terrorem* or
under the Unfair Terms in Consumer Contracts Regulations 1999".

under an interim certificate. Had the dispute concerned the payment of liquidated damages for delay, a payment might well have been ordered in favour of the consumer. There was no limit on the kind of dispute which could be referred to adjudication, and no imbalance of any degree arose. The court also noted that there had been no breach of the requirement as to openness. The adjudication terms were fully, clearly and legibly set out in the contract, and contained "no concealed pitfalls or traps".

It was also pointed out that the contractor neither deliberately nor unconsciously took any advantage of the consumers' necessity, indigence, lack of experience, unfamiliarity with the subject matter of the contract or of any weak bargaining position. In fact, as the court pointed out, the form of contract was insisted on by the architect employed by the defendant consumers, who were in any event knowledgeable business people who had engaged an architect and contract administrator and who also had legal advice. There was therefore, in the court's words, no departure from "good standards of commercial morality and practice".

The above case is closely related to that in *Westminster Building Co Ltd v Beckingham*.[159] This concerned an application to enforce the decision of an adjudicator. The contract between the parties contained a clause requiring disputes to be taken to adjudication, which had been done. It was now claimed that this clause was unfair.

The court noted, as the court had in *Lovell*, that the indicative list of prospective unfair terms in the Regulations contained an apparent reference to such a term as was here in dispute, but, although referring to that case, did not pause to consider whether the clause was in fact covered by the reference in the list. It did, however, note that case with approval and held that, here too, the clause was fair. It pointed out that the terms of the contract were decided upon by the consumer's agent who was a chartered surveyor. He had, therefore, available to him independent and objective advice as to the existence and effect of the arbitration clause. The builders did no more than accept the contract terms offered to them, and had no reasonable need to draw the consumer's attention to the potential pitfalls in and the operation of the disputed clause. The clause did not contravene the requirements of good faith nor create a significant imbalance in the consumer's rights.

10–071   The *Westminster* case was followed in *Allen Wilson Shopfitters v Buckingham*.[160] In essence, the facts of the case were the same, and the court came to the same conclusion.

In the course of its judgment in this last case, the court made reference to "the comprehensive review of the authorities" in *Bryen & Langley Ltd v Martin Rodney Boston*.[161] In that case, the judge noted that, while each case must depend on its own particular facts, it:

---

[159] [2004] EWHC 138 (TCC).
[160] [2005] EWHC 1165 (TCC).
[161] [2004] EWHC 2450 (TCC).

"was likely that in many cases in which an individual or a number of individuals enter into a contract under which building work is to be performed for him or them in a private, that is to say, non-business, capacity the facts and circumstances will be very similar. Unless the work is of small extent and value the individual or individuals will have professional advisers, such as an architect or a quantity surveyor or a contract administrator. Either in reliance upon his or their own judgment, or on advice from professional advisers, terms upon which it is considered appropriate to engage a contractor will be devised or selected and upon those terms tenders will be sought."

It had been argued that the disputed clause in this case was unfair because, first, a consumer could not be expected to have a detailed knowledge of a lengthy and technical form of contract such as the JCT Form; second, in practice adjudication is disadvantageous to employers under building contracts; and, third, it was the duty of the other contracting party to protect the consumer from the risk of being inadequately advised by his professional advisers.

Stressing again that each case fell to be judged on the basis of its own individual facts, the court accepted that, while it could be going too far to say that a building contractor who merely, without more, accepts a proposal from a "consumer" as to the terms of the contract to be made between them could never contravene the requirement of good faith, it was, even so: "difficult to envisage circumstances in which the criticism could properly be made that the contractor had acted contrary to the requirement of good faith in such a case".

The court also observed that it was not normally, in English law, the function of a party negotiating a contract to protect the other party to the negotiation from the consequences of his own folly, or from the negligence of third parties, such as the professional advisers to the other party. It then said that it would thus seem to be an unusual case:

"if such a case could be found at all, in which it would not be a complete answer to any suggestion that a building contractor had acted in bad faith in letting a 'consumer' choose to use a particular standard form of building contract, that the 'consumer' made his own decision, with or without the advice of a third party."

The court said that it was likely to be material to any consideration of the applicability of the Regulations (and hence now the 2014 Act) in any particular case of a building contract that the transaction was not of a normal "consumer" type, like buying a television set, but, for the individual or individuals concerned, a major project which, unless he or they are experienced in construction matters, would only be undertaken with the benefit of what was thought, at least, to be appropriate professional advice. **10–072**

The court also observed that, albeit with the specific exclusion of residential occupiers, Parliament had ordained the use of adjudication in the provisions of s.108(2) of the Housing Grants, Construction and Regeneration Act 1996. It seems, the court said:

"a bold thing to envisage that a procedure created and approved by Parliament for the resolution of disputes, albeit on an interim basis, by someone bound to act impartially and subject, at the enforcement stage, to a degree of supervision by the court, could properly be stigmatised as unfair or producing a significant imbalance in the rights of those potentially involved in the procedure."

It was irrelevant that there had been cases before the court in which the burden and cost of adjudication in particular circumstances had "been so enormous as to border on the scandalous". It said that the use made of a contractual term was not the target of the 1999 Regulations. The assessment whether a term was unfair fell to be made prospectively at the time the relevant contract was made, not retrospectively once advantage has been sought to be taken of the term.[162] The adjudication provision was accordingly fair. The court thus concluded that:

> "It is difficult to see that a provision in a contract by which a 'consumer' is bound to give a withholding notice by a given date if he wishes to exercise a right of set-off, at least if the specified date is fixed along the lines of that required by clause 30.1.1.4 of the JCT Form, creates a significant imbalance in the rights of the parties. As long as the 'consumer' is aware of the requirement, and alert to the possible need to comply with it, it does not affect his rights at all. If the requirement is contained in a form of agreement which he has himself put forward, any ignorance on his part of the term is not likely to be as a result of the opposite party failing to act in good faith."

In the Court of Appeal[163] the judge's approach was upheld, the court stating:

> "in light of the fact that it was Mr Boston, by his agent, who imposed these terms on B & L, I regard the suggestion that there was any lack of good faith or fair dealing by B & L with regard to the ultimate incorporation of these terms into the contract as repugnant to common sense. If they were to tender at all, B & L were being asked by Mr Boston to tender on (*inter alia*) the very terms of which Mr Boston now complains. It was not for B & L to take the matter up with him and ensure that he knew what he was doing: they knew that he had the benefit of the services of a professional, ... to advise him of the effects of the terms on which he was inviting tenders."

10–073 That each case is to be judged on its own facts received emphasis in *Steve Domsalla (t/a Domsalla Building Services) v Dyason*.[164] The applicant building contractor applied for summary judgment on its claim to enforce an adjudication award in its favour. The building contract was on the JCT Minor Building Works form of contract and had been signed by him and by the respondent who was a residential occupier as defined by the Housing Grants, Construction and Regeneration Act 1996 s.106(1). The latter's house had been so badly damaged by fire that it had to be demolished. His insurers agreed to reinstate. They appointed loss adjusters who advised on the selection of the applicant as builders. The works were not completed on time and many months later with the works still unfinished, the respondent suspended work because of ongoing disputes about its performance and the non-payment of certified sums. The applicant referred the disputes arising from non-payment to adjudication. The respondent signed a copy of the JCT adjudication agreement but contended that the adjudicator lacked jurisdiction because the adjudication and withholding notice clauses in the contract were unenforceable as a result of the application of the Unfair Terms in Consumer Contracts Regulations 1999. The adjudicator held that he had jurisdiction and gave a decision in the applicant's favour. He sought to enforce that award and applied for summary judgment.

---

[162] Reference was again made to the observations of Lord Bingham, *Director General of Fair Trading v First National Bank Plc* [2002] 1 All E.R 97.
[163] [2005] EWCA Civ 973.
[164] [2007] EWHC 1174 (TCC).

The respondent argued that the adjudication and withholding notice clauses in the contract were unenforceable as a result of the application of the 1999 Regulations, since he had not been instrumental in negotiating the contract or in determining its format but was a consumer who had been required to enter into it in order to obtain the reinstatement of his property to which his insurance policy entitled him.

The adjudication clause

The court concluded that this provision did not provide for a substantial **10–074** imbalance in the parties' rights, even though it was potentially unfair for the claimant to rely on the clause. It pointed out that the arbitration procedure was "a rapid, cheap and temporary legal process which determines the parties' rights". The court also pointed out that arbitration was to be conducted according to certain minimum standards as to fairness and impartiality, and that arbitration corresponded to the summary judgment procedures, but which could be undertaken more speedily and economically. Again, while an adjudicator might not be a lawyer, such person would have had relevant professional training. Just as with arbitration, "a legal background is not an essential prerequisite of a fair and impartial procedure". It was also to be borne in mind that decisions of an adjudicator could be overturned in litigation.

The withholding notice clause

In essence, the withholding clause required the consumer to give notice of such **10–075** amounts as he was withholding from payment. In the absence of such notice, no withholding was allowed. In the *Bryen & Langley* case, such a clause was upheld. The court stated that:

> "It is difficult to see that a provision in a contract by which a 'consumer' is bound to give a withholding notice by a given date if he wishes to exercise a right of set-off, at least if the specified date is fixed along the lines of that required by clause 30.1.1.4 of the JCT Form, creates a significant imbalance in the rights of the parties. As long as the 'consumer' is aware of the requirement, and alert to the possible need to comply with it, it does not affect his rights at all. If the requirement is contained in a form of agreement which he has himself put forward, any ignorance on his part of the term is not likely to be as a result of the opposite party failing to act in good faith."

In the *Domsalla* case, however, a different conclusion was reached, though it was stressed that the circumstances of the case were "unusual". The relevant factors were these:

(i)   The defendant had no hand in proffering or selecting the clause, no advice as to its existence, meaning or effect and no means of ascertaining that it was contained within the contract since he was not shown the contract conditions until he was provided with a copy to sign without being given any opportunity to read or consider them.

(ii)   He was not involved in certification or payment and all payments were to be made by the insurers. He was not entitled to issue withholding notices, it was the insurers and their agent the contract administrator who were concerned with whether, when and in what terms such notices should be issued.

(iii) His entitlement under the contract was to receive a reinstated home as close in design and construction to his original home as was possible. The workmanship was to be both good and in conformity with the standards of the contract. All money claims against the claimant available for breach of contract, whether for defects or delay, would be made in the defendant's name but would inure to the benefit of the insurers.

(iv) Domsalla could sue the insurers directly if so advised and, if they sued them through the medium of Dyason, could utilise the adjudication provisions of the contract.

(v) If a situation arose whereby Dyason became personally liable under the contract, the effect of the withholding provisions could substantially affect his rights. That was because they would not have been operated in his favour or to his advantage since they were only capable of being operated in favour of the insurers and Dyason was not able or entitled to operate them himself.

(vi) In consequence, Dyason would be unable to avoid the effect of an adverse adjudication decision relating to unpaid certificates even where there were good cross-claims for defects or delay because no withholding notices would have been served. This situation would arise in a contract which he would not ordinarily expect to pay out anything, where the insurers would expect to be able to rely on withholding notices in a similar situation and in which Dyason was only in the position of being an employer under a building contract because that was the way that his insurers had insisted that his entitlement to full reinstatement under his policy could be provided. He was not a voluntary employer, merely the agent of the insurers who did not wish to act as employer themselves notwithstanding the fire insurance reinstatement nature of the work being performed.

(vii) Domsalla could still rely on their rights to suspend work, as they apparently did, and could still proceed against the insurers directly. Thus, their rights would not be adversely affected if the withholding notice clause was held not to be binding whereas Dyason's rights and obligations would be very substantially affected if the clause remained binding against him.

The court also referred to the indicative list of unfair terms, and found the following to be of relevance:

"(1)   The following terms which have the object or effect of:
    (b)   inappropriately excluding or limiting the legal rights of the consumer vis-à-vis the supplier in the event of total or partial non-performance or inadequate performance by the supplier of any contractual obligations, including the option of offsetting a debt owed to the supplier against any claim which the consumer may have against him.
    (i)   irrevocably binding the consumer to terms which he had no real opportunity of becoming acquainted before the conclusion of the contract;
    (o)   obliging the consumer to fulfil all his obligations where the supplier does not perform his;

(q)   excluding or hindering the consumer's right to take legal action or exercise any other legal remedy, unduly restricting the evidence available to him . . .".

The court concluded that the disputed provisions were not binding on Dyason. The same finding that a clause in such category of contract was unfair was also made in *Mylcrist Builders Ltd v Buck*.[165] The applicant building company applied for permission to enforce an arbitration award against the respondent. The latter had contacted the builder to build an extension to her bungalow. She signed its standard terms and conditions, which contained a clause referring all disputes to arbitration. The builder commenced work, but a dispute later arose between the parties. He sought to commence arbitration and contacted an arbitrator, but following advice that the arbitration clause could be unfair, the respondent refused to submit to the arbitration. The arbitrator received an agreement to appoint that was signed only by the builder, but he confirmed his appointment and found in the builder's favour, who then sought to enforce the award.

It was held that the arbitration clause was unfair because, contrary to the   **10–076** requirement of good faith, it caused a significant imbalance in the parties' rights and obligations under the contract, to the detriment of the respondent. The existence of the arbitration clause together with the requirement for a mandatory stay under s.9 of the 1996 Act meant that the clause did exclude or hinder a consumer's right to take legal action. The court said that arbitration under the Act was not arbitration "covered by legal provisions" and therefore Sch.2, which contains the grey list of possibly unfair terms applied. Paragraph 1(q) (now Sch.2 para.20(a) in the 2014 Act) refers to terms: "Excluding or hindering a consumer's right to take legal action or exercise any other legal remedy particularly by requiring the consumer to take disputes exclusively to arbitration not covered by legal provisions . . .". The court said that the clause prevented the respondent from having access to the courts and caused an imbalance between the builder as a professional builder and the respondent as a lay person, to her detriment. The fees payable to the arbitrator were significant compared with the claim and that was a further element of imbalance to her detriment. Furthermore, although she had signed the contract containing the arbitration clause, its impact would not have been apparent to a lay person and had not been apparent to her, as evidenced by her subsequent conduct. The requirement of fair and open dealing meant that the clause and its effects needed to be "more fully, clearly and prominently set out than they were in the instant case". Although there was no suggestion that the builder had deliberately taken advantage of her lack of experience, unfamiliarity with the subject matter of the contract or her weak bargaining position, by including arbitration in its standard terms, the builder "clearly had taken such advantage, albeit unconsciously".

The arbitration clause was not binding and the award could not be enforced. The court also referred to what it called "useful approaches". These include:

"(a)   assessing the impact of an impugned term on the parties' rights and obligations by comparing the effect of the contract with the term and the effect it would have without it; and

---

[165] [2008] EWHC 2172 (TCC). See too *Zealander and Zealander v Lang Homes* [2000] TCLR 724.

(b)   considering the effect of the inclusion of the term on the substance or core of the transaction; whether if it were drawn to his attention the consumer would be likely to be surprised by it; whether the term is a standard term, not merely in similar non-negotiable consumer contracts, but in commercial contracts freely negotiated between parties acting on level terms and at arms' length; and whether, in such cases, the party adversely affected by the inclusion of the term or his lawyer might reasonably be expected to object to its inclusion and press for its deletion."

The court added that, where consumers have imposed the term either by their own choice or a choice made by their professional agent then it was "unlikely that there would be any lack of good faith or fair dealing with regard to the incorporation of the terms of the contract".

WRITTEN CONTRACTS AND TRANSPARENT LANGUAGE

10–077   Under the 1999 Regulations, reg.7 provided: (1) A seller or supplier shall ensure that any written term of a contract is expressed in plain, intelligible language. (2) If there is doubt about the meaning of a written term, the interpretation which is most favourable to the consumer shall prevail . . .".The 2014 Act is to the same effect, but set out differently. As noted already,[166] s.68(1) requires written terms to be "transparent". Section 69(1) states that: "If a term in a consumer contract, or a consumer notice, could have different meanings, the meaning that is most favourable to the consumer is to prevail". In practical terms, the Act does not differ from the Regulations.

In *Office of Fair Trading v Abbey National Plc*,[167] the court commented on the relationship between regs 7(1) and (2) thus:

"it does not follow that a written term is necessarily in plain intelligible language unless there is doubt about its true meaning. A term might be obscure and difficult to understand at all, but bear only one meaning for anyone who manages to fathom what it is saying. It was not suggested . . . that the meaning or application of the expression 'plain, intelligible language' is restricted to where Regulation 7(2) applies, and in my judgment no such restricted meaning is required by Regulation 7 or by the 1999 Regulations as a whole."

It was also noted that there was no real dispute between the parties that the question whether terms were in plain intelligible language was to be considered from the point of view of the typical or average consumer.

It had also been argued by the OFT that it was entitled to bring proceedings against sellers and suppliers to require them to put their written terms into plain intelligible language, it being suggested that the OFT might have such power under s.215 of the Enterprise Act. That provision allows the OFT (now the CMA) to obtain an enforcement order against a party committing a Community infringement, the 1999 Regulations (and now the 2014 Act) being within this category.[168] Given that reg.7(1) (and now s.68(1)) is mandatory in its wording, the OFT case does seem arguable. This question was, however, not fully argued and the court expressed no view.

---

[166] See para.10–038.
[167] [2008] EWHC 875 (Comm) per Andrew Smith J. This was not commented upon in either the Court of Appeal or the Supreme Court.
[168] Community infringements are discussed further at para.10–093.

In the Plymouth County Court, two examples have dealt with the ambiguity of written terms.[169] A plaintiff hired out a morning dress under a standard form contract which provided for compensation for late return. The judge held that the contract was ambiguous as to whether the specified compensation was daily or weekly and decided the ambiguity in the consumer's favour. In the other case, a local authority's car parking ticket was "not transferable" but was issued in standard format without specifying any particular car park. The judge ruled that "not transferable" restricted the transfer for the parking ticket from one motorist to another and not as from one local authority car park to another.

In *West v Ian Finlay and* Associates,[170] a "net contribution clause" ran: "... Our **10–078** liability for loss or damage will be limited to the amount that it is reasonable for us to pay in relation to the contractual responsibilities of other consultants, contractors and specialists appointed by you." Noting that any uncertainty had to be construed in favour of the consumer, the court in fact held such a construction would in any event accord with how both parties had read the clause anyway. It is of course possible that both trader and consumer might agree that a clause has a meaning adverse to the interests of the consumer, only for the court to rule that it is in fact ambiguous and then read it in favour of the consumer.

In *AJ Building and Plastering v Turner*,[171] it was accepted that the *contra proferentem* rule and the provisions of reg.7 were one and the same.[172] The court cautioned, however, against a too rapid finding of an ambiguity and stressed that the ordinary principles of construction were to apply.[173] The court then said this:

> "If the normal principles of construction lead to a firm conclusion as to the meaning of a document, there is no room for regulation 7 (2) to apply. However, if the process of construction does not lead to a firm conclusion, but the court is left with two or more interpretations that it cannot reject on other grounds, regulation 7 (2) will operate as a tie-breaker."

That reg.7 (now of course s.69 of the 2014 Act) will not apply where the normal principles of construction show that the clause lacks ambiguity is illustrated by *Du Plessis v Fontgary Leisure Parks Ltd*.[174] The court said that there was no room for the application of either the *contra proferentem* rule or reg.7 because, quite simply, "there is no ambiguity in the phrase under consideration".

---

[169] Consumer Law Today, November 1996.
[170] [2013] EWHC 868; [2014] EWCA Civ 316. The Court of Appeal differed from the High Court on the reading of the clause and made no comment on his observation.
[171] [2013] EWHC 484.
[172] In the course of his judgment in this case, the judge referred to and agreed with the observation of Andrew Smith J. in *Financial Services Authority v Asset LI Inc* [2013] EWHC 178 that reg.7 and the *contra proferentem* rule "were much to the same effect".
[173] Reference was made to the *West Bromwich* principles of construction discussed at para.2–002.
[174] [2012] EWCA Civ 409.

Disapplication of s.69

10–079   Section 69(2) of the 2014 Act provides that the provisions of s.69 do not apply on application for an injunction.[175] The reason for such disapplication was explained in *Commission of the European Communities v Spain*,[176] it was said that, in such applications, a court would necessarily be assessing contract terms in the abstract rather than in the concrete circumstances of a particular case and that, if the general principle of interpretation were applied to such claims, enforcement action against ambiguous terms might be rendered ineffective; the need to interpret such terms in the most favourable way to consumers would permit their continued use if, in the abstract, it were possible to construe them in a way that would render them not unfair.

Consequence of unfairness

10–080   Section 62(1), (2) of the 2014 Act provides that an unfair term in a contract or notice is not binding on the consumer, though subs.(3) adds that a consumer can still rely on unfair term if he wishes to. There was no such provision in the Regulations: no doubt that was the case previously by implication but it is now made explicit, though the circumstances where either party is likely to invoke it will be unusual at best. Section 67 further provides that, despite the presence of an unfair term the contract continues, "so far as practicable, to have effect in every other respect". The courts are not given the power to re-write the contract and such a provision would be incompatible with the Directive on which the Regulations and now the Act are based.

In *Banco Español de Crédito SA v Joaquín Calderón Camino*,[177] the European Court of Justice ruled that Spanish legislation allowing the national courts to rewrite an unfair term was invalid. The Court argued that that such a power, were it granted to the national court, would be liable to eliminate the deterrent effect on sellers or suppliers of the straightforward non-application of the unfair terms vis-à-vis consumers. For that reason, that power would ensure less effective protection of consumers than that resulting from non-application of those terms. If it were open to the national court to revise the content of unfair terms, sellers or suppliers would remain tempted to use those terms in the knowledge that, even if they were declared invalid, the contract could, nevertheless, be modified by the court in such a way as to safeguard their interests.

It is, however, otherwise if the term in question can be replaced by a provision permitted under national law:

> "Such an approach makes it possible to attain the Directive's objective, which consists, inter alia, in restoring a balance between the parties while preserving, as far as possible, the validity of the contract as a whole. If such a replacement were not permitted and the court were

---

[175] See para.10–085. The corresponding provision in the 1999 Regulations was reg.7(2).

[176] (C-70-03) [2004] ECR I-7999. This case was cited with approval in *AJ Building and Plastering v Turner* [2013] EWHC 484.

[177] (C-618/10) [2012] All ER (D) 110 (Sep). The ECJ has also ruled that national legislation can provide that the presence of an unfair term can render the whole contract void: *Pereničová v SOS financ spol sro* (C-453/10) [2012] C.M.L.R. 28.

required to annul the contract, the deterrent effect of the penalty of invalidity and the objective of consumer protection could be jeopardised. In the present case, the effect of such an annulment would be to render due the full amount of the balance of the loan. That, however, is liable to be beyond the consumer's financial capacities and, therefore, to penalise the consumer rather than the lender, who, in the light of that consequence, might not be encouraged to avoid including such terms in its contracts".[178]

Even though a term is unfair, however, It can still aid in the interpretation of other clauses In the contract: "The 2014 Act does not remove a term from a contract: it only specifies that it is not effective".[179]

The rule would appear to be, though it has never been tested in this context, that an entire term may be eliminated from a contract, yet leaving the contract in force, if it is merely subsidiary to the main purpose of the contract. If, however, it is substantially the whole of the consideration given for the other's promise, then the contract falls with it.[180]

In *Bankers Insurance Co Ltd v South*[181] the judge said it was only that part of the   **10–081**
disputed clause denying recovery whatever the consequences of the breach which was not binding on the insured, a conclusion he felt "at least" consistent with the spirit of the Regulations, noting the provision that the contract remains in existence as far as practicable.[182]

In the context of contracts for the sale of goods and supply of services, the central provisions will be the nature and identity of the goods or services on the one hand, and the price to be paid on the other. This approach is supported by the provisions relating to the core terms which are those defining the "main subject matter" of the contract and the price or charge.[183] The broad result would appear to be that virtually any clause ruled unfair would leave the contract standing since the central provisions would remain intact. The principal exception would lie when a core provision, not being in plain, intelligible language, was itself condemned as unfair.

PREVENTION OF CONTINUED USE OF UNFAIR TERMS

The relevant provisions of Council Directive 93/13 on unfair terms in consumer   **10–082**
contracts provide as follows:

> "7.(1)   Member states shall ensure that... adequate and effective means do exist to prevent the continued use of unfair terms in contracts concluded by sellers or suppliers.
>
> (2)   The means referred to in paragraph (1) shall include provisions whereby persons or organisations.... may take action... before the courts... for a decision as to whether contractual terms drawn up for general use are unfair, so that they can apply appropriate and effective means to prevent the continued use of such terms."

---

[178] *Kasler Arpad, Kaslerne Rabai Hajnalka v OTP Jelzalogbank Zrt* (C-26/13) Unreported February 12, 2014 (opinion of the Advocate-General). This view was endorsed by the European Court of Justice (April 30, 2014).

[179] *Spreadex Ltd v Cochrane* [2012] EWHC 1290.

[180] See for example *Goodinson v Goodinson* [1954] 2 Q.B. 118. See generally Cheshire, Fifoot and Furmston, *Law of Contract*, 15th edn, pp.541 and following.

[181] [2003] EWHC 380.

[182] See now Consumer Rights Act 2014 s.67.

[183] See para.10–027.

The Act is wider in that the Directive refers to the "continued" use of a term (thus implying that it has already appeared in at least one contract), whereas Sch.3 refers to a term which a person "is using, or proposing or recommending". Although Parliament may not have intended to go further than the Directive, this is in any event permitted by art.8 which allows any Member State to adopt more stringent provisions in the area which it covers.[184] The Act also covers oral terms, which the Regulations appeared not to do, so the Act now conforms to the intent of the Directive.

Similarly, the Regulations referred to terms drawn up for "general use" and this has not been retained by the Act, which is again more consonant with the Directive.

In *Office of Fair Trading v Foxtons Ltd*,[185] the OFT had issued proceedings against Foxtons challenging the fairness of certain terms in its standard form of contract. In the High Court, the judge distinguished between a general challenge, which a body such as the OFT (now the CMA) could make, and the challenge that an individual could make if sued. It held that Foxtons should not be prevented from enforcing individual contracts already entered into, as the circumstances of those contracts might establish that the relevant term was fair, even if, on the general challenge, the term had been held unfair. The OFT argued that the language of Directive 93/13 supported the view that general challenges were directed not only to future contracts but also to existing contracts. Foxtons argued that the court lacked the jurisdiction to grant declarations in a case where the parties before the court were not the parties to the contracts in which the terms appeared.

10–083   Reversing the High Court, the Court of Appeal ruled that art.7 of the Directive was clearly intended to cover existing as well as future contracts, and thus an issue on a general challenge could be the fairness of a term in a current contract. The Court of Appeal felt that it would be "quite inadequate protection to consumers" if a court on a general challenge, having found a term as used in current contracts to be unfair, had no power to prevent the supplier or seller from continuing to enforce that term in current contracts.[186] It was therefore most unlikely that the Directive intended that a general challenge should not relate to a standard term in current contracts and did not intend the courts of Member States to have the power to prevent continued reliance on that term by a supplier or service provider against a consumer. It was further held that, if the OFT succeeded in establishing the unfairness of any of the terms, it would be entitled to a declaration. It would be important to identify which term and what aspect of it was unfair, and it would be better to have that in declaration form rather than forcing people to analyse the judgment to assess precisely what it decided.

This ruling is in line with the decision of the European Court of Justice that a Member State may provide that an unfair contract term that has been declared void following an action brought in the public interest by a consumer protection

---

[184] See for example the ruling in *Pereničová v SOS financ spol sro* (C-453/10) [2012] C.M.L.R. 28.
[185] [2008] EWHC 1662 (Ch); [2009] EWCA Civ 288.
[186] The Court of Appeal noted the words of Lord Steyn in *Director General of Fair Trading v First National Bank Plc* [2002] 1 A.C. 481: "the system of pre-emptive challenges is a more effective way of preventing the continuing use of unfair terms . . . than ex casu actions".

authority against a seller or supplier is not binding on any consumer who has entered into a contract with that seller or supplier to which the same general business conditions apply.[187]

DEALING WITH COMPLAINTS

Under the Act, the CMA and any other specified regulator[188] may consider complaints made as to the fairness of a term or notice. The Regulations had made it mandatory to consider a complaint though, in relation to the CMA (then the Office of Fair Trading) it had become permissive under the provisions of the Public Bodies (The Office of Fair Trading Transfer of Consumer Advice Scheme Function and Modification of Enforcement Functions) Order 2013.[189] If a regulator other than the CMA intends to consider a relevant complaint, it must notify the CMA that it intends to do so, and must then consider the complaint. It must notify the CMA of the outcome of the application, and if an injunction is granted, the conditions on which, and the persons against whom, it is granted.

10–084

If a regulator considers a relevant complaint, but decides not to make an application for an injunction in relation to the complaint, it must give reasons for its decision to the person who made the complaint. A dissatisfied complainant could presumably seek judicial review.[190]

APPLICATION FOR AN INJUNCTION

An injunction can be sought under a broader range of provisions than under the Regulations. Whereas before, applications could relate solely to unfair terms, Sch.3 to the 2014 Act extends the power to terms seeking to exclude or restrict liability in relation to: goods contracts; digital content contracts; services contracts, or business liability for death or personal injury resulting from negligence. It may well have been that such terms could have been regarded as unfair under the old regime but the position is now made clear. The Act further brings within the scope of a complaint which is not transparent, this latter being defined by s.68 as meaning written in plain and intelligible language and, when written, legible.

10–085

Before making an application for an injunction, Sch.3 requires a regulator other than the CMA must notify the CMA that it intends to do so. The regulator may then make the application only if: (a) the period of 14 days beginning with the day on which the regulator notified the CMA has ended, or (b) before the end

---

[187] *Nemzeti Fogyasztovedelmi Hatosag v Invitel Tavkozlesi Zrt* (C-472/10) [2012] 3 C.M.L.R. 1; [2012] C.E.C. 1375 ECJ.

[188] Such other regulators being: the Department of Enterprise, Trade and Investment in Northern Ireland, a local weights and measures authority in Great Britain; the Financial Conduct Authority; the Office of Communications; the Information Commissioner, the Gas and Electricity Markets Authority, the Water Services Regulation Authority, the Office of Rail Regulation, the Northern Ireland Authority for Rail Regulation, the Northern Ireland Authority for Utility Regulation or the Consumers' Association.

[189] SI 2013/783.

[190] See generally Consumer Rights Act 2014 Sch.3.

of that period, the CMA agrees to the regulator making the application. It does not appear that the CMA can actually prevent the other regulator from seeking the injunction.

In deciding on an application for an injunction, the court may grant it on such conditions, and against such of the respondents as it thinks appropriate. Such injunction may include provision about (a) a term or notice to which the application relates, or (b) any term of a consumer contract, or any consumer notice, of a similar kind or with a similar effect.

This clearly envisages injunctions being in effect granted against parties not party to the particular action.

It is expressly provided by Sch.3 that the fact that the particular provision was already invalid because of some rule of law is no defence to an application for an injunction. This appears to strike in particular at those clauses rendered automatically void by the Act.[191]

In *Director General of Fair Trading v First National Bank Plc*,[192] after ruling that the term was unfair, the court said that "at first blush" an injunction would appear to be the appropriate form of relief. The defence, however, argued that the form of injunction sought by the claimant was too wide, since the notice of appeal had stated:

> "The Learned Judge ought to have held that clause 8 was unfair insofar as it was not limited by a proviso to the effect that the Defendant would not seek to rely on it after judgment
> (i)   in any case where the Court made an order for payment of the judgment debt by instalments, or
> (ii)   alternatively, in any such case unless a judge has specifically considered whether to exercise the Court's powers under sections 129 and 136 of the Consumer Credit Act 1974."

The Director General had appeared to recognise in this that the unfairness could be cured if an amendment were made to the clause. The court indicated that, if the Bank were to draft a suitable amendment to meet the Director General's objection, and give an undertaking to incorporate any such amendment into its standard terms, the court would be "minded to accept such undertaking, and the wider or any injunction would be unnecessary".[193]

Undertakings

10–086   As an alternative to an injunction, Sch.3 provides that a regulator may accept an undertaking. That undertaking may provide that the person will comply with the conditions that are agreed between the person and the regulator about the use of terms or notices, or terms or notices of a kind, specified in the undertaking. If a regulator other than the CMA accepts an undertaking, it must notify it of the conditions on which the undertaking is accepted, and the person who gave it.

---

[191]   See para.10–013.
[192]   [2000] 2 All E.R. 759.
[193]   [2000] 2 All E.R. 759 at 771, per Peter Gibson L.J.

INVESTIGATORY POWERS

Schedule 5 to the Act hands extensive powers to the "unfair contract terms enforcer".[194] This is any regulator[195] so long as that regulator is also a public authority within s.6 of the Human Rights Act 1998. Section 6(3) says only that such an authority includes "a court or tribunal, and any person certain of whose functions are functions of a public nature". Though accepting this definition is not exhaustive, it does appear not to include the Consumers' Association. This would be consistent with the Regulations which did not extend in this context to that regulator.

10–087

The purposes for which the unfair contract terms enforcer may exercise its functions are to enable the enforcer to exercise or to consider whether to exercise its power to seek an injunction or undertaking, and to ascertain whether a person has complied with or is complying with an injunction or undertaking. The powers available to an enforcer are: the power to make test purchases; the power to observe carrying on of business, etc.; the power to require the production of information[196]; the power to enter premises without warrant; the power to inspect goods, etc.; the power to require the production of documents; the power to entry premises with warrant; and the power to require assistance from person on premises. There is also an offence of obstruction.

PUBLICATION, INFORMATION AND ADVICE

The Act imposes certain duties on the CMA.[197] In particular, it must arrange the publication of details of:

10–088

(a)   any application it makes for an injunction;
(b)   any injunction; and
(c)   any undertaking.

It must respond to a request whether a term or notice, or one of a similar kind or with a similar effect, is or has been the subject of an injunction or undertaking. Where the term or notice, or one of a similar kind or with a similar effect, is or has been the subject of an injunction, the CMA must give the person making the request a copy of the injunction.

Where the term or notice, or one of a similar kind or with a similar effect, is or has been the subject of an undertaking, the CMA must give the person making the request:

(a)   details of the undertaking; and

---

[194] The Act also refers to domestic enforcers, EU enforcers and public designated enforcers; Sch.5 paras 3–5.
[195] As defined by Sch.3 para.8. See fn.190.
[196] The enforcer cannot exercise this power in relation to any action to use its powers in relation to unfair terms unless it has reasonable cause to suspect that a person is using, or proposing or recommending the use of, a contractual term or a notice following receipt of a complaint; Sch.5 para.13(8).
[197] Sch.3 para.7.

(b)　if the person giving the undertaking has agreed to amend the term or notice, a copy of the amendments.

The CMA may arrange the publication of advice and information about the provisions of the Act in relation to unfair contract terms.

APPLICABLE LAW

10–089　The provisions of the Act apply regardless of any contract term which applies or seeks to apply the law of a state outside the EEA[198] if the contract "has a close connection with the United Kingdom".[199] In the Regulations, the reference was to the EEA and not specifically the United Kingdom. Since the provisions of the Directive apply throughout the EEA, the consumer will still have the ability to bring an action according to the domestic law of the relevant EEA state if such state is the state of close connection.

No definition is given as to what is understood by "close connection". Some guidance may, however, be obtained from s.27(2) of the Unfair Contract Terms Act 1977 (now repealed by the 2014 Act) which provided that a choice of law outside the UK will have no effect if the consumer "was then habitually resident in the United Kingdom and the essential steps necessary for the making of the contract were taken there, whether by him or by others on his behalf". The Directive also uses only the phrase "close connection", and it may have been thought that to adopt the provisions of the 1977 Act could have imposed too restrictive a test. If this is so, then it may be enough to establish a sufficient connection that any essential step was taken in the United Kingdom, such as ordering the goods or services or the place of performance, regardless of where the contract was made or performance to be effected.

If the parties choose to make the law of the UK the proper law of the contract, when otherwise it would not be, then the provisions of the 2014 Act would seem to apply. This is in contrast to s.27(1) of the 1977 Act, which sub-section remains in force, which, in such a case, would disapply the reasonableness test. The difference in this context between the 1977 and 2014 Act is presumably the fact that the 1977 Act can also apply to business contracts and that it was felt essential not to discourage businesses choosing the law of the UK with the consequent possible flow of arbitration work. The application of the fairness test when making the United Kingdom the proper law would not have such an effect, particularly when the 2014 Act implements a Directive applying in the other countries of the EEA. If no choice of law is made, or the law of an EEA state is chosen, then s.74(2) applies Regulation (EC) No. 593/2008 of the European Parliament and of the Council of 17 June 2008 on the law applicable to contractual obligations.[200]

---

[198] That is to say, the 28 EU Member States, Iceland, Norway and Liechtenstein.

[199] Consumer Rights Act s.74(1). For "close connection", see *Martrade Shipping & Transport GMBH v United Enterprises Corp.* [2014] EWHC 1884.

[200] Generally, the choice of law cannot deprive consumers of the protection afforded to them by mandatory provisions of the law of the country where they have their habitual residence, provided that

It is to be noted that the Act does not make the choice of law clause invalid, stating only that it has no effect in relation to unfair terms. It might then be otherwise effective.

Criminal offences

The Act contains no provisions for the use of unfair terms to constitute a criminal offence. This might, however, be the case if the particular term is somehow in breach of the Consumer Protection from Unfair Trading Regulations 2008.[201]

10–090

ACTION UNDER OTHER ENACTMENTS

The use of unfair terms could be taken into account by the Financial Conduct Authority in the exercise of its licensing functions under the Consumer Credit Act 1974.[202] Consumers could also refer to any unfair terms in making use of those provisions of the Act as to unfair relationships.[203]

10–091

Domestic infringements

A domestic infringement is defined in the Enterprise Act 2002 (Pt 8 Domestic Infringements) Order 2003[204] to include an "act done or omission made in breach of contract for the supply of goods or services to a consumer. An act done or omission made in breach of a duty of care owed to a consumer under the law of tort or delict of negligence". As thus defined, a "domestic infringement" would not embrace unfair terms since use of an unfair term is not a breach of contract or of a duty of care.

10–092

Community infringement

A Community infringement is defined in the Enterprise Act 2002 Sch.13 as amended by the Enterprise Act 2002 (Pt 8 Community Infringements Specified UK Laws) Order 2003.[205] This includes a reference to the Consumer Rights Act and also to the Consumer Protection from Unfair Trading Regulations.

10–093

---

the other party pursues commercial or professional activities in that country or, by whatever means, directs such activities to that country or to several countries including that country, and the contract falls within the scope of such activities.

If no choice of law is made by the parties and the conditions just mentioned are satisfied, the consumer contract will be governed by the law of the country where the consumer is habitually resident. For further guidance, consult *http://europa.eu/legislation_summaries/justice_freedom_ security/judicial_cooperation_in_civil_matters/jl0006_en.htm*

[201] SI 2008/1277. See Ch.5.

[202] The FCA took over licensing responsibilities under the Consumer Credit Act 1974 on April 1, 2014 from the former OFT by virtue of the Financial Markets Act 2012 and the Financial Services and Markets Act 2000 (Regulated Activities) (Amendment) (No.2) Order 2013 (SI 2013/1881).

[203] See Consumer Credit Act 1974 s.140A–D as inserted by the Consumer Credit Act 2006.

[204] SI 2003/1593.

[205] SI 2003/1374, as amended by SI 2005/2418 and SI 2006/3372.

An enforcement order can be obtained under the Enterprise Act in relation to domestic and community infringements. Such an order can require the person:

- not to continue or repeat the particular conduct;
- not to engage in such conduct in the course of his or another's business; and
- not to consent or connive in the carrying out of such conduct by a body corporate.

An enforcement order may require the particular party to publish the order, or a corrective statement.

The court may accept an undertaking instead of an order. If an undertaking is breached, application can be made for an order. If an order, or undertaking given to the court, is infringed, the court can find the person in contempt and impose a fine. If the defendant is an individual, there can also be a sentence not exceeding two years.

Under s.221 of the Enterprise Act, a general or designated enforcer has the right to take proceedings in an EEA state other than the United Kingdom for the cessation or prohibition of a Community infringement.

Enforcers

General enforcers

10–094   The general enforcers designated by s.213 of the Enterprise Act are: CMA, Trading Standards Services in Great Britain; Department of Enterprise, Trade and Investment in Northern Ireland.

Designated enforcers

10–095   The following are designated enforcers[206]: CAA, Director General of Electricity Supply for Northern Ireland, Director General of Gas for Northern Ireland, Ofcom, The Water Services Regulation Authority, The Gas and Electricity Markets Authority, the Information Commissioner, ORR, the Consumers' Association and the Financial Conduct Authority.

---

[206] Enterprise Act 2002 (Pt 8 Designated Enforcers: Criteria for Designation, Designation of Public Bodies as Designated and Transitional Provisions) Order 2003 (SI 2003/1399); Enterprise Act 2002 (Pt 8) (Designation of the Financial Services Authority as a Designated Enforcer) Order 2004 (SI 2004/935); Enterprise Act 2002 (Pt 8 Designation of the Consumers' Association) Order 2005 (SI 2005/917); Enterprise Act 2002 (Water Services Regulation Authority) Order 2006 (SI 2006/522); The Enterprise Act 2002 (Pt 8) (Designation of the Financial Conduct Authority as a Designated Enforcer) Order 2013 (SI 2013/478).

Community enforcers

The Enterprise Act also refers to Community enforcers. These are entities from other EEA states listed in the Official Journal pursuant to the Injunctions Directive but who are not a general, designated or CPC enforcer.[207]   **10–096**

CPC enforcers

These are enforcers designated for the purposes of Regulation (EC) No.2006/2004 of the European Parliament and of the Council of October 27, 2004 on cooperation between national authorities responsible for the enforcement of consumer protection laws, as amended by Directive 2005/29/EC of the European Parliament and of the Council of May 11, 2005 concerning unfair business-to-consumer commercial practices in the internal market (the "CPC Regulation").   **10–097**

The CPC Regulation creates a network of enforcers which are responsible for taking action to eradicate cross border infringements of the EC consumer protection legislation set out in the Annex to that Regulation, and the Annex refers to the Unfair Terms Directive.

The enforcers are: CMA, CAA, Financial Conduct Authority, Secretary of State for Health, Department of Health, Social Services and Public Safety in Northern Ireland, Ofcom, Department of Enterprise, Trade and Investment in Northern Ireland, every local weights and measures authority in Great Britain, PhonePayPlus and the Information Commissioner.[208]

Enforcers who wish to apply for an enforcement order must first consult the person against whom the order would be made and with the CMA (unless the enforcer is the CMA). The CMA can itself take over the proceedings.[209]

Enhanced consumer measures

A major feature of the 2014 Act is what is called "enhanced consumer measures".[210]   **10–098**

Part 8 of the Enterprise Act enables certain enforcers to take civil action in respect of infringements of specified domestic/Community consumer legislation which harm the collective interests of consumers.

The enforcement procedure is set out at ss.214 to 223 of the Act. Central to this procedure is an application for an enforcement order.

The Consumer Rights Act Sch.7 amends Pt 8 of the 2002 Act to enable enforcement orders or undertakings to include new enhanced consumer measures, in addition to requirements that could be made under the existing legislation (i.e. generally a requirement to stop, or to not engage in the conduct that constitutes a breach of consumer law).

---

[207] i.e. Directive 98/27/EC of the European Parliament and Council of May 19, 1998 on injunctions for the protection of consumer interests. This is implemented in the UK by the Enterprise Act 2002. See text below for CPC enforcer.

[208] The Enterprise Act 2002 (Amendment) Regulations 2006 (SI 2006/3363).

[209] Enterprise Act 2002 ss.214, 216.

[210] See s.79 Sch.7. See further Enterprise Act 2002 s.219A.

The aim of the charges introduced by the 2014 Act is to provide greater flexibility for public enforcers[211] and the civil courts in relation to the contents of enforcement orders and undertakings made under Pt 8. If they are deemed suitable for a particular case, public enforcers and the civil courts will be able to attach (where they consider it just and reasonable) enhanced consumer measures to enforcement orders and undertakings. The enhanced consumer measures will need to fall into at least one of three specified categories (referred to as the redress, compliance and choice categories). Measures in the redress category will offer compensation or other redress to consumers who have suffered loss as a result of the breach of consumer law. Compliance measures are intended to increase business compliance with the law and to reduce the likelihood of further breaches. Measures in the choice category will help consumers obtain relevant market information about persons subject to enforcement orders or undertakings to enable them to make better purchasing decisions. Sections 210 and 211 of the 2002 Act are amended to widen the injunctive regime under Pt 8. This will enable enforcers to use it for infringements of domestic legislation that harm the collective interests of consumers where either the supplier or the consumer is in the UK.

Section 217(10A) of the 2002 Act provides a power for the court to attach enhanced consumer measures defined in s.219A to an enforcement order and for the court to specify an appropriate time period for the person to comply with the enhanced consumer measures.

Subsection (10B) allows the court to attach enhanced consumer measures to an undertaking accepted and for the court to specify an appropriate time period for the person to comply with the enhanced consumer measures.

Subsection (10C) provides that a private body can seek enhanced consumer measures under certain conditions.[212] Subsection (10D) allows the court to include in an enforcement order or undertaking a requirement that the person subject to the enforcement order or undertaking provide information or documentation to the court to show that they have complied with the enhanced consumer measures.

Section 219 (5ZA) enables public enforcers to include enhanced consumer measures in undertakings and to be provided with documentation from the person subject to the undertaking to specify an appropriate time period for the person to comply with the enhanced consumer measures and to require the person subject to the undertaking to provide information or documents to them. Subsection (5ZB) provides for the application of these provisions where the enforcer is not a public body.

The enhanced measures in detail

10–099   Section 219A(1) of the 2002 Act lists the three categories of enhanced consumer measures—redress, compliance and choice. Details of possible measures are not included in the legislation, the reasoning being that this could risk taking away flexibility from the courts and public enforcers to identify the most suitable

---

[211] These being the enforcers referred to at para.10–095.
[212] As to which, see Enterprise Act s.219C.

measure or measures to deal with a person subject to enforcement orders or undertakings. It could also take away the flexibility for a person who is subject to enforcement orders or undertakings to put forward their own measures, which could be deemed suitable, to the court or public enforcer.

Redress measures

Section 219A of the 2002 Act limits compensation or redress to those consumers **10–100** who have suffered loss as a result of the breach of consumer law. This is mirrored in s.219B(4)(a). Consumers retain the right to refuse offers of redress, whether in an enforcement order or undertaking, and take their own civil action against the person that has caused them detriment. Where the infringing conduct relates to a contract, subs.219(2)(b) states that measures in the redress category can include giving consumers the option to terminate that contract. Subsection (2)(c) allows for measures intended to be in the collective interests of consumers in cases where consumers who have suffered detriment cannot be identified or it would require a disproportionate cost to do so. Measures in these circumstances could include, for example, making a charitable donation equivalent to the value of the detriment caused to consumers (where that charity acts in the interests of consumers). Subsection (2)(c) only applies in the circumstances outlined above. It does not apply in circumstances where consumers who have been identified as suffering detriment choose to decline the redress offered.

Compliance and choice measures

Section 219A(3) and (4) describe the measures in the second and third **10–101** categories—the compliance and choice categories. Measures in these categories might include the person subject to the enforcement order or undertaking:

- appointing a compliance officer;
- introducing a complaints handling process;
- improving their record keeping;
- signing up to an established customer review / feedback site; or
- publicising details of the breach or potential breach in the local or national press.

The provisions of the 2002 Act which could require an offender to publish details of orders or undertakings do not apply in the case of the enhanced measures.

Matters related to the enhanced measures

Section 219B sets out the requirements that apply to the inclusion of enhanced **10–102** consumer measures within an enforcement order or undertaking. Section 219(B)(1) confirms that only just and reasonable enhanced consumer measures can be attached to enforcement orders or undertakings. Subsections (2) and (3) set out the factors the court or enforcer must take into account. These include a specific requirement that the measures must be proportionate, taking into account the costs of the measures (to business and consumers) and the benefit to consumers.

Subsections (4) to (5) make provision in relation to a loss case.[213] These provisions restrict the imposition of enhanced consumer measures in the redress category to cases where there has been a loss suffered by consumers and require that in those cases, the court or enforcer must be satisfied that the cost to the person subject to the enforcement order or undertaking of complying with the measures is unlikely to exceed the loss suffered by consumers. Administrative costs (i.e. the cost of setting up and running the scheme), however, should not be included in this calculation.

Provision is further made in subss.(6) and (7) for when an enforcement order or undertaking includes enhanced consumer measures offering compensation and a settlement agreement is entered into in connection with the payment of compensation. A waiver of a person's rights in the settlement agreement is not valid if it is a waiver of the right to bring civil proceedings in respect of conduct other than the conduct which has given rise to the enforcement order or undertaking. For example, the waiver will not be valid if it relates to additional goods or services that were not covered by the enforcement order or undertaking.

---

[213] In essence, a case where an order or undertaking has been given where there has been an infringement and a consumer has suffered loss; or where an undertaking has been given in the belief that an infringement has occurred followed by such loss: Enterprise Act 2002 Sch.7 paras (9), (10).

INDEX

This index has been prepared using Sweet and Maxwell's Legal Taxonomy. Main index entries conform to keywords provided by the Legal Taxonomy except where references to specific documents or non-standard terms (denoted by quotation marks) have been included. These keywords provide a means of identifying similar concepts in other Sweet and Maxwell publications and online services to which keywords from the Legal Taxonomy have been applied. Readers may find some minor differences between terms used in the text and those which appear in the index. Suggestions to *sweetandmaxwell.taxonomy@thomson.com*.

All references are to paragraph number

Acceptance
incorporation of exclusion clauses,
1–029—1–030
Acknowledgment
interpretation of exclusion clauses,
2–050—2–052
reasonableness of exclusion clauses,
9–042—9–043
Adjudication
unfair terms in consumer contracts, 10–074
Aggressive practices
unfair commercial practices, 5–012
Ambiguity
unfair commercial practices, 5–010
Anti-avoidance
Unfair Contract Terms Act 1977, 7–001
Applicable law
unfair terms in consumer contracts, 10–089
Apprenticeships
unfair terms in consumer contracts, 10–009
Arbitration agreements
interpretation of exclusion clauses, 2–049
Unfair Contract Terms Act 1977, 7–009
Arbitration clauses
incorporation of exclusion clauses, 1–027
Assumption of risk *see* **Volenti non fit injuria**
Auctions
unfair terms in consumer contracts, 10–008
Breach of a fundamental term *see* **Fundamental breach**
Breach of fiduciary duty
avoidance of exclusion clauses, 3–007
Breach of rules of natural justice *see* **Natural justice**

Building operations
unfair terms in consumer contracts
adjudication clauses, 10–074
generally, 10–069—10–073
withholding notice clause, 10–075—10–076
Burden of proof
avoidance of exclusion clauses, 3–002
Business contracts *see* **Unfair contract terms (commercial contracts)**
"By-pass provisions"
unfair commercial practices, 5–016
Cancellation
information rights, 6–014
Carriage by sea
Unfair Contract Terms Act 1977, 7–014—7–015
Charterparties
Unfair Contract Terms Act 1977, 7–022
Choice of law
Unfair Contract Terms Act 1977, 7–013
unfair terms in consumer contracts, 10–010
Community infringements
unfair terms in consumer contracts, 10–093
Company incorporation
Unfair Contract Terms Act 1977, 7–017
Complaints
unfair terms in consumer contracts, 10–084
Conduct
incorporation of exclusion clauses, 1–043
Consequential loss
interpretation of exclusion clauses,
2–042—2–045
Construction contracts
unfair terms in consumer contracts
adjudication clauses, 10–074
generally, 10–069—10–073
withholding notice clause, 10–075—10–076